The
CHILD-PARENT
RELATIONSHIP
in the
NEW TESTAMENT
and Its
ENVIRONMENT

The CHILD-PARENT RELATIONSHIP *in the* NEW TESTAMENT *and Its* ENVIRONMENT

Peter Balla

WIPF & STOCK · Eugene, Oregon

Wipf and Stock Publishers
199 W 8th Ave, Suite 3
Eugene, OR 97401

The Child-Parent Relationship in the New
Testament and Its Environment
By Balla, Peter
Copyright©2003 Mohr Siebeck
ISBN 13: 978-1-4982-7922-2
Publication date 12/9/2015
Previously published by Hendrickson, 2003

To my parents
Eszter Nagy and Tibor Balla

to my wife
Dr. Gyöngyi Hegedűs

to our children
Zsolt, Gergely, Csanád, Csenge

and to the memory of
my spiritual father
Professor John C. O'Neill
(8.12.1930–30.3.2003)

Preface

The present work was accepted for the degree of *Habilitation* (dr. habil.) at the Evangelical-Lutheran Theological University in Budapest, in October 2001. It has grown out of a twofold interest. On the one hand, my doctoral thesis, *Challenges to New Testament Theology*, had a primarily methodological emphasis, addressing issues in diverse areas in New Testament studies. For my research in connection with *Habilitation*, I wanted to turn to a new field, focussing on one particular theme. I have chosen the child-parent relationship from the viewpoint of the child: How did children honour their parents in the New Testament and its environment? This theme has enabled me to deal with many ancient sources outside the New Testament, and to concentrate on exegetical work in the New Testament itself. On the other hand, the theme is of special significance to me personally. My own life story is very much influenced by family relations: I am greatly indebted to my beloved parents; and I rejoice in living in my own family now. Their presence is a constant source of joy and strength to me. Therefore, I dedicate this work to my parents, to my wife, and to our children.

Apart from my family, many people and institutions have helped me in the process of carrying out this research. I was greatly helped by the *Hilfswerk der Evangelischen Kirchen der Schweiz*, which gave me a scholarship to study in Bern for seven months in 1997. I was able to spend another month in Bern in 1998, with the help of the Evangelical Faculty of the University of Bern. On the basis of the preparatory work carried out there, I was able to continue with research at home, and was in a position to apply for a scholarship from the Alexander von Humboldt Foundation. With their help, I spent twelve months at the University of Heidelberg in 1999/2000. Without these scholarships the present work could not have been brought to light. I should like to add with gratitude that the A. v. Humboldt Foundation has also generously contributed to the publishing costs. During my time abroad, I have received much help from Professor Ulrich Luz (Bern), and from Professor Gerd Theissen (Heidelberg), both of whom have helped me with many suggestions concerning the manuscript. Professor Theissen has also written a helpful criticism and evaluation in the form of an official *Gut-*

achten for the procedure of *Habilitation*. I thank both of them for much support and hospitality. I thank Professor emeritus Christoph Burchard (Heidelberg) and Professor emeritus Eduard Schweizer (Zurich) for comments on the first draft of the manuscript. I thank the whole Faculty at the Lutheran Theological University in Budapest for their willingness to receive me for their first procedure of *Habilitation* after the democratic changes in our country. I thank especially Professor Sándor Cserháti for his *Gutachten*. I thank my doctoral student, Rev. Ottó Pecsuk, for proofreading the Greek texts in my manuscript.

Special thanks are due to my doctoral supervisor, Professor John Cochrane O'Neill (Edinburgh), who had patiently improved the English of the manuscript both before its submission for the degree and also before I presented it for publication. He has helped me in so many ways over the years; I remain ever grateful for all his support. I should like to thank also all the staff of the publisher Mohr Siebeck for very helpful and professional work first in connection to my doctoral thesis and now, a second time, when they have taken on themselves even more of the editorial work. I thank the editors of *Wissenschaftliche Untersuchungen zum Neuen Testament* who have accepted this work in the series: Professors Jörg Frey, Martin Hengel, and Otfried Hofius. Professor Frey has also helped me with thorough comments on the manuscript and with his suggestion that this work be published in the prestigious first series of WUNT.

To some extent, one's teachers become one's "parents" as well. I thank all those who have taught me up to the present; among them Professor János Bolyki who guided my infant footsteps in New Testament studies and has inspired and encouraged me at every stage to prepare myself to carry forward the work at the Faculty of Theology of the Károli Gáspár Reformed University. As his successor now in the professorship, I express my gratitude to him, and also to the Colleagues and students in the Faculty.

Budapest, Hungary, September 2002   Peter Balla

Just after I had received the final proofs of the present work, the sad news reached me that Professor John C. O'Neill died on 30 March 2003 after a short illness. May this book contribute to keeping alive the memory of this great scholar.

P. B.

Table of Contents

Abbreviations XIII

Introduction 1

Part I: The Environment of the New Testament 5

Chapter One: From Homer to the End of the Greek Classical Period 6

1. Introduction 6
2. Traditional expectations concerning the duties of children towards their parents 10
3. Reasons and grounds for children's duties towards their parents . . 21
4. Limits to children's duties towards their parents 31
5. Summary and classification of the results 36

Chapter Two: Greek and Latin Sources from the Hellenistic Period to the Third Century A.D. 41

1. Introduction 41
2. The child-parent relationship in practice 44
   a) Preliminary remarks 44
   b) Expectations emerging from the social role of the father and of the mother 45
   c) Parents as husbands and wives 48
   d) Sons and daughters 50
   e) Differences between various segments of society 52
   f) How long did the influence of parents over their children last? . 53
   g) Children learning a trade or a profession 55
   h) Correspondence 56
   i) Conflicts between children and parents 58

	j) Anti-family ethos among the Cynics and the Stoics	60
3.	Norms and expectations about the behaviour of children to their parents	62
	a) Honour and reverence	63
	b) Provision for the old, funeral and veneration of the dead	64
	c) Some further duties	68
4.	Reasons and grounds for children's duties	70
5.	Limits to children's duties towards their parents	73
6.	Summary and classification of the results	76

Chapter Three: Jewish Sources in the Centuries around the Turn of the Era 80

1.	Introduction	80
2.	Some insights into real-life practice	82
	a) Children following their parents' teaching	82
	b) Obedience to parents in the matter of marriage	84
3.	Children's duties towards their parents	86
	a) Honour and respect	86
	b) Honour due to older people in general	91
	c) Respectful speech	92
	d) Obedience, loyalty, and gratitude	93
	e) Provision in old age	94
	f) Providing a funeral	95
4.	Reasons and grounds for children's duties	97
	a) God as the reason for duties	97
	b) Divine court and human court as combined reasons	99
	c) Further religious reasons for duties	99
	d) Nature calls for a debt to be repaid	100
	e) Virtue and other "logical reasons"	101
	f) Parents' authority and right to punish their children	102
	g) The promise attached to the Fifth Commandment: a long life	103
5.	Limits to children's duties	104
	a) Limit implied by ranking	104
	b) What is "just and profitable"	105
	c) Torah, temple, and conversion to "Judaism" as limits	106
	d) Enmity in the apocalyptic literature	108
6.	Summary and classification of the results	109

Table of Contents XI

Part II: The Child-Parent Relationship in the New Testament . . 113

Chapter Four: The Gospel Tradition 114

1. Introduction 114
2. "Honour your father and your mother" 117
   a) The Fifth Commandment in the Gospels 117
   b) Traditions assuming the duty of honouring parents 121
3. Tensions within the family 130
   a) Jesus calls his first disciples 131
   b) A new family? 133
   c) Conflict suffered as a consequence of discipleship 138
   d) The urgency of discipleship 142
   e) Jesus against "fathers on earth" and against "his (own) mother"? 149
4. Summary 155

Chapter Five: Traditions in the Pauline Corpus 157

1. Introduction 157
2. Texts concerning real child-parent relationships 160
   a) Undisputed Pauline letters 160
   b) The Household Codes in Colossians and Ephesians 165
   c) The Pastoral Epistles 178
3. Family imagery in a figurative sense 182
   a) Undisputed Pauline letters 182
   b) The Pastoral Epistles 196
4. Summary 198

Chapter Six: The Rest of the New Testament 202

1. Introduction 202
2. Texts concerning real child-parent relationships 203
3. Family imagery in a figurative sense 209
4. Summary 227

Conclusion 229

Bibliography 233

1. Editions of ancient texts 233
2. Literature on the environment of the New Testament 237
   a) Graeco-Roman environment 237
   b) Jewish environment 241
3. Literature related to the New Testament 244
   a) Commentaries 244
   b) Other works related to the New Testament 247

Index of References 261
Index of Authors 274
Index of Subjects 277

Abbreviations

As regards abbreviations, I follow Patrick H. Alexander *et al.* (eds.): *The SBL Handbook of Style: For Ancient Near Eastern, Biblical, and Early Christian Studies.* 1999, Peabody, Massachusetts: Hendrickson Publishers

The more frequent abbreviations are as follows:

EKKNT	Evangelisch-Katholischer Kommentar zum Neuen Testament
ET	English translation
fn.	footnote
Loeb	The Loeb Classical Library (see Bibliography, section 1)
LSJ	Liddell-Scott (see Bibliography, section 1)
LXX	Septuagint
NA27	Nestle-Aland, 27th edition (of *Novum Testamentum Graece*)
RSV	Revised Standard Version (Unless stated otherwise, this edition is used when quoting the Bible in English translation.)

In this work, references are made by giving the year of publication and the page number in brackets in the main text. If the same work is referred to in the same context more than once, after the first reference giving both year and page, page numbers alone are given in subsequent references. If more than one reference is made to the same page in the same context, then the page number is not repeated. The next occurrence of a page number indicates that the reference is made to another page. On occasion I repeat the page number for the sake of clarity (for example, in the case of a reference to a new theme). The page number is introduced by "p." if it is necessary in order to avoid a possible misunderstanding (for example, when there is a figure in the same context referring to a year or to a Bible verse). A page reference in a multi-volume work follows this pattern: vol. II , p. 453 is referred to as II/453. References in footnotes follow the same conventions.

Italics in quotations are always those of the author quoted.

When I use "he" for a non-specific pronoun in the third person, "he or she" should be understood. (As a justification for my usage I note that there is only one word for "he" and "she" in my native – Hungarian – language.)

Introduction

In recent decades there has emerged an increasing interest in family relationships in antiquity. Monographs and collections of essays have dealt with aspects of the Roman family. The number of publications on the Jewish family in antiquity has increased as well. Publications of papyri and inscriptions allow an insight into the life of Greek and Jewish families. Classical philologists, sociologists and biblical scholars alike turn their attention to the sociological dimensions of ancient family life. Some aspects have been studied extensively as, for example, the legal situation in the Roman family. In general, one may say that the child-parent relationship has been presented primarily from the perspective of the parents. In contrast to this prevailing emphasis in scholarship, the present monograph attempts to focus on the child-parent relationship especially from the point of view of the child, asking the question: How did they experience and fulfil the duties towards their parents? Or, to put it in another way, How did children honour their parents?

Within the New Testament there can be seen a twofold tension as regards the expectation that parents should be revered. On the one hand, there is a difference between reverence toward parents among the first followers of Jesus and in the settled congregations. The latter is represented, for example, by the Household Codes in the epistles to the Ephesians and Colossians, where children are addressed together with their fathers. This implies that the obedient children are together with their parents at home and even at the worship services of the household churches. This can be contrasted with passages in the Gospels that narrate that the first disciples of Jesus left their family homes when they followed their master.

On the other hand, there is a tension reflected even within the Gospel texts. Here we find, on the one hand, that Jesus subscribed to the commandment, "Honour your father and mother" (see e.g. Mark 7:9–13 in relation to the *Corban*; and Mark 10:17–27 par.: the passage concerning the "rich young ruler"). On the other hand, radical sayings concerning "leaving" one's parents are attributed to Jesus (see e.g.: Mark 10:29 and parallels) and also an extremely radical saying in Luke 14:26 about the necessity of "hating" one's father and mother.

Already in these few examples we can see that the duties of children to their parents applied to them even when they were grown-ups. This is reflected in the Greek term τέχνον, that can refer to the child-parent relationship irrespective of the age of the "child". Accordingly, I shall use the term "children" to refer to children in their relationship to their parents. Children, in this sense, remain "children" to their parents as long as their parents are alive; and even longer: when they venerate the memory of their deceased parents. Due to the fact that the majority of the New Testament texts under discussion refer to grown-up children, this will be the primary area of our interest also when looking at the environment of the New Testament.

Although most of the New Testament texts that contain references to our present field of study were not written with the purpose of describing family relationships, they nevertheless do reflect child-parent relationships among the early Christians. In this study, New Testament texts will be examined in relation to non-biblical family ethics and practices in order to find answers to the questions: To what extent did early Christianity fit into the pattern of its environment?; and, What were the characteristics peculiar to the first few generations of the followers of Jesus? In order to achieve this aim, the "environment" has to be surveyed, even if only from the limited aspect of the expectation that parents should be honoured.

It is a matter of course that in order to find answers to our primary question, How did children honour their parents?, – or, to put it in a more concrete way, Did the first Christians fulfill the expectation to honour their parents? – other related areas have to be touched upon as well. However, this question will guide us when looking at the sources. Other – often also very important – questions have to be left out of the focus of this study. For example, the aspect of education will be excluded, because it is mainly dealt with in our sources from the point of view of the parents: what were their duties in this regard toward children. On the other hand, this investigation should include cases where children failed to honour their parents, in as much as it can be seen as non-fulfilling existing expectations. When, to a limited extent, the obligations of parents toward their children will nevertheless surface, this will happen only because we have to see also what children could expect from their parents in order to understand what they were expected to owe their parents in return. Fulfilled – or even unfulfilled – expectations from their parents may have played a role in children's behaviour towards their parents.

When studying the New Testament texts as well as when examining their surrounding environment, practices of real life as well as the expectations and norms are important. A selection of texts will be quoted that describe the relationship between children and parents and that prescribe in a normative way what that relationship should involve. The two areas cannot and need not be separated too rigorously. It can be expected that we may be able to reconstruct norms from real-life experience; and, vice versa, normative texts may reflect what life in reality was like, as norms sometimes reflect rather than prescribe practice: legislation is sometimes a belated verbal fixing of already existing practices. However, due caution is to be exercised, because there may be normative texts which describe the ideal that never really existed.

The final aim has already been named: to find out what is shared by the first Christian generations with their non-Christian neighbours, Jewish and pagan, and what may be called Christian characteristics in which they differed from their surrounding world (if in fact they did differ). In order to achieve that aim, the present study will have a historical, descriptive character. The main questions to be posed to the sources are: What were the major norms, i.e. what were the duties of children towards their parents?, What were the grounds for those duties?, and, What were the limits or the boundaries to those duties, beyond which they need not be performed? As there are fewer sources that mention mothers and daughters than those concerning fathers and sons, a special attention will be given to sources that involve women.

The study divides into two main parts: first the "environment" of the New Testament is examined, then the relevant New Testament texts are discussed. For the first part, the period of ca. three centuries before and after the beginning of the Common Era will be in our focus, with a brief look into even earlier centuries in the case of the Greek sources. The pre-history of our theme in the Jewish world – for which our primary source is the Old Testament – will not be dealt with in a separate chapter, but it will be discussed in the chapter on the Jewish "environment" and in the chapters on the New Testament.

It has to be emphasised that an all-encompassing history of the child-parent relationship cannot be expected from the first part of this monograph. The aim of studying the environment is not that of writing a history of literature or a social history of childhood. The modest aim is to contribute to our knowledge in one particular branch of the scholarly study of classical antiquity: how children honoured their parents in the ancient world. It is necessary to point out in advance that the first part of this monograph does not want to give the impression that the texts mentioned would be familiar to the authors or to the addressees of the New Testament writings. The aim of this part is to summarise the main characteristics of the expectations with regard to honouring one's parents in the Jewish and pagan environment in which the early Christian movement lived its daily life. If the term "background" is used in this context, it should be understood as a reference to the social *milieu* of – various groups of – the early Christians. A brief description of that context helps to highlight how the early Christian movement may have appeared to its environment as representing a radically anti-family ethos; or, on the other hand, what aspects of the ethos of the child-parent relationship were – perhaps even in a natural, non-reflective way – shared by the early Christian communities and their Jewish and pagan neighbourhood.

In the second part, the New Testament texts are discussed in three groups: relevant passages in the Gospels will be discussed first, then the Pauline Corpus (with a special emphasis on the Household Codes), then a selection of other texts in the remaining parts of the New Testament that shed light on our theme. In this part, references to the findings of the first part will establish the link between the "environment" and the world of the early Christians, in order to see what was common to both and in what they differed.

Part I

The Environment of the New Testament

Chapter One

From Homer to the End of the Greek Classical Period

1. Introduction

The child-parent relationship is reflected in writings from the earliest periods of literary activity down to the turn of the era. It is difficult to trace particular thoughts about family relations, because we often have only the fragments that have survived. In general terms, there are cases where one can suppose that the ideas contained in earlier writings had an impact upon later authors, because we do know that the earlier writings were transmitted and discussed even centuries later. For example, the writings attributed to Homer were studied by later generations throughout the centuries.[1] In many cases, from later references we only know the fact that earlier writings were known, but the actual discussions are no longer extant. However, we also have some works that have survived to the present, for example, commentaries on Plato and Aristotle.[2]

The very fact that there were libraries established in the Hellenistic period – beginning with the *Museion* in Alexandria in the third century B.C. and the library at the royal court in Pergamum – can be seen as a proof that many writings from the earlier centuries were deliberately preserved. While these libraries were not open to the public, but only researched by a few experts, the libraries in Rome became open to the public from the end of the Republic.[3] The latter ones regularly included also a room for Greek books. It is also significant that catalogues were prepared in which the books of the libraries were listed. For example, the list of Kallimachos in Alexandria covered 120 volumes from many diverse authors, including references to the orator Demosthenes, to a poem which was – in his opinion – falsely attributed to Pythagoras, and to Euripides.[4]

---

[1] See the examples given by Nigel Wilson in Heinz-Günther Nesselrath 1997, 87–88, 91, 98, 101. I note that I confine my study to written sources. For a good introduction to the theme of children in ancient Greek art see, for example, the works of Hilde Rühfel (1984a, 1984b).

[2] See e.g. N. Wilson's examples in H-G. Nesselrath 1997, 101–102.

[3] See e.g. Tiziano Dorandi in H-G. Nesselrath 1997, 12–13.

[4] N. Wilson in H-G. Nesselrath 1997, 92. Wilson has marshalled many examples of how

1. Introduction

In order to be able to understand our pagan sources around the time of the New Testament in a more appropriate way, it is helpful first to discuss the periods that preceded the Hellenistic period. The aim of this inquiry is to look for ideas that remained influential in the centuries around the time of the New Testament. In this brief survey there is no attempt to describe child-parent relationships in the pre-Hellenistic period in an all-encompassing way; rather, the main question to be answered is: What norms were shared by the authors of later times, i.e. in the period ca. third century B.C. to the third century A.D.?

It is appropriate to reaffirm that whenever I mention "children", I use the term to express a relationship, and I do not refer to the age of children, unless it is specifically needed in a given context. It will be seen in many instances that the duties of children to their parents applied to them even when they were grown-ups. To give but one example, Plato thought that even adults had to be punished if they neglected their parents. In his *Laws* XI.932B–C,[5] he proposes that the wrongdoers have to be punished "with stripes and imprisonment if they are still strong – up to the age of thirty if they are men, while if they are women they shall suffer similar punishment up to the age of forty". Then, Plato gives no upper limit of age when he adds (*ibid.*, 932C):

And if, when they have passed these limits of age, they do not desist from the same acts of neglect towards their parents, but in some cases maltreat them, they shall be summoned before a court of 101 citizens, who shall be the oldest citizens of all; and if a man be convicted, the court shall assess what his fine or punishment must be, regarding no penalty as excluded which man can suffer or pay.

Most likely, this rule extended to men and women just as the earlier one did, because the Greek original does not speak about "men" only, as the translation would suggest. In the Greek text we can find the terms τις and ἄνθρωπος, both of which can refer to both sexes. Here we may note that the punishment is more severe if the "children" had passed the age of thirty in the case of men and forty in the case of women. On the one hand, this might imply that common sense can be expected from ever older grown-ups; on the other hand, it is likely that the growing age of the children is paired with an advance in the age of their parents. The older the parents are, the more it can be expected that their children do not neglect them. Perhaps it is presupposed that aged parents lose their power and children are tempted to neglect

---

later authors were engaged in a "philological" critical activity concerning works of earlier writers; see his section entitled "Griechische Philologie im Altertum" (in H-G. Nesselrath 1997, 87–103).

[5] In Loeb: vol. II., p. 453 (= II/453).

them. The more severe punishment over the age of thirty and forty implies that the moral obligation of the grown-up children toward their parents gets even stronger with the passing of time. Although the regulation is formulated from a negative perspective ("they do not desist from the same acts of neglect towards their parents", τῶν αὐτῶν ἀμελειῶν περὶ γονέας μὴ ἀφιστῶνται), this clearly implies the expectation that children should care for their aged parents. The immediate context contains also an affirmative statement as regards the duty of honour: πᾶς δὴ τιμάτω ... τοὺς αὐτοῦ γεννήτορας (932A). We further note that the punishment is to be decided by a human court. The oldest citizens have the right and duty to make sure that children do not maltreat (κακῶσι) their old parents. Thus in this passage an expectation is expressed together with the consequence of not fulfilling the duty expected. This consequence can also be seen as reason why the duty should not be neglected.

It is important to emphasise, as another introductory remark, that society in the Hellenistic as well as in the preceding period was largely influenced by patriarchal structures. This widely known phenomenon is of interest to us in as much as – together with other aspects of social life – the child-parent relationship, too, was influenced by male dominance. The role of women in society must have been reflected in the relationship between parents and their daughters, mothers and their children etc. Let us consider some examples as a general reminder; then we shall discuss the social role of fathers and mothers in the next chapter in more detail.

In his *Laws*, Plato lists in pairs the relationships which are not based on equality (XI.917A):[6]

... the better are the superiors of the worse, and the older in general of the younger; wherefore also parents are superior to their offspring, men to women and children, rulers to ruled. And it will be proper for all to revere all these classes of superiors, whether they be in other positions of authority or in offices of State above all ...

We note the double criterion, "better" and "older", as a basis for deciding who are the "superiors". One of the reasons why children owe reverence (αἰδεῖσθαι ... πρέπον)[7] to their parents is that parents are older than their offspring. Significantly, the pairs are extended in one case to a "triplet": men are superior to women and children. This structure of the statement indicates that women and children were in a similar position in this regard: they were subordinated to men.

---

[6] In Loeb: II/401.
[7] For αἰδεῖσθαι, cf. Prov 24:23; 4 Macc 5:7. In the latter, revering means respecting old age.

1. Introduction

We can find another example of the qualification "better", in Aristotle's *Nicomachean Ethics*. In a section where he discusses φιλία in various kinds of relationships, he affirms (1161a):[8]

The friendship between husband and wife again is the same as that which prevails between rulers and subjects in an aristocracy; for it is in proportion to excellence, and the better party receives the larger share, ... whilst each party receives what is appropriate to each ...

Both Plato and Aristotle use the same expression for "better" (Plato: οἱ ἀμείνους, Aristotle: τῷ ἀμείνονι). It is worth pointing out in what an unreflected way they both affirm that somebody is "better" than another. This may be an expression of thinking in terms of a patriarchal society. I note that both Plato and Aristotle refer to "nature" as a reason for a distinction among human beings. In the same context, Aristotle applies the notion of friendship between unequal partners also to the relationship between a father and his sons. A reference to "nature" is the only justification for the hierarchically structured relation (1161a):[9] φύσει τε γὰρ ἀρχικὸν πατὴρ υἱῶν. Plato uses the expression φύσει διατεταγμένων as a reason why children should fear and honour the prayers of parents (Πᾶς δὴ νοῦν ἔχων φοβεῖται καὶ τιμᾷ γονέων εὐχάς; *Laws* XI.932A).[10]

Thus, when in the following we shall consider the more specific relationship between children and parents, we also have to bear in mind this general background of a patriarchal society in antiquity.

In what follows, I shall discuss texts grouped under three headings: the duties of children towards their parents, the reasons or grounds for those duties, and the limits within which those duties were to be fulfilled. We have already met some examples on the occasion of the introductory remarks. As the passages will appear in full under one heading only, they will be referred to only briefly under the other headings, if they relate to more than one of these three areas. For the sake of clarity, all the important elements to be found will be listed in a summary at the end of the chapter.

The following texts are gathered as examples covering the centuries from Homer up to the Hellenistic period. Although they are taken from a wide range of genres, they are meant to be only representative of their authors and genres, without the claim that all the relevant texts are referred to.

---

[8] In Loeb: VIII.xi.4, p. 495.
[9] In Loeb: VIII.xi.2, p. 494.
[10] In Loeb: II/450.

2. Traditional expectations concerning the duties of children towards their parents

The expectation that children should honour their parents is expressed in numerous texts many centuries before the Christian era. A. Lumpe even risked the following generalising statement (1957, col. 1192): "Durch die gesamte griechische Literatur zieht sich die Forderung, den Eltern Ehrfurcht und Gehorsam zu erweisen".

Before we turn to some Greek examples, it is worth pointing out that although Jews were spread over most parts of the known world from the time of the Babylonian exile on, pagan texts do not betray any direct influence of the Mosaic commandment to honour one's father and mother. Rather, we may regard it as a general ethical norm that was widespread in the non-Jewish and pre-Christian world. We can agree with O. Larry Yarbrough's conclusion concerning the "requirement that children honor their parents found in Exodus and in Plato" that (1993, 56): "Neither is dependent on the other. They were both concerned with creating an 'ideal' legal system, but in this particular case we probably have to do with nothing more than what must be an almost universal component of morality and culture". The authors in antiquity were aware of this. In the same context Yarbrough points to a passage where Plato "refers to the claim of parents to rule over their children as 'universally just' (*Laws* 627A)".[11] This expression – like the appeal to "nature" noted above – can be seen as a reason or ground why parents should be honoured.

We shall see in the third chapter that many authors in Judaism in the Hellenistic period shared ideas and practices with their pagan contemporaries. In that period Hellenistic influence upon Judaism can be observed. Before we turn to texts from that age, let us consider briefly some examples from previous centuries where such close interrelation cannot be seen. When we look at examples of how the expectation of honouring one's parents appears in Greek literature, we shall find it expressed in very different genres of writings. We follow them roughly in their historical sequence. We can say that "honour" or "reverence" can be seen as an overarching duty. Many other duties are related to it in such a close way that we can regard them as concrete realizations of the duty of "honour".

We find examples already in early literary texts. In Homer's *Iliad* we read the following about a young man, Simoeisius, who was killed in a battle: "... yet paid he not back to his dear parents the recompense of his upbring-

---

[11] O.L. Yarbrough 1993, 56.

ing, and but brief was the span of his life, for that he was laid low by the spear of great-souled Aias" (*Iliad* 4,477–478).[12] The young man was prevented from fulfilling his obligation towards his parents by his early death, but the casual mentioning of the unfulfilled obligation shows the importance of the obligation for the narrator. We shall see below that even centuries later writers were concerned with the theme of children repaying (ἀπέδωκε) the "debt" they owed their parents for their labours in connection with bringing up their children when the children were young (θρέπτρα)[13]. The duty applies in most cases to grown-ups who are expected to care for their aged parents. As a reason or ground for this duty it is emphasised that it is but paying back that which was given to them when they had to rely upon the support of their parents.

A little while after the time of Homer's *Iliad*, Hesiod in his *Works and Days* describes the state of utmost evil in the following way (*Op.*, lines 182–189):[14] "The father will not agree with his children, nor the children with their father.... Men will dishonour their parents as they grow quickly old, and will carp at them, chiding them with bitter words, hard-hearted they, not knowing the fear of the gods. They will not repay their aged parents the cost of their nurture, for might shall be their right...".[15] The larger context of this passage lists the characteristics of the "fifth generation", which is the "race of iron" – when Hesiod lived (*Op.* 174–176) – as a time when "there will be no help against evil" (*Op.* 201). Thus the passage lists widespread negative behaviour, but from it we can see what would have been expected in positive terms: agreeing with one's parents – an aspect of obedience – (ὁμοίιος), honouring them (the opposite of ἀτιμήσουσι), speaking with respect, repaying the cost of nurture (θρεπτήρια). "Fear of the gods" (θεῶν ὄπιν εἰδότες) serves as a religious motivation for children's duties

---

[12] Homer in Loeb: I/189; οὐδὲ τοκεῦσι θρέπτρα φίλοις ἀπέδωκε, p. 188; a similar case is narrated in *Iliad* 17,301–302, in Loeb: II/252–253.

[13] Cf. Esth 2:7, where the Septuagint differs from the Massoretic Text. The verse begins in the LXX: καὶ ἦν τούτῳ παῖς θρεπτή. Liddell-Scott (= LSJ), p. 805, translate this passage as referring to Esther as a "slave bred in the house" of Mordecai. The Hebrew text means: "He had brought up Hadassah, that is Esther...". According to the Septuagint, Mordecai takes her as his wife, whereas in the MT "Mordecai adopted her as his own daughter" (RSV).

[14] Hesiod lived at the end of the eighth century B.C. (concerning the date of his autobiographical references in *Works and Days*, see Enzo Degani in H-G. Nesselrath 1997, 177). For the view that he influenced some authors in the Hellenistic period (e.g. Hermesianax, Phanokles, Kallimachos, Arat), see Richard Hunter in H-G. Nesselrath 1997, 261–64.

[15] Hesiod in Loeb, p. 17; for another example of warning against attacking one's old father with harsh words, see *Op.* 331–334, in Loeb, p. 27. We shall refer to it in the next section as well.

towards their parents.¹⁶ We may note the significance of father-child relationship: the characteristics of evil times include the disharmony between father and child. We shall see later that enmity between fathers and sons – or the overcoming of that enmity – appears as a sign of the end times in Jewish and Christian writings. ¹⁷

In the sixth century B.C., Solon secured in his laws for Athens that sons had to support their aged parents. Many later authors referred to this legislation; these sources are conveniently summarised by Antonius Martina's edition of references to Solon, in a section entitled "Lege iubet filios parentes alere".¹⁸ We quote but one of them, and then look at another source as well.

Aelian (ca. 170 – ca. 230 A.D.) has a long section on the lions where he writes that old lions do not risk hunting any longer, but their young children provide for them: "when they have obtained enough for themselves and for their sire, ... these young children summon their aged father to the feast".¹⁹ At the end of the passage, Aelian adds: "This is no order of Solon's to the Lions: it is Nature that teaches them...". From this we can see that he knew a law of Solon, which prescribed provision for the fathers (ταῦτα νομοθετῶν τρέφειν τοὺς πατέρας ἐπάναγκες).²⁰ We make two observations concerning this example from nature. On the one hand, "nature teaches" this duty (διδάσκει δὲ ἡ φύσις); as if the author said: men have to be taught by laws, but animals follow the same duties dictated them by nature. On the other hand, this example is significant, because we shall see in the next chapter that Philo has a similar passage on the example of the storks: how their young ones nourish the old storks who cannot leave their nests.²¹

Our next example from Solon shows what significance he attributed to the duty of burying one's father. This passage could be referred to under the heading "limits of duties" as well, but it is appropriate to quote it among the

---

[16] For ὄπις θεῶν, LSJ give the following extended translation (p. 1238): "*the vengeance or visitation* of the gods for transgressing divine laws".

[17] Cf. Mal 3:24 (= 3:23 LXX); Sir 48:10; Luke 1:17.

[18] *Solon.* 1968, pp. 226–28. He lists the following references: Demosth. (c. Timocr.) XXIV,105; Plut. Sol. 22,1 and 22,4; Aelian. Nat. anim. IX,1 and VI,61; Liban. Decl. XI,14; Liban. Epist. 1244 and 137; Aristoph. Av. 1353.

[19] Aelian: *On the Characteristics of Animals* IX,1; in Loeb, p. 221.

[20] *Ibid.*; I note that the Greek text is contained in the Solon testimonia edition of A. Martina (1968, 227), but it is added only in a footnote in the Loeb edition of Aelian (1959, p. 220, fn. 3).

[21] It is worth noting that in Aristophanes' comedy, *Clouds*, the rebellious son, Pheidippides, refers to a negative example from nature, in order to justify his own turning against his father: "Consider fowls and those other animals, how they retaliate against their fathers; and after all, what difference is there between them and us, except that they don't propose decrees?" (lines 1427–29, in A.H. Sommerstein 1982, 147).

2. Traditional expectations concerning the duties of children

examples of duties, because the "limitation" highlights the duty even more. Aeschines (fourth century B.C., but with reference to earlier lawgivers, above all to Solon) writes in his speech against Timarchus that: "the law frees a son, when he has become a man, from all obligation to support or to furnish a home to a father by whom he has been hired out for prostitution; but when the father is dead, the son is to bury him and perform the other customary rites" (... ἀποθανόντα δὲ θαπτέτω καὶ τἄλλα ποιείτω τὰ νομιζόμενα).[22] Aeschines draws the conclusion: "so long as the father is alive he is deprived of all the benefits of fatherhood, ... but when he is dead, and unconscious of the service that is being rendered him, and when it is the law and religion that receive the honour, then at last the lawgiver commands the son to bury him and perform the other customary rites."[23] The exemption shows that the normal case would have been that the son provides nourishment and even home for his aged father (τρέφειν τὸν πατέρα and οἴκησιν παρέχειν). It is significant for us that there is no exemption from the duty of burying the father, because we shall meet a case in the New Testament part, where Jesus instructs a son not to bury his father (Matt 8:22 par., see ch. 4, section 3d).

We learn from this passage in Aeschines further that, after the burial, "other" things were prescribed by the laws: the deceased were venerated by certain rites. In Solon's laws, although the father was unworthy, the veneration of the father was not cancelled. However, Aeschines argues that this can only be done because the unworthy father is not aware of it; in fact, "it is the law and religion that receive the honour" (τιμᾶται δὲ ὁ νόμος καὶ τὸ θεῖον) when a father is buried and venerated afterwards.

The fifth century tragedian, Sophocles, expresses the general view that the laws originated with the gods. The laws were not begotten by men, as the Chorus in *Oedipus Tyrannus* says: their "only father is Olympus" (lines 867–868).[24] In his essay entitled "Griechische Literatur bis 300 v. Chr.",[25] Enzo Degani points out the significant role played by the inherited laws of previous eras for Sophocles in his *Antigone*: "Antigone opfert sich im Namen dieser ewigen Prinzipien". Her conflict originated in her insisting on burying her brother in spite of the order of the king, Creon, who had for-

---

[22] Aeschines I,13; in Loeb, p. 15. I owe this reference to Gustav Wolff's edition of Sophocles' *Antigone*, where on page 6 we read: "Solon ... entband die Kinder von anderen Pflichten gegen den Vater, der sie zu gewissen Verbrechen anhielte, nur nicht von der Bestattung". Here, in footnote 2, we find the reference to Aeschines.
[23] Aeschines I,14; in Loeb, p. 15.
[24] Sophocles in Loeb: I/413.
[25] In H-G. Nesselrath 1997, 171–245; quotation from p. 227.

bidden the funeral. For Antigone, the necessity of a decent funeral belonged to those principles she observed.

Although there are variations in Sophocles' works on the matter of how Antigone's parents were to be buried, it is important for us that one of the versions, that of the play *Antigone*, tells us that she prepared the bodies of her parents for their funeral. Here Antigone says: "But when I come there, I am confident that I shall come dear to my father, dear to you, my mother, and dear to you, my own brother; since when you died it was I that with my own hands washed you and adorned you and poured libations on your graves; and now, Polynices, for burying your body I get this reward! Yet in the eyes of the wise I did well to honour you ...".[26] We note that the Greek verb τιμάω is used for giving honour in providing for the funeral.

Creon forbade the funeral and he asked Antigone how did she dare "to transgress these laws" (line 449; in Greek: ὑπερβαίνειν νόμους).[27] Antigone replied that the duty of providing for a funeral is stronger than Creon's proclamations: "... nor did I think your proclamations strong enough to have power to overrule, mortal as they were, the unwritten and unfailing ordinances of the gods".[28] Taking all these passages together, we can say that for Antigone the duty of burying her brother as well as her parents was ordered by the gods. She was willing to be sacrificed as a punishment for being obedient to these "ordinances of the gods".

Most of the philosophers who reflected on ethical matters included the relationship between parents and children.

We can find some examples in the thoughts attributed to Pythagoras and in the writings of the Pythagorean "school". When we look for texts concerning the relationship to parents, with due caution we may also refer to texts where old people are mentioned. If one is to honour old people in general, then we may assume that this would include one's own parents in particular. For example, Iamblichus (ca. 250 – ca. 325 A.D.) writes in his biography of Pythagoras: "he said that as soon as they [*sc*. boys] had entered on the path along which they intended to proceed for the remainder of their existence, they should imitate their predecessors, never contradicting those who were their seniors".[29] This implies the duty of learning from the older generations (including the parents) and that of obedience. Although it belongs to the theme of grounds for duties, it may be mentioned here that Pythagoras is said to have added the following practical reason to the above

---

[26] *Antigone*, lines 897–904, in Sophocles in Loeb: II/87.
[27] *Ibid.*, p. 43.
[28] *Ibid.*, p. 45.
[29] D. R. Fideler 1987, 68.

2. Traditional expectations concerning the duties of children 15

quoted duty: "For later on, when they themselves will have grown, they will justly expect not to be injured by their juniors."[30]

Iamblichus narrates how Pythagoras once entered a gymnasium and taught young people there. He encouraged them "to value their parents more than themselves: He said that they owed as much thanks to their parents as one deceased would owe to someone able to lead them back again to daylight. Further, it is right to cherish above all and never to pain those who have done one the first and greatest services. For only parents precede birth itself with their good deeds ..." (... πρὸς τὸ περὶ πλείονος ποιεῖσθαι τοὺς γονεῖς ἑαυτῶν, οἷς ἔφη τηλικαύτην ὀφείλειν αὐτοὺς χάριν ... ἔπειτα δίκαιον μὲν εἶναι τοὺς πρώτους καὶ τοὺς τὰ μέγιστα εὐηργετηκότας ὑπὲρ ἅπαντας ἀγαπᾶν καὶ μηδέποτε λυπεῖν ...).[31] Here the duty of children is summarised by the expressions "to love" parents above all (ὑπὲρ ἅπαντας ἀγαπᾶν) and "never to cause sadness" (μηδέποτε λυπεῖν) to them. Children owe gratitude (χάριν) to their parents. We shall see in the next section that Pythagoras is said to have taught the necessity of "obedience" to parents.[32]

The writing often referred to as the *Golden Verses of Pythagoras* may originate in some form with Pythagoras himself, but, more likely, with later members of the Pythagorean school. We do not know its exact date, but according to most scholars it does "epitomize the Pythagorean way of life";[33] therefore, it may be appropriate to mention it in this context. Its first four lines list the basis upon which other moral teaching is built up:

First honor the immortal gods, as the law demands;
Then reverence thy oath, and then the illustrious heroes;
Then venerate the divinities under the earth, due rites performing;
Then honor your parents, and all of your kindred.[34]

It is interesting that the abstract notion "oath" occurs in this list right after the immortal gods, interrupting the list of divine and human beings. Since an oath was often taken in a religious context, its presence here does not alter the fact that honour toward parents is closely related to honour toward gods. Perhaps we may infer from this list that honour is not only due to parents when they are alive, but also after they die, because it is possible that

---

[30] *Ibid.*, 68–69.
[31] Iamblichus: *On the Pythagorean Way of Life*, ch. 8, section 38; in J. Dillon – J. Hershbell 1991, 63.
[32] *Ibid.*, section 40.
[33] D. R. Fideler 1987, 163. I note that J. C. Thom suggests "a date of ca. 350–300 BC" (1995, 58).
[34] D. R. Fideler 1987, 163.

"illustrious heroes" refer to people who had been human beings in their earthly lives, but were elevated into the realm of divine beings after their death. Similarly, "divinities under the earth" may include deceased ancestors. We shall see more explicit examples of the expectation of venerating dead ancestors. This text does not say explicitly that it is the gods who demand the honouring of one's parents, but from the very fact that honour toward gods and parents are connected in a list we may infer that the former may be the ground for the latter.

On occasion, the elements of such a list do allow us to find out what may be the content of honouring gods and parents. In the following quotation attributed to Zaleucus (but possibly later than this contemporary of Pythagoras), the duty of honour toward parents appears together with that toward laws and rulers:

> Citizens should honor all the Gods according to the particular country's legal rites, which should be considered as the most beautiful of all. Citizens should, besides obeying the laws, show their respect for the rulers by rising before them and obeying their instructions. Men who are intelligent and wish to be saved should, after the Gods, divinities and heroes, most honor parents, laws and rulers.[35]

As in the case of laws and rulers the duty of obedience is explicitly stated, the subsequent list of "parents, laws and rulers" may suggest that honour and respect toward parents should also include obedience to them as leaders.

Leaving the circle of the Pythagoreans, we may find other examples in Plato (whose ideas were often taken up by contemporary and later Pythagoreans). We have seen in the introduction to this chapter that Plato used the term τιμάω when he formulated the norm: "Therefore let every man ... honour [τιμάτω] his own parents" (*Laws* XI.932A).[36] In the next section, we shall meet the duty of "reverence of speech" towards one's parents (*Laws* IV.717C–D).[37]

In Plato's *Laws* (IV.717B–718A)[38] we not only find the duty of paying back the "debt" to "living parents" and of "recompensing the old in their old age, when they need help most",[39] but also the duty of providing a "modest funeral" when the parents die. By the term "modest" Plato means that "the son neither exceeds the accustomed pomp, nor falls short of what his forefathers paid to their sires". Plato adds that "in like manner he [i.e. the son]

---

[35] D. R. Fideler 1987, 229.
[36] In Loeb: II/451.
[37] In Loeb: I/299.
[38] *Ibid.*
[39] For the similar expectation not to neglect and maltreat one's parents, see also the passage referred to in the introduction to this chapter: *Laws* XI.932A–C.

should duly bestow the yearly attentions, which ensure honour, on the rites already completed. He should always venerate them, by never failing to provide a continual memorial, and assigning to the deceased a due share of the means which fortune provides for expenditure".[40] Thus we can see that grown-up children are not only expected to care for their old parents and to provide a funeral when they die, but also to continue to venerate them after their death. I note that almost the whole section from Plato is also quoted by Aristoxenus in the fourth century B.C.[41] In the same context, an apophthegm of Aristoxenus mentions the duty of respecting one's parents in a list similar to those referred to above: "After divinity and divine spirits, the greatest respect should be paid to parents and the laws".[42]

Aristotle holds – with others whom we have discussed above – that "our parents have the first claim on us for maintenance, since we owe it to them as a debt"; and he even adds concerning the gratitude towards those to whom we owe our lives: "to support the authors of our being stands before self-preservation in moral nobility". We shall discuss this passage of the *Nicomachean Ethics* in the section on "limits" in more detail.[43] Here we simply note the duty of "maintenance" as well as that of honour (τιμή), expressed in the same passage.

Another genre where duties in the realm of the child-parent relationship are mentioned is the law court speeches of orators. In the next section, we shall meet a case of Isaeus whose eleven extant speeches deal with processes concerning hereditary law. Here we refer to an example from Lysias (ca. 445–380 B.C.), in whose speech number XIX ("On the Property of Aristophanes") the following is also mentioned among the speaker's virtues: "I am now thirty years old, and never yet have I either had a dispute with my father or been the subject of a complaint from any citizen".[44] In the Greek text we read οὔτε τῷ πατρὶ οὐδὲν πώποτε ἀντεῖπον, from which we can infer that "not to contradict" one's father was among the foremost virtues. This negative formulation might also imply the following positive expectations: speaking with reverence, and even obedience in general.

There are texts in several further genres where duties toward parents are

---

[40] In Loeb: I/299, 301.
[41] See T. Taylor 1822, 65–67; and D.R. Fideler 1987, 243.
[42] *Ibid.*
[43] 1165a, in Loeb: p. 527.
[44] In Loeb: *Lysias* XIX.55, p. 447. The background of the case is as follows: in ca. 390 B.C., a young Athenian man, Aristophanes, was executed and his property was confiscated. His father-in-law (who was acting as the guardian of Aristophanes' wife and children) was accused of withholding some part of the property. Since he died before he could be brought to trial, his son defended the case by this speech.

expressed or implied by the context. We shall meet examples in New Comedy (e.g. Menander) under the following heading. Here it may suffice to mention only one more literary example, and then focus upon another special genre.

Aristophanes (ca. 450 – ca. 386/5) – the only representative of Old Comedy from whom we have works extant in full – deals with problems of education in his comedy entitled *Clouds*. Although I have affirmed that I do not discuss the theme of education in this monograph, this work of Aristophanes deserves mentioning, because in the behaviour of the son, Pheidippides, we meet a character who is "selfish and thoughtless", who discards the "outward convention of filial obedience ... when he has been through Socrates' school", – as one of the editors of the *Clouds*, K. J. Dover has put it.[45] We have to add that the father is not a typical hero either. Dover describes him as "stupid and excitable, never truly resourceful, never in control of the situation, and at the end pitiable".[46] Nevertheless, in the contest of the personified Right and Wrong, ὁ κρείττων λόγος, i.e. "Right", as Dover translates the term, argues for the need of respecting one's parents.

The behaviour of the son is shown as a deliberate turning against old conventions. For example, Pheidippides is proud that he has learnt "subtle ideas" and is able to argue that "it is right to chastise one's father".[47] He argues as follows: his father beat him when he was a child (lines 1409–1410); "the old are in a second childhood" (line 1417, expressed in a proverbial way: δὶς παῖδες οἱ γέροντες);[48] thus it is time now that the sons "should beat their fathers in return" (line 1424). He says that the law that fathers should not suffer was made by a man (a thesis of the Sophists), so why should it be less open to him to "make a new law for sons in the future" (lines 1421–1424, ἧττόν τι δῆτ' ἔξεστι κἀμοὶ καινὸν αὖ τὸ λοιπὸν / θεῖναι νόμον τοῖς υἱέσιν, τοὺς πατέρας ἀντιτύπτειν;). Thus a general expectation of honouring one's parents is expressed in the work, although the comedy is probably a witness to the fact that there were challenges against that old convention in Aristophanes' time.

In a similar indirect way (as an unfulfilled duty), we can see that the father expected that his son should care for him in his old age in the same way as he cared for his son when he was an infant (lines 1380–90; the example is that the father brought drink and food for his child on its first "lisping utterance", and he carried him out of the doors and held him out when he said "kakka",

---

[45] *Aristophanes: Clouds*, p. xxviii.
[46] *Ibid.*, p. xxiii.
[47] *Clouds*, lines 1404–1405; in A. H. Sommerstein 1982, 145.
[48] *Ibid.*, p. 147.

2. Traditional expectations concerning the duties of children

and now the father is screaming in vain …). "Right", or, the "Better Argument", as Sommerstein translated the expression ὁ κρείττων λόγος, pleads that he should be chosen over against the "Worse Argument". Among the virtues he offers are the following: "you will know to hate the Agora and shun the bath-houses, … and to give up seats to your elders when they approach, and not to act rudely towards your own parents" (lines 991–995; … καὶ μὴ περὶ τοὺς σαυτοῦ γονέας σκαιουργεῖν).[49] Here we can see again that old people and parents are mentioned together, as if it would be argued that parents are expected to be honoured because they are "older".

A special genre in antiquity that dealt with the relationships within a household, oeconomics, originated and flourished in Athens in the fourth century B.C. Although there are writings that may be regarded as forerunners to this genre, yet the "earliest fully extant writing of this genre is Xenophon's 'Oikonomikos'".[50] We shall see that writings of this genre are significant for a better understanding of the Household Codes (*Haustafeln*) in Colossians and Ephesians; thus it is appropriate to mention a representative example here, too.

Xenophon's *Oeconomicus* may serve as a good example for our purposes from the point of view of its historical influence. As E. Dassmann and G. Schöllgen point out (1986, col. 817): "Das Werk hatte im Altertum eine vergleichsweise breite Wirkungsgeschichte". They also point to the fact that Cicero translated it into Latin (although that translation is no longer extant, *ibid.*). We must note, however, that Xenophon's work is of a didactic kind, so "it contains a medley of normative and idealistic thoughts on the Greek household", as its translator, Sarah Pomeroy states (1994, 33). The main character in the relevant passage of the *Oeconomicus* is Ischomachus, a wealthy man. His wife also belonged to the upper class, so their example cannot be viewed as representative of the whole of society. Nevertheless, they must have been referred to by Xenophon with the intention that his readers would learn from their example.

In *Oec.* VII.5–6, Socrates narrates to Critobulus his conversation with Ischomachus.[51] One of Ischomachus' answers to Socrates runs as follows:[52]

'What could she have known when I took her as my wife, Socrates? She was not yet fifteen when she came to me, and had spent her previous years under careful supervision so that she might see and hear and speak as little as possible. Don't you think it was adequate if she came to me knowing only how to take wool and produce a

---

[49] *Ibid.*, p. 107.
[50] E. Dassmann – G. Schöllgen 1986, col. 817.
[51] S. B. Pomeroy 1994, 138–39.
[52] *Ibid.*, p. 139.

cloak, and had seen how spinning tasks are allocated to the slaves? And besides, she had been very well trained to control her appetites, Socrates,' he said, 'and I think that sort of training is most important for man and woman alike'.

In this quotation first of all we may note how young the wife of Ischomachus was when he married her. Sarah Pomeroy affirms concerning the upper classes that "men tended to marry at about 30, but 14 was a normal age for the first marriage of an Athenian girl" (1994, 268). This phenomenon would have meant that prior to marriage a girl as a daughter was expected to be obedient to her parents. In our present example, obedience is implied by the expression "under careful supervision". Ischomachus' wife had to learn with obedience the virtues expected in that era from a wife.

From another passage we learn that this teaching was carried out by the parents. In VII.14–15 (p. 141) we read the following conversation between wife and husband: "'My mother told me that my duty is to practise self-control.' 'By Zeus, wife,' I said, 'my father said the same to me.'" Thus we can see that the husband, Ischomachus, was taught by his father. The key term, "self-control" (σωφρονεῖν), occurs in subsequent literature, too.

In Xenophon's *Oeconomicus* we also meet a specific occasion when a daughter was expected to be obedient to her parents: the parents decided whom she should marry. In VII.11–12 (p. 141), Ischomachus tells his young wife:

I, on my part, and your parents, on your behalf, considered who was the best partner we could choose for managing an estate and for children. And I chose you, and your parents, apparently, chose me, out of those who were eligible. (VII.12:) Now if some day the god grants us children, then we shall consider how to train them in the best way possible. For this will be a blessing to us both, to obtain the best allies and support in old age.

Another duty of a child (frequently met in our sources) is mentioned here as well: to provide support for one's aged parents (συμμάχων καὶ γηροβοσκῶν ὅτι βελτίστων τυγχάνειν, p. 140). In a beautifully-phrased passage, Ischomachus tells his wife that she can also rely on the benefits of this duty when she herself grows old (VII.42, p. 147):

But the sweetest experience of all will be this: if you prove to be better than I am and make me your servant. Then you will have no need to fear that as your years increase you will be less honoured [ἀτιμοτέρα]in the household; but you may be confident that when you become older, the better partner you have been to me, and the better guardian of the estate for the children, the greater the respect [τιμιωτέρα] you will enjoy in the household.[53]

---

[53] The Greek text from *ibid.*, p. 146. We note that τιμιωτέρα is used for the duty of respect.

The reference to "children" allows us to suggest that the respect she is to enjoy in the household will also include the respect from the side of her own children. In these quotations, then, we find an example that parents can expect to be honoured, and that there is an on-going process of children's duties: whatever they are expected to do to their parents, they can later expect from their own children in relation to themselves. Every child is part of a chain where he or she repays a debt owed to his or her parents; and that child will become a parent who can expect that a debt will be repaid to him or her. We may also note that the reference to being a good guardian of the estate also implies that the children will be grateful to their mother because she did her best in their upbringing.

We shall see in the next section that the duty of supporting one's parents was also expressed in a fourth century inscription found in Delphi.

As I shall summarise our findings at the end of the chapter, let us now turn to some texts where we can find further examples of grounds given for children's duties.

3. Reasons and grounds for children's duties towards their parents

We have already met some grounds for children's duties in the preceding section, as they often appear together with naming the expectations themselves. When I add further examples, again as representatives of various genres and centuries prior to the Hellenistic period, I also refer briefly to those already mentioned.

We have seen in the previous section that Hesiod referred to the fear of the gods as a reason for carrying out children's duties. In *Works and Days*, Hesiod further writes (*Op.*, lines 331–332): with the man "who abuses his old father at the cheerless threshold of old age and attacks him with harsh words, truly Zeus himself is angry, and at the last lays on him a heavy requittal for his evil doing".[54] Here we find one of the most frequently mentioned and most weighty grounds for all ethical conduct: the religious motivation. The threat of punishment from Zeus is an expression of the will of the gods: one should honour one's parents, otherwise there will follow punishment from the gods. Also in the context of the "fifth generation", seen in the previous section, we can find the idea of punishment as a reason not to dishonour one's parents: "Zeus will destroy this race of mortal men"

---

[54] In Loeb: p. 27.

(*Op.* 180). We note the duty we have met in the previous section – a duty that is implied by the negative formulation – that parents should not be harmed by irreverent speech. The man who "abuses" (νεικείῃ) his father picks a quarrel with him or attacks him verbally. The father referred to here is "at the cheerless threshold of old age". Liddell-Scott paraphrase the expression containing οὐδός in this way (LSJ, p. 1269): "on the *threshold* which is old age, i.e. perh., on the *threshold* that leads from life to death". A reverence for old age may be implied in this text as well.

In his *Life of Pythagoras*, Diogenes Laertius (third century A.D.) mentions older people and parents in two passages that are very near to one another (VIII.22, in Loeb, p. 339):

[Pythagoras] is said to have advised his disciples as follows: ... (p. 341:) To honour their elders, on the principle that precedence in time gives a greater title to respect; for as in the world sunrise comes before sunset, so in human life the beginning before the end, and in all organic life birth precedes death. (VIII.23:) And he further bade them to honour gods before demi-gods, heroes before men, and first among men their parents; and so to behave one to another as not to make friends into enemies, but to turn enemies into friends.[55]

We note the Pythagorean argument from natural life: he holds the principle that "precedence in time" calls for greater respect. He or she who is older, deserves a higher degree of honour (τοὺς τε πρεσβυτέρους τιμᾶν, τὸ προηγούμενον τῷ χρόνῳ τιμιώτερον ἡγουμένους).[56] It is significant for our theme that among human beings parents are to be honoured above all (καὶ θεοὺς μὲν δαιμόνων προτιμᾶν, ἥρωας δ' ἀνθρώπων, ἀνθρώπων δὲ μάλιστα τοὺς γονέας).

Iamblichus narrates that Pythagoras referred to the gods as a reason to honour and obey one's parents. On the same occasion when Pythagoras was addressing young people in a gymnasium, he is reported to have said concerning parents: "if we recognize that they are second to none in benefitting us, we cannot sin against the gods. And it is likely the gods would judge kindly those who honor their fathers second to none, for from our fathers we have learned to honor the divine".[57] Pythagoras here also refers to the

---

[55] This text has a very close parallel in Iamblichus: *On the Pythagorean Way of Life*, ch. 8, section 37. The editors of this work, John Dillon and Jackson Hershbell note that the two texts are "verbally quite close, as if the same document were available to them both", 1991, 63, fn. 4.

[56] For a monographic treatment of the theme that "the older is better", see P. Pilhofer 1990.

[57] Iamblichus: *On the Pythagorean Way of Life*, ch. 8, sections 38–39; in J. Dillon – J. Hershbell 1991, 63.

3. Reasons and grounds for children's duties towards their parents

example of Heracles, who, although being himself a god, was obedient to his father, Zeus. By this example, Pythagoras "showed the Crotoniates ... why it is necessary to obey willingly that which is ordered by parents" (διότι δεῖ τὸ προστατόμενον ἑκουσίως τοῖς γονεῦσιν ὑπακούειν).[58] The reference to "benefitting" from parents is a summary of what children owe them for their lives. We have seen among the duties that Pythagoras taught that children owe gratitude to their parents; the reason for this duty is that they gave life to their children. We note here the duty of "obedience" (ὑπακούειν).

We have already seen that there existed in antiquity the idea of a certain ranking, with parents mentioned in a list of those to whom honour is due. Parents follow after the gods, demi-gods and heroes, usually in the first place among human beings (see e.g. the *Golden Verses of Pythagoras* and Zaleucus in the previous section). We shall see that even in subsequent centuries parents appear in the second place or in the third place after the gods and the fatherland. The order of the lists implies that the duty of honouring one's parents follows from the duty of honouring the gods.

In the above quotation we not only meet a ranking, but also a reference to friends. Friendship (φιλία) was a key category for Pythagoras. He used this term even for internal family relationships, in a list similar to that seen above. Iamblichus writes that Pythagoras taught friendship "of all with all". In a long list of relationships he includes friendship "of a husband with a wife or children, brothers and relatives" (Φιλίαν δὲ διαφανέστατα πάντων πρὸς ἅπαντας Πυθαγόρας παρέδωκε, ... ἀνδρὸς δὲ πρὸς γυναῖκα ἢ τέκνα ἢ ἀδελφοὺς καὶ οἰκείους).[59] It is significant that this list begins with a reference to the friendship "of gods with human beings through piety and scientific worship" (... θεῶν μὲν πρὸς ἀνθρώπους δι' εὐσεβείας καὶ ἐπιστημονικῆς θεραπείας, *ibid.*).

Concerning the Pythagoreans, Iamblichus affirmed:[60] "These men, then, advised removal of competition and rivalry from true friendship especially, and from all friendship if possible; at least its removal from paternal friendship, and generally, from friendship with one's elders" (... ἐκ φιλίας ἀληθινῆς ἐξαιρεῖν ἀγῶνά τε καὶ φιλονεικίαν... ἔκ γε τῆς πατρικῆς καὶ

---

[58] *Ibid.*, section 40.
[59] Iamblichus: *On the Pythagorean Way of Life*, ch. 33, section 229; in J. Dillon – J. Hershbell 1991, 227. We have seen in the Introduction to this chapter that Aristotle, too, used the term "friendship" (φιλία) for the relationship between husband and wife.
[60] *Ibid.*, section 230. Because of the reference to Pythagoras I refer to this text here, although the Pythagoreans could be mentioned later. Once again, it has to be emphasised that chronology serves as a general guide in the course of our discussion, but is not followed rigidly.

καθόλου ἐκ τῆς πρὸς τοὺς πρεσβυτέρους). In this close connection of fathers and older people, the very juxtaposition implies that parents are also to be honoured because they are older.

Three great authors from fifth century B.C. literary works, in the genre of tragedy, provide further examples of grounds for children's duties. Aeschylus (525/4-456) in *The Suppliant Maidens*, after a call to worship the gods as the fathers did, goes on to speak of "reverence for parents – this standeth written third among the statutes of Justice, to whom honour supreme is due" (*Suppl.* 707–709).[61] Once again we note the religious reason for reverence towards parents. Here it is expressly stated that it is the will of the gods – written in statutes –, in this case that of *Dike*.

In our second example, in Sophocles' *Oedipus Tyrannus*, toward the end of the drama Oedipus tells the chorus that he has blinded himself, but it was Apollo "who accomplished these cruel, cruel sufferings ..." (*Oed. tyr.* 1329–1330).[62] Oedipus refers to himself as "the utterly lost, the thrice accursed, and moreover the one among mortals most hated by the gods!" (*Oed. tyr.* 1345–1346).[63] Oedipus killed his father and married his mother, although he did not know they were his own parents. He feels that Apollo's just anger over this deed cannot be atoned for. He gives the following reason why he put out his eyes by his own hands (*Oed. tyr.* 1371–1374):[64] "For I do not know with what eyes I could have looked upon my father when I went to Hades, or upon my unhappy mother, since upon them both I have done deeds that hanging could not atone for" (... οἷν ἐμοὶ δυοῖν ἔργ' ἐστὶ κρείσσον' ἀγχόνης εἰργασμένα). Here we can see the idea that acting against one's parents results in an unbearable burden. In his own eyes, he committed an act worse than anything else deserving execution.[65] His not knowing who they really were did not lessen the gravity of sinning against his own parents: it was a sin to be punished by the gods. We refer also to the previous section where we have seen that Antigone also thought she would have acted against the "ordinances of the gods" had she not buried her parents and her brother.

When Euripides (485/4-406) calls for reverence toward one's parents, he also uses the term σέβομαι, which is the expression mostly used of the honour to (or worship of) the gods. In Stobaeus' florilegium 79, a collection of

---

[61] In Greek: τὸ γὰρ τεκόντων σέβας / τρίτον τόδ' ἐν θεσμίοις / Δίκας γέγραπται μεγιστοτίμου (in Loeb: p. 70).
[62] Sophocles in Loeb: I/465.
[63] *Ibid.*, pp. 465 and 467.
[64] *Ibid.*, p. 469.
[65] LSJ translate our passage as "deeds too bad for *hanging*"; p. 17 (s.v. ἡ ἀγχόνη).

3. Reasons and grounds for children's duties towards their parents

sayings concerning the honour due to one's parents, we find the following quotation from Euripides:[66]

ὅστις δὲ τοὺς τεκόντας ἐν βίῳ σέβει,
ὅδ' ἐστὶ καὶ ζῶν καὶ θανὼν θεοῖς φίλος.

Here we find the clearly formulated religious ground for honouring one's parents: it is only this way that one can be "dear" to the gods in life and death, that is: eternally.

In the previous section, we have encountered in Aristophanes' *Clouds* two reasons for children's duties: that of owing gratitude for the father's caring help when the son was an infant; and also the reason that older people are to be honoured (and parents are older than their offspring).

We have already met two reasons for duties in Plato: the old age of parents and the threat of punishment in human courts.[67] In the previous section, we have also encountered Plato's reference to "what is universally just", as a reason without further specification (*Laws* 627A). Another reason cannot be separated from the duty of "recompensing" parents when they are old and need help. In as much as children are expected to pay back a "debt" owed to their parents for their own very existence and up-bringing, this duty is grounded in the parents' gift of life and up-bringing. Duty and its ground are like the two sides of a coin in this case.[68]

Plato gives a special example of reverence – that of speech – and the reason for it in one sweeping sentence (*Laws* IV.717C–D): "And throughout all his life he must diligently observe reverence of speech towards his parents above all things, seeing that for light and winged words there is a most heavy penalty, – for over all such matters Nemesis, messenger of Justice, is appointed to keep watch".[69] Plato can speak not only in negative terms about a penalty (ζημία), but he concludes his section on children's duties towards their parents by referring to what is due in return (τὴν ἀξίαν, 718A): "Every one of us, if we acted thus and observed these rules of life, would win always a due reward from the gods and from all that are mightier than ourselves, and would pass the greatest part of our lives in the enjoyment of hopes of happiness".[70] Penalty on the one hand from Nemesis, the "angel" of the goddess *Dike*, and reward from the gods stand as a warn-

---

[66] In C. Wachsmuth – O. Hense 1909, 619.
[67] *Laws* XI.932B–C (see the introduction to this chapter, fn. 5).
[68] For this duty and its reason, see the discussion of *Laws* IV.717B–718A in the previous section.
[69] In Loeb: I/299.
[70] In Loeb: I/301.

ing concerning the need to watch what words one uses in talking to parents.

Plato gives further grounds for duties towards parents.[71] He argues in his *Laws* (XI.931A–D) that if we honour the lifeless statues and images of gods, we believe that "the living gods beyond feel great good-will towards us and gratitude".[72] Likewise, our living parents should be honoured: "So if any man has a father or a mother, or one of their fathers or mothers, in his house laid up bed-ridden with age, let him never suppose that, while he has such a figure as this upon his hearth, any statue could be more potent, if so be that its owner tends it duly and rightly".[73] Plato distinguishes between gods whom we see (perhaps stars, cf. 821B) and those who cannot be seen. Of the latter, people erect statues. Here Plato refers to aged parents and grandparents as being more precious than the statues of the unseen gods. In this striking example living parents are due recipients of the same honour as due to gods, whereas other texts usually affirm that parents should receive this honour only after they die.[74] Klaus Schöpsdau notes in his Greek-German edition of Plato's *Laws*, that the term ἐν οἰκίᾳ, which is bracketed in most editions, should not be omitted. He argues – with a reference to Saunders – that we know from other places in Plato's *Laws* that it was forbidden to keep private places of worship in one's house (X.909D; 910B–C). Therefore, Plato probably wants to emphasise that in one's own house, honour toward one's parents replaces the forbidden private worship of the gods.[75]

Plato also affirms that the prayers of parents are heard by the gods, whether they pray for the good of the children or whether they curse them. After some references to cases where parents' curses upon their children were "granted by Heaven and fulfilled" (among them that of Oedipus), Plato affirms:

Let no man suppose, then, that when a father or a mother is dishonoured by the children, in that case it is natural for God to hearken especially to their prayers, whereas when the parent is honoured and is highly pleased and earnestly prays the

---

[71] These are also quoted at length later by Pempelus, see T. Taylor 1822, 67–69; D.R. Fideler 1987, 261. (I note that the dates of Pempelus are not given in LSJ; they simply write that he is to be found in Stobaeus.)

[72] In Loeb: II/447 and 449; quotation from 931A, p. 449.

[73] *Ibid.*

[74] I note that the Greek text is not easy to interpret, yet because of the reference to "old age" (ἀπειρηκότες γήρᾳ) it is certain that the parents are alive, though old and frail. To these parents is the term "shrine, statue" (ἵδρυμα) applied.

[75] *Platon, Werke*, VIII.2, p. 405, fn. 56.: "die gebotene Verehrung der Eltern wird somit zu einem 'Ersatz' für den verbotenen privaten Götterkult (so Saunders Notes Nr.112)".

3. Reasons and grounds for children's duties towards their parents

gods, in consequence, to bless his children – are we not to suppose that they hearken equally to prayers of this kind, and grant them to us?[76]

According to this passage, curses uttered by parents as well as prayers of parents for the blessing of their children are effective. Plato himself expressly states that with these arguments he provides grounds for honouring one's parents. He concludes the section on the prayers of parents by affirming that (931E–932A):[77]

> Every right-minded man fears and respects the prayers of parents, knowing that many times and in many cases they have proved effective. And since this is the ordinance of nature, to good men aged forefathers are a heavenly treasure while they live, up to the very last hours of life, and being propitious as they depart they are sorely regretted; but to the bad they are truly fearsome. Therefore let every man, in obedience to these counsels, honour his own parents with all the due legal honours.

In this argument we note that the verb "respects" is expressed by the term τιμᾷ in Greek. Once again we have an example in which "nature" serves as a reason for honouring one's aged parents (φύσις is referred to also in the previous quotation). The reference to "all the due legal honours" (πάσαις τιμαῖς ταῖς ἐννόμοις) leads us over to reasons and grounds in the human sphere.

Plato not only speaks about punishment by the gods, but he also holds that people's offences against their parents should be brought before human courts (932A–B):[78]

> If any person in this State be unduly neglectful of his parents, and fail to consider them in all things more than his sons or any of his offspring, or even himself, and to fulfil their wishes, let the parent who suffers any such neglect report it, either in person or by a messenger, to the three eldest Law-wardens, and to three of the women in charge of marriage; and these shall take the matter in hand, and shall punish the wrongdoers...

The prospect of punishment by legal courts, then, may be a further reason not to neglect one's parents. We note the expectation that parents should be considered to be "more" (μειζόνως) than one's own offspring and even more than oneself. We may contrast this statement with the Old Testament

---

[76] *Ibid.* 931B–C; quotation from 931C, p. 449. We note that both father and mother are mentioned here. The next passage emphasises the honour due to mothers in an even more pointed way: "in the eyes of the gods we can possess no image more worthy of honour than a father or forefather laid up with old age, or a mother in the same condition" (τὴν αὐτὴν δύναμιν ἐχουσῶν); *Laws* XI.931D.

[77] In Loeb: p. 451.

[78] *Ibid.*, pp. 451 and 453.

law – quoted by Jesus in the New Testament: "you shall love your neighbour as yourself" (Lev 19:18).[79]

We note that Aristotle gave the following reason for providing "maintenance" for parents: "since we owe it to them as a debt".[80]

That a man would be held responsible before human courts for neglecting his parents can be seen also in the example of an inscription, found in 1937 in a wall just outside the western entrance of the Temple of Apollo in Delphi (L. Lerat 1943, 62). On the basis of the names of those who are mentioned in the text, Lerat dates the marble inscription towards the end of the fourth century, or the beginning of the third century B.C. (pp. 69–70). For reasons which we are not told, the Council in Delphi voted to carve into marble the laws concerning parents. Lerat notes that most likely the law itself is even older than the time of the marble stele, but the Council, perhaps because of the lack of observance toward that law, thought it important to keep it in front of the eyes of the Delphians (p. 70). Part of Lerat's reconstruction of the Greek text runs as follows (pp. 62–63):[81]

[ὅστ]ις κα μὴ τρέφηι τὸν πατέρα κα[ὶ τ]ὰν ματέρα, ἐπεί κα [π]οτανγέ[λλη]ται πο[ὶ τ]ὰν βουλάν, ἁ βουλὰ κατ[αδε]ίτω τὸν μὴ τρέφοντα καὶ ἀγ[έτω ἐ]ν τὰν δαμοσίαν οἰκίαν ἔντ[ε κα ...

Unfortunately, the rest of the inscription is not extant. On the basis of other evidence, Lerat argues that the term δαμοσίαν οἰκίαν must mean "prison" (67). Again, we do not know exactly what the negligence of μὴ τρέφηι ("n'assure pas la subsistance") meant, but it is clear from this inscription that some kind of (food-) provision was expected from the children towards their parents. To fail to carry out that duty was punished by imprisonment. We may note that the first word of the inscription is reconstructed by Lerat as [Θε]ός (p. 62). As the context is lost, we should not read too much into the presence of this word, but with due caution we may raise the possibility that the regulations of the law court were in some connection with the religious life of the day. However that may be, here we can see a threat toward negligent children as a motivation to keep laws concerning their duties toward their parents. If they disobey those laws, they face punishment, even that of imprisonment.

We can find also a material reason why children should care for their par-

---

[79] For a discussion of this verse in the Old Testament and in the Synoptic Gospels, see Hubert Meisinger 1996, 7–69.

[80] *Nicomachean Ethics* 1165a, in Loeb: p. 527.

[81] L. Lerat translates this section as follows (p. 63): "Si quelqu'un n'assure pas la subsistance de son père et de sa mère, lorsqu'il sera dénoncé auprès du Conseil, que le Conseil fasse enchaîner le coupable et le fasse conduire en prison jusqu'à ce que (ou tant que)...".

3. Reasons and grounds for children's duties towards their parents

ents: children inherit from their parents when they die, so they should provide for them while they are still alive. In this context we may add that a child's duty to provide for his or her aging parents was also extended to the expectation of provision for grandparents and great-grandparents. The orators deal with hereditary issues at length. This is a special genre, where reference is made to laws, and at the same time the laws are applied to real life situations. For example, in legal arguments in the works of Isaeus, a fourth century B.C. orator, we find the following reason why a grandchild of the deceased should inherit rather than the children of the deceased person's brother:[82]

... if my grandfather were alive and in want of necessities of life, we, and not our opponent, would be liable to prosecution for neglect. For the law enjoins us to support our parents, meaning by "parents" father, mother, grandfather, and grandmother, and their father and mother, if they are still alive; for they are the source of the family, and their property is transmitted to their descendants, and so the latter are bound to support them even if they have nothing to bequeath to them. How then can it be right that, if they have nothing to leave, we should be liable to prosecution for neglecting them, yet that, if they have something to leave, our opponent should be the heir and not we? Surely it cannot be right.

We note a number of significant elements in this speech. Firstly, here we meet again the reference to legal punishment, or prosecution (ἡμᾶς ὑποδίκους εἶναι τῆς κακώσεως), if children do not obey the law that parents (and grandparents) should be supported and cared for (κελεύει γὰρ τρέφειν τοὺς γονέας). Secondly, it is affirmed that parents (and grandparents) are the "source" of life of the family (ἀρχὴ τοῦ γένους εἰσί). It follows that children owe a debt in return for their lives. Thirdly, the argument that children will inherit from them serves as a reason why children have to provide for their parents; though it is worth pointing out that even if their parents or grandparents cannot leave any inheritance behind, the duty of supporting them remains valid.[83]

Finally, we consider some quotations preserved by Stobaeus. According to him, Timocles (fourth century B.C.) held that if one reveres his father, then one will be a good citizen and one will be successful against the enemy:[84]

ὅστις φοβεῖται τὸν πατέρα καὶ αἰσχύνεται, οὗτος πολίτης ἀγαθὸς ἔσται κατὰ λόγον καὶ τοὺς πολεμίους δυνάμενος κακῶς ποιεῖν.

---

[82] Speech XIII: "Against Agoratus"; in Loeb: p. 309.
[83] For further examples from the orators, see the excellent chapter by Giulia Sissa, "Die Familie im griechischen Stadtstaat", in A. Burguière et al., 1996, 237–76.
[84] In C. Wachsmuth – O. Hense 1909, 622–23.

The reference to being a good citizen implies that one obeys the laws of the city. It may also be seen as a pointer to the close link between the *polis* and the family. In a similar way, Aristotle – disagreeing with Plato's abolishing the significance of the family based on blood relations – emphasised the necessity of maintaining the family as the basic unit of the state. We shall return to this important view on the occasion of discussing the New Testament Household Codes.[85]

We note the terminology used by Timocles: φοβεῖται τὸν πατέρα καὶ αἰσχύνεται. As we find here a reference to "fear" and a feeling of "shame" before a father only, it is worth pointing out that Stobaeus cites several sayings which relate to one's "mother". In a quotation from Euripides, where children are encouraged to love their mother (here the term ἐρᾶν is used),[86] the reason for this love is simply that there is nothing dearer for the children than their mother (Οὐκ ἔστιν οὐδὲν μητρὸς ἥδιον τέκνοις). This is a reason taken from "nature".

The next quotations lead us to the writers of New Comedy. These authors are significant, because it can be clearly seen that they influenced later Roman authors.[87] Although with these authors we reach the turn of the fourth and third centuries, we mention them here, whereas their followers and adaptors writing in Latin, Plautus and Terence, belong to the period covered in our next chapter. In a quotation from Philemo, a mother is addressed with these words: ἔτεκές με, μῆτερ, καὶ γένοιτό σοι τέκνων ὄνησις, ὥσπερ καὶ δίκαιον ἔστι σοι.[88] Here mothers are entitled to "enjoyment of their children" because this is just (or right). The reason is not specified; it may be seen as a summary of several arguments we have met: nature tells us that it is just that parents "profit or delight" from their children,[89] since they have given much to their children earlier; or, it may be the will of the gods, especially of *Dike*, that children cause their parents to delight.

In our last example, Menander (ca. 342–291 B.C.) refers to the "law"

---

[85] For a discussion of the relevant passages in Book I. of Aristotle's *Politics*, see G. Sissa's article in A. Burguière *et al.*, 1996, especially pp. 237–43. Sissa argues: "Gegen die platonische Utopie verteidigt Aristoteles, was er als wahres Wesen der Familie in der griechischen Gesellschaft ansieht..." (p. 243).

[86] In C. Wachsmuth – O. Hense 1909, 620: "Εὐριπίδου Ἐρεχθεῖ (fr. 358 N.2) ... ἐρᾶτε μητρός, παῖδες ...".

[87] For a list of works of Plautus and Terence, which were influenced by – and often even bore the title of – works of Greek authors in New Comedy, see Richard Hunter's article entitled "Hellenismus", in H-G. Nesselrath 1997, 246–68, especially p. 253.

[88] In C. Wachsmuth – O. Hense 1909, 621.

[89] LSJ, p. 1231, translate ὄνησις as "*enjoyment of* a thing, *profit* or *delight* from it" (italics theirs).

when he affirms that one has to pay the same honour to parents as to the gods:[90] Νόμος γονεῦσιν ἰσοθέους τιμὰς νέμειν. We can leave open the question whether this ambiguous reference to the law, as the ground for honouring one's parents, refers to divine law or human law, because the two spheres are often related to one another in an inseparable way. When closing this section, we note the importance of the "genre" of New Comedy for our topic, because these writers often deal with problems arising in the family. In as much as tension between children and parents (often in connection with marriage plans) is a frequent theme for comedy, it is the more significant that one of the greatest authors of New Comedy emphasised the duty of honouring one's parents.[91]

We now turn to texts which relate to the question of whether or not a child's duty to his or her parents should recognise some limits.

4. Limits to children's duties towards their parents

Some of our sources in antiquity refer to limitations concerning children's duties towards their parents. They are of high significance for our present project, because we shall see in the part on the New Testament that there was a tension in the child-parent relationship in the Jesus movement; or, to put it in another way, there were cases with limitations in carrying out the duty of honouring one's parents among Jesus' first followers.

In chronological order, our first example can be found in the laws of Solon, in Athens, at the beginning of the sixth century B.C. As Plutarch tells us, the following limit is set (*Lives,* Solon XXII.1): "[Solon] enacted a law that no son who had not been taught a trade should be compelled to support his father" (νόμον ἔγραψεν υἱῷ τρέφειν τὸν πατέρα μὴ διδαξάμενον τέχνην ἐπάναγκες μὴ εἶναι).[92] It must be acknowledged, however, that this rule is not a general principle in Solon's laws; it has to be understood within its context. By introducing this law, Solon wanted to solve the problem which arose from the fact that too many people migrated to Attica. As there were many people who had no skill and no jobs either, Solon wanted to turn

---

[90] In C. Wachsmuth – O. Hense 1909, 623.

[91] Cf. the summarising note of the editor and translator of Menander's works in the Loeb series, W. G. Arnott (vol. 1, p. xxxi): "In every play one or two love affairs come through obstacles to a happy conclusion. The obstacles are always the same: differences of class or background, shortage of cash, parental opposition."

[92] Plutarch: *Lives,* Solon XXII; in Loeb: p. 465.

"the attention of the citizens to the arts of manufacture".[93] We note that the negative formulation (ἐπάναγκες μὴ εἶναι) affirms the duty in an indirect way: what is not compulsory in this case, would be the normal expectation in general. In this context we may assume that the above mentioned law had a twofold purpose: on the one hand, it encouraged fathers to pay attention to the training of their children; and on the other hand, if children did not support their fathers, it must have meant that "fathers", i.e. older people were encouraged to carry out useful work and not simply to rely on the care provided by their children. In as much as we can see the "practical" aim of that law, it is an important example, because it shows that Solon must have thought that the duty toward one's parents was not thought of as an absolute one by the society of his day.

In the light of the argument met earlier that children owe a debt to be repaid to their parents, we may infer from this example that if a father did not provide the teaching a trade for his son, this may have been regarded as negligence in terms of upbringing. Perhaps the son was exempt from his duty of support because he owed a lesser debt than those children whose upbringing included training in a trade. We may note that Solon spoke about sons and fathers and not about children and parents in general; this may be due to the context which deals with teaching "manufacturing" professions.

In Solon's laws, at the end of the section seen above, we encounter another case when a son was exempt from the duty of supporting his father: if the son was illegitimate. It is clear from this example that the duty is affirmed by Solon as a necessity, yet a necessity that has to recognise certain limits:

But that provision of his was yet more severe, which, as Heracleides Ponticus informs us, relieved the sons who were born out of wedlock from the necessity of supporting their fathers at all. For he that avoids the honourable state of marriage, clearly takes a woman to himself not for the sake of children, but of pleasure; and he has his reward, in that he robs himself of all right to upbraid his sons for neglecting him, since he has made their very existence a reproach to them.[94]

Behind this exemption from the duty of support stands a reason we meet widely spread in antiquity: the main goal of marriage is that of begetting children. A man who goes to *hetairai*, does not honour marriage, but seeks pleasure only. A child out of this union is not equal with a child that was born as a fulfillment of marriage. Solon further argues that the father is responsible for the difficult life an illegitimate child had to face. The father is

---

[93] *Ibid.*
[94] Plutarch: *Lives*, Solon XXII.4; in Loeb: p. 467.

4. Limits to children's duties towards their parents

to bear the consequence of his deed: when he grows old, he cannot count on the support of his child, a support that would have been obligatory for his legitimate son (τὸ μηδὲ τοῖς ἐξ ἑταίρας γενομένοις ἐπάναγκες εἶναι τοὺς πατέρας τρέφειν).

We have already met the third reason why a grown-up son is relieved from his duty to support his father: in the case that the father had hired him out for prostitution when he was a child. We note, however, that even in this case the son was obliged to bury his father when he died and he had to "perform the other customary rites".[95]

We observe, then, that the duty of supporting one's father is a strong expectation; indeed, it is a necessity, or obligation. Nevertheless, it is not an absolute one: under certain circumstances a son was exempt from it. It is significant that in all the cases in Solon's laws the exemption from the duty is justified by the unworthy behaviour of the father. We note that the above-mentioned limitations belong to the human sphere; they are based on the mutuality of duties and not on a "religious" priority of parents.

In the preceding sections, we have encountered many examples of lists where gods were named before parents as the due recipients of honour. The very ranking can be seen as a limitation: gods come before parents.[96] In the lists there is no concrete limit expressed; they serve as a general reminder of priorities. We shall see that the matter of priority shall remain important also in the Hellenistic period and also for the Jesus movement. It will play a significant role in our understanding of many difficult New Testament texts.

In literary works, the priority of the gods over one's parents is often expressed directly by the commands given by gods in oracles; these commands have to be obeyed. To give but one example from the genre of tragedy, in the *Electra* of Sophocles we can find an example that the gods can even order the killing of one's parent.[97] We may argue that in as much as gods order human beings to honour their parents, it is the gods who can revoke that duty. As Enzo Degani has put it: "In der *Elektra* ist selbst der Muttermord, da von Apollons Orakel angeordnet, eine erlaubte und sogar geschuldete Tat".[98] This limit, of course, is not an arbitrary order from the gods; it is in relation to the sin committed by Electra's mother: she killed

---

[95] Aeschines I,13 (Speech against Timarchus), p. 15.
[96] See e.g. the Pythagoreans: the *Golden Verses of Pythagoras*, fn. 34; Zaleucus, fn. 35; Aristoxenus, fn. 42.
[97] At the beginning of the play, Orestes narrates that he went to the "Pythian oracle" to learn in what way he can take revenge for his father's violent death. See e.g. lines 32–37; in Sophocles in Loeb: I/171.
[98] E. Degani in H-G. Nesselrath 1997, 227.

Electra's father. Electra's participation in killing her own mother – together with Electra's brother, Orestes – was an act of revenge. It is significant that this limitation in honouring the mother was based on Apollo's order.

In Plato, we find two reasons why children are entitled to disagree with their parents. One of these reasons is if the parent in question has become insane (*Laws* XI.928D–E).[99] From the context it seems that Plato is not happy to mention this possibility at all. Most likely, he thought that a child could act in such a way that an "enmity" would not arise. However, he mentions as a possibility – or perhaps even as a fact[100] – that sons may "claim permission to indict their fathers for insanity when they are in a shameful condition owing to illness or old age".[101] Plato also names a condition: the son can initiate the procedure of indictment only if his father "regards himself as master of his own property and wastes his goods".[102] If the "Law-wardens" decide that the son's opinion about his father was right, then "the father that is convicted shall thenceforward have no power to administer even the smallest tittle of his property, and shall be counted as a child in the house for the rest of his life".[103] We note that in the State envisaged by Plato the limitation of a father's power is decided upon by the representatives of the legal system.

Plato further affirms that a child is entitled to disagree with his or her father's will. According to Plato (*Laws* XI.926B–C),[104] children might have "a complaint against the ordained laws concerning testaments in respect of any detail; and especially of those relating to marriage". In cases where children can prove that they would be unduly wronged by the will, they can turn to "Law-wardens", whose "verdict shall be carried out as final" (926D).[105]

In his *Life of Pythagoras*, Iamblichus recalls the following tradition:[106] "The Pythagoreans likewise said that it is more necessary to pay attention to philosophy, than to parents or to agriculture; for no doubt it is owing to the

---

[99] In Loeb: II/441.

[100] For the possibility that Plato refers to an existing phenomenon, see his phrase at the beginning of the section (928D): "Between fathers and their children, and children and their fathers, there arise differences greater than is right" (Διαφοραὶ πατέρων τε πρὸς αὐτῶν παῖδας γίγνονται καὶ παίδων πρὸς γεννητὰς μείζους ἢ χρεών).

[101] 928E, in Loeb: p. 441. In Greek, παράνοια is used for madness. As a law-term, γράφεσθαι is used for "to indict" (see LSJ, p. 360).

[102] 929D–E, p. 443.

[103] 929E, p. 445.

[104] In Loeb: II/433.

[105] *Ibid.*

[106] D. R. Fideler 1987, 116.

4. Limits to children's duties towards their parents 35

latter that we live, but philosophers and preceptors are the causes of our living well, and becoming wise, on discovering the right mode of discipline and instruction." It is difficult to decide in what concrete ways this tradition imposes a "limit" in carrying out duties toward parents. It is clear, however, that it wishes to express the high value of philosophy: it has a priority before parents. We have seen above that the Pythagoreans also affirmed children's duty to honour their parents after the gods. Even though the two statements may be in tension, we have to note this reference to philosophy which should come before "parents" and "agriculture". This limitation gains significance when compared with the radical sayings of Jesus concerning the disciples leaving their parents (to be discussed in the fourth chapter).

We note that in Aristophanes' *Clouds* it is philosophical teaching that opens the eye of the son of Strepsiades so that he can now argue against old conventions, including that of obedience to his father. Although Aristophanes did not approve of the Sophists, we may say that in the figure of the son, Pheidippides, he probably depicted an existing phenomenon of his age.[107]

Aristotle, too, acknowledges certain "limits" in honouring one's parents, although he does not say explicitly what those limits are. He simply affirms that different honours are due to different people. In his *Nicomachean Ethics* he writes (1165a):[108] "all people have not the same claim upon us,... even a father's claim is not unlimited" (ὅτι μὲν οὖν οὐ ταὐτὰ πᾶσιν ἀποδοτέον, οὐδὲ τῷ πατρὶ πάντα). The limitation that not everything is to be given to one's father as his due is justified by a "religious" argument: "...just as Zeus does not have all the sacrifices".[109]

Although Aristotle does not say *what* honour is "appropriate to a father" and to "one's mother", it is important that he refers to a distinction when he lists the following recipients of our duties:

Honour also is due to parents, as it is to the gods, though not indiscriminate ["not all", οὐ πᾶσαν] honour: one does not owe to one's father the same honour as to one's mother, nor yet the honour due to a great philosopher or general, but one owes

---

[107] We can leave open the question to what extent Aristophanes' picture of Socrates is a fair or unfair presentation. A. H. Sommerstein makes a good point when he affirms: "That Socrates was far from a typical sophist, Aristophanes either did not know or did not care: he may not have taught dishonest rhetoric, but he certainly (like the Worse Argument in the play) questioned and confuted those whose zeal for traditional beliefs was stronger than their understanding of the grounds on which these beliefs might be based, and his young admirers will have been encouraged by his example to do likewise ..." (*The Comedies of Aristophanes: Clouds*, p. 3).

[108] In Loeb: IX.ii.7–9, p. 527; Greek text: p. 526.

[109] 1165a, Loeb p. 527.

to one's father the honour appropriate to a father, and to one's mother that appropriate to her.[110]

The Greek text clearly limits the extent of the honour due to one's parents: καὶ τιμὴν δὲ γονεῦσι καθάπερ θεοῖς, οὐ πᾶσαν δέ.[111] Without being able to be more specific, we note the limitation expressed by the term "not all honour". We further note the reference to the honour due to the gods in the context of honour due to parents.

Having found many examples of duties, reasons and grounds for, and limits to, duties, we may now summarise them in a short list of the most important items.

5. Summary and classification of the results

We have frequently met the expectation that a child should "honour" or "revere" his or her parents. This general duty is often expressed by various forms of τιμάω (Hesiod, Pythagoras, the Pythagoreans [to whom the *Golden Verses of Pythagoras* may be attributed], Zaleucus, Plato, Aristotle, Aristoxenus, Xenophon, Menander). Pythagoras is said to have used the term ἀγαπάω as well. Euripides also uses the term σέβομαι; in Plato we have also found αἰδέομαι. Aeschylus uses τὸ σέβας for "reverence". In Timocles, φοβέομαι, "fear", is used with respect to one's father. We can say that this overarching expectation can be fulfilled by carrying out a number of concrete duties which can be summarised as follows.

In most of our examples, grown-up "children" owe a "debt" to be "repaid" to their parents when they grow old: children should provide for their old or ill parents, just as their parents provided for them when they were little children, and because they owe their very lives to their parents (Homer, Hesiod, Solon, Pythagoras, Aristophanes, Xenophon, Isaeus, Aristotle, – also the law at Delphi prescribes provision); to put it in another way: grown-up children should not neglect and maltreat their parents (Plato). This duty is related to the more general duty of gratitude (Pythagoras, Xenophon, the Pythagoreans).

Children should "imitate their predecessors", i.e. learn from them (Pythagoras); learning includes the appropriating of virtues like self-control, and also the learning of a skill or trade (Xenophon).

Children should not disagree with their parents (Hesiod, Pythagoras, Ly-

---

[110] *Ibid.*
[111] *Ibid.*, p. 526.

5. Summary and classification of the results

sias; implied also by Aristophanes). Closely related to this duty is the following: children have to obey what their parents say (Pythagoras, Zaleucus, Lysias). "Obedience" had also as its consequence that parents could decide whom their daughter should marry (Xenophon).

Children are expected to observe a respectful speech towards their parents (Hesiod, Plato, perhaps Lysias).

Children have to provide a funeral for their parents (Solon, Sophocles, Plato). Parents are to be venerated even after their deaths; this includes practising certain rites (Solon, Plato, and perhaps the Pythagoreans (*Golden Verses*); Aeschines approved of Solon's law).

The main duties of children can be listed in the following table:

While parents are alive *(due to them as superiors:)*	*After they die* *(due to them as superiors:)*
being obedient to them; learning from them; speaking to them respectfully;	venerating them (as divine beings);
(providing for them when weak:)	*(providing for them as mortals:)*
caring for them when they are old.	providing a funeral.[112]

To sum up, honour is a general expectation; it should be shown above all in obedience, provision in old age, and "provision" for the deceased: funeral rites and veneration afterwards.

We have found reasons and grounds for children's duties both in the divine and in the human spheres. Grounds related to the divine sphere are as follows:

Only those people can please the gods who revere their parents; fear of the gods serves as a ground (Hesiod, Pythagoras, Euripides, Plato; implied perhaps by Aeschylus, Aristotle and Philemo). Closely related to this is the following: children face punishment from the gods if they neglect or dishonour their parents; this implies that dishonouring one's parents is a sin against the gods (Hesiod, Sophocles, Plato). Apart from punishment, reward from the gods serves as a reason (Plato).

There is a ranking of beings, often expressed by the order of appearance in a list. In that rank, one or more "places" after the gods, parents are mentioned as due recipients of honour (Pythagoras, the Pythagoreans [*Golden Verses*], Zaleucus, Aristoxenus).

---

[112] I thank Professor Gerd Theissen for his helpful comments on structuring the table.

There are divine statutes that prescribe children's duties (Aeschylus, perhaps also implied by Plato, Philemo and Menander).

Prayers of parents are heard by the gods, both when they pray for the blessing or for the punishing of their children (Plato). This may be regarded as an expression of reciprocity usually referred to as the *do ut des* morality in religion.

We have encountered the following grounds and reasons for duties in the human sphere:

Laws prescribe children's duties (Solon, Plato, Isaeus, perhaps Menander). Accordingly, children will be responsible in front of human courts; neglecting one's duties toward one's parents is a crime (a crime which may be punished even by imprisonment according to the law at Delphi; Plato, Isaeus). By honouring one's parents one will be a good citizen (Timocles; implied also by Aristotle). It belongs to the sphere of law that children are going to inherit from their parents. This is a further reason why they are expected to provide for their parents while they are alive (Isaeus).

We have seen the expectation that children owe a great "debt" to their parents. From this it follows that children can thank their parents for their very existence, their nurture and upbringing (Homer, Hesiod, Pythagoras, Aristophanes, Plato, Isaeus, Aristotle). This serves as a reason for the duty. It can be extended to an on-going process: when "children" grow up, they will expect that younger people will respect them; in other words: children should bear in mind that one day they will become parents to their children; therefore, people should act to their parents as they are going to expect their own children to act (Pythagoras, Xenophon). This may be regarded as an another example of a *do ut des* morality (the same may be said about acting because of the prospect of future inheritance, seen above).

"By nature" parents are superior to their offspring (Plato also refers to this as being "universally just"; Aristotle; perhaps also Euripides and Philemo with respect to one's mother). Nature also provides a rule: precedence in time calls for respect; this means that parents are to be respected because they are older than their children (Pythagoras, Plato; implied also by Hesiod and Aristophanes).

We have met the following limits of children's duties:

Most often parents were mentioned in a list after the gods; this implies that the honour due to the gods comes before the honour due to parents (Pythagoras, the Pythagoreans [*Golden Verses*], Zaleucus, Aristoxenus). Since it is the will of the gods to honour parents, gods can set a limit to their own order, as in the case of Apollo's oracle in Sophocles. This concrete order, however, was a punishment of the unworthy behaviour of a parent.

5. Summary and classification of the results

Solon introduced the limitation that if a son was not taught a trade by his father, the son is exempt from the duty of providing for his father. The same exemption applied to illegitimate sons. A son that had been hired out for prostitution by his father, later did not have to support his father, but he was obliged to bury him.

Plato proposed that an insane parent does not have to be obeyed, and that an unjust will of a father can be challenged.

The Pythagoreans held that philosophy comes before parents. Aristophanes' *Clouds* may imply a knowledge of this view (although he himself criticised it), in as much as philosophical teaching was responsible for turning Pheidippides against his father.

We have to emphasise again that our list is not a comprehensive one. Nevertheless, with due caution we can observe two phenomena. First, as the gods order respect toward parents, it is the gods who can limit that respect. This view seems to be constant through the centuries. Secondly, a certain widening of the sphere of limits during the period from the sixth to the fourth centuries can be observed: Solon exempted from the duty of providing for parents those sons who were not taught a trade, those who were born outside the boundary of a legitimate marriage, and those who had been hired out for prostitution by their fathers. Plato held that insane fathers can be indicted and that an unjust will can be attacked. The Pythagoreans left the sphere of law, and they did not justify any limitation by unworthy behaviour on the parent's side: they set the priority of philosophy itself as a limit to the honour due to parents. We shall be interested to see whether the process of "widening" the sphere of limits is continued in the Hellenistic period.

The following table may help us to have an overview of the main reasons for duties and the main limits of duties.

reasons	in the divine sphere	in the human sphere
status of parents	in lists together with gods	parents are older and superior
source of the norm	will/(fear) of the gods	nature; what is universally just
form of the norm	statutes of gods	human laws
consequences		
– of negligence	punishment/curse	tried in courts; imprisonment
– of honour	reward/pleasing the gods	good citizens (pleasing men)
"do ut des"	gods answer parents' prayers	expecting support from children; expecting inheritance
other:		paying back a debt to parents

limits	in the divine sphere	in the human sphere
due to status	gods first in lists	insane (mad) father
source of limit	oracle	law: unjust will
behaviour	god's judgment ...	... over mother killing husband; father – begot illegitimate son; – did not teach his son a trade; – hired out son for prostitution
other:		the priority of philosophy

It is a matter of course that any classification is somewhat forced; not every item in the above table has an exact parallel. We note the two main cases where there is no parallel in the divine sphere: 1. the expectation of owing a debt to parents as a reason why one should provide for the parents (paying back the debt); 2. the limitation set by a priority within the human sphere; this priority is due to be given to philosophy.

We shall see in the following chapters that most of the views expressed in the sources discussed in this chapter had a continued history; they surface also in the period which lasted ca. from the third century B.C. until to the third century A.D. It is important for us to see that they were not new ideas when the Jesus movement began. In the following two chapters, we shall look out for ideas new to that period and also for those that were taken up from earlier centuries. The aim of our investigation will be to determine the *milieu* in which the early Christians lived.

Chapter Two

Greek and Latin Sources from the Hellenistic Period to the Third Century A.D.

1. Introduction

In this chapter we look at the Greek and Latin sources; in the next chapter we shall focus on Jewish sources in the same period. In drawing rather wide boundaries for the period to be discussed, we must emphasise one great risk we run: societies may change considerably during the course of three (and more) centuries. Our main focus will be the first century B.C. and the first two centuries of the Christian era, but the justification for widening the time span of the focus of our study lies in the similarities we find in the views and practices of the three centuries before and after the time of Jesus and his first followers. As the aim of this book is to discuss the New Testament against the background of its surrounding world, it is of significance that we find certain characteristics of the child-parent relationship that were fairly constant over a longer period of time.

I have decided to discuss the Greek and Latin sources together. Although they represent two different cultures (and I shall point out some differences later), in the period of our interest there were many common features in these two cultures. As an example, we may refer to the wide use of the Greek language in the Roman Empire. As H. I. Marrou puts it (1956, 255): "from the time of Horace onwards an educated Roman was proficient in the two languages, Greek and Latin". As regards the provinces, Marrou affirms (256): "The fact is that Greek culture had such tremendous prestige that the Roman State never made any serious attempt to impose Latin on its Eastern subjects."

Concerning the attitude of the Romans to their subjects, we may say that two general rules complemented one another: on the one hand, the legal rulings of Rome were – in general terms – valid all over the Empire; on the other hand, "the Romans usually took over the legal institutions of conquered countries without making any fundamental changes".[1] Thus in order

---

[1] V. A. Tcherikover – A. Fuks 1957, vol. 1., p. 7.

to be able to make a comparison between the New Testament and its surrounding world, it is necessary to establish the conditions which applied in the Roman Empire.²

Some further introductory remarks concern the social differences reflected in our sources. Firstly, our sources are mainly documents written by men.³ Susan Treggiari's verdict may be applied to various relationships within a family (1991a, 183): "The authors of Graeco-Roman literature, being male, were less acute in their observation of husbands". Secondly, we do not have the same amount of material on the various relationships within the family. As Beryl Rawson argues (1986b, 15–16): "the aspects which have been most treated have been those of husband-wife relations and of the male head's role." Thirdly, not much has survived written by children in antiquity. Rawson's remark – though somewhat exaggerated – can serve as an overall warning (1991b, 7): "There is virtually no material generated by children themselves in the Roman world". We shall see below some valuable exceptions: letters written by sons and daughters.⁴

I have already mentioned earlier that throughout my thesis I refer to the term "child" as an expression of a relationship, and not as an automatic indication of age. An adult is still the child of his or her parents. In spite of this usage, it seems necessary to affirm that "childhood" was also regarded as a specific stage of life in antiquity. Although there exists the view in scholarship that "the concept of childhood as a separate stage is a relatively modern invention",⁵ Emiel Eyben expresses the majority view in recent times (1991, 142): "There can be no doubt that Romans had a clear recognition not only of 'childhood' but also of 'youth' as distinctive phases of development".⁶ I agree with this latter view.⁷

---

² We may note a warning sounded by Beryl Rawson. She states that: "Although Christian families were already in Rome by the middle of the first century AD, their influence was slight: Rome was essentially a non-Christian society in the period to be discussed" (1986b, 6). We may add that this does not make it superfluous to study Roman society as the environment of the early Christians.

³ We shall especially value the few exceptions, like Perictyone and Phintys; see below, sections 2, 4, and 5.

⁴ Peter Müller emphasises the sparsity of evidence on education (1992, 89): "Eigenständige Schriften zur Erziehung von Kindern finden sich in der gesamten griechisch-römischen Antike ... äußerst selten. Die einzige griechische Schrift, die sich ganz diesem Gegenstand widmet, ist die unter dem Namen des Plutarch überlieferte Abhandlung Περὶ παίδων ἀγωγῆς."

⁵ By this remark, Suzanne Dixon (1991, 109) refers to the work of P. Ariès (*Centuries of Childhood*, 1962).

⁶ As examples, Suzanne Dixon refers to the "ritual connected with birth and other *rites de passage*": "At the age of about fifteen a boy would undergo a ceremony at which he set aside

1. Introduction

For our present study, the environment in which children grew up in antiquity is also of significance. Most scholars of family life in antiquity emphasise that the Roman legal term *familia* (as well as the term οἶκος in the Greek world) included not only parents and children, but others as well. For example, Beryl Rawson states:[8] "The Roman *familia* consisted of the conjugal family plus dependants (i.e. a man, his wife, and their unmarried children, together with the slaves and sometimes freedmen and fosterchildren who lived in the same household)." Children often grew up in a fellowship where they were exposed to many relationships. They learnt not only from their parents,[9] but from other people, too. Children were often emotionally attached to their nurses and *paedagogi* to such an extent that that relationship remained even when they had grown up.[10] We should remember these general observations when we focus our discussion on childparent relationships.

---

the *bulla* and the tunic (*toga praetexta*) of his childhood and took on a man's dress (*toga virilis*)" (1992, 101). There were many Greek terms which differentiated between the stages of life. In Philo, *Cher.* 114 we find the following sequence: βρέφος, παῖς, ἀντίπαις, ἡβῶν, μειράκιον, πρωτογένειος, νεανίας, τέλειος ἀνήρ (Ulrich Luz 1997, III/123, fn. 26, with further examples).

[7] See also Emiel Eyben's recent article on "Jugend" in *RAC* 19, 1999, cols. 388–442.
[8] 1986b, 7; see also T. Wiedemann 1989, 143–44.
[9] We can find a beautiful example of a father teaching his son, in Plutarch, *Cato the Elder* 20,4–7: "Cato himself taught him letters, taught him the laws and taught him athletics. He instructed him in how to throw a spear, fight in armour, to ride on horseback and to box; he also taught him to endure heat and cold, and to swim through whirlpools and river-rapids. He says that he wrote the book entitled the 'Histories' in his own hand and in large letters to enable his son to learn about the laws and customs of Rome at home. And he was as careful to avoid saying anything inappropriate in his son's presence as in that of a vestal virgin" (see J. F. Gardner and T. Wiedemann 1991, 102).
[10] J. F. Gardner and T. Wiedemann quote the text of an epitaph erected by a *paedagogus* to his erstwhile charge "who died on the day when the later Emperor Claudius was to have married her" (1991, 105; *CIL* 10.6561): "To Medullina, daughter of Camillus, espoused to Tiberius Claudius Nero Germanicus. The freedman Acratus, her *paedagogus*."

As indicated in the Introduction to our monograph, the theme of education is not dealt with in this thesis. For our purposes it is sufficient to note that children were exposed to impulses from others than their parents, as well. For the theme of education see e.g. H. I. Marrou's monograph, *A History of Education in Antiquity*, 1956; and the article on "Erziehung" by P. Blomenkamp in *RAC* 6, 1966, cols. 502–559.

2. The child-parent relationship in practice

a) Preliminary remarks

In the following, I shall discuss some phenomena of social life in antiquity that most likely had a bearing also on the child-parent relationship. As a preliminary remark we must note that our sources reveal much more about the upper-class (and perhaps the middle-class) than about lower classes. We cannot do anything but follow our sources; however, we must bear in mind the limitations caused by the selective – or often random – character of those very sources. The fact that the larger proportion of our sources concern the upper-class may not correspond to the social picture of early Christianity; though it is worth noting that the upper classes often set the pattern for the classes below them. In as much as there were Christians belonging to different classes of society (including the upper-class),[11] all the sources are relevant for our present aim: to collect non-biblical material which allows an insight into the environment of the early Christians.

One kind of the source that allows us an insight into real life in antiquity is found in documents written on papyri. The papyri finds are of high significance for our research, because they can often be dated. Official writings like marriage contracts and wills are dated by the authors themselves. However, when we deal with the materials contained in the papyri we must remember that they do not represent the whole society of that time. On the one hand, they are geographically restricted. Most of the papyri were found in Egypt where the climate allowed papyri to survive. This restriction, however, can have an advantage, too, namely that we often have an insight into the life of a village where the finds were recovered.

Another restriction is that literacy was rather low in antiquity. On many official documents there is a final clause which states who wrote and signed the document for somebody else who was illiterate. This phenomenon should warn us that we cannot expect a wide range of personal letters among family members. Literacy was most likely to be found among the members of the middle or upper classes who could afford the costs of education. Yet again, we should not underestimate the level of literacy either, as

---

[11] See e.g. Gerd Theissen's study from 1977, especially p. 46: "Wir finden in ihr [i.e. in der Jesusbewegung] sowohl Mitglieder und Sympathisanten der neuen Oberschicht, ... als auch Angehörige mittlerer Schichten ...". We also know that there were slaves among the early Christians (see e.g. 1 Cor 7:21–22; and the Letter to Philemon). For a discussion of the social classes in the Corinthian church, see G. Theissen 1989c (originally published in 1974).

we have a great number of letters extant from the times of antiquity. The fact that we also have letters written by (and to) women indicates that education was available to (at least some) girls, too.[12]

In this chapter, we shall first consider examples of every-day life in sources that describe reality, and then turn to sources which reveal norms that were "prescribed" to children in respect of their relationship to their parents. As in the previous chapter, we do not attempt to summarise the social history of the period, but try to collect the main things that were expected of children in relation to their parents from both practical examples and normative ones.

b) Expectations emerging from the social role of the father and of the mother

We have seen in the previous chapter how self-evident it was in the pre-Hellenistic period that society was based on a patriarchal structure. This remains true for the period of our present discussion. Let us examine some examples of this fact; and let us consider the social role of the father and of the mother.

W. K. Lacey has pointed to major differences between Greek and Roman societies as regards the relationship between family and state. In a recent article, he refers to his earlier monograph on the family in Greece[13] in which he argued that "the *oikos* was the institution through which one could reach an understanding of Greek society and the Greeks" (1986, 121). The main task of the state was to defend the *oikos* (122). Lacey has put forward the thesis that – in contrast with the situation in Greece – "it was *patria potestas* which was the fundamental institution underlying Roman institutions" (123). Lacey adds that "in consequence, public life followed the assumptions of private life, and not vice versa".

Although there were differences in the Greek and Latin societies as regards the role of the father, attention has to be paid to the Roman term *patria potestas*.[14] In earlier works on this legal expression, emphasis fell on the

---

[12] Examples of the above mentioned phenomena can be found, for example, in the first volume of the *Select Papyri* (Loeb edition, 1970), to which source I shall refer repeatedly in this chapter.

[13] 1968 (German transl. 1983).

[14] E. Eyben (1991, 115) refers to Dionysius of Halicarnassus who "pointed to the exceptional authority of the Roman *patria potestas*", and "to the differences between the Roman and the Greek world where the son was subject to his father's authority for only a short time (e.g. as long as he was unmarried or under eighteen years of age or until his name was entered in the public registers)". Eyben, however, argues that by the time when Dionysius

power accorded to the *patria potestas*.¹⁵ Recent works, however, point out that, from very early times on, *pietas* served as a restriction on the power exercised by the *paterfamilias*.¹⁶ It is true that the oldest male ancestor in a Roman family, the *paterfamilias*, had a lifelong paternal power over his children.¹⁷ Yet this power was limited by the increasing social independence of the children,¹⁸ and, as J. Gaudemet puts it, "durch die Bräuche, durch die Meinung der aufmerksamen Nachbarn und schließlich durch die Furcht vor den Göttern" (1969, 331). Emiel Eyben argues that by the time of the beginning of the Empire, "public opinion developed a distaste for undue strictness" (1991, 115). He claims that: "From the days of Empire onwards the legislators adapted themselves gradually to the altered mentality and took as their rule of thumb the maxim we find in the writing of the third-century jurist Marcianus: 'paternal authority must be based on affection, not on cruelty (*patria potestas in pietate debet, non atrocitate consistere*)'".¹⁹ *Pietas* was not only a one-sided obligation on children, but a mutual obligation on parents as well as on children (see e.g. R. Saller 1991, 147).

We shall see the significance of the role of the *paterfamilias* when we discuss the Household Codes in Ephesians and Colossians (in chapter five). The three pairs of addressees are based on the leading role of the *paterfamilias* as a husband, a father, and a master of slaves. It is also significant – perhaps as an expression of the limits of his power – that the "weaker" parts are addressed first: wives, children, and slaves.

To sum up, the father was the head of the Roman (and in a more limited way of the Greek) family. Judith Hallett has listed the numerous Latin words which derive from *pater*,²⁰ and she pointed to the fact that: "No anal-

---

wrote, "this portrait of a *paterfamilias* was largely a theoretical and anachronistic one". (For an English translation of Dionysius' text, 2.26.1ff, see for example J.F. Gardner – T. Wiedemann 1991, 12–13.)

[15] For example, E. Sachers writes in his detailed article on *patria potestas* in PW: "Die röm. *p.p.* war ursprünglich die volle, rücksichtslos durchgeführte, hausherrliche Gewalt über die Ehefrau, über die in der Ehe erzeugten Kinder und die sonstige agnatische Deszendenz" (vol. XXII/1, 1953, col. 1054).

[16] See e.g. E. Eyben 1991, 115.
[17] See e.g. Max Kaser 1971, 341.
[18] M. Kaser 1971, 341.
[19] 1991, 115; Cf. also Richard Saller's statement (1994, 72): "it is a gross oversimplification to represent Roman fathers as endowed with unlimited power, obeyed by children under unlimited obligation underwritten by the duty of *pietas*." Saller concludes: "Roman culture drew a clear distinction between the father's relationship with his children, characterized by mutual obligation and concern, and the master's exploitative power over his slaves" (73).

[20] 1984, 27–28, e.g.: *patronus, patricii, patria*.

2. The child-parent relationship in practice

ogy for such linguistic formations, which associate the word *pater* with power, ownership, and achievement, may be adduced among the Latin words built from *mater*, mother".[21] We have seen that *pietas* was expected from children (and also from fathers).

Fathers usually decided whom their daughters should marry. This implies an expectation of obedience in a concrete sphere of life, as we have also seen in the previous chapter. It is possible that even sons had to ask for the assent of their fathers in relation to marriage.[22] The fact that marriages were "arranged" may have meant that – at least in the initial period of marriage – husband-wife relationships were not necessarily filled with emotion. J. Gaudemet notes that apart from the time of the exile of Cicero, we cannot find any kind words to his wife in his letters (1969, 334). Gaudemet adds: "Cicero zeigt dagegen zärtliche Gefühle für seine Kinder". Of course, that this may have had many reasons, and one cannot generalise. Nevertheless, it may have been true at least in some of the marriages that parent-child bonds were as strong (or even stronger) than those between husband and wife.[23] One might also add that the arrival of children brought husband and wife closer to one another. These aspects of marriage arrangements may be instructive when dealing with New Testament passages related to advice on marriage (or even on non-married life), e.g. in 1 Corinthians and in 1 Timothy.

In the upper classes of Roman society there were women who exercised political influence and attained a high social esteem and significance. This is significant for us, because there are some women from the higher classes explicitly mentioned in the New Testament (Acts 17:4.12.34), and, perhaps, their presence can be presupposed in some further NT texts, too. Judith Hallett remarks (1984, 31):

although upper-class women exerted the greatest social and political impact, and elicited the most esteem from men, in *maternal* roles, ... they also commanded respect from, and because of, ties with the male blood kin who were their approximate contemporaries, and were assigned value from infancy as daughters of their fathers.

In all these phenomena we can observe important characteristics of the environment of the New Testament.

---

[21] 1984, 28; see also W. Kunkel on *mater familias* in PW, 1930, cols. 2183–84.
[22] See e.g. J. Gaudemet 1969, col. 318.
[23] As J. Hallett notes (1984, 243): "An upper-class Roman woman of the classical era may not ... have or have been expected to receive much emotional sustenance from her husband nor to make much of an emotional investment in him".

c) Parents as husbands and wives

Let us review some examples of texts concerning the social roles of men and women as husbands and wives – again with a view to consequences for child-parent relationships.

In the opinion of Ocellus Lucanus, "the law of nature" is the reason why wives should not rule over their husbands.[24] Ocellus writes: "the wife who surpasses her husband in wealth, in birth, or in friends, is desirous of ruling over him, contrary to the law of nature".[25] (We note the significance of this idea for our understanding of the Household Codes.)

In his writing entitled *On the Felicity of Families*, Callicratidas argues that the family, like the universe should be "organized with reference to one particular thing, which is the most excellent, and also with a view to benefit the majority".[26] In the case of the family, the father is "the best thing"; and "unanimity" is the "common advantage".[27] We note that "felicity" is named as a goal of family life.

When describing family relationships, Callicratidas can also make use of the term "governing". He affirms: "In the family's domestic part there are three divisions: the governor (the husband), the governed (the wife), and the auxiliary (the offspring)."[28] We may note that children are ranked here on a lower level than women. It is clear, however, that obedience is expected not only from wives but also from children. Among other texts, this example may be significant as a background to the Household Codes in the New Testament, since it can be argued that there is also a hierarchical order among those from whom obedience is expected (wives, children, and slaves).

There were very few women authors in antiquity. Therefore, we are especially interested in their view concerning their society. We find two examples of women writers, Perictyone and Phintys, whose writings, unfortunately, are difficult to date.[29] Perictyone (third or second century B.C.)

---

[24] Ocellus was an "early Pythagorean", whose *On the Nature of the Universe* may be a "post-Aristotelian" writing, according to D.R. Fideler (1987, 203).

[25] D.R. Fideler 1987, 210.

[26] The writing is dated to the third century B.C. by H. Thesleff (1961, 115); quotation from D.R. Fideler 1987, 235.

[27] *Ibid.*

[28] *Ibid.*

[29] It is appropriate to mention a caution here that applies to "Pythagorean texts" in general. We know that Pythagoras himself lived in the sixth century B.C., but he left no writings behind (D.R. Fideler 1987, 19). His thoughts are preserved in later biographies and in fragments that survive from Pythagorean and Neopythagorean philosophers (most of these fragments have been preserved by Stobaeus, fifth century A.D.). It is difficult to date the thinkers

wrote a treatise entitled *On the Harmony of a Woman*. In this work she gives numerous pieces of advice as to how a woman should behave, what virtues she should develop. She mentions the possibility that women may happen "to rule over cities and nations", and she adds: "as we see is sometimes the case in a kingdom".[30] Nevertheless, the treatise seems to presuppose that women as wives should be subordinated to their husbands. For example, Perictyone affirms concerning the duty of a woman:[31]

she ought to live with her husband legally and kindly, claiming nothing as her own property but preserving and protecting his bed, for this protection contains all things.... She should likewise patiently bear his anger, ... and whatever other faults he may inherit from his nature.

Perictyone even seems to accept the general view in her society that a husband may have a "connection with other women", but this "last error" is not "granted" to women.[32] These unbalanced "rights" and duties suggest that she regarded the patriarchal structure of society as a given fact which she did not question. It is within this framework that a woman has to acquire her virtues "so that she may be just, brave, prudent, frugal, and hating vainglory".[33] A woman can make use of these virtues in all her relationships, including those towards her children. As Perictyone puts it: "Furnished with these virtues she will, when she becomes a wife, act worthily towards herself, her husband, her children and her family".[34] This implies an on-going process throughout generations as daughters become mothers: daughters learn virtues (including prudence, σωφροσύνη) from their mothers. We

---

of the latter category and their writings (D.R. Fideler 1987, 19). As E. Dassmann affirms (1986, col. 819): "Die Datierung dieser größtenteils in fingiertem Altdorisch verfaßten Werke... geht sehr weit auseinander. Sie reicht vom 3.Jh. vC.... bis zum 2.Jh. nC." I shall not make an attempt to date the individual texts here. As a general approach, I accept H. Thesleff's thesis that much of the material often referred to as "Neopythagorean" should be regarded as "Pythagorean". He dates the majority of these writings to the third century B.C. (1961, 99; I note that his view remained "essentially unchanged" even when he published the Greek texts somewhat later, 1965, iii).

What makes the dating of the writings of Perictyone and Phintys even more difficult is the probability that these may be names adopted from older times by later writers. They were either Neopythagoreans, possibly from as late as the second century A.D., or Pythagoreans perhaps already from the third or second century B.C. As in the case of the other Pythagorean authors, I accept this latter view, expressed by H. Thesleff (1961, 115), on the basis of his detailed study on the writings in question.

[30] D.R. Fideler 1987, 239.
[31] D.R. Fideler 1987, 240.
[32] *Ibid.*
[33] D.R. Fideler 1987, 239.
[34] *Ibid.*

note in advance the significance of the root σωφρο- in NT texts also in relation to women, e.g. 1 Tim 2:9 and Titus 2:4–5.

Phintys wrote a treatise entitled *On Woman's Temperance*.[35] In this work she argues that "there are certain employments specialized to each sex", and that "there are some common to both man and woman".[36] In her opinion, "Female avocations are to guard the house, to stay at home, to receive and minister to her husband".[37] The expectation that a woman would stay at home is qualified in another passage: "Neither should a woman go out from her house at dawn or dusk, but openly when the forum is full of people, accompanied by one or at the most two servants, to see something or to shop".[38] From the expectation that a woman is "to guard the house" and "to stay at home" we can infer that mothers spent significantly more time with their children than fathers did. They were to pass on the expected virtues to their offspring; this implies obedient learning on the children's side.

d) Sons and daughters

It may be appropriate to mention here some of the similarities and differences between sons and daughters in antiquity, in connection with their relationship to their parents.

An important role of the father in ancient society was to perform sacrifices in the family circle at home.[39] For example, Phintys writes concerning women:[40]

> As to sacrifices of the Gods, ... she should abstain from celebration of the rites and the Cybelean sacrifice performed at home, for the municipal law forbids them to women.

We can infer from this phenomenon that sons watched their fathers performing rituals with an increasing sense of responsibility: they will have to carry on these rituals one day when they become fathers with the role of a *paterfamilias* in their own families. Sons had to learn certain social functions from their fathers: in general, we may say that they had to learn how to behave later as the head of their own family.

Although from a legal point of view fathers played a leading role in the

---

[35] The work is dated to the third century by H. Thesleff (1961, 115).
[36] D.R. Fideler 1987, 263.
[37] *Ibid.*
[38] D.R. Fideler 1987, 264.
[39] E. Sachers affirms in his article on *paterfamilias* in PW (vol. XVIII/4): "Die Darbringung von Opfern für die Familie... oblag dem *p.f.* allein", 1949, col. 2140).
[40] D.R. Fideler 1987, 264.

2. The child-parent relationship in practice 51

family, mothers were also respected by their children. For example, E. Eyben writes (1993, 213): "In Rome a *materfamilias*, too, was held in high regard (more so than was the case in Greece), and managed to impress her stamp on her children, both girls and boys". In both Greek and Roman cultures, the mother was responsible for the upbringing of children in their first few years of life.[41] Concerning Roman customs, P. Blomenkamp argues: "Die Mutter zieht das Kind in den ersten Jahren auf. Sie wird hoch geachtet u. behält einen großen Einfluß auf das weitere Leben ihrer Kinder.... Die Mädchen bleiben der mütterlichen Aufsicht unterstellt, bis sie heiraten".[42] Thus, we can see that children, both sons and daughters, were expected to honour their mother for the care in their upbringing (an expectation we have met in the previous chapter as well).

Judith Hallett marshals examples of good relationships between mothers and sons.[43] For example, she refers to Plutarch who "states that the legendary Coriolanus always believed he ought to bestow upon his widowed and evidently brotherless mother all the filial affection which would have ordinarily been lavished on his father".[44] Hallett also argues that because "Roman women were generally married while in their early teens,... the age difference between a mother and her son would not be much greater than that separating her from her husband".[45] Hallett also draws the conclusion that "Roman mothers and sons could expect to spend more of their lifetimes together than fathers could with their offspring".[46] It is, then, a natural inference to suggest that there developed a special emotional link between many mothers and sons in ancient Rome. Since it was widespread practice also in Judaism that girls married rather early, the above mentioned special affection between mothers and sons may serve as a background to the whole New Testament (whether Jewish or non-Jewish families are concerned; see e.g. the mother of the sons of Zebedee, or texts concerning Jesus and his mother).

We may note briefly a phenomenon that is not directly relevant to the New Testament. Adoption served as a means of providing legitimate heirs in upper-class Roman society. Although there are some examples of the adoption of young children and also of females, the majority of adoptions concerned adult men.[47] As a reason Beryl Rawson remarks (1986b, 12):

---

[41] P. Blomenkamp 1966, cols. 507 and 510.
[42] *Ibid.*, col. 510.
[43] See her chapter entitled "Mater et Liberi", 1984, 243ff.
[44] *Ibid.*, 251.
[45] *Ibid.*, 252.
[46] *Ibid.*, 252–53.
[47] S. Dixon 1992, 112.

"by then, chances of survival were greater and the adopting father could see what he was getting as a son and heir".[48] She shows that the adopted son was "to continue the family and to observe the various family rites when the father had died". Suzanne Dixon emphasises that "the law still observed certain obligations between the adopted child and his biological father".[49] Nevertheless, by adoption a person was transferred "into the agnatic family of the adopter". In relation to his new "father", the adoptee "was subject to the same legal privileges and limitations of a legitimate biological son".[50] Adoption does not have direct parallels in the non-Jewish circles witnessed to in the New Testament.[51] It may be noted that adoption was also known among the Jews. As regards the infancy narratives in the Gospels of Matthew and Luke, Joseph may have feared that rumors would arise as to whether Jesus was an illegitimate son. Even if he was not the father, by adoption he would have conferred on Jesus all the rights of a son.

e) Differences between various segments of society

Apart from the different social role of fathers and mothers, parents and children, we have to mention briefly the major differences between what may be called "classes" in ancient society. These differences also had a bearing upon the relationship between children and parents.

The most fundamental difference in ancient society is that between free persons and slaves. This difference had a significant effect also on relationships within the family. As J. F. Gardner and T. Wiedemann argue (1991, 43–44): "a slave-owner could do whatever he wished with his slaves. Consequently the law of the classical period could not recognise any family relationships (e.g., parent/child, husband/wife) among slaves; the only formal relationship they had was with their master". We have to bear this in mind when we study New Testament text involving slaves (e.g. the Household Codes).

The difference between the upper and lower classes has already been mentioned. It is reflected, for example, in the sphere of education. Peter Müller has emphasised the financial aspect of education in antiquity where

---

[48] S. Dixon reminds us that it was a society with "relatively poor life chances of infants and young children" (1992, 99).
[49] *Ibid.*, p.112.
[50] *Ibid.*
[51] Perhaps, in a figurative sense, Christians can be seen as adopted by God. Günter Haufe argues that the idea of sonship in Gal 4:4–6 implies adoption (1979, col. 637): "nach Paulus sind die Christen 'Kinder Gottes' als die um Christi willen von Gott Adoptierten."

education was provided mainly by private teachers (1992, 115). Müller adds that the texts that deal with education in antiquity reflect the milieu of the city (116). This observation points to another aspect of differences between social segments: the difference between the population of the cities and that of the countryside.[52] When discussing New Testament texts, we shall have to pay attention to the location of the people involved; for example, in the case of some letters it is significant that the addressees lived in cities like Corinth or Rome.

f) How long did the influence of parents over their children last?

There were many factors which determined how long a child remained under the influence of his or her parents. We have already seen that in antiquity girls usually got married earlier than boys. Although the Roman *paterfamilias* retained his power lifelong,[53] we might assume that the marriage of a child did cause some distancing from the influence of the parents. Around the time of the New Testament, the majority of marriages were *sine manu*,[54] i.e. women did not pass under the authority (*manus*) of their husband, but remained under the authority of their father.[55] Even their property remained under the supervision of their father.[56] Nevertheless, in everyday life, they must have had some freedom from the oversight of their father. For example, Max Kaser states (1971, 329–30):

> Die Praxis bietet demgegenüber jedoch ein anderes Bild. Ist die Ehe gesund, pflegt das Vermögen jedes Gatten beiden zugutezukommen. Die Frau überläßt ihres der Verwaltung des Mannes. Die Sachen, die dem häuslichen Gebrauch dienen, werden gemeinsam benutzt; der Mann gewährt der Frau Unterhalt im gemeinsamen Haushalt.

In the same way, we may assume that sons, having got married, lived at some distance from the close influence of their parents. We may add that male slaves – and people of the lower classes in general – got married ear-

---

[52] See e.g. J. Gaudemet 1969, col. 333: "Große Unterschiede taten sich auf zwischen der Familie auf dem Lande und der in den großen Städten".

[53] See e.g. M. Kaser's statement (1971, 349): "Die Gewalt des bisherigen *paterfamilias* endet mit dem Tod und mit der *capitis deminutio* des Vaters oder des Kindes". We have to add that a father also had the right to emancipate his child. Concerning *emancipatio*, Kaser notes (p. 350): "Der Vollzug der Emanzipation bleibt dem Belieben des *paterfamilias* überlassen; nur ausnahmsweise können Hauskinder ihre Emanzipation im Verfahren *extra ordinem* erzwingen".

[54] See e.g. Mireille Corbier 1991, 48–49.

[55] See e.g. M. Kaser 1971, 312.

[56] See e.g. M. Kaser 1971, 329.

lier than men belonging to the higher classes. For example, Beryl Rawson writes (1986 b, 22):

> The humblest epitaphs set up in Rome (the *sepulcrales*, in *CIL* 6), many of them for slaves or ex-slaves, reveal a wide age range for 'marriage', but the biggest groups whose age of marriage is indicated belong to the range of 12 to 18 for women and 19 to 21 for men.[57]

Geographical distance, in general, is of significance for studying the child-parent relationship in the New Testament, because we have many cases where people mentioned in the New Testament travelled large distances (to mention but a few: Paul, Timothy, Epaphras, Aquila and Prisca). As the image of a soldier surfaces in Ephesians and 1 Timothy, it may be of interest to see from the example of a "real" soldier that soldiers often travelled far from their family. Our soldier in question writes a letter addressed to his son and to Tachonis (who is most likely his wife). The worry of this soldier concerning his family is expressed in a way that provides a very nice picture of his relation to his child:[58]

> Heraklas to Horos and Tachonis, greetings and good health. Don't worry about us. Since we've been on military duty we have been sailing in the boat for eight days. With the gods' will in three days we shall be on shipboard. As for the child keep an eye on him as you would an oil lamp, since I am worried about you.... Farewell... and to Horos his son.

At the end of this sub-section a word of general caution may be appropriate. If we meet a certain "silence" in our sources concerning parents this does not necessarily mean lack of contact between children and parents. It is also possible that the person's parents were not alive at all. Suzanne Dixon rightly warns us that average life expectancy in antiquity was rather low. She writes concerning the Roman family (1992, 149): "the median life expectancy was about twenty-seven years for women and about thirty-seven for men and relatively few people lived to see their grandchildren". Dixon adds that in spite of this phenomenon, Cicero and Seneca seem to take "the

---

[57] P.R.C. Weaver adopts a similar view when he writes (1991, 189): "childbearing for female slaves began about age fifteen, and ... male slaves first 'married' about age twenty or slightly later". I note that B. Rawson explains her usage of inverted commas with the term "marriage" as "the beginning of a lasting union" (1986b, 50). – Rawson also states in a generalising way that (1986c, 197): "the period of childhood – at least for the lower classes – was short" in antiquity. As a counterpart to this statement she adds that for "upper-class children, especially boys, there does seem to have been a concept of adolescence between childhood and adulthood" (p. 200).

[58] In G.H.R. Horsley, *New Documents*, 1981, I/52; the letter is dated to the turn of the Era (p. 51).

age of sixty as the approximate beginning of old age" (p. 150). Nevertheless, her remark remains true that "a much smaller proportion of the ancient population attained this age" than in our times. We note that it is often mentioned in commentaries that the possible reason why Jesus' father, Joseph, does not appear in the Gospels after the infancy narratives is that he might have died early. The phenomenon of early death is to be kept in mind when discussing the passage concerning "widows" in 1 Timothy.

g) Children learning a trade or a profession

As we have seen, child-parent relationships were naturally more intensive while the children were young, especially before they got married. Mention has already been made of the role of parents in education. Although we do not discuss this field in the present monograph, the other side of the coin is worth mentioning: children learning a trade or a profession. We often find in our sources that children followed the trade of their father. Apart from the upper class, children followed the trade of their parents because it frequently occurred that husband and wife worked together at the same trade. Miriam Peskowitz states that, for Rome, this phenomenon is "indicated by inscriptional evidence" (1993, 32). She also points to the example of Aquila and Priscilla, the married couple in Acts 18:2–3, "who work together as tent makers" (*ibid.*).

Suzanne Dixon points to a difference between the wealthy and the poor in respect of teaching children a trade or a profession. In the upper classes, parents could afford to "send their sons abroad to learn certain liberal arts from professional teachers" (1992, 117). She observes that even these parents "prized those skills which were transmitted in traditional fashion on the model of home-based, practical learning". The latter characterised the lower classes.

We note that, according to Mark 6:3, Jesus followed the trade of his father, because here Jesus is referred to as a "carpenter" (in the majority of the MSS; some MSS refer to Jesus as the "carpenter's son"). M. Peskowitz points also to the example of James and John (in Mark 1:19) who "worked as fishermen with their father Zebedee" (1993, 32).[59] As regards daughters, Keith Bradley argues (1991a, 108): "daughters in artisanal families, like their counterparts in upper-class society at Rome, may not normally have been trained for work other than that of a traditional, domestic sort, but

---

[59] It is interesting to note that even if a son was sent to be an apprentice to another master, later he returned to his father to work with him. See e.g. M. Peskowitz 1993, 32.

were instead prepared only for marriage and childbearing in the seclusive manner typical of women's life in antiquity as a whole".

Architectural evidence suggests that a family's home and workshop – and even shop – were often to be found in the same building. M. Peskowitz has pointed to "the close architectural proximity, in fact, overlay, of shopfronts and workshops to living quarters in Rome" (1993, 32). B. Rawson makes a significant distinction when she observes that the rich were likely to provide a more child-centred environment than the poorer strata of society (1991b, 21):

> For a great many Romans home and work must have been combined in one smallish area combining residential and commercial or 'industrial' activities. For the élite, this was much less so and one might argue that for these families greater privacy combined with greater affluence, leisure, and education to provide a more child-centred environment.[60]

This is of significance for our discussion of the child-parent relationship in early Christian city congregations in general, where they were gathering at rich people's houses. For example, the Household Codes presuppose that children (of course not only those of the host) were together with their parents when they listened to the member of the congregation who read aloud Colossians or Ephesians.

To sum up, there was a strong tradition of children following their parents' trade and profession in antiquity. In the case of the artisans, this often implied that children would work "at home", i.e. in the workshop of their parents.

h) Correspondence

There was often a widely extended correspondence between children and their parents in antiquity. Correspondence often expresses honour on the children's side; on occasion gratitude for provision extended by the parents. We read on more than one occasion that a child writing to his or her parents mentions that he or she writes many times to them. For example, in a letter dated 130 B.C. we find:[61] "Esthladas to his father and mother greeting and

---

[60] See also the study of Andrew Wallace-Hadrill on the architectural evidence of Pompeii and Herculaneum. He also distinguishes between Greek and Roman houses (1991, 197): "If the classical Greek evidence points to democratic societies with *oikoi* of regular and predictable size, ... Pompeii and Herculaneum surely suggest a society with very unequal distributions, whether of wealth or of family or household size".

[61] *Select Papyri* (= SP) vol. I., pp. 289 and 291. (In my quotations from Loeb's editions, the

2. The child-parent relationship in practice 57

good health. As I have often written to you to keep a stout heart and take care of yourself until things settle down, once again please exhort yourself and our dependants to take courage."

We find another example in a recruit's letter to his mother:[62] "And whenever I find a messenger I will write to you; never will I be slow to write." Or, a mother writes to her son:[63] "Write to me constantly about your health, in order that I may have consolation". This request does not necessarily imply that the son was ill, because wishes concerning good health are frequently recurring themes in the letters. One can understand that welfare was one of the most important matters when someone was far away from his or her relatives. This expression may simply be a request for regular correspondence.

We have to be cautious about generalisations as to whether fathers or mothers are more often represented in the letters. We often simply do not know whether the father or mother (the one who does not appear in a letter) was alive at all, or whether he or she was not divorced. If we think of the fact that men played a more important role in society than women then we may cautiously say that we do nevertheless have a large number or letters written to or by mothers. A very moving example is a letter of a "penitent son" addressed to his mother:[64] "I go about in filth. I wrote to you that I am naked. I beg you, mother, be reconciled to me. Well, I know what I have brought on myself. I have received a fitting lesson. I know that I have sinned" (οἶδα ὅτι ἡμάρτηκα). This letter implies that the son honours his mother, so he is sorry for causing sadness to her. This setting offers a striking parallel to the parable of the lost son in Luke 15.

A mother when writing to her son who is away from home to study (aided by an attendant, παιδαγωγός) not only offers financial help, but is even interested in what her son is learning about. We read in her letter:[65] "do not hesitate to write to me about anything which you require from me (ἐ[ὰ]ν χρείαν ἔχῃς).... I took care to send and inquire about your health and to learn what you were reading.... So now, my child, you and your attendant must take care to have you placed under a suitable teacher". From this letter one can feel the attentive responsibility of the mother. It is as if the attendant and the teacher were the extension of the mother. The mother is responsible

---

Greek and Latin texts are taken always from the previous (even) page in relation to the English translation which has always an odd page number.)
[62] SP I/303; the papyrus is dated by the editors to the second century A.D.
[63] SP I/309; dated to the second century A.D.
[64] SP I/317 and 319; the papyrus is dated by the editors to the second century A.D.
[65] SP I/335; second or third century. A.D.

for the education of the child, but she exercises this function with the aid of other skilled people.

Thus, our sources express a certain mutuality of correspondence also in relation to financial help. Children could ask for money and parents were ready to help. In another example, in an ostracon letter from a father to a son, we learn how money could be sent even from a distance:[66] "if you need some money write to me and I will send it to you with any trusty person I can find". Such care and provision was expected to be repaid by children when their parents needed help in their old age or ill-health.

i) Conflicts between children and parents

While surveying child-parent relationships in practice, we have already seen some examples of tensions between children and parents. As the theme of conflict will recur also in our discussion of the New Testament, it is worth looking at some more examples of conflicts between children and parents.

Although we do not know its circumstances, we find an example of disagreement between a son and a father in a "question to an oracle". It is significant that the father turned to the gods with his concern:[67] "O Lord Sarapis Helios, beneficent one. (Say) whether it is fitting that Phanias my son and his wife should not agree now with his father, but oppose him [ἀντιλέγειν] and not make a contract. Tell me this truly. Goodbye." In this case we may reckon with two possibilities. On the one hand, it is possible that the invocation implies that the father expected support from the oracle: the god being evoked should confirm that a son ought not disagree with his father. On the other hand, it may be implied that the father thought that a child should not disagree with his father in general, but that there may be exceptions; the god should tell him whether it is an exceptional case. In both cases, it is taken for granted that a son should not disagree with his father (though in the latter case there are possible limits to that norm). Thus this text confirms that the general expectation is obedience of a son toward his father.

A. Lumpe pointed to the literature of astrology when he observed in commenting on some fragments of Nechepso and Petosiris (ca. 150–120 B.C.; 1957, col. 1193): "Zu den kosmisch bedingten Katastrophen rechnen die Vertreter der Astrologie auch den Zwist zwischen Eltern und Kindern". This observation is the more significant as we shall meet a similar view in

---

[66] In G. H. R. Horsley, *New Documents*, 1981, I/59; it is dated to the second century A.D.
[67] SP I/437; first century A.D.

our study of the Jewish sources in the next chapter.[68] This important theme will have to be addressed also during the discussion of certain New Testament texts (e.g. Mark 13:12).

We have already seen how a son asked his mother in a letter to forgive him because he has changed. In another letter we find how a child "threatens" his father with breaking off contact because his father did not take him with him on a trip. E. Eyben interprets the letter as coming from a "spoiled child", who writes "in truly childish fashion" (1991, 132):[69] "If you won't take me with you to Alexandria I won't write you a letter or speak to you or say goodbye to you; and if you go to Alexandria I won't take your hand nor ever greet you again. That is what will happen if you won't take me". As the child finishes his letter by thanking his father for presents and asking for a lyre, we can agree with Eyben that these threats are not all that "serious". From the way the son expresses his "threats" we can infer that the general expectation was respectful speech and greeting words; the son wanted to "punish" his father by deviating from these norms.

Many ancient authors discussed the question whether it is right or wrong if fathers take severe measures against their children. With a reference to Livy (1.50.9), Eyben argues that (1991, 121): "When father and son disagreed, no discussion was possible, or even necessary". On the basis of Valerius Maximus' work (5.8.4), Eyben also refers to the case of M. Scaurus "who did not want any contact with his son any more because of the latter's cowardly behaviour on the battlefield, thus driving him to commit suicide (101 BC)" (1991, 122). Eyben adds that "such harshness must always have been extremely rare" in the private sphere; it could mainly occur in the case of "offences against the (early) Republic" (*ibid.*). Most of the discussion in the ancient sources relate to the question of disciplining children who did something wrong. As in these cases the conflict arises from disobedience in the sense of some wrongdoing, I shall not discuss it in detail. A comment from Seneca may suffice. In his work entitled *On Mercy* (1.16.3), he calls the "worst sort of father" (*pessimus pater*) him "who controls his children by constant whippings even for the most trivial offences".[70] We shall see that the early Christian congregations probably did not practice severe measures against children (see especially the discussion of the Household Codes in the chapter on the *Corpus Paulinum*).

---

[68] See e.g. O. Larry Yarbrough 1993, 59; he refers to *1 En.* 100:1–2.
[69] E. Eyben quotes here P.Oxy. 1.119, a papyrus dated "*c.* AD 200" (1991, 132).
[70] In Loeb: I/405. See also E. Eyben 1991, 122.

j) Anti-family ethos among the Cynics and the Stoics

The movement of the Cynic philosophers is of special significance for our theme. There are attempts to describe the Jesus movement as influenced by Cynic ideas.[71] Even if one does not consider Jesus to be a Cynic preacher, the Cynic movement is part of the environment of early Christianity; it can provide an insight into the social implications of a "conversion to philosophy". This expression from an earlier significant work of A. D. Nock has recently been taken up by Stephen Barton, and applied to Cynic views.[72] Apart from a few concrete examples from the lives of Cynic philosophers, Barton refers to Epictetus' work (*Discourses* III.xxii) which "gives a detailed and certainly Stoicizing account of the ideal Cynic" (1994, 48). According to Epictetus, the Cynics wanted to be "wholly devoted to the service of God", so they preferred not to marry and not to have children in order to avoid any "distraction" (p. 49). Epictetus is worth quoting at some length (*Discourses* III.xxii.45–47,50):[73]

> And how is it possible for a man who has nothing, who is naked, without home ... to live serenely? Behold, God has sent you the man who will show in practice that it is possible. "Look at me," he says, "I am without a home.... I sleep on the ground;[74] I have neither wife nor children [οὐ γυνή, οὐ παιδία]...." (50) Lo, these are words that befit a Cynic, this is his character, and his plan of life.[75]

We must note here the religious motivation of commitment to philosophy. The Cynic philosopher refers to God who sent him. This implies that God is named as the ground of the lifestyle of the philosopher. In the next part of this chapter, we shall look for grounds and reasons for the duties of children. Here we note God as a "ground" of an anti-family ethos. Barton emphasises that there are similarities as well as differences between Cynicism and the Jesus movement. Concerning the latter, he argues that "where Cynicism is explicitly anti-social and opposed – or at best, indifferent – to marriage and family ties *per se*, the gospels are communal and take house-

---

[71] See, for example, J. D. Crossan (1992) and F. G. Downing (1992 and 1996).

[72] See A. D. Nock 1952, ch. 11 (pp. 164–86) entitled "Conversion to Philosophy", and S. Barton 1994, especially p. 47 with a reference to Nock.

[73] In Loeb, vol. II, pp. 147 and 149. For a comparison between Epictetus and the Gospel material, see, for example, the monograph of Adolf Bonhöffer (1911) and the article of J. N. Sevenster (1966).

[74] S. Barton (1994, 51) points to the similarity between this way of life and the Gospel tradition about the Son of Man who "has nowhere to lay his head" (Matt 8:20 par. Luke 9:58). The saying on the dead burying the dead, next to this saying, shall be of special significance for us in the chapter on the Gospel traditions.

[75] For further examples from other Cynics, see S. Barton 1994, 50–51.

hold institutions and family ties for granted" (1994, 51). It is also worth pointing out that the Cynics did not "leave" their family; rather they remained unmarried. This is a significant difference when compared with the disciples of Jesus who left their family when they followed Jesus.[76]

It is important to contrast Cynic philosophy with the ideas of Stoics like Musonius Rufus (first century A.D.) and his pupil, Epictetus (ca. A.D. 55–135). According to Barton, the latter are much more positive towards "marital ties and the raising of children" than the Cynic philosophers (p. 52). Nevertheless, Barton holds that for Epictetus, too, "the philosopher's commitment to the good transcends even ties of filial respect" (p. 53). Barton quotes the following passage from Epictetus (*Discourses* III.iii.5–6, p. 54; I quote from Loeb II/31):

> That is why the good is preferred above every form of kinship. My father is nothing to me, but only the good [οὐδὲν ἐμοὶ καὶ τῷ πατρί, ἀλλὰ τῷ ἀγαθῷ[77]].... For that reason, if the good is something different from the noble and the just, then father and brother and country [πατρίς] and all relationships simply disappear.

However, this passage should not be taken out of its context. In the passage preceding this quotation (III.iii.2), Epictetus argues that "it is the nature of every soul to assent to the true, dissent from the false".[78] A little later he writes: "My father is taking away my money."[79] Thus the context as well as the second part of Barton's quotation seen above suggest that if a father would lead away from what is good then the good should be followed rather than the father. The fact that also in the opinion of Epictetus parents are to be respected can be seen, for example, from the following remark (III.vii.25–28):[80]

> ... in the case of man, it is not his material substance that we should honour, his bits of flesh, but the principal things [τὰ προηγούμενα]. What are these? The duties of citizenship, marriage, begetting children, reverence to God, care of parents [γονέων ἐπιμελεῖσθαι] ...

Thus, although Barton's analysis has to be complemented, on the whole he is right in pointing out that here we have an example of "a justification for the relativization of family – and specifically filial – ties" (p. 54). That is why this part of the environment is of significance for New Testament texts where there is a tension within the family.

---

[76] We shall return to this matter in our study of the New Testament texts.
[77] Cf. the similar idiom in John 2:4.
[78] In Loeb: II/29.
[79] III.iii.9; in Loeb: II/31.
[80] In Loeb: II/57.

Although Epictetus himself does not give concrete examples of conflicts arising from this commitment to the "good" and to philosophy, we shall see later that Musonius Rufus does give a detailed example where he argues that philosophy is for the good of mankind: it is in the end the will of the gods. Musonius' example will strengthen our observation that this allegiance to philosophy has a religious motivation. In our present example, the "good" offered by philosophy serves as a limit to the duty of a child toward his or her father. "Limits" of duties will be collected in a separate section.

From these examples we may summarisingly affirm that conflicts between children and parents arose on the basis of philosophical (and at the same time religious) commitments. As Barton puts it (p. 54): "conversion to philosophy ... involved an allegiance higher than ties of kinship and household". Therefore, we shall have to return to this theme when we discuss the family ethos of Jesus.

Having considered some examples of how child-parent relationship worked in practice (and what expectations this practice presupposed), we shall now turn to the theme of norms within the realm of that relationship. We shall follow the pattern set in the previous chapter, i.e. we shall discuss texts with regard to the duties of children towards their parents, the grounds for those duties, and the limits to the fulfilling of those duties. This will enable us to make a comparison between our findings in these chapters.

3. Norms and expectations about the behaviour of children to their parents

We have found the following duties in the texts reflecting the social circumstances of the Hellenistic period up to the end of the third century A.D.: *pietas*, obedience in general (e.g. Callicratidas), obedience in marriage, respectful speech, a daughter should learn σωφροσύνη (prudence) from her mother (e.g. Perictyone and Phintys), a son should learn from his father how to become a *paterfamilias*, to honour his mother in gratitude for upbringing and financial help, not to disagree with his parents. We have already noted that these duties were also known in the centuries before the period in question. In this section, we collect further examples of these and other duties.

3. Norms and expectations about the behaviour of children to their parents 63

a) Honour and reverence

The first duty to be mentioned is the general expectation that a child would honour or revere his or her parents. This general expectation is "filled in" with concrete content in various duties; thus it may be argued that honour is an overarching duty to be shown in many concrete ways.

We can find a high appreciation of a mother – and, indeed, of both parents – expressed in a letter addressed to the brother of the letter-writer:[81] "... for we ought to revere our mother as a goddess, especially one so good as ours. This I have written to you, brother, because I know how sweet a possession our revered parents are." We shall see later that parents and gods were often referred to in the same context. Here we note that a mother deserves the same reverence as a goddess. We note the Greek term for revering, σέβεσθε (the editor corrects to σέβεσθαι). The son who writes this letter is expressing his personal feelings, but this is surely also a concrete expression of a more general rule.

Just as we have found lists of those to whom honour is due in earlier centuries, we also find them in the period of our present focus. Diogenes Laertius writes:[82] "The Stoics approve also of honouring parents [γονέας σέβεσθαι] and brothers in the second place next after the gods [ἐν δευτέρᾳ μοίρᾳ μετὰ θεούς]. They further maintain that parental affection for children is natural to the good, but not to the bad". We note the reference to nature as a reason why parents love their children; this implies the same reason why children should return that love. The very connection expressed by the phrase "next after the gods", may also imply that the gods are the ground of honouring parents.

We can find further examples in the writings of Hierocles.[83] The titles given by him to the sections imply a certain ranking: he first discusses conduct towards the gods then that towards one's country.[84] Then he writes:[85] "After considering the gods and our country, what person deserves to be mentioned more than, or prior to our parents? ... No mistake, therefore, will

---

[81] SP I/321; dated to the second century A.D.

[82] VII.120 (in the section on Zeno); in Loeb: vol. 2., p. 225.

[83] Karl Praechter has marshalled arguments in favour of his thesis that the fragments of Hierocles preserved by Stobaeus are best understood as the work of a Stoic; *Hierokles der Stoiker*, 1901. I quote the texts in D. R. Fideler's translation, 1987, 275–79. It is difficult to date Hierocles' work. Even if it is to be dated to the fifth century A.D. (as an *ad quem*, due to the date of Stobaeus), its ideas may reflect the views of Stoics in the period we discuss in this chapter.

[84] D. R. Fideler 1987, 275–77.

[85] *Ibid.*, 277; Greek text in K. Praechter 1901, 45.

be made by him who says that they are as it were secondary or terrestrial divinities" (οὓς δευτέρους καὶ ἐπιγείους τινὰς θεοὺς εἰπὼν οὐκ ἂν ἁμάρτοι τις). Although between the gods and parents there is mention of the fatherland, it is nevertheless clear that parents are also related to the gods. The text implies honour as a duty, and the gods also serve as a "reason" for the duty. Cicero has a similar sequence of the triad, gods – country – parents, in *Off*. 1.45.160: "even in the social relations themselves there are gradations of duty [*gradus officiorum*] so well defined that it can easily be seen which duty takes precedence of any other: our first duty is to the immortal gods; our second, to country; our third, to parents; and so on, in a descending scale, to the rest."[86] He can also refer to the "fatherland" (*patria*) and parents without mentioning the gods (*Off*. 1.17.58):

> Now, if a contrast and comparison were to be made to find out where most of our moral obligation is due, country would come first, and parents; for their services have laid us under the heaviest obligation; next come children and the whole family, who look to us alone for support and have no other protection...[87]

We note the argument that parents support and protect their children; this implies that children owe them a return. The speaker is under an obligation to his parents and he is to protect his own children: this implies an on-going process in which children of ever new generations are expected to return provision to their parents.

It can be argued that honour is not simply one duty among others, but is an all-encompassing term: other duties are aspects of the duty of honouring one's parents. It is only for the sake of clarity that we collect them under separate headings.

b) Provision for the old, funeral and veneration of the dead

Two duties of children frequently recur in our sources (on occasion together): to provide for their parents when they get older; and to bury them when they die. We have a beautiful expression of these duties in a letter of a

---

[86] In Loeb: (vol. XXI) p. 165. Cf. also E. Eyben's observation (1993, 206): "Like the Stoics, Cicero ranked the *pietas* owed to parents third after the respect owed to the gods and to the fatherland".

[87] In Loeb: p. 61. The Latin text refers to the "benefits" we receive from parents (in Loeb: p. 60; also in the edition of C.F.W. Müller 1906, 21): "Sed si contentio quaedam et comparatio fiat, quibus plurimum tribuendum sit officii, principes sint patria et parentes, quorum beneficiis maximis obligati sumus, proximi liberi totaque domus, quae spectat in nos solos neque aliud ullum potest habere perfugium...".

3. Norms and expectations about the behaviour of children to their parents 65

son to his father.[88] Before the son urges his father to come to him and spend at least a season with them, he addresses his father in this way:[89] "Nothing truly will be dearer to me than to protect you for the rest of your life in a manner worthy of you and of myself, and if the fate of mankind befalls you, to see that you enjoy all due honours [τυχεῖν σε πάντων τῶν καλῶν]; this will be my chief desire, honourably to protect you [προστατῆσαι] both while you live and when you have departed to the gods." Writing a personal letter, Philonides expresses in a roundabout way – but nevertheless clearly – that he will provide for a burial that would express the honour due to his father.

These two most frequently mentioned obligations of a child are expressed in a less poetic – and therefore more straightforward – way in a will from 284 B.C. The testament makes clear that the children will not only inherit when their parents die, but receive financial support while their parents are still alive. Right after the mention of this provision – as if as a counterpart to it – the duties of the children are listed:[90] "If in their lifetime Dionysius or Callista [i.e. the father or the mother] is in need or in debt, all the sons in common shall support them and contribute to pay their debts. If any one of them refuses to support them or contribute or does not help to bury them [ἐὰν δέ τις αὐτῶν μὴ θέληι ἢ τράφειν ἢ συναποτίνειν ἢ μὴ συνθάπτωσιν], he shall forfeit 1000 drachmae of silver and there shall be right of execution on him who is insubordinate and does not act in the manner stated." The fact that these duties had to be stated in a will implies that there must have been children negligent in respect of their duties. However, the content of the will most likely expresses wide-spread habits and expectations concerning what a child owes to his or her parents.

The obligation of provision, mutually expected from parents and children, were codified under the Empire.[91] We may add, however, that legislation often followed developments within everyday life's practice. The duty of provision is often included in the term *pietas*. A. Lumpe stresses that coins often pictured the piety of the imperial family, "und symbolisierten sie durch das Bild des Storches, der als besonders rücksichtsvoll gegen seine Eltern galt".[92] We shall see in the next chapter that Philo also re-

---

[88] The editors of the papyrus provide the following information: the son, Philonides, was living in Alexandria; the father, Cleon, was a chief engineer in the Fayum. The papyrus is dated about 255 B.C., SP I/279.
[89] *Ibid.*
[90] SP I/237 and 239.
[91] A. Lumpe refers to Dig. 25,3,5; 28,7,9 when he states (1957, col. 1197): "In der Kaiserzeit wurde die gegenseitige Unterhaltspflicht zwischen Eltern und Kindern rechtlich festgelegt".
[92] *Ibid.*

ferred to the example of the stork. Seneca writes: "not to love one's parents is to be unfilial" (*parentes suos non amare impietas est*; *Ben.* 3.1.5).[93] Thus love and *pietas* are inseparable. Seneca also says that children "owe" their parents the provision of care. In *Ben.* 6.23.5 he writes: "We owe filial duty to our parents" (*debemus parentibus nostris pietatem*).[94] In this latter context he refers to the gods as well as to nature as providing for us; in as much as they give life to children through their parents, the gods and nature can be seen as the ground for saying that children owe their parents provision in return. Seneca argues that we are indebted to our parents for our lives even if they did not "plan" our birth. He continues in *Ben.* 6.23.5:

> But it is not possible for us to suppose that the gods did not know what they would accomplish when they promptly supplied to all men food and support, nor were those for whom they produced so many blessings begotten without purpose. Nature took thought of us before she created us...[95]

Lumpe points to the significance of the existence of two temples in Rome which were dedicated to *pietas* between parents and children (1957, col. 1197). In the founding legend of the Republican Temple to Pietas we find a "tale of a daughter's devoted protection of her mother" (R. Saller 1994, 107); so *pietas* did not apply only to the relationship of a son to his father.[96] Valerius Maximus (5.4.7) recalls this legend, according to which a mother sentenced to starvation in a prison was kept alive by her daughter who eased "the mother's hunger with the aid of her own milk". He concludes the story by saying that "the first law of nature is to love (*diligere*) parents".[97] Here we note the reference to nature as a ground for the duty. Although we do not know the origin of the legend, it is probably safe to say that it connects the obligation of *pietas* in this period with the same expectation in earlier centuries.

On the basis of *pietas*, parents expected from their children that they would look after them when they grew old. Parents who lost their children were anxious about their old age, as we can see on some epitaphs dedicated

---

[93] In Loeb: vol. III, p. 129.

[94] In Loeb: III/409.

[95] *Ibid.*, p. 411.

[96] R. Saller (*ibid.*) also points to Pliny the Elder (*Nat.* 7.121) for whom "this *exemplum* surpasses all others from around the world as an act of *pietas*". Pliny uses in this section the expression "pietatis exempla", see in Loeb: II/586.

[97] The work of Valerius Maximus, *Facta et dicta memorabilia* is dated to ca. A.D. 31 or 32; see the section on "Die Literatur der Kaiserzeit" by Gian Biagio Conte in Fritz Graf, *Einleitung in die lateinische Philologie*, 1997, 192–227. Conte writes (225): "Das Werk ist nicht so sehr ein Geschichtswerk als vielmehr eine Sammlung von moralischen Exempla zuhanden der Rhetorenschule."

3. Norms and expectations about the behaviour of children to their parents 67

to deceased children. Suzanne Dixon remarks that such parents "grieved for the loss of the many services the children would in the normal course of events have performed for them" (1992, 111–12).[98] To quote but one example, we may refer to a husband who writes the following as the epitaph to his wife:

> Children had been our hope, which for some considerable time Fate had begrudged us. If Fortune had borne to continue taking care of us in her established way, what would either of us have failed to obtain? ... When you despaired of your fertility, and lamented my childlessness lest, by retaining you in marriage, I might resign my hope of having children and as a result suffer misfortune, you spoke plainly about divorce.[99]

We learn from the epitaph that the husband did not accept this offer. On the contrary, they lived in an unusually long and happy marriage, as the first lines of the inscription affirm: "Uncommon are marriages which last so long, brought to an end by death, not broken apart by divorce; for it was our happy lot that it should be prolonged to the 41st year without estrangement". Here we not only have an insight into the significance of children for their parents as their hope in old age, but we can also find a reference to a possible "solution" to childless marriages: that of divorce. We note that the husband regarded their own example of a long marriage as the exception in their society (*Rara sunt tam diuturna matrimonia*).[100]

Thus we may see from our examples that in a society where a "pension" was not provided for by the state, children were the only hope of parents for care when they grew old (except, of course, when the parents were rich themselves).

The carrying out of the duty of burying one's parents can be seen from epitaphs. It is a matter of course that we find other examples as well, e.g. of parents burying their children or husbands burying their wives. There are, however, frequent examples of children organising the funeral for their deceased parents. On a stone monument erected for a woman by her second husband, we find the following text as is spoken by the woman:[101]

> ... my mother was Athenian, my father from Hermione, and my name was Epiphania. I have seen many a land, and sailed every sea: for my father and husband were ship-owners, (both of) whom I buried with pure hands in a tomb when they died. But

---

[98] See also her references to *CIL* 6.19914, 22066, 28644, 27866 (p. 219).
[99] In G. H. R. Horsley, *New Documents*, 1983, III/34; the Latin text found in Rome is dated to ca. 18–2 B.C.
[100] *Ibid.*, p. 33. For a discussion of divorce in ancient Rome, see Susan Treggiari 1991 b.
[101] G. H. R. Horsley, *New Documents*, 1982, II/55; the monument is dated to the second or third century A.D.

previously my life was happy: I was born among the Muses, and shared in wisdom. And to friends abandoned, as woman to women I provided much, with a view to piety [εἰς εὐσεβίην ἀφορῶσα].

Apart from the reference to burying her father, we note that the term "piety" is used for Epiphania's motivation for helping other people.

Having mentioned the obligation of providing for parents while they are alive, and then a decent funeral for deceased parents, it is appropriate to add at this point that parents were to be revered by children even after they died. A. Lumpe has summarised this duty of children in the following way (1957, col. 1197):

Die Geister der Toten Eltern und Voreltern wurden von den Römern als weiterhin über dem Hause waltend gedacht und als göttliche Wesen (dii parentes, divi parentum, auch dii Manes = die Guten genannt) verehrt (Cic. leg. 2,22 u. 55); ihnen wurden vor allem an den Parentalien (13.–21. Febr., ...) die Totenopfer dargebracht, welcher Akt mit dem Verb parentare bezeichnet wurde.

It is notable that parents were not venerated as divine beings by early Christians (at least the New Testament texts are silent on this matter). However, we have to bear in mind that for their environment, this obligation was also included in their duties toward parents.

c) Some further duties

The term *pietas* has a very rich meaning. We have already seen its meaning as "provision". There is a further aspect to the term: that of an obedient, submissive attitude. S. Dixon refers to Cicero's own family as an example of *pietas* in this latter sense. From Cicero's letters to Atticus we learn "that Terentia [Cicero's wife] sometimes behaved badly to her daughter but that Tullia bore this well" (1988, 221). Cicero praised the *pietas* of his daughter, Tullia, toward her mother.[102] Dixon adds that: "Such *pietas* was expected of children of all ages and both sexes". This *pietas*, then, meant a certain kind of submission, obedience: the acceptance of a mother's decisions. Valerius Maximus (7.8.2) also preserves an example of how a certain daughter even accepted the unjust will of her mother; and this she did on the basis of her *pietas*.[103]

Next we may mention that the notion of "love" – as probably distinct from *pietas* – also surfaces in our sources. As an example, E. Eyben (1991, 117) summarises a passage in Cicero as follows (*Partitiones oratoriae*

---

[102] S. Dixon (*ibid.*) refers to Cicero, *Att.* 11.17 (and to *Fam.* 14.11 as a comparison).
[103] See e.g. S. Dixon 1988, 221–22.

3. Norms and expectations about the behaviour of children to their parents 69

25.88): "not only *caritas* but especially *amor* unites parents and children, brothers, husbands". Quintilian writes that a father, a tutor, or a husband should be moderate to those who wronged them, since "they emphasise their affection [*caritatem*] for the wrongdoer and there is no desire to do anything that will excite dislike against them save by the manifestation of the fact that they still love them [*amare ipsi videntur*]" (6.2.14).[104] We find an exhortation to have a strong love toward parents in the first century A.D. author Chaeremon: Βεβαιοτέραν ἔχε τὴν φιλίαν πρὸς τοὺς γονεῖς.[105]

Hierocles, the Stoic, mentions several duties of children:[106] they ought to repay the benefits received from their parents; they owe "piety and gratitude" to parents. We note that Hierocles also witnesses to the strong expectation seen above that children should provide food, "a bed, sleep, massage, a bath, and proper garments, in short, the necessities of the body" when their parents are old. Perhaps all these are referred to by Seneca when he summarisingly affirms:[107] "a duty is performed by a son, or a wife, or by persons that are stirred by the ties of kinship, which impels them to bear aid" (*officium esse filii, ... ferre opem iubet*).

We have already mentioned in the previous chapter that there exists another link between the pre-Hellenistic period and the centuries just before the Common Era: authors of New Comedy, like Menander and Apollodorus, have exerted such an influence on some late writers (Plautus and Terence) that the latter often even took over the titles of the works of the former. To give but one example, Terence's final play, *Adelphoe* ("The Brothers", dated to 160 B.C.) is named after the work of Menander under the same title in Greek: Ἀδελφοί.[108] Sidney G. Ashmore observed that (1962, 37): "The principal figures in Terence's dramas are the following: two old men, one severe, the other mild and indulgent; two young men, one openly dissipated, the other exemplary". This applies to *The Brothers* as well. In this play, the author praises obedience based on love rather than on fear. It is true, this is depicted in the relationship between Micio and the son of his brother. Micio has adopted Aeschinus. Micio narrates in moving words in the first scene (lines 40–79) how he hopes that his (adopted) son will not lie to him, because he treats him with openness and trust. Herbert Rädle has stated in a *Nachwort* to his edition of the play (1977, 123): "Ganz

---

[104] Transl. by H.E. Butler 1921, II/425.
[105] Quoted by Stobaeus, *Flor.* 79, in C. Wachsmuth – O. Hense 1909, 625.
[106] D.R. Fideler 1987, 277.
[107] Seneca, *Moral Essays. On Benefits* 3.18.1, in Loeb: vol. 3, p. 159 (Latin text on p. 158).
[108] S. Ireland (1990, 2) observes that although the Latin adaptations of Plautus and Terence were "taken from Greek plays", they "were never mere translations."

offensichtlich steht der hellenistische Dichter ... auf der Seite des Micio." Since it is a play, it can be argued that the expectations concerning a child's duties reflect either the author's view which he wanted to offer as an ideal to his audience, or a wide-spread view concerning which the author could expect agreement on the side of the audience. In one way or another it is a witness to the expectation that a child should be honest and obedient to his father (also as to an "old" man).

As we shall summarise our findings at the end of this chapter, we turn to texts that show the grounds given for children's duties towards their parents.

4. Reasons and grounds for children's duties

As we saw in the case of the pre-Hellenistic period, grounds for duties relate to divine as well as to "earthly" spheres in the three centuries before and after the beginning of the Common Era. We recall that already in the previous sections we have found examples for the following grounds and reasons: the gods (e.g. the Cynics), this is also implied by a sequence listing the gods, country, and parents (Hierocles who also calls parents "terrestrial divinities", Cicero), *pietas* as motivation (Cicero and Seneca), nature (e.g. the Stoics, Valerius Maximus), parents' earlier support has to be returned by their children (Cicero, Seneca), inheritance.

We can find references both to the gods and to nature as grounds for duties also in the writing of Pempelus, entitled *On Parents*:[109]

Neither divinity nor anyone possessing the least wisdom will ever advise anyone to neglect his parents.... For he who honors his parents by gifts will be recompensed by God, for without this the divinities will not pay any attention to the prayers of such parents for their children.... Nature having disposed the matter thus, prudent and modest men will consider their living aged progenitors a treasure, to the extremity of life ...[110]

As we saw in the previous chapter, these thoughts are most likely based on Plato's *Laws*, Book XI. Thus this quotation also repeats the idea that the

---

[109] Preserved by Stobaeus; dated by H. Thesleff to the third or second century B.C. (1961, 115). I quote here the translation of D. R. Fideler (1987, 261).

[110] Hierocles the Stoic also refers to both the divine sphere and to nature as grounds for duties when he writes (D. R. Fideler 1987, 278): "children should be persuaded that they dwell in their father's house, as if they were ministers and priests in a temple, appointed and consecrated for this purpose by nature herself, who entrusted to their care a reverential attention to their parents". From this quotation we can see that "nature" can be personified, we might even say, deified; thus nature is inseparable from the sphere of the gods.

4. Reasons and grounds for children's duties 71

gods will only hear the prayers of parents for their children if the children honour them. This serves as a further reason for the duty. There is an element of the *do ut des* principle also involved in this condition for a prayer to be answered.

A writing attributed to Charondas connects sin against the gods with sin against parents:[111] "let contempt of the gods be considered as the greatest of iniquities, including voluntary injury to parents, neglecting of rulers and laws, and voluntary dishonoring of justice." He adds in a positive formulation:[112] "Let him be considered as a most just and holy citizen who honors these things, and indicates to the rulers and the citizens those that despise them". We note here the interrelation between sin against gods and crime against law. These connected spheres serve as a ground for duty towards parents.

From among the few women writers of this period, Perictyone mentioned the following duties among those listed by her for women:[113] "She should venerate the Gods, thereby hoping to achieve felicity, also by obeying the laws and sacred institutions of her country. After the Gods, she should honor and venerate her parents, who cooperate with the Gods in benefiting their children." We may infer from this quotation three grounds for the duties towards parents. Not only is the duty of honouring gods connected to that of honouring one's parents, but parents and gods are in close relationship as regards the ground for duties as well: they cooperate *for the good* of the children. From this we may further infer that parents should be honoured because they *cooperate with the gods*. We may also say that this is a general rule, so that the women who are addressed here should become parents who would cooperate with the Gods for the benefit of their own children. Thus there emerges another ground – besides the religious one –, namely, the *ongoing succession* of parents and of children who in turn become parents themselves.[114] We have seen this ground also in the chapter on the preceding period.

Perictyone adds a further ground for honouring one's parents: that of being judged by the gods. She writes:[115] "He who despises his parents will both among the living and the dead be condemned for this crime by the

---

[111] Third century B.C., see H. Thesleff 1961, 115. Quotation from D.R. Fideler 1987, 232.
[112] D.R. Fideler 1987, 232.
[113] D.R. Fideler 1987, 239–40.
[114] A. Lumpe gives another example as a "ground" of duty that has a reference to future (1957, col. 1197): "Die Liebe der Eltern ist das beste Unterpfand zukünftigen Glücks (Verg. ecl. 4, 60/3)".
[115] D.R. Fideler 1987, 240.

Gods, will be hated by men, and under earth will, together with the impious, be eternally punished in the same place by Justice, and the subterranean Gods, whose province it is to inspect things of this kind." This means that not to honour one's parents is a crime against the gods. This crime deserves punishment which is executed by the gods – by the goddess Justice and by other gods. The matter of honouring one's parents is seen here as a matter of piety. Perictyone concludes her treatise: "For no greater error or injustice can be committed by men than to act impiously towards their parents."[116]

We find an interesting combination of grounds for the duty of honouring one's parents in an aretalogy of Isis discovered in 1969 in Maroneia, Macedonia.[117] In a long list of what Isis is praised for, we encounter also the following:

You gave laws [νόμους], but they were called *thesmoi* originally. Accordingly, cities enjoyed tranquillity, having discovered not violence legalised, but law without violence. You made parents honoured by their children [σὺ τιμᾶσθαι γονεῖς ὑπὸ [τ]έκνων ἐποίησας], in that you cared for them not only as fathers, but also as gods. Accordingly, the favour is greater when a goddess also drew up as law what is necessary in nature [ἡ χάρις κρείσσων ὅτε τῆς φύσεως τὴν ἀνάγκην καὶ θεὰ νόμον ἔγραψεν].

Reference is made here to written law, which law originates with the goddess Isis. This god-given law is in harmony with nature; indeed, it is a necessity of nature. Once again, we can observe how the spheres of divinity and humanity are intertwined, the latter incorporating both the legal system and nature in general.

According to Hierocles, children owe gratitude to their parents because children can thank their very existence to their parents: they "were once produced by them".[118] When children provide for their aged parents, they "imitate" the care of their parents to them when they were infants. Hierocles states: "By the benefits they formerly conferred upon us, our parents became to us the preceptors of what we ought to bestow upon them".[119]

We may also mention that in antiquity the duty of burying one's parents was a condition of earning an inheritance. Concerning the "office of burial", Suzanne Dixon notes that it "tended to be associated in Roman culture with the duties and privileges of inheritance" (1992, 109). In other words,

---

[116] *Ibid.* 241.
[117] In G. H. R. Horsley, *New Documents*, 1981, I/11; the inscription is dated to the second half of the second century or the first half of the first century B.C. (p. 10).
[118] D. R. Fideler 1987, 278.
[119] *Ibid.*

children who were to inherit from their parents were expected to fulfil their duty of burying their deceased parents.[120] Finally, in the light of these examples we may conclude that children's duties towards their parents were regarded as "natural", or self-evident. The grounds of their duties did not even have to be listed, but were supposed to be well-known. Although in the following quotation from Epictetus children are not mentioned specifically, the general character of the advice would, no doubt, also apply to them:[121] "Next, if you sit in the town council of some city, remember that you are a councillor; if you are young, remember that you are young; if old, that you are an elder; if a father, that you are a father. For each of these designations, when duly considered, always suggests the acts that are appropriate to it." As an other example we may refer to Musonius who lists a number of questions concerning proper conduct (including questions concerning the limits to the necessity of obeying one's father, to which we return below). Musonius interrupts these question by asking whether he should ask them at all: ἢ οὐδὲ ἐρωτᾶν τοῦτό γε ἄξιον.[122] The casual way of asking this question implies that the answers are self-evident for his hearers.

Before we summarise children's duties and their grounds, in the next section we raise the issue: Were there limits to children's duties towards their parents? If so, What were those limits or what were the reasons which exempted children from fulfilling the duties described above?

5. Limits to children's duties towards their parents

Most of our sources affirm the duty to honour one's parents; only rarely are limits mentioned beyond which one was not obliged to carry out that duty. Some texts seem to be so inclusive as if they expressed the requirement of a "limitless" honour towards one's parents. For example, Perictyone states:[123] "We should reverence parents both while living and dead, and never oppose them in anything they say or do." We have seen in the previous chapter that Plato exempted children of a "mad" father from their duty toward him. Perictyone differs from Plato in making clear in a long list of conditions that

---

[120] Concerning Roman law, M. Kaser remarks (1971, 734): "Für die Bestattung zu sorgen, kann der Erblasser jemandem anheimgeben.... Andernfalls obliegt die Bestattung den Erben".
[121] Book II. ch. X.10–12 (in Loeb: p. 277).
[122] Musonius, ed. by R. Nickel 1994, 502.
[123] D.R. Fideler 1987, 241.

even insane parents have to be revered by obedience and submission on their children's side:[124]

Parents ought not to be injured in word or deed; and whatever their rank in life, great or small, they should be obeyed. Children should remain with them, and never forsake them, and almost submit to them even when they are insane, in every allotted condition of soul or body, or external circumstances, in peace, war, health, sickness, riches, poverty, renown, ignominy, class, or magistrate's rank. Such conduct will be wisely and cheerfully adopted by the pious.

We also point to the expectation that children should stay with their parents. As we have seen earlier, it was expected of women that they would not be away from home for long periods of time. Here we find a similar remark concerning children in the writing of a woman author. We have already noticed the point, expressed again in this quotation, that such behaviour is pious. A religious motivation lies behind all the duties mentioned. These duties seem not to have any limits.

The following quotation from Epictetus shows an almost "unlimited" character of the duties it mentions. Epictetus writes:[125] "Next bear in mind that you are a Son. What is the profession of this character? To treat everything that is his own as belonging to his father, to be obedient to him in all things, never to speak ill of him to anyone else, nor to say or do anything that will harm him, to give way to him in everything and yield him precedence, helping him as far as is within his power."

In this quotation the only "limit" implied is the limitations of human beings as it is expressed in the last phrase: "... as far as is within his power". However, we have seen in the section on the Cynics and the Stoics that the former claimed that God called them to a life without a family (which claim probably means they did not marry), whereas Epictetus held that the commitment to the "good" had preference even in his relationship to his father. In that context we have mentioned Musonius Rufus to whom we promised to return.

A writing entitled *Must One Obey One's Parents Under All Circumstances?* (Εἰ πάντα πειστέον τοῖς γονεῦσιν) tells us how Musonius was asked this question by a youth who wanted to study philosophy when his father would not let him. In his detailed answer, Musonius indicates the limit to children's duty to obey their parents with the following arguments.[126] A father does not have to be obeyed if he asks something evil, un-

---

[124] D. R. Fideler 1987, 240; for another translation see T. Taylor 1822, 63–65.
[125] Book II, ch. X,7 (Loeb p. 277).
[126] Musonius, ed. by R. Nickel 1994, 500–511.

5. Limits to children's duties towards their parents

just, or shameful (κακά ... ἢ ἄδικα ἢ αἰσχρά).[127] Zeus wants people to be good (ἀγαθός).[128] To be "good" equals to be a philosopher. Thus the person who asked the question should put philosophy before his father's wish, because he should put Zeus – who is the common father of all human beings – before his own father.[129] Thus here we find a threefold argument for limitation in carrying out children's duties: first, philosophy is to be given preference; second (inseparably from the previous point), it is affirmed the Zeus stands behind the expectation that people should become "good" by becoming philosophers. We shall meet the phenomenon also in Part II, dealing with the New Testament. In the Jesus movement the Kingdom of God, and in the end God himself, stands behind the expectation that some disciples should leave their parents when becoming followers of Jesus. Third, a father commanding a wrong does not have to be obeyed.

We may briefly refer here to the "lists" of those to whom honour is due, discussed in the previous section. A certain limit to children's duties is implied in the ranking expressed in those "lists" (see Diogenes Laertius on the Stoics). In as much as parents come after the gods and one's country in some of those "lists", the gods and one's *patria* limit the duties which are due to parents.[130]

As a final example, we may point to the phenomenon that parent's testaments could be challenged if the child felt that he or she was unduly hurt (neglected) by the will. To mention but one example, Keith Bradley refers to the court case in which Pliny (the narrator of the event) served as an advocate for Attia Viriola, "a woman who had been disinherited by her aged father" (1991a, 172). Pliny writes that the act of disinheriting occurred when the old father got married and "brought home a stepmother for his daughter".[131] Bradley implies that this was not a unique case, but something available to people disagreeing with a testament: "Attia Viriola had thus been compelled to go to court to recover her inheritance".[132] Although this refers to the legal sphere, it may be regarded as a special case of "contradicting" one's father.

---

[127] *Ibid.*, 502. Cf. also the second century A.D. writer, Aulus Gellius (*Attic Nights* 2.7.1–10), who suggests that a father should not be obeyed when he commands one to do something wrong; see O. Larry Yarbrough 1993, 54–55.

[128] *Ibid.*, 508. The term ἀγαθός has a variety of meanings. R. Nickel rightly translates it here as "tugendhaft" (1994, 509).

[129] *Ibid.*

[130] See, for example, Cicero, *Off.* 1.45.160 and 1.17.58, in our section on duties.

[131] K. R. Bradley 1991a, 172; Pliny, *Letters* 6.33.

[132] K. R. Bradley 1991a, 172–73; See other examples in Valerius Maximus (7.7.4) referred to by S. Dixon 1988, 222.

We now summarise our findings concerning norms and duties presented in this chapter. When doing so, we have to emphasise that this summary should not be regarded as a unified picture of the Hellenistic period. Some aspects occurred in a few sources only; some might have been specific to their very author. Caution is due against any generalisation. Rather, the following is to be seen as a gathering of the phenomena we have encountered in our sources. This will enable us to compare the phenomena found in the previous period (and those to be listed from Jewish sources in the next chapter).

6. Summary and classification of the results

As regards *duties*, we have found in our Greek and Latin sources in the period between ca. the third century B.C. and the third century A.D. that the duty of children to honour their parents is widely attested. As we have looked at "everyday life" as well, on occasion a witness of a duty is not a philosopher or playwright, but, for example, an otherwise unknown writer of a letter or someone mentioned on a funerary inscription. Our main focus in this period is not so much *who* is our source, but *what* duty is expressed. Honour and reverence as duties are attested in a great variety of sources (e.g. in personal letters and in the moral writings of the Pythagoreans) with more than one Greek word: τιμάω (e.g. ordered by the goddess Isis) and σέβομαι (e.g. the Stoics, according to Diogenes Laertius). We have also found terms for love as a duty: φιλία (e.g. Chaeremon), *amare* (e.g. Seneca), and *diligere* (e.g. Valerius Maximus). Although the expectation of *pietas* originates in legends of older times, the term surfaces in this era abundantly.

We have met the duty of gratitude which is often expected to be shown by providing for aged or old parents (e.g. Epictetus). This is a kind of repaying a debt owed to parents for childbearing (e.g. Hierocles, Seneca), upbringing, and financial support even toward grown-up children. Children will become parents; thus children of ever new generations are expected to provide for their parents (e.g. Cicero).

A general expectation of obedience is on occasion put in concrete terms: obedience in accepting their parents' decision as to whom they should marry; obedience in learning the virtues of a women (daughters learning from their mother, e.g. Perictyone and Phintys) or in learning the role of the *paterfamilias* (sons learning from their father). Learning the trade of the parents is also an important feature. Obedience also includes the submission to the testament of parents (e.g. Valerius Maximus).

6. Summary and classification of the results

Respectful speech is expected from children (e.g. Epictetus). This means that parents ought not to be harmed by words, but also that they should not be "contradicted" (this being a special case of obedience as well).

It is a strong expectation that children should provide the funeral of their parents; then an on-going ritual to the honour of the deceased parents is expected.

We can summarise the duties in the following table:

While parents are alive *(due to them as superiors:)*	After they die *(due to them as superiors:)*
obedience; learning; respectful speech;	veneration;
(providing for them when weak:)	*(providing for them as mortals:)*
provision, *pietas*.	funeral.

Once again, it is appropriate to emphasise that these are all expressions of honour and reverence toward parents. When compared to the duties found in the previous period, this list confirms that the duties and expectations are the same in the period discussed in this chapter; the overall expectation that a child should honour his or her parents is very strong in the pagan environment of the New Testament.

We have encountered *grounds and reasons* for duties both in the divine and the human spheres. They are as follows.

As regards the *divine sphere*, it is affirmed that it is the will of the gods (the goddess Isis) that parents should be honoured. This is attested in god-given laws (that governed what is necessary in nature). The gods reward children who honour their parents (Pempelus); and they punish the children who fail to honour their parents (injury to parents is also a crime against the gods; Perictyone refers to *Dike*, the goddess of Justice).

Parents have to be honoured because they appear together with the gods in lists which show to whom honour is due (Hierocles, Cicero).

Only the prayers of the parents of respectful children will be heard by the gods (Pempelus).

As regards the *human sphere*, children have to care for their parents because their parents brought them to life and nurtured them when they were infants (e.g. Hierocles). Children ought to remember that one day they will become parents themselves. In the Latin speaking world, *pietas* is named as motivation (Cicero and Seneca). The on-going process of children becoming parents serves as a further ground (e.g. Perictyone). Parents are to be respected and obeyed also because they belong to the older generation (e.g. Terence).

Nature requires that children should honour their parents (e.g. Pempelus, the Stoics, Valerius Maximus). It is also maintained that nature requires what the gods require; to that extent this reason can belong to the divine sphere as well (Isis inscription).

Children owe provision (especially the duty of burial) to their parents from whom they will gain inheritance. This reasoning belongs to the area of law; the same is true of the view that children honouring their parents are regarded as good citizens (Charondas).

We have met the following views concerning the *limits* of children's duties:

There is no limit to children's duties towards their parents (e.g. Perictyone). Even insane parents are not to be neglected.

Gods are to be honoured before parents; this is implied by their place before parents in lists (e.g. the Stoics, Cicero).

One's country has precedence before one's parents; this is implied by *patria* (country) mentioned before parents in lists by Cicero.

A philosopher's commitment to the good has to be given priority (Epictetus, Musonius Rufus; the latter also claiming that this is the will of Zeus).

Parents do not have to be obeyed if they require something wrong to be done (Musonius Rufus, Aulus Gellius; implied also by Epictetus). Unjust wills can be challenged in law courts (Pliny).

The reasons (grounds) for duties and limits of duties can be summed up in the following tables.

reasons	*in the divine sphere*	*in the human sphere*
status of parents	in lists together with gods	parents are older
source of the norm	will of the gods	nature (also as god's will)
form of the norm	god-given law	legal area
consequences		
– of negligence	punishment	
– of honour	reward from the gods	good citizens
"do ut des"	answer to parents' prayers	expecting support from children; expecting inheritance
other:		paying back a debt to parents

6. Summary and classification of the results

limits	in the divine sphere	in the human sphere
due to status	gods first in lists	(honour also insane parents!) one's country
source of limit		unjust will
behaviour		father commanding a wrong thing
other:	Zeus stands behind ...	... the priority of philosophy

If we compare these tables with those in the previous chapter, we can state that almost all the reasons and limits found in the pre-Hellenistic period surface also in the three centuries before and after Jesus' time. In our present tables, we miss an explicit reference to punishment by human legal courts among the reasons; and the behaviour of an unworthy parent is not discussed in great detail among the limits. Among the differences, we observe the appearance of the view that parents (including parents who become insane) deserve unlimited honour from their children. Although this view emerges, views concerning limits also extend to this period. We have encountered *patria* (one's country) also among these limits. The priority of philosophy is strengthened by the argument that Zeus stands behind this limit; and even nature is more clearly connected to the gods as a ground for duties.

To sum up, it seems that honour due to parents is expected even more emphatically in this period. On the one hand, there are fewer limits to this expectation. On the other hand, nature as a ground for duty as well as the priority of philosophy as a limit is strengthened by a reference to the gods.

In the next chapter we shall turn to the writings of Jewish authors in the same period, i.e. the third century B.C. to the third century A.D. We shall look for views shared by the non-Jewish environment and those peculiar to our Jewish sources. This will conclude our investigation of the "environment". Then we shall discuss the New Testament material against the background of the non-Christian sources.

Chapter Three

Jewish Sources in the Centuries around the Turn of the Era

1. Introduction

Before we turn to Jewish sources on our subject, a few introductory remarks are in order. As we shall see, the theme of the child-parent relationship is dealt with by a few sources at some length and by many sources in short remarks. Compared with the sources on the Graeco-Roman world, we have much less on Jewish everyday life and practice. Concerning our sources, Shaye Cohen affirms (1993 b, 3): "Much of the evidence derives from Wisdom literature (Proverbs, Ben Sira), Philo, and rabbinic literature; all of the evidence is prescriptive". In this chapter, our main sources are the Apocrypha and the Pseudepigrapha, Philo, Josephus and the Qumran documents. We do not discuss sources that are later than the first century. Apart from a few references, we do not include in our present research the rabbinic writings, though it is admitted that the documents that were written later than the time of the New Testament may also incorporate traditions that go back to the first century. Since the dating of rabbinic traditions is an unsolved problem of present day scholarship, we exclude this field from our inquiry into the Jewish "environment" of the New Testament. As regards secondary literature, the topic of the Jewish family in antiquity has not been studied in such detail as the family in Greek and Latin societies.[1]

These phenomena will determine our investigation in this chapter: we shall focus on the sources which yield most of the material and we shall in-

---

[1] In recent years, scholars focus on this field with an increasing interest. Shaye Cohen has edited a volume of essays entitled *The Jewish Family in Antiquity* (1993 a). In the Introduction of this significant work, Cohen affirms (1993 b, 1): "I know of no monograph-length study of the subject". A further important contribution to the theme is a more recent volume entitled *Families in Ancient Israel*, the chapters of which are written by four distinguished biblical scholars (Leo Perdue *et al.*, 1997). S. Safrai's earlier chapter, entitled "Home and Family", in the major textbook edited by himself on "the Jewish people in the first century", is still worth consulting (1976, vol. 2, ch. 14, pp. 728–92). For further literature, see S. Joubert and J.W. van Henten who summarise recent works in this field (1996, esp. 122–27).

1. Introduction

clude the shorter remarks of diverse sources at relevant places. In the case of motifs that have a pre-history in the Old Testament, we shall mention the relevant OT passages in discussing the motif in the Jewish sources around the turn of the era.[2]

One of our main sources is Philo of Alexandria. Philo has numerous short remarks on the relationship between children and parents. In her excellent essay entitled "Parents and Children: a Philonic Perspective", Adele Reinhartz affirms that comments related to the parent-child relationship appear "in every extant treatise of the *Exposition*" (1993, 62). Philo has also three longer sections where he discusses the Fifth Commandment. We shall focus mainly on these passages.

In his treatise entitled *On the Decalogue*, Philo treats the Fifth Commandment twice: first as it comes at its own place in the line of the Ten Commandments (*Decal.* 106–120); and then on the occasion of a summary towards the end of the treatise (165–167). He discusses it again in his treatise entitled *On the Special Laws* (2.224–241). It is of significance to observe with the translator of these treatises in the Loeb edition, F. H. Colson (vol. VII, p. xiii), that: "As a matter of fact allegory is almost entirely absent from the *De Dec.* itself and only appears occasionally in the civil or social laws of the *Spec. Leg.*"

We note that Colson disagrees with Goodenough on the question, Is Philo's exposition of the Mosaic law his own interpretation or a reflection of "Jewish jurisprudence in Egypt"? Colson is not convinced by this latter position, promoted by Goodenough. Colson (VII/xii–xiii) argues that our limited knowledge of how Jews in Alexandria administered law does not enable us "to determine whether, when Philo departs from the substance of the Terah [*sic!*], he is adjusting it to what was administered or to what he himself thought reasonable". However, while taking due note of this caution, it can be added that there are numerous passages in Philo which would suggest that Philo not only deals with norms and duties but also refers to "real life" practices. For example, concerning the duties toward God and toward fellow human beings, Philo remarks (*Decal.* 108): "Now we have known some who associate themselves with one of the two sides and are

---

[2] I am aware of the problematic character of using the term "Old Testament", especially when referring to the Bible of the Jewish people. I adopt the term as a shorthand reference to the sacred writings of the Jewish people, acknowledging that the boundaries of the OT canon were not clearly defined at the time of many of the sources discussed in this chapter. For a summary of the problems involved in referring to the different "canons" of the Jewish people, see James Sanders's article in *ABD*, entitled "Canon: Hebrew Bible" (1992, esp. 838–43).

seen to neglect the other". There are also other passages where he refers to negative examples; these are better understood if we think that Philo had concrete cases (and persons) in mind.³ Although Philo is later than some of our other Jewish sources under consideration, occasionally I mention him first in the subsections, since he is the most extended source on our theme. We give special attention to the cases in which Philo differs substantially from the OT and from the other Jewish literature referred to in this chapter.

2. Some insights into real-life practice

It is difficult to differentiate between what is described in our sources in a normative way and what is reflection of existing practices. Nevertheless, we first point to some examples where our texts may yield an insight into practice, and then we shall discuss texts from the point of view of the norms they affirm or imply in a separate section. As regards everyday practice, we point to two areas of the child-parent relationship that have parallels both in the pagan environment and in the New Testament. The first applies primarily to sons and the second relates to daughters.

a) Children following their parents' teaching

From Old Testament times on, the father of the house had as one of his main roles to teach his children.⁴ We find examples of this also in Jewish writings in the centuries around the turn of the era. For example, at the end of a passage on Sabbath meetings in *Hypothetica* (8.7.14), Philo writes concerning the participants of these meetings:⁵

And so they do not resort to persons learned in the law with questions as to what they should do or not do, nor yet by keeping independent do they transgress in ignorance of the law, but any one of them whom you attack with inquiries about their ancestral institutions can answer you readily and easily. The husband seems competent to transmit knowledge of the laws to his wife, the father to his children, the master to his slaves.

Here we can observe that it is the father's duty to teach their children the

---

³ Cf. Philo's following remarks (*Decal.* 110–112): "In such bestial savagery the first place will be taken by those who disregard parents.... For to whom else will they show kindness if they despise the closest of their kinsfolk...?"
⁴ For a discussion of the themes, "God as Teacher", "God as Head of the Household", and "God as Mother" in the OT, see Leo Perdue, in Perdue *et al.*, 1997, 228–29.
⁵ In Loeb: IX/433.

2. Some insights into real-life practice

law. The leading role of the head of the household is affirmed in each of these pairs. We note the similarity to the pairs in the Household Codes in Ephesians and Colossians; and also that, in contrast to the Codes, there is no "reciprocity" between the parts of the pairs in this Philonic passage (see ch. 5 on the Pauline Corpus).[6]

In Jubilees we read that Joseph did not surrender himself to the desires of his master's wife, "but he remembered the Lord and the words which Jacob, his father, used to read, which were from the words of Abraham, that there is no man who (may) fornicate with a woman who has a husband" (*Jub.* 39.6).[7] We note the significance of the teaching passed on through generations from fathers to sons. It is interesting to see that according to this passage the patriarchs left their teaching behind in writing. According to *Jub.* 11.16, Abram's father taught him writing.

A beautiful summary of an outstanding father's teaching activity is narrated by the mother of the seven martyrs in 4 Maccabees. First, the mother says to her sons (18:10): "While he was still with you, he taught you the law and the prophets". Then she gives a long list of examples what their father read to them from various parts of Scripture and how he sang the songs of David.

Education is often connected with the idea of discipline. For example, Sir 7:23 gives the following advice: "Do you have children? Discipline them, and make them obedient from their youth".[8] In chapter 22, verses 3 and 6 we read: "It is a disgrace to be the father of an undisciplined son.... Like music in mourning is a tale told at the wrong time, but chastising and disci-

---

[6] For the father's teaching role in the Old Testament, see e.g. Deut 6:6–9; Exod 13:14; Josh 4:6.21; Prov 4:1–4 (note the presence of the mother in this last passage). See also John J. Collins in L.G. Perdue *et al.*, 1997, 141. Collins observes that (p. 142): "The education of girls consisted primarily in preparation for marriage." Cf. also Ross Kraemer 1993. – As we study the child-parent relationship from the perspective of the child, the theme of teaching and education is of interest to us only to the extent to which it implies obedience on the children's side.

[7] O.S. Wintermute (in J.H. Charlesworth 1985, II/44) argues for dating the document between 161–140 B.C. He also argues that the author "was a Jew who lived in Palestine" (p. 45); he "probably belonged to a priestly family" and "to the Hasidic or Essene branch of Judaism". – Unless otherwise stated, I usually quote the Pseudepigrapha from Charlesworth (1983 and 1985); and the Apocrypha from the Revised Standard Version (see e.g. B.M. Metzger, 1977). The date of these writings is often controversial; that is why I do not always attempt to refer to them in their chronological order.

[8] Georg Sauer observes that the Hebrew original of the work must have remained significant in Palestine, whereas the Greek translation made by the grandson of the author was prepared in Egypt; thus the work entered Diaspora Judaism (1981, 490). The Hebrew version may be ascribed to the first quarter of the 2nd century B.C., and the translation some time after 132 B.C., i.e. the grandson's arrival in Egypt (p. 490).

pline are wisdom at all times" (cf. Prov 1:8–9; 3:11–12; 17:25 [here both father and mother mentioned]; see also Heb 12:6–7).

The following longer passage in Sirach also mentions beating as a possible punishment (30:1–6):

> He who loves his son will whip him often, in order that he may rejoice at the way he turns out. He who disciplines his son will profit by him, and will boast of him among acquaintances. He who teaches his son will make his enemies envious, and will glory in him in the presence of friends. The father may die, and yet he is not dead, for he has left behind him one like himself; while alive he saw and rejoiced, and when he died he was not grieved; he has left behind him an avenger against his enemies, and one to repay the kindness of his friends.[9]

In this passage, we note the aim of teaching: to leave behind someone like the father himself.

Josephus emphasises the necessity to "imitate" forefathers. According to *C. Ap.* 2.204, the Law orders that children "shall be taught to read, and shall learn both the laws and the deeds of their forefathers, in order that they may imitate the latter". Here we note that many preceding generations are included in the term "forefathers". The aim of learning is to imitate the forefathers, naturally including parents as well.

In the New Testament we learn that Timothy was taught Scriptures by his Jewish mother (and grandmother; see 2 Tim 1:5; 3:15; cf. Acts 16:1). We have seen in the previous chapters that learning from parents was among children's duties in the non-Jewish environment as well. We note in advance that in the New Testament Epistles early Christian leaders naturally used paternal imagery in giving advice which they expected the congregations to follow (see chs. 5 and 6).

b) Obedience to parents in the matter of marriage

There is a strong tradition in Judaism (which goes back to Old Testament times) that the parents – and especially the father – had the decisive role in giving their daughters in marriage.

In Sir 7:24–25 we find the following observation: "Do you have daughters? Be concerned for their chastity, and do not show yourself too indulgent with them. Give a daughter in marriage; you will have finished a great task. But give her to a man of understanding". Sirach mentions daughters in other passages, too. In 22:3–5 we read: "the birth of a daughter is a loss. A sensible daughter obtains her husband, but one who acts shamefully brings

---

[9] See also Sir 30:12.

grief to her father. An impudent daughter disgraces father and husband, and will be despised by both". It is difficult to tell from this context whether 22:3b should belong to v. 3a (which refers to the undisciplined son, seen above). If so, then the parallelism would probably mean that it is difficult to discipline a daughter. However, v. 3b may be seen in the context of the following verses as well. In this case it may be another reference to the "problem" of a father in finding a suitable marriage for her daughter.

This "problem" is expressed in a longer passage in Sirach (42:9–11):

A daughter keeps her father secretly wakeful, and worry over her robs him of sleep; when she is young, lest she do not marry, or if married, lest she be hated; while a virgin, lest she be defiled or become pregnant in her father's house; or having a husband, lest she prove unfaithful, or, though married, lest she be barren. Keep strict watch over a headstrong daughter, lest she make you a laughingstock to your enemies, a byword in the city and notorious among the people, and put you to shame before the great multitude.

Perhaps, it is related to the great number of concerns involved in a daughter's marriage that it was often preferred if wife and husband came from the same larger family circle. S. Safrai notes (1976, II/754): "The Book of Judith, for example, informs us that the heroine's husband, Manasseh, was also of her family and clan. This endogamy is particularly emphasized in the Book of Tobit; the author of the *Book of Jubilees* likewise stresses the importance of it, although he does not specifically require it, and in his usual manner he tells us that the patriarchs adhered to this norm".[10]

Finally, in Josephus we see that a girl who is to be married is not free in her decision: she has to be asked for "from him who is authorized to give her away", most probably meaning the father (*C.Ap.* 2.200).[11]

---

[10] Safrai refers to the following passages: Jdt 8:2; Tob 1:9; 3:15–17; 4:12; *Jub.* 4:15.16.20. 27.28.33; 8:6; 11:7.14. – As an example concerning the patriarchs, see Gen 28:1–7; it is worth noting that v. 7 stresses the obedience of Isaac to his father and mother. – For the theme of marriage and divorce, see the chapter by J.J. Collins in the volume by L.G. Perdue *et al.* (1997). Collins's chapter is entitled "Marriage, Divorce, and Family in Second Temple Judaism", pp. 104–162. – S. Joubert and J.W. van Henten (1996, esp. 132–39) rightly point to the Book of Judith in which it is "a-typical" that a widowed woman does not remarry, but maintains the estate herself as a household leader: "Judith is depicted as an ideal woman, a model for Israel" (p. 133).

[11] Although S. Safrai also refers to many talmudic examples, the dates of which may be open to dispute, his section entitled "Betrothal and marriage" gives much insight into practical details (1976, II/752–60). For example, he notes that (p. 752): "There was an early halakic argument as to whether the parents were allowed to negotiate and agree on the financial side of the marriage on the sabbath" (he refers to *Shabbat* 16:22; *b.Shabbat* 12a; 150a). Safrai here also observes that: "A late midrashic source indicates that marriage brokers existed in the second century C.E., but it is not known whether the use of an intermediary was general in the first century."

We now turn to the theme of children's duties. We discuss our sources in three sections in the same sequence as in the previous chapters: first we collect norms and expectations concerning children's duties toward their parents; then we gather the reasons and grounds (or motivations) of those duties; finally, we look at the theme of limits that are set in carrying out the duties. We shall summarise the results of the sections at the end of the chapter.

3. Children's duties towards their parents

We have already seen two concrete duties of children, which also surfaced in the non-Jewish sources: the duty of learning from the parents and that of obeying them in the matter of whom one should marry. In the following, we collect examples of further duties; first, we discuss the overarching theme of honour and then we turn to more concrete duties.

a) Honour and respect

In our previous chapters, we have seen the significance of the duty of honouring one's parents. That parents should be honoured is frequently expressed in our Jewish sources as well. We found in Greek and Latin writings that parents appeared in certain "rankings". Philo also "ranks" parents; they come immediately after God (*Spec.* 2.235):[12] "Honour therefore, he says, next to God (μετὰ θεόν) thy father and thy mother, who are crowned with a laurel of the second rank assigned to them by nature, the arbitress of the contest". It is interesting to observe here that even in a passage where Philo refers to the commandment itself, he expounds it with his own interpretation by referring to "nature". We shall see the significance of nature for Philo also in other passages.

As we have seen, Philo deals with the commandments not only in his treatise entitled *On the Special Laws*, but he has also a special treatment of the Ten Commandments, entitled *On the Decalogue*. We shall return to these writings in more detail in the section on the reasons for duties. Here

---

[12] In a letter dated 17.04.1997, Gerd Theissen has shared with me his observation that: "Im Diasporajudentum hätte man als die beiden höchsten Gebote weniger das Gebot der Liebe zu Gott und zum Nächsten als die Verehrung Gottes und Eltern genannt". I am indebted to him for this remark. – I note Theissen's argument that "tendencies both to extend and to limit love of neighbour stand side by side in early Judaism, as they do (later) in primitive Christianity" (1999, 64–71, quotation at 65).

3. Children's duties towards their parents

we briefly mention Philo's emphasis on the duty of honouring parents according to the Fifth Commandment.[13] Philo deals with this commandment in *Decal.* 106–120, introducing this section with the following summary (106): "After dealing with the seventh day, He gives the fifth commandment on the honour due to parents" (παραγγέλλει πέμπτον παράγγελμα τὸ περὶ γονέων τιμῆς).[14] We note that Philo summarises the reference to "father and mother" in the Fifth Commandment as "parents".[15] He divides the Ten Commandments into two sets of five. Concerning the Fifth Commandment, he affirms (106): "This commandment He placed on the borderline between the two sets of five; it is the last of the first set in which the most sacred injunctions are given and it adjoins the second set which contains the duties of man to man." This implies a very high view on parents, since the duty toward them is placed as the conclusion of the list of duties toward God. In as much as the OT does not tell us how the commandments are divided on the two tables of stone, Philo goes beyond the OT when distinguishing the Fifth Commandment from other commandments concerning duties towards fellow human beings, and placing it on the "border-line between the mortal and the immortal side of existence" (*Decal.* 107).[16] We shall see also in the section on reasons for duties that Philo argues by referring to the procreative function of parents (107): They belong not only to

---

[13] Although the Commandments are not numbered in the Old Testament, Philo numbers them. I adopt his numbering which coincides with the numbering in my home church, and in the Reformed churches in general. The Lutheran and Catholic churches refer to the commandment to honour father and mother as the Fourth Commandment.

[14] In Loeb: vol. VII, pp. 61–69; *Decal.* 106 and 107 on p. 61 (the Greek text on p. 60).

[15] The Fifth Commandment is transmitted in the OT in two different versions in the two accounts of the Decalogue. In the Septuagint text of Exod 20:12 we read: τίμα τὸν πατέρα σου καὶ τὴν μητέρα, ἵνα εὖ σοι γένηται, καὶ ἵνα μακροχρόνιος γένῃ ἐπὶ τῆς γῆς τῆς ἀγαθῆς, ἧς κύριος ὁ θεός σου δίδωσίν σοι. The MT is shorter: only P.Nash and LXX have "that it may go well with you"; and only LXX has "good" (τῆς ἀγαθῆς) as an adjective with "land". Deuteronomy 5:16 (LXX) reads as follows: τίμα τὸν πατέρα σου καὶ τὴν μητέρα σου, ὃν τρόπον ἐνετείλατό σοι κύριος ὁ θεός σου, ἵνα εὖ σοι γένηται, καὶ ἵνα μακροχρόνιος γένῃ ἐπὶ τῆς γῆς, ἧς κύριος ὁ θεός σου δίδωσίν σοι. The MT has a different order: "... that your days may be prolonged, and that it may go well with you ...". For a recent, detailed study of this commandment in the biblical tradition, see Harry Jungbauer, 2002. (This excellent work has reached me after the completion of my manuscript. Part B, pp. 7–135, is devoted to *Das Elterngebot im Alten Testament.* Part C deals with the intertestamental literature, pp. 139–253; see especially the section on Philo, pp. 217–230.) – We note that in the OT there are other commandments beside the Fifth Commandment that require honour toward parents; see e.g. Lev 19:3; cf. also Exod 21:15.17.

[16] I owe this point to Professor Eduard Schweizer. He made the following observation in a letter dated 27.11.98: "Theologisch wäre hochinteressant, dass einerseits Philo weitergeht als das AT es (mindestens im Grossen und Ganzen) tut, andererseits aber weit über den Hellenismus hinaus an die enge Beziehung des Schöpfergotts zum Menschen erinnert."

the mortal, but also to "... the immortal [side of existence] because the act of generation assimilates them to God, the generator of the All" (ἀθανάτου δὲ διὰ τὴν τοῦ γεννᾶν πρὸς θεὸν τὸν γεννητὴν ὅλων ἐξομοίωσιν).

The *Letter of Aristeas* refers to the duty as required by God's commandment.[17] The letter has a long section which relates how during the seven days of a banquet the Egyptian king put questions to each of the translators of the Septuagint (Aristeas 187–294). In Aristeas 228 we read that the king "asked the sixth guest to answer. His question was, 'To whom must one show favour?' The answer was, 'To his parents, always, for God's very great commandment concerns the honor due to parents. Next (and closely connected) he reckons the honor due to friends, calling the friend an equal of one's own self. You do well if you bring all men into friendship with yourself'". Here we observe the significance of friends; but also the priority of parents. We note the reference to God's commandment as the reason for the duty.

The *Sibylline Oracles* has a passage with a certain "ranking", possibly coming from Egypt as well.[18] In the third book, lines 573–574 provide the context for our relevant passage: "There will again be a sacred race of pious men who attend to the counsels and intention of the Most High". Then in lines 593–594 we read: "and they honor only the Immortal who always rules, and then their parents". We note that in these two examples the appearance of the duty right after the duty of honouring God can be seen as a ground for that duty. We have met this phenomenon also in the non-Jewish environment.

Pseudo-Phocylides provides further evidence for the presence of this duty in Alexandria, expressed in a form that we may call a "ranking".[19] Line 8 reads: "Honor God foremost, and afterward your parents" (πρῶτα

---

[17] R. J. H. Shutt (in J. H. Charlesworth 1985, II/9) argues that the *Letter of Aristeas* was written probably by a Jew from Alexandria. He argues for a date around 170 B.C., but he notes that we can only say with certainty that the writing "was written between approximately 250 B.C. and A.D. 100" (p. 8).

[18] The *Sibylline Oracles* are notoriously difficult to date. J. J. Collins (in J. H. Charlesworth 1983, I/322) notes that book 3 was "known to Clement of Alexandria at the end of the second century". On the basis of the internal evidence, Collins argues for a date about 163–45 B.C., as regards the main corpus to which he ascribes our relevant passage as well (pp. 354–55). Concerning provenance, Collins affirms (p. 355): "There is no doubt that Sibylline Oracles 3 was written in Egypt". He ascribes it to "Egyptian Judaism" (p. 356). In his opinion, "it was written in the circles associated with the priest Onias, founder of the temple at Leontopolis", and not in Alexandria as is usually argued (p. 355).

[19] P.W. van der Horst (in J. H. Charlesworth 1985, II/565) affirms that the text has an "undeniably Jewish character" in spite of the efforts of the author to hide this. He dates the writing between 30 B.C. and A.D. 40 (p. 568). He argues for an Alexandrian provenance (*ibid.*).

θεὸν τιμᾶν, μετέπειτα δὲ σεῖο γονῆας). Pseudo-Phocylides is a significant source in the realm of ethical conduct in the household, on which he has a long passage (lines 175–227). We shall see its significance as regards formal parallels to the Household Codes in Colossians and Ephesians.

Jubilees mentions parents and neighbours as those to whom honour is due; once again, neighbours come only after the parents. If *Jubilees* originates in Palestine, then we have a significant parallelism between the above-mentioned writings from Alexandria and a writing from Palestine. In *Jub.* 7.20 we read: "And in the twenty-eighth jubilee Noah began to command his grandsons with ordinances and commandments and all the judgments which he knew. And he bore witness to his sons so that they might do justice and cover the shame of their flesh and bless the one who created them and honor father and mother, and each one love his neighbor and preserve themselves from fornication and pollution and from all injustice". Though *Jubilees* refers to Noah here, it seems likely that the Fifth Commandment and the commandment to love one's neighbour from Leviticus can be supposed to be in the background. We observe the significant order: 1. to bless the creator; 2. to honour father and mother; 3. to love one's neighbour.

Fragments from Qumran also confirm the presence of the duty of honouring one's parents in Palestine. In 4Q416, frag. 2, col. iii, lines 10b–19a we read:[20]

To Him who glorifies thee give honour, *11* And praise His name continually, For out of poverty He has lifted up thy head, And with *the* nobles has He made thee to be seated, And over a glorious *heritage 12* has he placed thee in authority; Seek out His good will continually. Thou art needy; do not say 'I am needy, And I *will* n[ot] *13 study* (?) knowledge'. Bring thy shoulder under all instruction, And with all [ ]... *refine* (?) thy heart, And with abundance of understanding *14* (sc. refine) thy thought*s*. Study the mystery that is to come, And understand all the ways of Truth, And all the roots of iniquity *15* thou shalt contemplate. Then thou shalt know what is bitter for a man, And what is sweet for a *person*. Honour thy father in thy poverty, *16* And thy mother in thy *low estate*. For as God (*scarcely* 'the Father') is to a man, so is his own father; And as *the Lord* is to a person, so is his mother; For *17* they are 'the *womb that was pregnant with thee*'; And just as He has set them in authority over thee And *fashioned (thee)* according to the Spirit, So serve thou them, And as *18 they* have uncovered thy ear to the mystery that is to come, Honour thou them for the sake of thine own honour And *with [reverence] venerate* their *persons*, *19* For the sake of thy life and of the length of thy days. *vacat.*

---

[20] In Emanuel Tov 1999, 113. (Cf. also the text in F. G. Martínez 1994, 384.) In another fragment we find the same text: 4Q418 9–10. Tov's translation is based on a composite text (italics his).

The fragment is generally referred to as sapiential text (so e.g. in the subtitle of E. Tov's edition in 1999; cf. also F. G. Martínez 1994, 384), i.e. it is classified as wisdom literature. Other sections of the document strengthen this view, but even in the passage quoted here we may note the references to "instruction" and "understanding" as possible pointers to this genre. Although it is not stated explicitly, "instruction" (in Martínez's edition: "discipline") may refer to the role of the parents, as it does in other wisdom literature. Although the Fifth Commandment is not quoted in this passage, we may assume that it is alluded to. The end of the section is fragmentary, but one might argue that the expression "the length of thy days" is a reference to the promise attached to the Fifth Commandment in the Old Testament (Exod 20:12): "Honour your father and your mother, that your days may be long in the land which the Lord your God gives you". Emanuel Tov has commented on the words in line 19 of the fragment in this way: "This paraphrases the formula at the end of this commandment in Exod 20:12 or Deut 5:16" (1999, 122). The commandment and the promise attached to it (cf. also Eph 6:2–3) may be supposed to be reasons for the duty.

Because Sirach was written in Palestine and translated into Greek in Egypt, it may be cited as a witness to the presence of the duty of honouring one's parents both in Palestine and the Egyptian Diaspora. Sirach 3:11 says that: "a man's glory comes from honouring his father, and it is a disgrace for children not to respect their mother". In another passage, we find a parallel structure between two verses, 7:27a and 7:29a: "With all your heart honour your father ...; (7:29a) With all your soul fear the Lord".[21] The second member of the parallelism is an allusion to Deut 6:5, and the parallelism formulates children's duty toward their parents in the same way. Sirach 7:27b mentions one's mother as well, even though it is not stated explicitly that she should be honoured as it was in the Fifth Commandment. Due honour is nevertheless probably implied, because she is referred to as the giver of life. Together with v. 28, these verses point to the debt children owe to their parents for their lives: "(27b) ...and do not forget the birth pangs of your mother. (28) Remember that through your parents you were born; and what can you give back to them that equals their gift to you?"

In this section, we can see how widely attested is the duty of honouring one's parents. We have met examples in writings from different locations and dates. We must note that these writings tend to be philosophical; many

---

[21] Verse 28 interrupts this parallelism, which can be seen in the Greek translation of the work. Concerning these two verses, Professor Gerd Theissen pointed out to me in the letter referred to above that: "Die beiden Gebote... sind bewußt parallel gestaltet". I thank him for this and other helpful comments (see fn. 12).

of them can be ascribed to wisdom literature. We have seen in the preceding chapters that this duty was wide-spread also in the non-Jewish world. In Judaism, the Fifth Commandment plays a prominent role; however, the duty itself can be expressed without explicit reference to the commandment.

In the following sections, certain individual duties will be referred to. Although they are not so widely attested – and this must serve as a caution against generalisations –, nevertheless it can be argued that most of them are also in some sense related to the main duty: the duty of honour towards parents. Some of them are special cases of honour; some are consequences of it. In these cases we might assume that they were widely observed even if they do not surface in as many sources as the prime duty of "honour".

b) Honour due to older people in general

Some of our sources extend the duty of honouring one's parents also to include old people in general as the recipients of this duty.

Sirach 3:12–13 refers to old fathers, thus combining the two spheres of duty: that toward old people and that toward parents: "O son, help your father in his old age, and do not grieve him as long as he lives; (13) even if he is lacking in understanding, show forbearance; in all your strength do not despise him." We remember that Plato exempted children from their duty if their father was "insane". In Sirach, even when an aging father "lacks in understanding", this does not serve as a limit to the children's duty of providing for fathers.

In Pseudo-Phocylides, lines 220–222 read: "Revere those with gray hair on the temples and yield your seat and all privileges to aged persons. To an old man of equal descent and of the same age as your father give the same honors". It can be argued that the honour due to parents and the honour due to old people are the two sides of the same coin. On the one hand, one can say that parents have to be respected, because they are older; the parents of a grown-up child must have been regarded as "old" in antiquity, due to the comparatively low life-expectancy. On the other hand, old people are to be revered because they are similar in age to one's parents; thus honour due to parents is to be transferred also to old people (as in the quotation above).

It is significant that in Josephus the duty of respecting older people is mentioned right after the duty towards parents (*C. Ap.* 2.206), as if an extension to the latter. Josephus affirms that the Law "requires respect to be paid by the young to all their elders". We note Josephus' argument as a reason for this duty: it is to be carried out "because God is the most Ancient of all" (cf. Dan 7:9). Josephus' reference to the Law serves as a ground for the duty.[22]

c) Respectful speech

In a passing comment we also learn that for Philo "good words" are included in a child's duty of honouring parents. While arguing that the amputation of hands is not enough punishment for those who strike their parents (cf. Exod 21:15, "Whoever strikes his father or his mother shall be put to death"), Philo affirms concerning such a son (*Spec.* 2.248): "And even if while making no assault with his hands he uses abusive language to those to whom good words are owed as a bounden duty, or in any other way does anything to dishonour his parents, let him die". Philo probably refers to Exod 21:17 ("Whoever curses his father or his mother shall be put to death"); we observe his strictness in requiring the death penalty in the case of "abusive language" as well as in the case of doing anything to dishonour parents. Perhaps this is an example of Philo being more radical than the Torah (cf. Jesus' radical sayings in Matt 5:21ff).

Sirach 3:8 emphasises the importance of respectful speech, too: "Honour your father by word and deed". This verse occurs in a long passage on children's duties toward their parents (3:1–18). It is significant that the immediate context refers to the Lord (and one's mother) as well (3:6–7): "Whoever glorifies his father will have long life, and whoever obeys the Lord will refresh his mother; (7) he will serve his parents as his masters."

As a final example, we mention that the the second book of the *Sibylline Oracles* lists also those who "disobeyed or answered back an unruly word to their parents" among the impious to be destroyed (lines 275–276).[23] We remember that the strong emphasis on this concrete sphere of honouring parents, the honour expressed in speech, is also paralleled in the non-Jewish environment.

---

[22] In Lev 19:32 we read: "You shall rise up before the hoary head, and honor the face of an old man, and you shall fear your God: I am the Lord." We note the "fear of God" as a ground for the duty in the OT. In Isa 3:5 it is a sign of the time of God's judgment if "the youth will be insolent to the elder, and the base fellow to the honorable." The parallelism implies the inferior character of the young people when compared with the old. – For a further example concerning old age in the Jewish "environment", see Philo *Spec.* 2.237. – For a discussion of the priority of the "older" in Jewish literature, see P. Pilhofer 1990.

[23] J.J. Collins argues that the Jewish substratum of books 1 and 2 comes from Phrygia (in J.H. Charlesworth 1983, I/332). He dates this stratum "about the turn of the era". Our lines belong to a passage concerning which Collins remarks that it is "not necessarily Christian".

3. Children's duties towards their parents

d) Obedience, loyalty, and gratitude

In *Decal*. 165–167, Philo summarises those areas of the law which are in relation to the Fifth Commandment. He sets up four pairs: old – young; rulers – subjects; benefactors – benefited; masters – slaves (165). According to Philo, "parents belong to the superior class of the above-mentioned pairs, ... while children occupy the lower position with juniors, subjects, receivers of benefits and slaves" (166).[24] Here it seems to be implied that laws which address those relationships also apply to child-parent relationships. In this way Philo extends the sphere of validity of the Fifth Commandment beyond the parent-child relationship.

Philo does not quote any concrete laws here; he affirms in a generalising way that "there are many other instructions given" (167). Those "other" instructions must mean, in this context, laws that are understood by Philo as applications of the Fifth Commandment. Thus we may conclude that children in relation to their parents should observe instructions given "to the young on courtesy to the old (εἰς ἀποδοχὴν γήρως), ... to subjects on obeying their rulers (εἰς πειθαρχίαν ἡγεμόνων), ... to recipients of benefits on requiting them with gratitude (εἰς χαρίτων ἀμοιβάς), ... to servants on rendering an affectionate loyalty to their masters (εἰς ὑπηρεσίαν φιλοδεσπότον)" (167). Here we note the list of duties including courtesy, obedience, gratitude, and loyalty.

The demand for obedience is frequently expressed in the *Testaments of the Twelve Patriarchs*;[25] especially obedience to the admonitions of the father (*T. Reu.* 3.8; *T. Jud.* 1.4; *T. Zeb.* 10.2). It is also brought into connection with obedience to God. For example, in *T. Jud.* 13.1 we read: "And now, whatever I command you, listen, children (τέκνα), to your father, and keep all my words, to perform the ordinances of the Lord and to obey the com-

---

[24] In Loeb: VII/89; Greek text on p. 88: παῖδες δὲ ἐν τῇ καταδεεστέρᾳ (τάξει), ἐν ᾗ νεώτεροι, ὑπήκοοι, εὖ πεπονθότες, δοῦλοι.

[25] Concerning these writings, H.W. Hollander and M. de Jonge affirm that the "terminus ad quem" is the beginning of the third century A.D., because Origen used the Testaments (1985, 82). They leave the possibility open that the Testaments "may represent a thorough and to a considerable degree consistent reworking of an earlier Jewish writing" (p. 83). Because of the very fragmentary character of the documents found in Qumran which show similarities to the Testaments extant in Greek, they express their caution (p. 85): "it is practically impossible to answer the question whether there ever existed Jewish Testaments in some form". H. C. Kee is bolder in his conclusions. He proposes "the Maccabean period as the date of origin of the Testaments" (in J. H. Charlesworth 1983, I/778). He affirms that this writing (apart from the Christian interpolations) was composed by a "hellenized Jew" (p. 777). As regards provenance, Kee argues for a Syrian origin (p. 778). My quotations are always from the work of H.W. Hollander – M. de Jonge (1985).

mandment of the Lord God". It is worth noting that although Judah himself "transgressed the commandment" of the Lord and of his fathers (13.7), he nevertheless claims that he did whatsoever his father said (17.3–4). We observe the high level of authority of the father; the ethical expectations are implied already in the very *genre* of the "testament".

In our example from *T. Jud.* 13.1, obedience to one's father is asked for, because the father teaches God's commandments. "Obedience" here seems to be an overarching notion: it covers everything required by the duty of "honour". We shall see in the part on the NT that honour and obedience are, on occasion, so closely related that both can be used as a summary of children's duties toward parents.

e) Provision in old age

We have seen in non-Jewish sources that provision for parents who grow old and weak is one of the most important duties for children; indeed a duty which applies to adult people as well, who remain "children" to their parents lifelong. This duty is expressed in Jewish sources as well.

The *Sibylline Oracles* may attest this duty for Phrygia.[26] In the second book, line 245 provides the context for a longer passage when it says that the impious will be destroyed. A little later, lines 273–275 list the following among the impious: "as many as abandoned their parents in old age, not making return at all, not providing nourishment to their parents in turn".

In 4Q416, frag. 2, col. iii, line 17 we find the term "serve" in relation to parents. Because of the authority of their parents over them, children are admonished to serve them. "And just as He has set them in authority over thee And *fashioned (thee)* according to the Spirit, So serve thou them" (see in E. Tov 1999, 113). It is possible that a general attitude is described here: children are under the authority of their parents. However, we raise the possibility that provision for older parents is also included in this "service".

We would argue in a similar way concerning a verse in Sirach. Here again, the text may refer to a general expression of obedience: "he will serve his parents as his masters" (3:7). However, in the light of other literature, we may well see a reference to the duty of provision for old age included in the term "serve". This interpretations is strengthened by the context noted above, since in Sir 3:12 we read: "O son, help your father in his old age, and do not grieve him as long as he lives".

Philo uses the example of storks to argue that children should provide for

---

[26] See J. J. Collins in J. H. Charlesworth 1983, I/332, referred to above.

their aged parents in return for their care when the children were young. With a reference to old storks Philo emphasizes that their children gather "provision for the needs of their parents" (*Decal.* 116). We shall see in the next section that Philo uses this argument from nature as a ground for the duty of providing for parents.

Though probably earlier than the above-mentioned examples, a passage in Tobit concludes this section, because it naturally leads on to our next theme.[27] The passage mentions the duty of caring for old parents as well as that of burying them when they die. Tobit 4:3 reads: "My son, when I die, bury me, and do not neglect your mother. Honour her all the days of your life ...". The order not to neglect the mother after her husband's death may be seen as a call to provide for her: when need arises, in terms of food, and also by everyday help in general. We note that this duty is valid for one's whole life. Although we have seen that this duty plays a significant role also in the pagan world, it is likely that in our Jewish sources it has such a high esteem because it was regarded as the main concrete content of the Fifth Commandment.[28]

f) Providing a funeral

From the time of the patriarchs on, a decent funeral was significant in the eyes of the Jewish people. This duty they shared with their non-Jewish neighbours as well. It is a matter of course that people other than one's children could provide a funeral, but it was also regarded as the duty of a child. Notice the particular emphasis in the passage from Tobit 4:3–4 just cited on the duty of a child to bury his parents. Tobit called his son Tobias, and said: "My son, when I die, bury me, and do not neglect your mother. Honour her all the days of your life; do what is pleasing to her, and do not grieve her. Remember, my son, that she faced many dangers for you while you were yet unborn. When she dies bury her beside me in the same grave". Here we note the distinct mention of both father and mother as the recipi-

---

[27] R. Meyer says about the date and provenance of Tobit (in *RGG*³, VI/907): "Da nach 14,5 der herodianische Tempel (20 vChr) noch nicht steht und die 4Q-Texte wohl dem I. Jh. vChr angehören, wird das Tobitbuch um oder vor 200 vChr verfaßt sein, und zwar eher in der östlichen Diaspora als in Palästina".

[28] Leo Perdue (in Perdue *et al.*, 1997, 190) states: "To honor the parents meant not only to obey them but also to care for them in their old age and to provide them a proper burial." – As a later reference we may refer to *b. T Qidd.* 31b, towards the end of that section. Here honourable behaviour includes: to give one's father to eat, to drink, and to clothe him; to lead him in and out. The latter implies that the father is old or weak; that is why he needs his child's providing care.

ents of their children's duty to bury them. The reference to the dangers faced by the mother before the child was born implies that children should honour their mother because they thank her for their own lives. This ground for the duty surfaces in the pagan environment and in the NT as well.

In the *Testaments of the Twelve Patriarchs* we read (*T. Gad* 8.3): "My children, obey your father, and bury me near to my fathers". At the end of the individual Testaments the burial of the testator, carried out by his children, is also recorded. For example, in *T. Reu.* 7.1–2 we read: "And Reuben died, having given these commands to his sons. And they placed him in a coffin, until they brought him up from Egypt and buried him in Hebron in the double cave, where his fathers were".[29]

As regards funerals, Josephus is not so explicit as the above sources. He simply states that the "funeral ceremony is to be undertaken by the nearest relatives" (*C. Ap.* 2.205). However, the context suggests that children are meant first of all, as the next section speaks of children's duty of honouring their parents (2.206). In *B.J.* 5.545 we find indirect evidence for this duty. When Josephus' mother hears the false news that her son is dead she laments over her loss because she expected that her son would bury her.[30]

We observe that the ancestor cult does not surface directly in our sources around the turn of the era. This is surprising, if we compare this period with earlier centuries of Israel's life, as reflected in the OT, where dead kinsmen "in some obscure sense entered into the sphere of divinity, reflected in occasional references to dead ancestors as '*elohîm*, 'divinities.'"[31] Pieter Craffert (1999c, 32) has pointed to archeological evidence showing that the custom of putting "possessions and objects for daily use" in coffins and tombs was practised in the Second Temple period. However, he adds that "what is missing here is any suggestion of worship of the dead. The dead are conceived as going down to the nether world where they are sustained and well supplied by the living" (p. 33). It seems, then, that Judaism around the time of the NT honoured ancestors only in the sense that they provided for them

---

[29] Joseph commands his children that they should bring with them also the bones of Zilpah (*T. Jos.* 20.3): "And carry up Zilpah your mother and bury her close to Bilhah, by the Hippodrome, near Rachel". – In the OT, cf. the stories in which the patriarchs are buried by their sons, e.g. Gen 25:9; 35:29; 49:29.

[30] For a further attestation of this duty, see *Jub.* 23.7; 36.1–2,18.

[31] So Joseph Blenkinsopp, in L. G. Perdue *et al.*, 1997, 81. As examples, Blenkinsopp points to 1 Sam 28:13; 2 Sam 14:16; Isa 8:19–20 (n. 67 on p. 101). For the theme of the veneration of ancestors in the OT, see *ibid.* 81–82; see also Leo Perdue, in Perdue *et al.*, 1997, 206. – I note that caring for the tombs of the prophets is witnessed to in NT times, see Matt 23:29 (cf. Pieter Craffert 1999c, 40). However, "deification" is not implied in the Matthean text.

in the afterlife just as they had provided for them when they were old in their earthly life. Sirach 7:33 may confirm this: "Give graciously to all the living, and withhold not kindness from the dead." In Tobit 4:17 we find an even more concrete instruction: "Place your bread on the grave of the righteous, but give none to sinners."

The lack of evidence for worshipping the dead as divine beings distinguishes Judaism from its pagan environment. We shall see that the NT is silent on any veneration or deification of dead parents. In this regard, early Christians (among whom many were of Jewish origin) probably shared the views of their Jewish neighbours who did not become Christians. Jewish emphasis on monotheism may have caused a change in practice even in comparison with the OT.

4. Reasons and grounds for children's duties

a) God as the reason for duties

We have already seen in the previous section that parents are mentioned immediately after God in Philo, in the *Sibylline Oracles*, and in Pseudo-Phocylides. This "ranking" implies that God is seen as the reason for duties toward parents. We recall that we have encountered this kind of argument also in non-Jewish sources. We have seen further that God's commandment serves as a ground for duty in the *Letter of Aristeas* and seems to be implied in a Qumran fragment as well.

Before Philo begins his exposition of the Ten Commandments, he discusses how they are to be divided. In *Decal.* 50–51 he states that God divided the ten into two sets of five (εἰς δύο πεντάδας).[32] According to Philo, "the first five obtained the first place"; he also calls these the "superior set of five" (ἡ μὲν οὖν ἀμείνων πεντάς). The Fifth Commandment treats "the duty of honouring parents, each separately and both in common". Here Philo advances an argument which he frequently repeats elsewhere: the commandment concerning parents belongs to the first set because parents "copy" God's nature "by begetting particular persons" (οἱ μιμούμενοι τὴν ἐκείνου φύσιν γεννῶσι τοὺς ἐπὶ μέρους). As we have already seen, in *Decal.* 107 Philo argues as follows:[33] "we see that parents by their nature stand on the border-line between the mortal and the immortal side of existence, the mor-

---

[32] In Loeb: VII/31 and 33.
[33] In Loeb: VII/61.

tal because of their kinship with men and other animals through the perishableness of the body; the immortal because the act of generation assimilates them to God, the generator of the All". Thus parents, while they are human beings, deserve honour because of their participation in God's work. Honour is due to God; that is why honour is due to parents as well.

In *Decal.* 120, Philo refers to some "bolder spirits" who say "that a father and a mother are in fact gods revealed to sight (ἄρα πατὴρ καὶ μήτηρ ἐμφανεῖς εἰσι θεοί)". Adele Reinhartz (1993, 68) argues that Philo "is distancing himself" from those "bolder spirits" whom he quotes. Even if we accept this observation, it is clear that Philo does not deny this view. As it stands, Philo's reference to these ideas serves as a positive argument for the duty of obeying one's parents.[34] I think that Philo can refer to this view because he has already made it clear that parents are human beings. They share in the honour due to God only as his "imitators" in begetting. Thus Philo concludes this section – and leads over to the discussion of the next five commandments – by saying (121): "With these wise words on honouring parents (περὶ γονέων τιμῆς) He [i.e. God] closes the one set of five which is more concerned with the divine".

In his treatise *On the Special Laws*, Philo not only repeats his view that "parents are midway between the natures of God and man, and partake of both", but he states explicitly (*Spec.* 2.225):[35] "Parents, in my opinion, are to their children what God is to the world". Here again, his argument is that parents "imitate" God in that they "immortalize the race" by begetting children.

Jesus ben Sirach in Sirach 3:2 emphasizes his right to be listened to by his children "for the Lord honoured the father above the children, and he confirmed the right of the mother over her sons". In the long passage that follows, God (or the Lord) is referred to repeatedly as the justification of children's duty. For example, in 3:16 we read: "Whoever forsakes his father is like a blasphemer, and whoever angers his mother is cursed by the Lord." We observe that both father and mother are mentioned.[36] We note that in Sirach the children are warned not to anger their mothers, whereas in the NT fathers are warned not to anger their children (see Col 3:21 and especially Eph 6:4 in which the same verb, παροργίζω, is used, as in Sir 3:16).

---

[34] A. Reinhartz also notes this point, which weakens her proposal concerning the "distancing" on Philo's side (1993, 68).

[35] In Loeb: VII/447.

[36] J.J. Collins notes (in L.G. Perdue *et al.*, 1997, 141): "Ben Sira accords equal honor to fathers and mothers, although he mentions the father more often." – For the role of women in the OT, see the section entitled "Females" by Leo Perdue, in Perdue *et al.*, 1997, 180–82.

4. Reasons and grounds for children's duties

b) Divine court and human court as combined reasons

In accordance with the place of the Fifth Commandment on the "borderline" between what people owe to God and what they owe to fellow human beings, Philo gives a combined reason for the duty of honouring one's parents. On the one hand, those who neglect this duty are convicted "in the divine court" (*Decal.* 111). In accordance with his own argument, Philo mentions here also the "due respect to those who brought them forth from nonexistence to existence and in this were imitators of God". On the other hand, those who neglect their parents are also convicted "in the human court, [namely,] of inhumanity". We recall that children's duty was based on a reference to divine and human courts also in non-Jewish texts.

c) Further religious reasons for duties

The third chapter in Sirach not only refers to the Lord, but also to further religious reasons as motivations for children's duties. In Sirach 3:3–4 we read: "Whoever honours his father atones for sins, and whoever glorifies his mother is like one who lays up treasure". We observe how in this *parallelismus membrorum* both father and mother are mentioned, as it is often the case in wisdom literature. We note the striking affirmation that the honouring of one's parents has an atoning effect. This motivation reappears in Sir 3:14–15, where we read: "For kindness to a father will not be forgotten, and against your sins it will be credited to you; in the day of your affliction it will be remembered in your favor; as frost in fair weather, your sins will melt away".[37] Perhaps this may be seen as the closest parallel to Philo's high esteem of parents when he emphasises parents' participation in God's creating activity.

Blessing and curse dispensed by one's parents are also mentioned as grounds for children's duties. In Sirach 3:8–9 we read: "Honour your father by word and deed, that a blessing from him may come upon you. For a father's blessing strengthens the houses of the children, but a mother's curse uproots their foundations". Blessing and curse can be seen as prayers. Thus this reference to blessing may be a close parallel to the argument found in texts from the non-Jewish environment that God will listen to parents' prayers only if their children honour them. In Sir 3:5 it is explicitly said that the man who honours his father will receive an answer to his prayers

---

[37] J. J. Collins (in L. G. Perdue *et al.*, 1997, 141) makes the following observation in connection with this passage in Sirach: "There is a tendency in second temple Judaism to associate atonement with good works (cf. Dan. 4:24 [ET 4:27])."

(whereas in the previous example it was the father who was honoured by his children who received answers to prayer): "Whoever honours his father will be gladdened by his own children, and when he prays he will be heard". The ongoing line of parents and children serves as the reason for honouring parents.

d) Nature calls for a debt to be repaid

As we have already mentioned, Philo also argues from nature: from the examples of lions, watch-dogs, sheep-dogs and storks (*Decal.* 113–117).[38] From his long discussion of the example of the stork we learn Philo's view with regard to the child-parent relationship. It is significant that here we find a certain reciprocity between the duties of "children and parents", because in general terms, as A. Reinhartz rightly argues (1993, 66), the "basis for every Philonic discussion of family life is the assumption of the hierarchical nature of the parent-child relationship".[39] As regards the old storks who are unable to fly, children gather "provision for the needs of their parents" (*Decal.* 116). The "inactivity" of the old is "justified by their age" (117). The younger birds are "moved by piety (εὐσεβεῖν) and the expectation that the same treatment will be meted to them by their offspring". Mutuality, then, is justified by the logic that those who are now children will eventually become parents themselves. Another aspect of mutuality is expressed in the argument that help is "a debt both incurred and discharged at the proper time – namely that in which one or the other of the parties is unable to maintain itself, the children in the first stage of their existence, the parents at the end of their lives" (117). We note that although the whole treatment occurs in the discussion of a Mosaic law, this framework does allow room for Philo to refer to nature as a ground for duty. In relation to the above mentioned behaviour of the storks he uses the terms αὐτοδίδακτος and φύσις.

We have encountered the argument that children owe a debt to their parents also in non-Jewish literature. As a further example in Jewish literature, we may add to the Philo passage the reference we have already mentioned from Sirach (7:27–28): "With all your heart honour your father, and do not forget the birth pangs of your mother. Remember that through your parents you were born; and what can you give back to them that equals their gift to you?"

---

[38] In Loeb: VII/65 and 67.

[39] It is for this reason that A. Reinhartz discusses "parent-child" relationships and not the other way round. She does have, however, a section on the "Responsibilities of children towards their parents" (1993, 77–81).

4. Reasons and grounds for children's duties   101

We have already met a passage in the second book of the *Sibylline Oracles* where, among the wicked who will be destroyed are "as many as abandoned their parents in old age, not making return at all, not providing nourishment to their parents in turn" (lines 273–275). The term "return" implies the repaying of the debt children owe to their parents. Josephus expresses the same idea when he speaks of a son's duty to "respond" to the benefits received from his parents (*C. Ap.* 2.206).

From some of the above examples we can also see that among the phenomena of "nature" that entail moral duties is included the phenomenon of child-bearing. We have to add, however, that for Philo the procreation of life is both a demand of nature and a certain partaking in God's creative activity. When Philo applies the example of the storks to human beings, he returns to his "hierarchical" arguments mentioned above. First, he affirms that "children have nothing of their own which does not come from their parents" (*Decal.* 118). Then, in his repeated reference to God, we even learn the main aim of marriage (119): "For parents are the servants of God for the task of begetting children (θεοῦ γὰρ ὑπηρέται πρὸς τέκνων σπορὰν οἱ γονεῖς), and he who dishonours the servant dishonours also the Lord". Thus here we find a double aspect of the child-parent relationship: it is the order of nature that generations should follow one another; at the same time it is God's will. For Philo, "nature" and "God's will" are the two sides of the one coin.[40] The ongoing line of procreation should remind children of the debt they owe to their parents for their lives.

e) Virtue and other "logical reasons"

We have already met in Philo a list of children's duties. Philo makes use of a list also in his argumentation. He marshals the four pairs we have seen above and he even adds a new element to the list: the pair of teacher and pupil. He argues (*Spec.* 2.226): "And a father and mother deserve honour (ἄξιοι... τιμῆς).... For in the judgement of those who take account of virtue, seniors are placed above juniors, teachers above pupils, benefactors above beneficiaries, rulers above subjects, and masters above servants". Philo then goes on to affirm that "sons and daughters are placed in the lower order" of these pairs (227).[41]

---

[40] I owe this point to Professor Christoph Burchard, Heidelberg, who has formulated it to me in this way: "Die Natur ist Gottes inkorporierter Wille."
[41] A. Reinhartz observes that there is a "male-female hierarchy" in Philo (1993, 86; she points e.g. to *Spec.* 1.200–201). It is, therefore, significant that in this context mothers appear together with fathers (probably because both are mentioned in the Fifth Command-

We note his reference to "virtue" (ἀρετή) as a reason for duty. In the sentence which closes this section (227) and leads over to the next one, he gives similar reasons: "That none of these statements is false is self-evident, but logical proofs will ratify their truth still further". Among the "logical proofs" we find again the arguments that "the maker is always senior to the thing made" (*Spec.* 2.228; cf. Heb 3:3), and that parents gave children their very existence, then nurtured them and educated them (*Spec.* 2.229). The latter reasons surface also in the non-Jewish environment.

f) Parents' authority and right to punish their children

In *Spec.* 2.231, Philo uses the term ἀρχή when affirming that "parents have also received authority over their offspring". This "authority" means that fathers have the right to beat their children (232). Father and mother together can decide even "to extend the punishment to death" (232, also expounded in 243ff).[42] F. H. Colson notes that "Philo's language suggests a more independent action on the part of the parents than Deuteronomy",[43] since in Deut 21:18–21 the parents have to bring their disobedient, "stubborn and rebellious" son to the elders at the gate, and if they find him guilty, "then all the men of the city shall stone him to death with stones" (v. 21). Thus here we have another case in which Philo goes beyond the Torah. We do not know whether this law was carried out in practice; at least Philo does not mention any examples. Nevertheless, the threat of punishment can be seen as a further ground for children's duties.

We have also seen a reference to the death penalty in the context of a passing comment on "good words" (*Spec.* 2.248). We recall how Philo extends the field of offence by a son to include every possible act of dishonour to his parents: if he "in any other way does anything to dishonour his parents, let him die". We may add that while Philo probably has passages from Scripture in mind,[44] he also refers to the good of the community as an argument. Anyone dishonouring his parents is described by Philo as follows (248):[45]

---

ment) and that sons and daughters also appear together. Reinhartz goes on to say (1993, 65): "It would seem, however, that the relationship which is of greatest interest and concern to Philo is that between father and son. His remarks to 'parents' and 'children' are in reality addressed primarily to males in their roles as fathers and sons".

[42] I note that Adele Reinhartz agrees with earlier Philo scholars, Heinemann and Goodenough, that "Philo's understanding of parent-child relationships may indeed have been influenced by the Roman concept of *patria potestas*" (1993, 76–77; quotation from p. 77).

[43] In Loeb: VII/452.

[44] See e.g. Exod 21:15,17; Lev 20:9; cf. Deut 27:16.

[45] In Loeb: VII/461 and 463.

4. Reasons and grounds for children's duties

"He is the common and indeed the national enemy of all. For who could find kindness from him who is not kind even to the authors of his life?"

As regards punishment for children who are negligent towards their parents, Josephus, too, refers to the death penalty (*C. Ap.* 2.206): "if a son does not respond to the benefits received from them – for the slightest failure in his duty towards them – it [i.e. the Law] hands him over to be stoned". This is probably a reference to Deut 21:18ff, as in Philo (though without giving the right of punishing into the hands of the parents). When Josephus and Philo take over the idea of the death penalty from the OT, they show how high an esteem parents have for them. This is true even if it is only stated as a warning and does not reflect actual practice.

*g) The promise attached to the Fifth Commandment:
a long life*

Philo emphasises that the first four commandments have their reward in the very "action" of keeping them. In as much as the Fifth Commandment belongs to the first set of five, it can be said that "he who shews respect to his parents should not seek anything further, for if he look he will find his guerdon in the action itself" (*Spec.* 2.261). However, since the Fifth Commandment is also concerned "with mortal things", God also gave a further encouragement to it. Here Philo quotes the Fifth Commandment: "Honour thy father and thy mother, that it may be well with thee and that thy time may be long".[46] Philo expounds the commandment in the following way (*Spec.* 2.262): "Here He names two rewards: one is the possession of virtue, for 'well' is virtue or cannot exist without virtue, the other in very truth is salvation from death given by prolonged vitality and agelong life which thou wilt keep thriving even while in the body, if thou live with a soul purged clean of all impurity".

Philo interprets the promise as a reference to "prolonged vitality". We have to note that the original reference to "long life" in the Fifth Commandment probably does not only mean the prolongation of one's own life, but also the life of future generations. As Franck Alvarez-Péreyre and Florence Hey-

---

[46] We shall see the significance of the fact that a promise is attached to the Fifth Commandment also in our discussion of the New Testament; see e.g. the discussion of Eph 6:2–3. We note that Philo quotes the Fifth Commandment also on another occasion, in his treatise entitled *The Worse attacks the Better (Quod Deterius Potiori insidiari soleat)*, 52. Here he uses it for an allegorical interpretation: νοῦς is the father, and αἴσθησις is the mother. A little further on, in section 54, the "Maker of the world" is called "father", and σοφία is called "mother". He who honours these, shall experience the "good" (εὖ) promised in Exod 20:12 and Deut 5:16.

mann have put it: "'Damit deine Tage lang werden' muß nicht wörtlich als Zusage von Langlebigkeit, sondern vor allem im Sinne von Nachkommen verstanden werden, ohne die es keine historische Kontinuität geben kann."[47]

We also encounter the reference to long life in Sirach, probably originating in the Fifth Commandment as well (3:6): "Whoever glorifies his father will have long life, and whoever obeys the Lord will refresh his mother". In this parallelism we note that the term "Lord" (rather than "mother") in the second part corresponds to "father" in the first part.

As mentioned earlier, one could argue that the expression of "the length of thy days" may be a reference to the promise attached to the Fifth Commandment also in a fragment from Qumran. In 4Q416, frag. 2, col. iii, lines 18–19 children are addressed with regard to their parents: "Honour thou them for the sake of thine own honour And *with [reverence] venerate* their *persons, 19* For the sake of thy life and of the length of thy days".

Though in the Jewish sources "long life" as a motivation for duties originates in the Fifth Commandment, its implication concerning future generations can be seen as a parallel to the idea met in the non-Jewish sources: the very hope for an ongoing process of children becoming parents serves as a reason for honouring parents.

5. Limits to children's duties

In general terms, it is expressed or presupposed in our sources that God's first place implies a limit to the honour people owe to their parents. Before we turn to some examples, we recall that Sirach seems to differ from the view we encountered in Plato that an old father who loses his sense does not have to be obeyed. Ben Sirach opposes this "limit" when he admonishes a son concerning his aged father (3:13): "even if he is lacking in understanding, show forbearance; in all your strength do not despise him".

a) Limit implied by ranking

When we discussed the duties of children above, we noted texts that show a certain ranking between God and one's parents. These texts imply a limit, by ranking parents after God. Apart from the passages cited above

---

[47] F. Alvarez-Péreyre and F. Heymann, in A. Burguière *et al.*, 1996, 204. Their chapter in this major work on "Altertum" is entitled "Ein Streben nach Transzendenz: Das hebräische Muster der Familie und die jüdische Praxis", pp. 196–235.

(Philo, the *Sibylline Oracles*, Pseudo-Phocylides), we may refer to Josephus on the same theme. In *C. Ap.* 2.206 he writes: The Law "ranks honour to parents second only to honour to God". This statement implies two significant consequences: 1) parents are ranked very high, indeed, the highest among human beings, right after God (μετὰ τὴν πρὸς θεὸν δευτέραν); 2) but the same expression indicates a limit to honour due to parents: honour to God must have precedence over honour towards parents. It is not stated explicitly, but a sentence like this also implies that if the commandment of God is contradicted by the orders of parents, the former must be obeyed.

We have met the same implication of ranking in lists also in the non-Jewish sources. This idea shall be significant for our understanding of some sayings in the Gospels in which Jesus calls disciples to become special servants of God's Kingdom and in which he calls some disciples to follow him, the unique envoy of that Kingdom. The duty of honouring God on the first place does not require dishonouring one's parents; it only emphasises the right priorities.

b) What is "just and profitable"

In Philo, we encounter one passage that may be seen as a "limit" to children's obligation of obeying their parents. Philo writes (*Spec.* 2.236):

For parents have little thought for their own personal interests and find the consummation of happiness in the high excellence of their children (τέλος εὐδαιμονίας νομίζουσι τὴν τῶν παίδων καλοκἀγαθίαν), and to gain this the children will be willing to hearken to their commands and to obey them in everything that is just and profitable (τοῖς δικαίοις καὶ συμφέρουσιν); for the true father will give no instruction to his son that is foreign to virtue (οὐδὲν γὰρ ἀλλότριον ἀρετῆς ὁ ταῖς ἀληθείαις ὑφηγήσεται πατὴρ παιδί).

The limits to the duty of obedience are expressed here by the terms which qualify the area in which one has to obey one's parents: in matters "just and profitable". Adele Reinhartz notes that "this passage raises the question of whether one is obligated to obey paternal instruction which is foreign to virtue" (1993, 79). She adds that "Philo nowhere addresses this question directly". On the basis of "Philo's world-view as a whole", Reinhartz thinks that for Philo "in a conflict between virtue and filial obedience, the former must prevail". We may add that in Philo's own formulation this question should not arise at all. A "true father" will not come into conflict with virtue; accordingly, a father who asks something which is against virtue is not a true father. However, Reinhartz may be right in taking Philo's statement as an implication of a limit to children's obedience.[48]

c) Torah, temple, and conversion to "Judaism" as limits

A certain type of text deserves mentioning in this context in general, namely stories about the willingness to die for the Mosaic laws, or for the temple. In these stories we often find the motif that family ties are ranked second after the Torah; and fidelity to the Torah and to the temple might involve readiness to suffer martyrdom.

For example, in connection with the Maccabean revolt, Jewish people's attitude is described in the following words in 2 Macc 15:18: "Their concern for wives and children, and also for brethren and relatives, lay upon them less heavily; their greatest and first fear was for the consecrated sanctuary".[49] Although this sentence is written from the perspective of soldiers, we may assume that it describes the views of families in general.[50]

4 Maccabees puts a strong emphasis on martyrdom. Perhaps a more general passage can be viewed against this background as well. In 4 Macc 2:9b–13 we read:[51]

In all... matters we can recognize that reason rules the emotions. For the law prevails even over affection for parents, so that virtue is not abandoned for their sakes. It is superior to love for one's wife, so that one rebukes her when she breaks the law. It takes precedence over love for children, so that one punishes them for misdeeds. It is sovereign over the relationship of friends, so that one rebukes friends when they act wickedly.

---

[48] We must also notice how Philo changes from the plural of parents to the father when it comes to instructions. Παῖς can be both masculine and feminine; so, perhaps the translation "child" may be allowed here instead of "son".

[49] C. Habicht summarises the provenance of 2 Macc as follows. The work of Jason of Cyrenaica was abridged by an author whose name remains unknown. We do not know where he lived (1976, 169). Both Jason (p. 170) and the author of 2 Macc must have been Jews (p. 189). Habicht affirms that 2 Macc is a literary product "durchaus von griechischer Art und Form". Scholars ascribe it various dates; the dates vary between 124 B.C. and the first half of the first century A.D. (p. 169).

[50] See another example of a similar kind in Josephus, *B.J.* 2.197.

[51] H. Anderson (in J.H. Charlesworth 1985, II/532) states that the author of the work "is unquestionably a Jew... profoundly influenced by Greek philosophical thought". As regards date and provenance, Anderson argues for the following view: "4 Maccabees was written outside of Palestine by an unknown author in the period of 63 B.C. – A.D. 70" (p. 533). He notes that many commentators argue for Alexandria as the place of origin of *4 Macc* (p. 534), others for Syrian Antioch (pp. 535–36), but he himself prefers leaving the question open, or at most "contemplating only some possible location in the coastal lands of Asia Minor" (p. 537).

Once again, we note the subordination of "family ties" in general, including "affection for parents" in particular. These texts are significant as a background to our discussion of the New Testament. We shall meet passages in the Jesus tradition where family relationships are put in the second place when compared to matters of God's Kingdom.

We may mention Josephus as an example in connection with limits to duties within a family. He emphasises the openness of the Jewish community to those who want to observe the Mosaic laws (*C. Ap.* 2.210). In this context he formulates a limit to duties required by family ties: "To all who desire to come and live under the same laws with us, he [i.e. "our legislator" (ὁ νομοθέτης)] gives a gracious welcome, holding that it is not family ties alone (οὐ τῷ γένει μόνον) which constitute relationship, but agreement in the principles of conduct".[52]

Stephen Barton has pointed out that many Jewish writings narrate cases where a distancing from one's family is something worthy of praise.[53] For example, in *Jub.* 11.16 concerning Abram we read: "And his father taught him writing. And he was two weeks of years old. And he separated from his father so that he might not worship the idols with him". In the *Apocalypse of Abraham*, chapters 1–8 narrate the story of Abraham's youth.[54] At the end of this long narrative concerning the futility of the gods of his father, we read Abraham's words (8.1–6): "And it came to pass as I was thinking things like these with regard to my father Terah in the court of my house, the voice of the Mighty One came down from the heavens in a stream of fire, saying ... 'Go out from Terah, your father, and go out of the house, that you may not be slain in the sins of your father's house'. And I went out". Verse 6 tells us that his father and his house was burnt by a thunder. In *Joseph and*

---

[52] It is worth noting that in relation to this theme Josephus claims a similarity between Plato's ideas and the Mosaic laws. Josephus writes (II/257): "In two points, in particular, Plato followed the example (μεμίμηται) of our legislator. He prescribed as the primary duty of the citizens a study of their laws, which they must all learn word for word by heart. Again, he took precautions to prevent foreigners from mixing with them at random, and to keep the state pure and confined to law-abiding citizens". Perhaps Josephus means that a good legislator like Plato naturally had to come to the same conclusions as the "legislator" of the Jews. We note that Josephus could refer to Plato as a "parallel" to his own considerations of the Mosaic law.

[53] See 1994, 24ff *passim* and 55.

[54] R. Rubinkievicz argues for a date "sometime after A.D. 70 and before the middle of the second century" (in J. H. Charlesworth 1983, I/683). As regards provenance, he cautiously remarks: "If the original language of the Apocalypse of Abraham is Hebrew, then it was most likely composed in Palestine". Rubinkievicz brings arguments for the case that it "was written in a Semitic language, probably in Hebrew" (p. 682), but he warns us that "it is preserved in Slavonic manuscripts that are far removed from the conjectured time and place of the original composition" (p. 683).

Aseneth we learn Aseneth's thoughts which she said in her heart (11.4):[55] "All people have come to hate me, and on top of those my father and my mother, because I, too, have come to hate their gods and have destroyed them". The passage does not say that Aseneth hated her parents, but the hope of marrying Joseph resulted in her hating the pagan gods of her former family.

Although these latter examples refer back to the times of the patriarchs, they were probably intended by their authors to serve as encouragement for prospective converts to Judaism at the time of their writing. These examples, then, can be seen as limits to children's duties: for the sake of the God of the people of Israel one has to be prepared to leave a pagan background, including family house and parents. We shall see in the NT that the question of mixed marriages is mentioned, but the theme of the tension between children and parents caused by the difference between faith and paganism is not addressed. We shall meet another kind of difference in "faith", namely the tension in the family caused by a new adherence to Jesus (see e.g. on Matt 10:34ff, in ch. 4).

d) Enmity in the apocalyptic literature

Although Jewish apocalyptic literature does not speak directly about any "limit" in children's duties toward parents, enmity within a family is seen as a sign of the last days. The context of God's judgment shows that the enmity is regarded clearly as a negative phenomenon, but it cannot be avoided. In this sense, children's duties will be "limited", though this will happen against the will of God. For example, in *1 En.* 100.1–2 we read:[56] "In those days, ... a man shall not be able to withhold his hands from his sons nor from (his) sons' sons in order to kill them. Nor is it possible for the sinner to withhold his hands from his honored brother. From dawn until the sun sets, they shall slay each other". Verse 4 shows us the context clearly: "And the Most

---

[55] C. Burchard writes that "we are probably safe to say that the book was written between 100 B.C. and Hadrian's edict against circumcision, which has to do with the Second Jewish War of A.D. 132–135" (in J. H. Charlesworth 1985, II/187). Burchard says that the work "does appear to have originated in Egypt". If it is the case, then "the Jewish revolt under Trajan (c. A.D. 115–117) is the latest possible date".

[56] E. Isaac summarises the consensus view of scholars before the discovery of fragments of *1 Enoch* among the Dead Sea Scrolls when ascribing to our relevant passage the date c. 105–104 B.C. (in J. H. Charlesworth 1983, I/7). This date can be maintained even now, strengthened by the fact that fragments from the longer section, of which our passage is part (chs. 91–107), were also found at Qumran. On the basis of the Qumran fragments, Isaac affirms that "it is clear that the work originated in Judea" (p. 8).

High will arise on that day of judgment in order to execute a great judgment upon all the sinners". Although we do not find here a reciprocity between father and son, the second pair, sinner and his brother, shows that severe enmity within the family is a sign of the last days.[57] We shall see in the part on the NT that both Gospel texts as well as epistles in the Pauline Corpus mention enmity in the family as an unavoidable sign of the apocalyptic end times.

6. Summary and classification of the results

From the above examples we can see how much of the views concerning the child-parent relationship was shared by Jews and non-Jews in the centuries around the time of the New Testament. There are also a number of differences. When summarising our results, we follow the pattern set in the first two chapters.

From our Jewish sources we can put together lists of duties and grounds for duties very similar to those seen in the chapters on pagan texts. To quote Shaye Cohen in summarizing the articles in a significant volume on our theme (1993b, 2): "The striking conclusion that emerges from all four papers ... is that the Jewish family in antiquity seems not to have been distinctive by the power of its Jewishness; rather, its structure, ideals, and dynamics seem to have been virtually identical with those of its ambient culture(s)".

The following *duties* of children surfaced in our sources. The duty of honour and respect is widely attested (e.g. Philo, Josephus, Sirach, Pseudo-Phocylides, the *Sibylline Oracles*, the *Letter of Aristeas, Jubilees*, Qumran). Honour due to older people in general stands in close connection to the same duty toward parents (e.g. Philo, Josephus, Pseudo-Phocylides). Respectful speech is a concrete application of the duty of honour (e.g. Philo, Sirach, the *Sibylline Oracles*). Obedience, loyalty, and gratitude also follow from honour; obedience can be an overarching duty in the same way as honour (Philo, *Testaments of the Twelve Patriarchs*). Obedience includes learning from parents (e.g. Philo, Josephus, Sirach, 4 Maccabees, *Jubilees*) as well as being obedient to them in the matter of marriage (Josephus, Sirach). Provision for old parents is also significant; it is possible to argue that the Fifth Commandment implies this duty as well (e.g. Philo, Sirach, Tobit, the *Sibylline Oracles*, Qumran). Providing a funeral is a further essential

---

[57] Cf. also *1 En.* 56.7; 99.5; *Jub.* 23.16; *2 (Syr) Bar.* 70.6; from the OT see Zech 13:3.

example of honouring parents (e.g. Josephus, *Testaments of the Twelve Patriarchs*, Tobit). We have observed that veneration appeared in the sense of providing for parents even in the afterlife, and not in the sense of venerating them as divine beings. Apart from this latter phenomenon, which shows a significant difference when compared with the pagan environment, the main duties are shared by Jews and pagans around the time of the New Testament. In order to show the similarities, we summarise the main duties in the following table:

While parents are alive *(due to them as superiors:)*	After they die *(due to them as superiors:)*
being obedient to them; learning from them; speaking to them respectfully;	providing for them in the afterlife;
(providing for them when weak:)	*(providing for them as mortals:)*
caring for them when they are old.	providing a funeral.

We have encountered the following reasons and grounds for children's duties. Reference to "God" serves as the reason for children's duty, including cases in which parents' "ranking" after God implies the ground for the duty (Philo, Pseudo-Phocylides, the *Sibylline Oracles*). The sanctions of the divine court and of the human court are regarded as combined reasons (Philo). There are further religious reasons for duties, including the idea that honour toward parents atones for sins (Sirach); the condition under which the blessings of parents and the prayers of children are heard is the rendering of honour (Sirach). Nature calls for a debt to be repaid (Philo, Josephus, Sirach, the *Sibylline Oracles*). Virtue and other "logical reasons" are named by Philo as the ground for duties. Parents' authority and right to punish their children are reasons for children's duty (Philo, Josephus). In addition to the above reasons (which surface also in the pagan sources), the Fifth Commandment is a ground for duty in the Jewish sources. The promise attached to the Fifth Commandment, a long life, is also unique to the Jewish sources (and shared by Ephesians in the NT), though its meaning probably includes the prospect of children who will, in their turn, care for their parents (Philo, Sirach, Qumran).

As regards limits to children's duties in the Jewish sources, we have seen that senility of old parents is not a "limit" (Sirach; contrast Plato's view in ch. 1, but note the similarity to Perictyone in ch. 2). God's priority in rank-

6. Summary and classification of the results

ing implies a limit in duties toward parents (Philo, Josephus, Pseudo-Phocylides, the *Sibylline Oracles*). What is "just and profitable" is a possible limit, according to Philo. The Torah, the temple, and conversion to "Judaism" serve as limits only in our Jewish sources (Josephus, 2 Maccabees, 4 Maccabees, *Jubilees, Apocalypse of Abraham, Joseph and Aseneth*); but the loyalty to the Torah can be seen as parallel to the loyalty to the higher good in philosophy (see ch. 2). In Jewish apocalyptic literature, enmity within the family is seen as an unavoidable sign of the last days when God's judgment will be executed (*1 Enoch*).

The following tables may serve as a summary:

reasons	*in the divine sphere*	*in the human sphere*
status of parents	ranking right after God participation in "creation"	parents are older
source of the norm	will of God	nature (also as God's will)
form of the norm	God's commandments	
consequences		
– of negligence	punishment/curse	threat by the death penalty
– of honour	blessing, long life	pleasing those who observe virtue
	atoning for sins	
"*do ut des*"	answer to parents' prayer	expecting support from children;
	answer to one's own prayer	
other:		paying back a debt to parents

limits	*in the divine sphere*	*in the human sphere*
due to status	God ranking first	(honour even a senile father!)
other:	Torah, temple, conversion	what is "just and profitable"
cause of tension:	the end times	

It is understandable that our Jewish sources have reasons and limits unique to them in the environment, if they are either directly related to the "Old Testament" (see the references to the Law, e.g. the Fifth Commandment), or reflect traditions that claim to be in connection with the earlier periods of Israel (see e.g. the *Testaments of the Twelve Patriarchs*). We shall see in the second part of this monograph that both pagan and Jewish views on children's duties are relevant to our interpretation of the New Testament. It is against this background that we shall attempt to understand the traditions of the early Christians.

Part II

The Child-Parent Relationship in the New Testament

When discussing the child-parent relationship in the New Testament, I shall briefly refer back to the characteristics found in the world surrounding early Christianity. On occasion, I shall quote some texts not yet referred to, whenever a parallel idea is met with in the New Testament text under discussion. Our main aim is to find out to what extent early Christianity shared ideas and practices with its environment, and what (if any) was its own peculiarity.

I shall discuss the New Testament in three chapters, treating the Gospels, the *Corpus Paulinum* and the remaining books of the New Testament in turn. As a matter of course, further differentiation will be necessary within the chapters; however, it may be said in advance that there is no attempt to solve introductory problems on which scholarship cannot find wide agreement up to the present day. Our primary focus is the early Christian world in general. That is why it is not of supreme importance to decide whether a certain view was held, for example, by Paul himself, by a disciple of his, or even by an early Christian community that saw itself in some way connected to the apostle. However, I shall also make an attempt to show what our results may mean for the hypotheses that differentiate between Pauline, and Deuteropauline Epistles, and even the Pastorals.

In this monograph, our field of interest is first-century Christianity, its views and practices, so that two or three decades difference in the dating of certain writings does not seriously challenge our enterprise. It is necessary that debates and differences within early Christianity should be addressed, yet it is more important to find the relationship between views and practices attested to by the New Testament and those found in its environment.

Chapter Four

The Gospel Tradition

1. Introduction

As regards the ordering of the material, there are two major possibilities: we can either reconstruct the historical sequence of the tradition, or we can discuss the individual canonical books. In what follows, the second possibility will be preferred, because it is notoriously difficult to date individual sayings in the gospels. Another reason for this decision is that the major aim of our present project is to describe the child-parent relationship in early Christianity. Therefore, it is not essential to attempt to ascertain in the case of sayings of the Jesus tradition whether they go back to the historical Jesus, or whether they reflect the views and practices of the second or third generation in Christianity. We shall try to present various possible interpretations, and we shall not necessarily attempt to settle on one of the possibilities with the claim that it and it alone can be shown conclusively to be right. We shall see that there are radical sayings of Jesus, concerning the consequence of discipleship, that are accepted as authentic by the majority of scholars; however, we shall have reason to hold that Jesus also adhered to the commandment to honour one's parents.

First, we shall discuss the Synoptic Gospels, then the Fourth Gospel. Exegetes working on Synoptic texts are expected to indicate on what hypothesis they base their discussion. The following exposition is based on the view that every individual pericope or saying has to be examined afresh as regards the question of original wording and possible dependence. On occasion, a Matthean version of a saying in the triple tradition may be older than Mark, or a Lukan version may be independent of both Mark and Matthew. This approach is compatible with the Two-Document Hypothesis, provided the possibility is left open that Jesus' sayings also continued to be passed on in an oral form after they had been put into writing. The oral traditions could have influenced the Gospels of Matthew and Luke as well. However, the argument will always be presented in such a way as could be accepted also by exegetes who have doubts concerning the Two-Document Hypothesis.

1. Introduction

For practical reasons, first we shall discuss texts to be found in the shortest Gospel, Mark, and in either or both of the other two Synoptics. Then we turn to traditions attested to by both Matthew and Luke, and then to material peculiar to any one of the Gospels. This ordering of the material also fits the Two-Document Hypothesis.

Some short passages will not be discussed on their own, but rather together with passages similar in content. In this case, the above mentioned order may change. The passages will not be examined in detail; however, some exegetical observations will be necessary in order to understand more clearly what the passages say about our main theme.

It is appropriate to mention in advance how the present project relates to the thesis of Gerd Theissen that emphasises the difference between two major types of early Christian ways of life (and thus two different kinds of "Sitz im Leben" of the transmission of texts): that of itinerant charismatics and of settled congregations.[1] We shall see that the present project supports the overall picture to a large extent; it is confirmed that there are radical sayings of Jesus that involve "leaving" one's parents, whereas family life in the first settled congregations shows a different picture: families are together and children are expected to obey their parents. However, it will be argued also that – in the case of the child-parent relationship – the difference between the two types of Christianity is not as great as it is argued by Gerd Theissen. Texts that seem to witness to Jesus' ethos as inimical to the family (e.g. Luke 14:26) can be interpreted in a different way.[2] Our project attempts to show that the "general rule" in early Christianity is a kind of child-parent relationship which was seen in the pagan and Jewish environment of the New Testament: honouring one's parents is strongly expected from children. It is also argued that the radicalism of Jesus' own way of life (and that of the wandering charismatics in the early church) does not deny the validity of that rule; it only sets certain limits to it in as much as Jesus

---

[1] See his analysis of "Wanderradikalismus" (originally published in 1973), 1989d. – For the characterisation of the settled congregations on the basis of the Corinthians' example, see Theissen 1989c (originally published in 1974); especially his exposition of the term "Liebespatriarchalismus" (1989c, 268–71).

[2] Theissen writes (1989d, 83): "Die Logien vertreten ferner ein afamiliäres Ethos. Die Aufgabe der stabilitas loci schließt den Abbruch familiärer Beziehungen ein. Bedingung der Nachfolge ist der Haß von Vater und Mutter, Frau und Kindern, Bruder und Schwester (Lk 14,26)." He refers to Luke 14:26 at other places as well, always taking it in the literal meaning as a reference to "hatred"; see e.g. 1977, 185; 1989e, 42 – though in the latter context (p. 43) Theissen adds that orders ("Gebote") are always more radical than actual behaviour. He points to 1 Cor 9:4–5 which shows that some disciples took their wives with them; thus they did not break with their families as would have been expected on the basis of Luke 14:26 where wives are also mentioned.

and the Kingdom preached by him require that priority is to be given to them. It will be further argued (though this aspect of the Gospel tradition cannot be discussed in detail here) that Jesus' claim of a special relationship to God implied that ultimately it was God's will that the disciples obeyed when they followed Jesus. If so, then even the "limits" set to the general expectation of honour toward parents was not a unique element in the Jesus movement; rather, a main reason for the limits found in the environment were applied to Jesus: God comes before parents. This overall thesis requires to be substantiated by close examination of a host of New Testament texts, and from that examination will emerge the conclusion that the texts are best interpreted in the light of the expectations (and limits) found in the environment.

I mention in advance also that I follow Theissen's criticism of the view that Jesus' radical sayings can be seen as examples of a wandering Cynic philosopher. Theissen acknowledges that there are "structural similarities" between the movement of Cynic philosophers and of early Christians: the ethos of both is characterised by a renunciation of home, family and property.[3] However, the major difference is that the philosophers distanced themselves from conventions by contrasting nature and law. "Die urchristlichen Wanderprediger taten dasselbe in mythischen Bildern, indem sie der alten, zum Untergang verurteilten Welt eine neue Welt entgegensetzten."[4]

The material falls naturally into two parts. We begin by discussing passages that clearly affirm or imply that children are expected to honour their parents; then we turn to passages that, at first sight, seem to witness to disagreement within the child-parent relationship, i.e. where children fail to honour their parents. Our main question will be whether these latter texts show that Jesus and his first followers taught or acted against children's duty to honour their parents.

In this chapter priority is given to texts that address real child-parent relationships; figurative usage of family imagery will be excluded (e.g. as when God is addressed as "father"). We shall see that in the *Corpus Paulinum* and the rest of the NT the figurative usage becomes much more dominant; that is why we include family imagery in our field of study in the last two chapters.

---

[3] "Heimat-, Familien- und Besitzlosigkeit", 1989 d, 90.
[4] *Ibid.*

2. "Honour your father and your mother"

a) The Fifth Commandment in the Gospels

There are two passages in the Synoptic Gospels where the Fifth Commandment, "Honour your father and your mother" (RSV), is quoted in a context where it is implied that the Ten Commandments are to be observed;[5] they are seen by Jesus and his first followers as the primary Old Testament texts that direct their behaviour. There are also passages where the Fifth Commandment is not referred to, but sayings or actions of people imply the validity of the content of it. These texts affirm that Jesus and his disciples shared the norm of their environment: parents are to be honoured; they are to be obeyed and, when they grow old, they are to be cared for.

The first occurrence of the Fifth Commandment in Mark is at 7:10, in the *Corban* pericope (7:9–13). This passage has a parallel only in Matthew (15:1–9), where it is located in the same context: the preceding and following pericopes correspond to those that surround the Markan passage. As regards the whole of the pericope, Matthew's version is shorter than that of Mark. In the verse containing the Fifth Commandment, there are differences as well as agreements. The major agreement is that both Mark and Matthew have a double quotation: after Exod 20:12a (or Deut 5:16a) they also quote Exod 21:16 (LXX; in MT 21:17; cf. also Lev 20:9, which has a similar content). In the second quotation, they agree verbatim with one another (ὁ κακολογῶν πατέρα ἢ μητέρα θανάτῳ τελευτάτω), and they both differ slightly from the Septuagint version of Exod 21:16 (ὁ κακολογῶν πατέρα αὐτοῦ ἢ μητέρα αὐτοῦ τελευτήσει θανάτῳ). This difference in the reference to the death penalty may be due to the phenomenon that the same Hebrew expression, מוֹת יוּמָת, is translated in three different ways in three consecutive verses in the Septuagint, and the ending found in Mark and Matthew is the same as the ending of the verse immediately following the one they quote from the Septuagint. Whatever the exact wording, it is significant that this second quotation is one of the concrete applications of the duty of honouring one's parents we have met in the previous chapters on the environment: "Whoever curses his father or his mother shall be put to death". To speak evil things against one's parents was widely condemned in

---

[5] Although the commandments are not numbered in the Bible, I follow the numbering we have met in Philo. I note that the Reformed tradition of Protestantism follows this numbering, whereas the "Fifth Commandment" is referred to by Lutheran and Roman Catholic Christians as the "Fourth Commandment".

the world surrounding the New Testament. We may add that in the Old Testament context of the saying there is a further application of failing to honour parents: "Whoever strikes his father or his mother shall be put to death" (Exod 21:15 MT).

The differences between Mark 7:10 and its parallel, Matt 15:4, are the following: Mark introduces the quotations by saying: "For Moses said", whereas Matthew writes: "For God said" (or, in some variants: "For God commanded, saying ..."); and in many manuscripts of Matthew, the possessive pronoun, "your", is missing either after "father", or after "mother", or after both, so that the editors of Nestle-Aland 27 (= NA27) omit it in both cases in their main text. Although the Markan text has it both times (τίμα τὸν πατέρα σου καὶ τὴν μητέρα σου), it is worth noting that only Deut 5:16a LXX has it in both cases; in Exod 20:12 it appears only after "father".

I think we can maintain the authenticity of this Old Testament quotation on Jesus' lips.[6] As a Jew, Jesus most probably acknowledged the validity of the Ten Commandments. He shared with his Jewish and pagan environment the expectation that parents have to be honoured. It is significant that in this passage, reporting on a dispute with "Pharisees and scribes from Jerusalem", the Fifth Commandment is reported to have been quoted by Jesus himself both in Mark's and in Matthew's version. The early church probably held that this attitude was an important element of the picture they had of Jesus.

Having said this, it is to be acknowledged that our very passage also claims that the norm was not universally followed. Mark uses the Hebrew and Aramaic term "Corban", a gift offered to the temple, and its correct Greek equivalent, δῶρον, whereas Matthew uses only the latter,[7] when they present the opponents of Jesus as finding an excuse not to fulfil the commandment. In Mark's version (7:11–13): "but you say, 'If a man tells his father or his mother, What you would have gained from me is Corban' (that is, given to God) then you no longer permit him to do anything for his father or mother, thus making void the word of God through your tradition which you hand on." In v. 12, the idea of "doing" something for parents probably means caring for them when they are old. The parallel version, Matt 15:5 clearly claims that helping one's parents equals honouring them: "But you say, If any one tells his father or his mother, What you would have gained from me is given to God, he need not honour his father." Here we have an example for the phenomenon we have encountered in the environment of

---

[6] For a different view, see Harry Jungbauer 2002, 266.
[7] U. Luz 1996, vol. 2, p. 422, fn. 49.

the New Testament: aged parents can expect that their grown-up children will care for them; they will support them even financially.

Ulrich Luz summarises the two major possibilities as to how Matthew's view on the Mosaic law relates to that of Mark:[8] 1. Matthew largely agrees with Mark in accepting moral law as remaining valid and in rejecting ritual law (i.e. Matthew edits Mark mainly in stylistic matters); 2. Matthew does not reject ritual law; but he holds that in certain conflict situations ritual law should be ranked behind the Love Commandment and moral law in general. For our purposes, it is not necessary to decide which picture is more likely to be true. In either case, both Mark and Matthew (and/or the communities they represent) held that the Fifth Commandment was valid and should be observed without looking for reasons for exceptions. We observe that the Fifth Commandment is used here as an example of differentiating between the commandment of God and human tradition (cf. 7:8.13). It is significant that the child-parent relationship is taken as an example; this shows that this area has a special place in God's will. In our pericope the verb "to honour" (τιμᾶν) points to this connection: God is honoured with the lips alone (v. 6); this lip-service becomes evident from the fact that parents are not honoured (vv. 10–13).[9]

Concerning the environment of the New Testament, we have already seen how widespread was the expectation that parents should be honoured. It seems that in Diaspora Judaism the two major Old Testament commandments, to love God and to love one's neighbour (Deut 6:5 and Lev 19:18), were often expressed in the form of demanding honour to God and to parents (see e.g. Philo *Spec.* 2.235; Josephus *C. Ap.* 2.190; 2.206; Ps.-Phoc. 8; *Sib. Or.* 3.593; Aristeas 132; 228; Sir 7:27–29).[10] For example, Ps.-Phoc. 8 says: πρῶτα θεὸν τιμᾶν, μετέπειτα δὲ σεῖο γονῆας. We note the Greek verb, τιμᾶν, which is not only used in the Septuagint text of the Fifth Commandment, but is frequently encountered in other texts of the environment of the New Testament as well. A clear example for seeing these due honours as the fulfilling of the above-mentioned double commandment can be found in Sir 7:27a and 29a, where we find the following parallelism: "With all your heart honour your father, ... With all your soul fear the Lord" (as we have seen in our third chapter).

Gerd Theissen argues that "love of neighbour" is to be extended to outsiders (enemies, strangers, sinners) in the Jesus tradition, but, at the same

---

[8] *Ibid.*, p. 418.
[9] I owe this observation to Professor Gerd Theissen, Heidelberg (letter dated 6.1.2001).
[10] I thank Professor Gerd Theissen for this comment; see my reference to his letter dated 17.04.1997, in ch. 3, fn. 12.

time, it is "combined with a renunciation of love of the closest members of one's family".[11] He refers to Luke 14:26 as an example. We shall see that I interpret that verse in a different way. I argue that the early Christians observed both the Fifth Commandment and the commandment to love one's neighbour. This can be seen more clearly in the next passage to be discussed (as well as in our chapter on Pauline writings, cf. Rom 13:9).

The other occurrence of the Fifth Commandment in Mark is at 10:19. The pericope of the "Rich Man", often referred to as the "rich young ruler", is transmitted by all three Synoptic Gospels (Mark 10:17–27; par. Matt 19:16–26 and Luke 18:18–27). The commandment to honour one's father and mother is quoted by Jesus in all three versions.[12] It appears in a list of those elements of the Ten Commandments which concern fellow human beings – sometimes referred to as the second of the two tables of stones. The three versions are not exactly identical in content and order (and there are even variant readings within the individual gospel traditions), but they all agree in putting the commandment to honour father and mother at the end of the list.[13] The position of the commandment may be emphatic: the last member of the list has a special significance. The form of the commandment may highlight this special role: it is formulated in a positive way after prohibitions starting with μή.

We remember that Philo argued that this commandment is deliberately put at the boundary between obligations toward God and those toward fellow human beings. We may add that the position at the end of the list in the Synoptic Gospels can also be regarded as an emphasis. I agree with Joachim Gnilka who affirms that this position implies that the Fifth (or in his numbering the "Fourth") Commandment is to be understood against the background of social duties toward parents.[14] The text does not say anything about the parents of the man who approached Jesus, but if he was indeed "rich" and "young" (as a conflation of the various Synoptic accounts imply), then the social duties expressed by the commandments quoted may have been intended to have a special appeal to him: he probably did not kill anybody, but what about fair treatment toward the poor and provision for his own parents?[15]

---

[11] G. Theissen 1999, 66.

[12] I note that according to Harry Jungbauer the citation of the commandment does not go back to Jesus, but is an addition of an early Christian "compiler" of this "catechetical piece" (2002, 282–83).

[13] For a clear summary of views of scholars on the differences of content in the lists, see Joel F. Williams 1994, p. 144, fn. 2.

[14] J. Gnilka 1979, II/87.

[15] In connection with this pericope, David L. Mealand has argued that the resemblance between "wandering Cynic mendicants and itinerant disciples of Jesus... does not go very

2. *"Honour your father and your mother"* 121

We observe that the man claims that he has fulfilled these commandments, and Jesus does not challenge this claim (Mark 10:20–21). This raises the question how this pericope relates to the following one, which is about the disciples leaving everything behind. This latter pericope will be discussed among the texts that seem to witness tensions in the families of Jesus and his first followers. It is appropriate to remark at this point, that there are two possible interpretations. It may be argued that the latter pericope throws light upon the former, i.e. the rich man was also asked to leave his family when he was to sell everything.[16] I would argue that the first pericope throws light on the second: observing the Fifth Commandment is expected, and the disciples' leaving everything behind has to be seen against this background. In Matthew's version, after the last part of the list from the Ten Commandment, that is, after the commandment to honour father and mother, Lev 19:18 is also added: "You shall love your neighbour as yourself." Thus, at least for Matthew (and/or his community) these commandments belonged together and they were both valid.

b) Traditions assuming the duty of honouring parents

There are other Synoptic passages where it is assumed that children fulfilled the commandment to honour their parents. This honouring could be practised in various ways – just as we have seen when studying the environment of the New Testament. In the above examples, "children" were adult people who remained responsible for their parents even when the parents grew old. In some of the other examples, children prior to their coming of age are also involved.[17]

In Mark 5:21–43 (par. Matt 9:18–26; Luke 8:40–56), we meet one of the

---

deep" (1981, 71). His key arguments are: the Cynics "do not seem to have developed a common life", and they were not "interested in the Kingdom of God or the law of Moses (Mark 10.19)."

[16] So e.g. Harry Jungbauer, who gave the following title to his chapter discussing this passage: "Die Suspension des Elterngebots in der Nachfolge Jesu nach Markus 10,17–31 par." (2002, 275).

[17] Although the passages where Jesus points to children as examples do not explicitly address the issue of the child-parent relationship, it is significant that Jesus attaches a high value to children (see Mark 9:33–37 par. Matt 18:1–5 and Luke 9:46–48; Mark 10:13–16 par. Matt 19:13–15 and Luke 18:15–17). The texts do not give much detail as to why children are an example, but it is probable that their trustful obedience to their parents is also implied. The expression "to humble oneself" (Matt 18:4) may include obedience toward parents. For a discussion of passages that point to the significance of children in Jesus' teaching, see Hans-Hartmut Schroeder 1972; Günter Haufe 1979; Peter Müller 1992; Bettina Eltrop 1996; William Strange 1996; John Carroll 2001.

several occasions where it is reported in the Gospels that a parent brings an ill child to be healed by Jesus. These are examples of the care with which parents look after their children while they are too little to provide for themselves (cf. also the bread of the children in Mark 7:28 par. Matt 15:26). Although it is not stated in these passages, we have seen in the environment of the New Testament that grown-up children were expected to pay back this debt they owed their parents for their very existence and upbringing.[18]

However, we encounter the element of obedience in these passages. The healed child is given back to his or her parents and it is naturally assumed that he or she remains with them in their home. We note that in our example just mentioned, Jairus, a synagogue ruler, approaches Jesus asking for healing for his daughter (in Matthew's version, for raising his daughter who is already dead at the time of the request), but in the very act of healing (by that time raising from death also in Mark and Luke) Jesus invites both father and mother to the room (Mark 5:40; not in Matthew; Luke 8:51). After the healing (raising) he commands that the twelve-year-old girl should be given something to eat (Mark 5:43; not in Matthew; Luke 8:55). By that it is implied that she is returned into the providing care of her parents.

We may note that the story is narrated in such a way in all of the Synoptic Gospels that it is interrupted by the story of the Haemorrhaging Woman.[19] The two stories have many striking similarities; for example, the number "twelve" as the age of the girl and the length of the illness of the woman. For our theme it is significant that the woman is addressed as "daughter" by Jesus (Mark 5:34; Matt 9:22; Luke 8:48), and the same term (θυγάτηρ) appears in the next verse (in Matthew in the second following verse, and with a different Greek word, κοράσιον) again as the story of Jairus' daughter is continued. Joel Williams suggests that "Jesus' address of the woman as daughter reveals the depth of his compassion toward her", on a parallel with Jairus' care for his daughter.[20] While accepting this comment, we may add that the wording may also imply a claim of authority on Jesus' side.

The term "father" implies authority also in other Gospel texts, for

---

[18] For further examples, see Mark 9:14–29 (par. Matt 17:14–21 and Luke 9:37–43a), a father asking for healing for his son – note especially Mark 9:17, "I brought my son to you", this expression is slightly different in the Matthean parallel: "I brought him to your disciples"; it is not there in the Lukan parallel, but only Luke ends the story by affirming that Jesus healed the boy, "and gave him back to his father" (9:42). Cf. also Mark 7:24–30, a mother asking healing for her daughter (par. Matt 15:21–28).

[19] J.F. Williams (1994, 112) argues – in agreement with many commentators – that: "The intercalation of one episode within another is a common literary technique in Mark's Gospel" (see fn. 3 on the same page for a list of passages).

[20] Ibid., 116.

example, in passages where the name of the father is given when referring to children: Bartimaeus, the son of Timaeus (Mark 10:46; in the Matthean and Lukan parallels the name is not given);[21] Simon, the father of Alexander and Rufus (Mark 15:21, see G. M. Lee 1975, 303; in par. Matt 27:32 and Luke 23:26 it is not mentioned that Simon is anyone's father; in John 19:17 Jesus carries his cross himself, so Simon is not mentioned at all). It is even more significant for our theme that the sons of Zebedee were referred to by giving their father's name even after they had left their profession as fishermen, and even after they had left their father when they followed Jesus. We shall return to these texts later, but here we point out that James and John continued to be referred to as "the sons of Zebedee" until the end of the Gospels, according to the following passages: Mark 10:35 par. Matt 20:20; the Lukan parallel does not refer to concrete disciples; but see also Matt 26:37; Luke 5:10; John 21:2, where the references to the "sons of Zebedee" are clearly later than the time when they left their father.[22] One wonders whether this would have been possible had they left their father in such a scandalous way that they were regarded as ungrateful children. We may add that according to Matt 20:20 their mother is among those who followed Jesus, together with her sons.

There is one short passage in the Synoptic Gospels that also points in the same direction. In the pericope about Jesus healing the mother-in-law of Peter (Mark 1:29–31 par. Matt 8:14–15 and Luke 4:38–39), it is narrated with a certain naturalness that the mother of Peter's wife lived with them in their house. It is, of course, possible that she was there only because she was ill, but it is in any case significant that Peter and his wife cared for her, thus fulfilling one of the most important duties of a child encountered in the environment of the New Testament.[23]

It is clearly stated that Jesus entered the "house" (οἰκία) of the disciples,[24] although the parallel versions do not agree in naming the owner of

---

[21] For a detailed argument for the significant role Bartimaeus plays in Mark's Gospel, see chapter four in Williams's work, *ibid.*, 151–71. Williams concludes by saying (p. 170): "Through the identification with Bartimaeus and subsequent minor characters, the reader is encouraged to move beyond faith in Jesus and his power toward a more faithful acceptance of the demands and values of Jesus."

[22] I note that the term "mother" has a similar significance, probably in line with the view, seen in texts in the environment of the New Testament, that older people are to be respected. See, for example, the reference to "Mary the mother of James the younger and of Joses" in Mark 15:40 par. Matt 27:56. The latter verse also has the rather circumstantial phrase: "the mother of the sons of Zebedee".

[23] Zoltán Dóka also emphasises that "Simon is not taken out of his family relations and responsibilities by his radical following of Jesus" (1996, 32; translated from Hungarian).

[24] For a discussion of the term οἰκία (in comparison with οἶκος), see P-Y. Brandt and

the house: "the house of Simon and Andrew" (Mark 1:29); "Peter's house" (Matt 8:14); "Simon's house" (Luke 4:38, Codex Bezae and a few other MSS add here Andrew as well).[25] The significance of this short passage lies in its unpretentious character.

We have to keep this passage in mind also when we discuss passages about Jesus' disciples leaving their parents. It may serve as an argument for the view that – at least in the case of Peter's wife – the disciples did not cut off all relations with their parents, and – if need required – they could return to their parents. We note that according to 1 Corinthians 9:5, many years later Peter's wife accompanied him on (at least some of) his journeys. We do not know how early she began to follow her "wandering" husband; it remains important that (if we can trust the sequence of the Gospels) Peter and his wife fulfilled the duty of providing for old or ill parents even after Peter was called to follow Jesus. Provision in this case included asking for healing.

There are some further texts in which it is presupposed that children should honour their parents, this including various concrete manifestations of that honour, like, for example, obedience, provision in old age. The following examples are referred to as corroborating the evidence we have already seen, but it has to be acknowledged that they are either implicit (i.e. they presuppose a picture rather than prove it), or they are witnessed to by one source only. Concerning the latter, I note that, since it is not an aim of our project to set apart "authentic" sayings of Jesus, even texts whose historicity is doubted by the majority of exegetes can be regarded as useful for the present thesis, as they witness – at least – to the existence of a view in some part(s) of early Christianity (and this is the main focus of our study, as we have stated earlier).[26]

There are some passages where Jesus tells a story in which it is naturally presupposed that children should obey their parents. For example, in Mark 12:1–12 (par. Matt 21:33–46; Luke 20:9–19; cf. also The Gospel of Thomas

---

A. Lukinovich 1997. They conclude (532): "Marc et Luc ont des usages inverses de οἶκος et οἰκία. Lorsqu'il s'agit d'insister sur la relation entre celui qui accueille et celui qui est reçu, Luc utilise οἶκος et Marc οἰκία."

[25] We shall see later, that the "house" was an important place for early Christians; they gathered in houses of rich disciples even for worship. In the Gospel tradition, a house gathering like the one at Levi's house (see Mark 2:15, and also its parallels) may be seen as an anticipation of later church meetings (see e.g. Elizabeth S. Malbon, 1985; David M. May, 1993).

[26] It has to be noted that the criteria for authenticity are not discussed in this thesis either. Multiple attestation is, of course, only one of several important criteria; it is mentioned here by the way of example in order to indicate a significant theme that is not addressed in the present project.

2. "Honour your father and your mother"   125

65) we read in a parable that a certain father sent his son to collect the rent of the vineyard he had let out to tenants. In all three Synoptic Gospels it is narrated in a self-evident way that the son obeyed his father. As regards the origin of the story, there are two main possible interpretations.

It may be argued that the story is a creation of the post-Easter church and modelled on the obedience of Jesus, the Son of God. Expressing a majority view, Joachim Gnilka affirms that the story is to be assigned to the Hellenistic Jewish-Christian congregation, and it is not to be attributed to Jesus.[27] His main argument is that in the parable the son is the heir to the election and promises of Israel.[28] He also argues that the allusions to Isa 5:1–5, the sending motif, the sequence of sending servants and son, suggest that the interpreter should look to the Old Testament as the source of the ideas presented in this story.[29] For many scholars, our passage belongs to the milieu of the Son of God sayings, most of which they cannot accept as authentic. Without entering the debate on the origin of the Son of God sayings, here we simply note the possible support given by these texts to our thesis: the Son of God sayings presuppose a view of child-parent relationship in which obedience is expected from the child. We shall return to the implications of these texts for our thesis in the final chapter.[30]

However, it is worth pointing out that there are some scholars who argue that even the motif of sending the son could be a pre-Easter element in the story. Gnilka rightly observed that in the Matthean and Lukan versions the killing of the son takes place outside the walls,[31] but he fails to see the im-

---

[27] J. Gnilka 1979, II/148; see Matt 21:39 and Luke 20:15.

[28] *Ibid.*, 144.

[29] *Ibid.*, 145. It has to be noted that there is an increasing number of scholars in our days who do not follow the "dissimilarity test", but rather argue that it is a better methodological presupposition to hold that "Jesus did use the Scriptures", than to affirm that "if a concept or pattern is traceable to ... a scriptural background, it cannot have come from Jesus" (R. E. Brown, *The Death of the Messiah*, 1994, II/1478 and 1479). Cf. also the view of G. Theissen and A. Merz: "Das Differenzkriterium ist durch das *historische Plausibilitätskriterium* zu ersetzen, das mit *Wirkungen* Jesu auf das Urchristentum und seiner Einbindung in einen jüdischen *Kontext* rechnet" (*Der historische Jesus*, 1997, 117; italics theirs).

[30] For a recent analysis of the titles in Mark's Gospel, see Edwin K. Broadhead, *Naming Jesus: Titular Christology in the Gospel of Mark*, 1999, especially the chapter entitled "Son of God", pp. 116–23. Broadhead affirms (121): "The power of the coming Son of Man is connected to Jesus' sonship (14.61–62). Alongside this authority, the submission of the Son is focused. The son is pleasing God (1.11), and he knows less than the Father (9.7)."

[31] J. Gnilka 1979, II/147. It is worth noting that D, Θ, the Old Latin witnesses, the church father Lucifer (died ca. 371) and the Armenian translation of Irenaeus have the "Markan" sequence, i.e. "killing and throwing out" in the Matthean parallel (21:39), but not in the Lukan parallel. If it is an adjustment to the Markan text, then it is difficult to explain why theses witnesses did not adjust the Lukan text as well.

portance of the fact that the Markan text does not correspond to the fate of Jesus: the son is first killed and then thrown out (Mark 12:8). Gerd Theissen and Annette Merz also point to other elements in the story that do not agree with the following data of Jesus' death: he was executed by the Romans and he was buried.[32] They argue that in the case of a post-Easter creation, one would expect a greater correspondence between the parable and the actual events around Jesus' death. They conclude concerning the motif of the killing of the son who was sent last: "Trotz nachösterlicher Allegorisierung könnte hier ein vorösterlicher Zug erhalten sein".[33] This pre-Easter element can be seen as reflecting a possible case in the society of the day. It can be added to other elements of the story that fit the contemporary Palestinian setting (readily acknowledged by scholars who regard the story as a post-Easter creation).[34]

For this latter interpretation, it is also important that the idea of "heritage" can not only be a theologically motivated reference to the heirs of Israel's promises, but it is also part of everyday social life. We have seen in the first chapter that being an heir was one of the reasons why a child was expected to honour his parents. Although the motifs of obedience and inheritance are not connected explicitly in our story, we should not fail to see that its pattern fits in the environment of the New Testament: a son as the heir obeys his father.

This picture is strengthened by another parable, preserved only in Matthew's Gospel, concerning the two sons who were sent by their father to work in the vineyard (Matt 21:28–32). Although the crucial verses (29 and 30) have survived in several variants differing in wording, some of which result in the changing of the order of the two types of answers, it is clear that one of the sons first agreed then did not go, while the other first refused then changed his mind and went. The manuscripts agree in the summarising question (v. 31): "Which of the two did the will of his father?" (RSV, the Greek text does not have the possessive pronoun, "his", but simply: "the will of the father"). The whole story is based on the following presupposition: the listeners (readers) share the view of the story teller that a son is expected to obey his father. The summarising question implies a difference in the moral value between the not obeying and the obeying son. The storyteller expects that the listeners should pronounce judgment upon the son who did not obey. This is so natural that it does not have to be said ex-

---

[32] G. Theissen and A. Merz 1997, 378–79.
[33] *Ibid.*, 379.
[34] See e.g. W. Schmithals 1986, II/514.

2. "Honour your father and your mother" 127

plicitly. Jesus is said to have applied this unexpressed consequence immediately: he warns the listeners that the "tax collectors and the harlots" go into the kingdom of God before them. The implied conclusion (it is better to say "no" first and then to repent, than not to repent at all) can only work if the assumption is agreed by story-teller and listeners: a son should obey his father's will. This story, attributed to Jesus by Matthew (and/or his community), shows that in – at least – one early Christian circle, the expectation found in the "environment" was shared that sons should obey (and by obeying show honour to) their father.

At the end of this section we discuss briefly three further pericopes that support the picture gained in the exegesis of the previous passages. Each of them is special material of the Gospel in which it is preserved: two from Luke and one from the Fourth Gospel.

In Luke 2:41–52, the story of the twelve-year-old Jesus is narrated only by Luke, and even he brings it in only at the end of the birth narrative.[35] There are scholars who doubt the historicity of this story.[36] Without attempting to solve this problem, I simply note that on the surface of the story we find a contradiction in Jesus' behaviour. On the one hand, he causes worry for his parents by staying behind in Jerusalem without any notice (Luke 2:48); though it has to be emphasised that it is not indicated either by the parents of Jesus nor by the evangelist that Jesus was disobedient. On the other hand, at the end of the story Jesus joins his parents and returns with them to Nazareth. The text even stresses his obedience (2:51).

There is no real contradiction here. Jesus simply follows the general rule we have seen in the chapters on the environment (expressed also in lists of those to whom honour is due): God comes always before parents.[37] Accordingly, Jesus' answer to his parents indicates that he has his heavenly father in mind;[38] so the RSV inserts the term "house" into its translation (2:49) in

---

[35] Walter Kirchschläger rightly observes that the passage is located after the "Vorgeschichten" and before the presentation of Jesus' activities (1996, 368). He also points out that Jesus being twelve years of age is not a "child" any longer, because in Jewish perception he has reached the threshold of adulthood (*ibid.*).

[36] François Bovon calls it an "anecdote" (EKKNT III/1, 1989, p. 154). According to him, Luke took it over from the tradition, and re-worked it.

[37] As Kirchschläger puts it (1996, 369): "Historische Rückfragen können getrost als nebensächlich außer acht gelassen werden, denn dem Evangelisten geht es um etwas anderes: ... Der heranwachsende Jesus begreift Gott in einzigartiger Weise als die Mitte seines Lebens, als seinen Vater, und er setzt eine entsprechende Priorität".

[38] We note that if God is called "father", this implies that honour is due to fathers in general. For a discussion of the fatherhood of God in Jesus' sayings, see Dieter Zeller 1981. He argues that Jesus did not speak "to his Father exclusively" (124). Rather, Jesus used the term "father" as it was known to his listeners from the "Old Testament" (118–120). Zeller con-

rendering ἐν τοῖς τοῦ πατρός μου: "How is it that you sought me? Did you not know that I must be in my Father's house?" Whether this story is to be labelled a legend (or anecdote) or not, we note that according to this story Jesus grew up in his parents' home and it was presupposed in a natural way that he obeyed them.

Our second passage from Luke is the parable of the Lost Son (often referred to as the Prodigal Son; Luke 15:11–32). The parable is deeply rooted in the everyday life around Jesus, as is shown (apart from others) by Wolfgang Pöhlmann in his detailed monograph from 1993.[39] Pöhlmann's analysis is especially helpful for our project, because he discusses the parable against the background of the views concerning the household represented in the literary genre *oeconomicus*. We shall return to this theme when we discuss the Household Codes of Colossians and Ephesians in the next chapter. Here it is enough to emphasise the significance of that background even for the world of Jesus. As Pöhlmann affirms with reference to Jesus' wandering lifestyle (1993, 48): "Auch wer nicht in die Ordnung des Hauses eingefügt ist, kann nicht übersehen, daß das Haus die soziale Grundordnung jeder antiken Gesellschaft ist."[40]

It is clear from the whole structure (and main message) of the parable that the hearers are expected to share the following view of the story-teller: it was not usual that the younger son requested his share of the heritage in advance (v. 12; see Pöhlmann 1993, 186). Although it was legally possible to claim the heritage before the father's death by agreement (see Howard Marshall 1979, 607), the expectation would have been that he remains at home, as the older son did, and would have cared for his father (supposing the father would have lived long and become weak toward the end of his life). This would have been the "ethos of the house" (Pöhlmann 1993, 186). The younger son only becomes a positive hero when he repents and returns home. By doing so, he acknowledged that he would obey his father in the

---

cludes that (125): "The Father, whom Jesus brings close to his listeners, remains the faithful God of Israel".

[39] For a discussion of the authenticity (with detailed arguments against the view that it is a Lukan creation), see W. Pöhlmann 1993, 153–60.

[40] For a discussion of the similarities in the theme "contrasting brothers" between Terence's Adelphoe (a work we referred to in the second chapter) and the parable of the Lost Son, see W. Pöhlmann 1993, 98–102. He rightly emphasises the main difference between the two (102): "Jesus erzählt nicht vom Standpunkt des Erziehers aus.... In der Umformung seiner Erzählung geschieht die Befreiung eines Menschen, der seine Lebensmöglichkeit verwirkt hat, zu einer neuen Existenz." Nevertheless, the parallel to the genre of comedy remains significant in the theme of the sons' relationship to their fathers. Honour is expected in both cases.

future (indeed, he would have been prepared to obey him even as his servant, see v. 19).

We should also note that the older son is not a negative figure; the two-part story was probably told in order that people in the position of the older son would also rejoice in the return of the lost ones. As Howard Marshall has put it (1979, 604): "will the elder brother share the father's joy at the return of the prodigal? – this is the unanswered question which is addressed to the hearers of the parable."

The older son summarises what was expected from a son (Luke 15:29a): "Lo, these many years I have served you, and I never disobeyed your command". By going out to the older son (v. 28b) the father acknowledges that he had done the right thing by remaining at home and working for him. We can even hear praise in his words (15:31): "Son, you are always with me, and all that is mine is yours." The story envisages a picture implying that, when the whole family is together, sons duly honour their father. When life returns to normal setting, it is a real cause for rejoicing – as the concluding words of the father (and of the story) imply (15:32): "It was fitting to make merry and be glad, for this your brother was dead, and is alive; he was lost, and is found."

We conclude this section by briefly mentioning a passage from the end of Jesus' earthly life: Jesus' conversation from the cross with his mother and with the beloved disciple, as narrated in John 19:25–27. In vv. 26–27 we read: "When Jesus saw his mother, and the disciple whom he loved standing near, he said to his mother, 'Woman, behold, your son!' (27) Then he said to the disciple, 'Behold, your mother!' And from that hour the disciple took her to his own home."

This little scene is often said to be editorial work designed to provide a basis for the Johannine congregation (so e.g. Udo Schnelle 1998, 288–89). Jean Zumstein has argued that, together with the scene of the first sign at Cana in John 2, they form an *inclusio* (1997, 150; see also János Bolyki 2001, 490–91). Zumstein (*ibid.*) lists four points of contact between the two stories: 1) the expression "mother [of Jesus]", without giving her name; 2) the address "woman" in the vocative (γύναι); 3) mention of the "hour"; 4) closeness and intimacy ("Nähe und Vertrautheit") between mother and son in both scenes. Irrespective of one's view regarding the historicity of the scene at the cross, it is clear that the author of the Fourth Gospel (and/or his circle) did not see any problem in "relating the fact that the dying Jesus provided for the care of his mother after his death".[41] This can be seen as a

---

[41] So R. E. Brown 1970, p. 923.

special way of fulfilling the expectation that children had to provide for their aged parents. As Schnelle has put it (1998, 288): "Der Lieblingsjünger tritt an die Stelle Jesu, er ist nun der Sohn Marias. Zugleich erfüllt Jesus die einem Sohn nach Ex. 20,12 aufgetragene Rechtspflicht, für die Mutter zu sorgen."[42] It is striking in Schnelle's exposition that whereas he holds that the scene is formed by the evangelist (*ibid.*), he does not say why the evangelist pictures Jesus as caring for his mother. It is possible to argue that the evangelist intended to counter some of the sayings of Jesus inimical to the family (to be discussed in the next section). However, it is also plausible to maintain that the early church (or at least some part of it) thought that Jesus fulfilled the general expectation we have also met in the environment of the New Testament.

3. Tensions within the family

According to the Synoptic Gospels, right from the beginning of his public activity Jesus called certain people to follow him as his disciples. In some cases this call resulted in the disciples leaving their parents. At a first sight, this seems to witness to a radically anti-family attitude on Jesus' side. Gerd Theissen has coined the phrase "Wanderradikalismus" to describe the phenomenon that while people literally followed Jesus, they left behind their home, family, and fortune.[43] In the following, the radicalism of Jesus' ethos will not be questioned; rather, it will be discussed with the question in mind whether this radicalism meant a break with the duty of honouring parents.

---

[42] One of the arguments of J. Zumstein against the historicity of the scene is that the earthly Jesus should have entrusted his mother to one of his relatives rather than to one of his disciples (1997, 132). Zumstein's aim is to show the symbolic character of the scene (and of its context). One might add, however, that the symbolic meaning (that the pre-Easter fellowship of Jesus is to continue around the figure of the beloved disciple) can be accepted even as an element of the event taken as history: Jesus on the cross may not only have provided for his mother, but also for his followers. – For a discussion of the possibility of the taking up of this little scene in a non-canonical writing (the *Gospel of Philip*), see Hans-Josef Klauck 1992b.

[43] G. Theissen 1989d (originally published in 1973); see esp. p. 83. The same features, *Heimatlosigkeit, Familienlosigkeit, Besitzlosigkeit* (complemented by defencelessness, *Schutzlosigkeit*) characterize "wandering charismatics" in early Christianity (Theissen 1997, 14–21; originally published in 1977).

a) Jesus calls his first disciples

We find a report of Jesus calling his first disciples in all four canonical gospels; Mark 1:16–20 and Matt 4:18–22 are similar enough to be called parallels, but Luke and John have different stories concerning the call (Luke 5:1–11; John 1:35–51). It is explicitly stated about James and John that they "left their father" (Mark 1:20b): καὶ ἀφέντες τὸν πατέρα αὐτῶν Ζεβεδαῖον ἐν τῷ πλοίῳ μετὰ τῶν μισθωτῶν ἀπῆλθον ὀπίσω αὐτοῦ. Matthew says they left the boat and their father, but he does not mention the hired servants (the codices W and 33 omit the full section on these brothers, i.e. Matt 4:21–22). Luke says in a concluding sentence (5:11) that they left "everything" (πάντα; the term "everything", a neuter plural, can include persons as well).[44]

First we note that one pair of brothers, James and John, were working in the same trade as their father: they were fishing together. Although it is not stated explicitly, we may presume that the same was true for the other pair of brothers, for Simon (Peter) and Andrew. They are reported to have left the boat, but there is no mention of their father (Codex Bezae and the Old Latin witnesses have πάντα in Mark 1:18; this may be an assimilation to Luke 5:11). There is no enmity between children and parents implied in the calling narratives. As we have seen in the previous section, James and John continued to be called the sons of Zebedee even after they became disciples of Jesus, and Peter cared for the ill mother of his wife. Nothing compels us to presuppose that they would not have provided for their father later if any need should have arisen.

Peter was prepared to return to his fishing business after Jesus' death. Irrespective of the question of the authenticity of this scene reported only by the Fourth Gospel (John 21:3),[45] it makes best sense if we presuppose that the author of the Fourth Gospel did not think that there was any enmity between Peter and his family (although once again it has to be emphasized that we do not hear anything about the parents of Peter in the Gospels).

We emphasise again that the scene concerns Jesus calling disciples. As Walter Schmithals rightly observes with regard to Luke 5:11 (1979, 113; italics his): "Auch die abschließende Feststellung, daß Simon sein Schiff verließ und Jesus nachfolgte, muß primär im Rahmen einer *Jünger*berufung

---

[44] For an example where the neuter plural πάντα refers to people, see the variant reading at Rom 11:32.

[45] Even if one regards Luke 5:1–11 as a parallel of John 21:1–11, i.e. as a post-Easter story retrojected into Jesus' earthly life, this "parallel" does not have the element of "returning" to fishing: in Luke it is presented as a call to discipleship at the beginning of Jesus' ministry (see D. L. Mealand 1981, 76, esp. fn. 75).

verstanden werden." In their first context, texts about *Nachfolge* may be regarded as referring to exceptional cases, i.e. they do not apply to all disciples.[46] As Martin Hengel has put it: "Jesu Ruf in die 'Nachfolge' gilt nur dem einzelnen Gerufenen".[47] David Mealand contends that the group of those who "left behind their home and family ... probably exceeded twelve in number", but he adds that "not all Jesus's hearers followed him in the literal sense" (1981, 73). In the following, there will be other passages, too, where the key to the interpretation will be the view that Jesus had two kinds of disciples: some who had to follow him, and those who returned to their homes right after they became disciples of Jesus. Thus not every saying applied to all of them. J. C. O'Neill takes this view a step further when he argues that some "hard sayings about discipleship – sayings about taking up the cross, about leaving all, about not loving father or mother more than him – ... are only for the few who are called to rule" as ministers (1984, 84). Whether or not one makes this further step of speaking about the rulers of the communities, one can agree with the distinction between circles of disciples to whom the individual sayings applied.

This is not to deny the radicalism of the call. To some extent, we might see it as a parallel to what we have seen in the environment: giving priority to a higher good in the circle of Stoic philosophers; or following the lifestyle of a teacher, as in the case of Josephus who spent some years as a pupil of Bannus, the ascetic (*Vita* 11). David Mealand has argued that in the case of those "who took up the Cynic way of life, it was often financial ruin or exile which made a man turn to philosophy" (1981, 76). He also affirms that "Jesus and his first disciples were not thoroughgoing ascetics" (*ibid.*). Thus the parallels from other movements may "help a little, but do not fully explain the way in which Jesus and his disciples abandoned family, and home, and previous occupation" (75). The question arises as to what kind of a leader Jesus was held to be by his first followers. I hold with Mealand (*ibid.*) that:

---

[46] Ulrich Luz (1989a, I/176) rightly points out that in the usage of the early church these texts were generalised: they were applied to all members of the congregation. Matthew uses the term "to follow" (ἀκολουθέω) also about the crowds; this shows that he did not differentiate between the disciples and the people who were sympathetic to Jesus (see also U. Luz 2002, I/242). However, this observation does not challenge the view that Jesus did not call everybody to the same kind of "following". We may add that Mark too uses the term ἀκολουθέω for the crowds, see e.g. Mark 3:7 (with variations in the MS tradition) and 5:24.

[47] M. Hengel 1968, 68. The sentence is the title of the fifth section of Hengel's work, summarising his view in a thesis-like form. – As a historical parallel, we can mention that according to Pliny the Elder (*Nat.* 5.17.4) the Essenes were joined by recruits who left their families.

3. Tensions within the family

The character of Jesus's ministry arose from his conviction that the Reign of God was imminent, and that its coming must be announced throughout the land. It is from this necessity that the itinerant nature of his ministry came about.

In this thesis we cannot discuss the views concerning Jesus' understanding of the Kingdom, and concerning his messianic consciousness, nor can we enter into the debate about how the early church came to call him the Messiah. I simply acknowledge that my working hypothesis is to suppose some kind of a messianic claim on Jesus' side, and a positive response to it already by his first followers. This will be especially relevant in the course of discussing other passages where a call to follow Jesus is involved.

b) A new family?

In the Synoptic Gospels, there is a report of a direct confrontation between Jesus and his mother and brothers (Mark 3:31–35 par. Matt 12:46–50 and Luke 8:19–21). There is no agreement among scholars as regards the historicity of this passage, or to what extent it reflects the situation of the household churches. It can be argued that it presupposes the separation of the Christian community from the synagogue (so W. Schmithals 1979, 212). However, it can also be argued that it is not likely that the early church created a story with such a negative attitude from Jesus' family. As G. Theissen and A. Merz argue (1997, 104): "Der Vorwurf der Familie, Jesus sei verrückt (Mk 3,20ff), ist angesichts der großen Bedeutung der Familie Jesu nach Ostern gewiß keine Rückprojektion". The other two synoptic Gospels introduce this scene in another context. It is significant that a preparatory comment is only to be found in Mark (3:21): "And when his family heard it, they went out to seize him, for people were saying, 'He is beside himself.'"[48] In this translation, there are hidden two exegetical problems. First, the Greek text, οἱ παρ' αὐτοῦ ("those with him"), is not unambiguous: it can refer to the disciples or to the relatives of Jesus. It is more likely that the latter sense is to be applied here, because otherwise the scene reported in 3:31–35 is difficult to understand: why does Jesus refuse his mother and brothers if they had not given any reason for wanting to call him away?[49]

---

[48] Robert Guelich notes (1989, 168): in Mark 3:20–21 we find "either the remains of a biographical apothegm or the first part of the second pronouncement story" (i.e. 3:31–35).

[49] For further arguments in favour of this exegetical decision, see Timothy Dwyer 1996, 106. He argues also against the other translation possibility according to which the text would refer to the disciples wishing to calm down the crowds (104–105). It is also to be noted that D, W and the Old Latin witnesses have another subject for the verb "heard" in place of οἱ παρ' αὐτοῦ: "the scribes and the others".

Secondly, "people" is inserted in the translation; in the Greek the subject of ἔλεγον is not specified. This ambiguous expression may have referred to Jesus' relatives as the speakers.[50]

Thus, even if Mark 3:20–21 is a Markan addition to an earlier tradition, it is a necessary explanation of the background of the scene. For our understanding of vv. 31–35, the inclusion of vv. 20–21 means that Jesus' identification of his true family was not meant to involve the abandoning of his blood relations. It can be seen as an answer to the intended action of his non-understanding parents. Taeseong Roh has rightly pointed to the difference between Jesus' own attitude and that which was expected from the disciples (2001, 112). Whereas Jesus defines his own new family (v. 34: "And looking around on those who sat about him, he said, 'Here are my mother and my brothers!'"), there is no expectation of any breach with one's family on the side of the listeners. We may add that Jesus was provoked by his "non-believing" family to praise those who were accepting what he taught (for a tradition that Jesus' brethren did not believe in him during his earthly ministry, see also John 7:5). Thus this passage does not address the child-parent relationship in the case of the disciples. In Jesus' case, it was not his own initiative; rather it was a response to hostile behaviour on the side of his family.[51] He did not follow them when they wanted to hinder him in his teaching ministry. The content of his teaching is not narrated, but from the concluding (perhaps editorial) word we may infer that it was the priority of the will of God, the heavenly Father, that caused him to be disobedient to his mother and brothers.[52] We shall see in the next passage that this decision was not without some pain for Jesus.

Jesus is not only reported to have had to face enmity from his relatives, but also from his "country" (Mark 6:1–6a par. Matt 13:53–58; cf. Luke 4:16–30 and John 4:44; 6:42; Nazareth is only named in Luke's version). We have met the same term, πατρίς, in Epictetus where "the good" is pre-

---

[50] For this view, see T. Dwyer 1996, 106. Matthew and Luke do not have the negative claim made by Jesus' relatives. Perhaps these evangelists did not transmit this tradition because of the later positive role of the relatives of Jesus. Ulrich Luz suggests that Matthew omitted the strong statement in Mark 3:21 (1996, II/287).

[51] George Aichele has argued that there is a significant connection between the Beelzebub pericope and our pericope that surrounds it in Mark. His suggestion, put in the form of questions, points in the same direction as our exposition in as much as it sees the crowd as the active side to which Jesus passively responds (1999, 45): "[I]s the strong man (in his house) to be somehow equated with the demands of one's own family? ... does Jesus' willingness to have the crowd possess (or bind) him as son and brother somehow affirm the insinuation that he is possessed by Beelzebub? Or by the Holy Spirit?"

[52] T. Roh (2001, 108-110) agrees with Dibelius in regarding Mark 3:35 as a redactional application of the preceding verses to "anyone" who is willing to do the will of God.

3. Tensions within the family

ferred to it (*Diatr.* III.iii.6: "... father and brother and country ... disappear"). We note that some manuscripts do not refer to Jesus as a "carpenter", but as the "son of a carpenter" (Matthew has only this latter textual tradition). As we have seen in previous chapters, it is plausible that Jesus followed the trade of his father, as many sons did in antiquity. The pericope does not say that Jesus felt any animosity against his country; rather, "he marvelled because of their unbelief" (Mark 6:6a). He summarises the feelings of his fellow countrymen (and not his own feelings) in a proverbial way (Mark 6:4): "A prophet is not without honour, except in his own country, and among his own kin, and in his own house" (cf. also Matt 13:57; John 4:44). According to this passage, Jesus clearly did not initiate enmity with his own country, but he had to suffer their "non-belief".

As we follow the order of the pericopes relevant to our theme as they appear in Mark, we may mention briefly a passage that speaks of leaving one's parents: a son leaving his father and mother when getting married. In the pericope concerning divorce (Mark 10:1–12 par. Matt 19:1–9; cf. also Luke 16:18 and Matt 5:31–32), Jesus is reported to have quoted Gen 2:24. In Mark 10:7 we read: "For this reason a man shall leave his father and mother and be joined to his wife".[53] The term καταλείψει is the same as in the Septuagint version of Gen 2:24. The institution of marriage was regarded as the will of God by Jews, as it can be seen also by Jesus' reference to the Old Testament text.[54] Although it was customary in both the Graeco-Roman and the Jewish environment that in the case of a marriage the newly wedded couple became the nucleus of a new family, this was so much not against the parents that – as we have seen in the previous chapters – parents often played a decisive role even in determining whom their child should marry. We have also seen that – if circumstances permitted – the new family remained in the house of the parents: physical "leaving" was not always involved. Whether or not the new couple remained in their parents' home, the use of the verb καταλείπω here is not the same as in Luke 5:28 (not in its

---

[53] The second half of the verse, "and be joined to his wife", is omitted by the codices Sinaiticus, Vaticanus, and some other witnesses. It is possible that it was omitted by accident due to *homoioteleuton*, because Codex Sinaiticus (unlike some other MSS) has αὐτοῦ both after "mother" and "wife". The full text (with some variations) is given by Matthew. The quotation of Gen 2:24 continues ("and the two shall become one flesh") in manuscripts omitting the middle of the verse, so it may be a real "omission" (though it is possible that it was added in order that the full Septuagint text be quoted, so e.g. J. Gnilka 1979, II/73, fn. 23).

[54] Joachim Gnilka points to the significance of Gen 1:27 also being quoted in the Markan pericope (1979, II/73): "Es kommt auf die Verbindung von zwei von Gott füreinander bestimmte Menschen an. Beide – das ist ein dem Alten Testament gegenüber neuer Gesichtspunkt – verlassen das Elternhaus, um den Schöpfungsauftrag zu erfüllen."

parallels) concerning Levi: "And he left everything, and rose and followed him." This latter example has its parallel rather in passages where the verb ἀφίημι is used to express that the disciples left their parents and homes when they followed Jesus. We turn now to these texts.

We have already seen that in each of the Synoptic Gospels the passage on the rich young ruler is followed by a short discussion between the disciples and Jesus (Mark 10:28–31 par. Matt 19:27–30 and Luke 18:28–30). It is in this pericope that Jesus speaks about the reward for the disciples leaving everything behind. The Synoptics present the scene with a very similar content, but there are also many differences. To point to but a few: only in Matthew do we read Peter's question ("What then shall we have?") added to his statement that the disciples have left everything. Even in the indicative sentence ("Lo, we have left everything and followed you"; Mark 10:28) there are some variations in the manuscripts: in Mark some manuscripts have the perfect of the verb "followed" (ἠκολουθήκαμεν), some have the aorist (ἠκολουθήσαμεν); all MSS of Matthew and Luke have the aorist. NA27 prints the perfect in Mark as the main text (and the editors suggest that the aorist is due to the parallels); in this case there is a "minor agreement" between Matthew and Luke.

Matthew and Mark alone conclude the scene with the saying: "But many that are first will be last, and the last first" (Mark 10:31; Matt 19:30). Matthew repeats this saying at the end of his next pericope (his special material), the parable of the workers in the vineyard (20:16). Luke brings it as the conclusion of the saying on the people coming from all four winds to sit at table in the Kingdom of God (13:30), with little changes in wording and in a reversed order. One might ask whether the meaning of this saying in Matthew and Mark at the end of our pericope differs from its meaning in the other places. Perhaps here it refers to the disciples who are last in the eyes of their fellow countrymen, because they have no financial security since they left their homes and families (and to those who think they are "first" because they keep to the good order of a settled family life who are in fact the "last" if they do not follow Jesus).

In Mark's version, however, there is another difference from Matthew and Luke: in Jesus' answer, Matthew and Luke bring only the list of those whom the disciples have left, whereas in Mark's version Jesus repeats the list when he assures the disciples of the reward for their following him. These lists are not exactly the same. In Matthew, some manuscripts have "houses or brothers or sisters or father or mother or children or lands" (NA27 print this as the main text, based primarily on the Codex Vaticanus), many manuscripts (including the Byzantine "majority") add "or wife" after "lands", and some (including family 1) have "parents" instead of "father or mother". Some have a variation in order: they bring "houses" as the last item in the list. In Luke's version, the codices Vaticanus, Sinaiticus (and some other MSS) have "house or wife or brothers or parents or children". Many manuscripts (including the Byzantine "majority") have the same list but in a reverse order in the middle ("parents or brothers or wife"). Some manuscripts have this reverse order and not only "brothers", but also "sisters". Although there are variations in both lists, it is clear that Matthew and Luke do not have the same list. (Note also the single of "house" in all the MSS of Luke, whereas Matthew has the plural, "houses"; note further that the MSS of Luke do not have "lands" in the list.)

As we have indicated above, Mark has two lists. In the Codex Vaticanus and the Byzantine "majority", Jesus' saying reads as follows (Mark 10:29–30):

Truly, I say to you, there is no one who has left house or brothers or sisters or mother or father or children or lands, for my sake and for the gospel, (10:30) who will not receive a hundredfold now in this time, houses and brothers and sisters and mothers and children and lands, with persecutions, and in the age to come eternal life.

The original "hand" of the Codex Sinaiticus does not have the second list, its first corrector adds it with "mother" in the singular, and a second corrector (with some further MSS) add "father". Codex Bezae brings the second list as a new sentence: "whoever left... [list with some changes, e.g. "house" in singular, "sisters and brothers"]... will receive". It is to be noted that the second list does not have "father" in most of the manuscripts. Taeseong Roh has rightly pointed out that the sequence "mother and father" is unusual; in view of the leading role of the father in the family in antiquity, one would expect that the father should be mentioned first (2001, 127). He offers the following solution to the manuscript evidence seen above: Matthew has changed it to the "usual order" and Luke has chosen the summarising term "parents". Roh argues that the Markan order (together with the sequence of Mark 3:35, "brother, and sister, and mother") point to the community of "settled sympathisers" of Jesus ("eine Gemeinschaft unter ortsansässigen Sympathisanten", p. 128). Roh suggests that the omission of "father" in the second list (in Mark 10:30) is due to a view of community which has only God as "father" (p. 136), and wants to resist the claim of wandering missionaries to become their leaders: they are accepted as brothers and not as fathers (p. 132).

Roh has taken up and applied to these texts the overall thesis of Gerd Theissen seen earlier. The present text is one of the significant passages for the thesis of Theissen; however, it has to be seen also in the light of how we understand the other relevant passages.[55]

It is important to see that the context of the Jesus saying in Mark 10:29–30 (and par.) indicates what is at stake here in the eye of the evangelists: the discipleship of Jesus. It is not only the radicalism of Jesus' call to the rich young ruler that is to be emphasised as a context for our pericope. It is equally important to see that the validity of the commandment to honour father and mother is acknowledged by Jesus just before he speaks to his disciples about the reward of following him. Each of the Synoptics indicate that the "leaving" occurs for the sake of the discipleship of Jesus: for Jesus' name's sake (Matt 19:29); for Jesus' and the gospel's sake (Mark 10:29); for the sake of the Kingdom of God (Luke 18:29). It may be argued that the disciples' leaving everything is not as radical as Jesus' call to the rich young ruler to sell everything and give the proceeds to the poor. We have already seen that the disciples did have a home to return to even after they followed Jesus. This saying has to be seen in the context of a call to discipleship. It concerns priorities; it is addressed to some of the disciples and not to all of them. This saying does not deny the continuing validity of the Fifth Commandment.

c) Conflict suffered as a consequence of discipleship

There are several sayings attributed to Jesus that affirm that children will rise against their parents. Some have strong similarities, e.g. Mark 13:12 par. Matt 10:21. This verse is printed without an indication of a variant in NA27 in the Markan text, and there is a little grammatical variation in the Matthean version. The verse reads (RSV): "And brother will deliver up brother to death, and the father his child, and children will rise against parents and have them put to death". The variant in Matthew is more likely a grammatical correction: the majority of the witnesses give the verb "rise" in the third person plural, whereas the Codex Vaticanus and some other codices bring the more correct third person singular, because the subject, "children" (a plural neuter in the Greek) would require this. What is striking in this case is that the verse is part of a longer unit that has a parallel in Matthew in a different context: Mark 13:9–13 is part of the "little apocalypse",

---

[55] See G. Theissen 1977. In this article – which has Mark 10:28 as its title – Theissen concedes that from a religious point of view the existence of following Jesus ("Nachfolgeexistenz"; p. 161) is a consequence of meeting the Holy One ("Begegnung mit dem Heiligen"), but his own main task is to show from a sociological perspective that this existence is a variant of social uprootedness ("eine Variante sozialer Entwurzelung").

whereas its parallel, Matt 10:17–22 occurs in Jesus' speech concerning the sending out of the disciples. Luke 21:10–19 is a parallel passage (in a speech of Jesus concerning the last days, as in Mark), but in the very parallel to our verse the reference to children rising up against parents is missing. Luke 21:16 reads: "You will be delivered up even by parents and brothers and kinsmen and friends, and some of you they will put to death". In all three Synoptics, the saying is followed by Jesus' affirmation: "you will be hated by all for my name's sake". In Mark and Matthew Jesus concludes the little unit, but not the speech, with exactly the same words: "But he who endures to the end will be saved". Luke has a further saying first (omitted by Marcion and a Syriac version: "But not a hair of your head will perish"), then the same content as the conclusion in the parallels, but with a different wording: "By your endurance you will gain your lives".

One might argue that the unit stood originally in the apocalyptic speech as in Mark (and Luke), and Matthew transferred it into a different context: Jesus' speech at the sending out of the disciples (so e.g. U. Luz 1996, II/105).[56] It is significant that even in Matthew's context there is an apocalyptic tone to the saying, due to the reference to "enduring to the end" (10:22b). Joachim Gnilka (1979, II/192) observes that the term "the end" (τέλος) is ambivalent: it may have meant "death" in the "Vorlage" of Mark, but in Mark 13:12 it probably means the end-time, since it is used with this sense in verse 7 already. He also points to 4 Ezra 6:25 as a parallel apocalyptic saying: "And it shall be that whoever remains after all that I have foretold to you shall himself be saved and shall see my salvation and the end of my world." Gnilka also raises the possibility that Mic 7:6 may stand behind Mark 13:12 and its Matthean parallel (p. 191; U. Luz affirms the same for the latter, 1996, II/106). It is possible that the content of the verse is in the background, but its wording is different. The only real parallel is the verb "rise", in the third person singular, as it refers to the daughter (in the singular) rising against her mother: "for the son treats the father with contempt, the daughter rises up against her mother, the daughter-in-law against her mother-in-law; a man's enemies are the men of his own house." We shall see that there is a reference to this verse in Matthew a little later, in 10:35, but that verse in Matthew does not have a Markan parallel (and it omits the very reference to "rising against").

To be sure, the expression "children will rise against parents and have

---

[56] It is worth noting that Martin Hengel (1984, 1–45) sees the Neronian persecution in the background of Mark 13:12. He argues that, according to Tacitus (*Ann.* XV,44), Christians under severe torture betrayed the names of their fellow Christians. Thus "brothers" (members of the Christian congregation) handed over "brothers" to death.

them put to death" indicates enmity within the family to the bitter end. This is an extremely hard saying as regards children's behaviour. We have to observe, however, that the context clearly shows that the enmity arises against the followers of Jesus: It is because of Jesus' name that they will be persecuted. This persecution is carried out with such emotion that even family members turn against one another. This does not imply that Jesus' own followers would turn against their parents; rather, Jesus warns his disciples that they will be persecuted by their parents or even by their children.

Thus when Jesus speaks here of an enmity between children and parents, he refers to the consequences of discipleship, which are not intended by the disciples, but have to be suffered by them unavoidably. This enmity is described with a reference to apocalyptic circumstances, whether the end would come soon in Jesus' opinion (cf. Matt 10:23, the immediately following verse), or at a non-specified time even in the possibly distant future. Ulrich Luz (1996, II/112–13) argues that the reference to "brethren" (in Matt 10:21 and its Markan parallel taken over by Matthew) points to the experience of Jewish Christians from the side of their fellow-Israelites; but he also adds that the experience of persecution is extended to be of general validity, since it is also affirmed in Jesus' saying to the disciples that: "you will be hated by all" (Matt 10:22).

Thus hatred is the reaction of some people to the message of Jesus, the main theme of the mission of his disciples. William Davies and Dale Allison explain the reference to Jesus' "name" in this way (1991, II/187): it "explains the persecution as arising from the disciples' identification with Jesus and their confession of him (cf. 1 Pet 4.14; Polycarp, *Ep.* 8.2; Justin, *1 Apol.* 4)." The disciples have to be prepared to suffer this even from their family members; it is not implied that they would behave in the same way to their persecutors.

We have concluded the discussion of texts that are to be found in Mark (and in other Gospel parallels). In the following, we turn to passages witnessed to by Matthew and Luke, or by only one of the canonical Gospels.

Matthew 10:34–36 (par. Luke 12:51–53) is often assigned by scholars to Q; though if it comes from Q, then in the case of these verses Matthew's and Luke's Q-versions were different (so U. Luz 1996, II/134). The reminiscence of Mic 7:6 raises the possibility that the text was produced by the early Christian community which explained its own situation by this Old Testament verse. However, Ulrich Luz argues that Mic 7:6 played a role also in Judaism in connection with the end-times (cf. *m. Sotah* 9:15), and Jesus caused schism in his own immediate family (Mark 3:31–35), so one can presuppose Jesus-logia in these verses (p. 135).

3. Tensions within the family

On the surface, it seems that according to this saying it is Jesus who initiates enmity. The grammatical form (ἦλθον + the infinitive) indicates the aim or goal of the coming of Jesus (so U. Luz 1996, II/138, fn. 42). The verse reads: "Do not think that I have come to bring peace on earth; I have not come to bring peace, but a sword." Verse 35 begins with a repetition of the term "I have come", which may be an editorial strengthening of the parallelism (so U. Luz 1996, II/134, fn. 2). In verses 35–36 we read: "For I have come to set a man against his father, and a daughter against her mother, and a daughter-in-law against her mother-in-law; (36) and a man's foes will be those of his own household."

Ulrich Luz notes that Matt 10:35–36 is more remote ("eher weiter entfernt") from the Septuagint text of Mic 7:6, than its Lukan parallel, though only Matthew concludes by quoting the reference to the household (p. 134). However, it remains significant that the Old Testament reference has end-time connotations even in our passage. The immediate context of the quotation, Mic 7:7 refers to looking forward to the God of salvation: "But as for me, I will look to the Lord, I will wait for the God of my salvation; my God will hear me", and the remaining part of the whole of chapter 7 is a consolation with future promises, including a reference to "that day" (Mic 7:12). Despite the grammatical form, the saying concerns the preparation of the disciples for what will happen to them. Although the two chapters, Matt 10 and Luke 12 are not parallels as such (only some parts of them), both of them are long collections of sayings concerning discipleship. It can be argued in the case of both that just as we have seen in connection with the previous passage, Matt 10:21–23, our present sayings address the theme of what the disciples have to suffer as a consequence of their decision to follow Jesus. William Davies and Dale Allison have rightly pointed to Matt 5:9 (where Jesus praises peacemakers) and to Matt 10:12–15 as significant contexts of the present passage (1991, II/217, fn. 22). Although they emphasise the contrast in the form of a question: "How could Jesus praise peacemakers and then announce that he did not come to bring peace but a sword?", they add with a reference to Jesus' speech at the sending out of the disciples: "When Jesus and his messengers are not received [i.e. they reject the blessing of peace], there cannot but be conflict and division." This point strengthens our interpretation that Jesus' disciples suffer because of the negative answer of others to the gospel, and they do not initiate enmity in the family. As Darrell Bock has put it (1998, II/1189): Jesus' remark concerning the division in families "clearly recognizes that people respond differently to the hope he offers."

William Davies and Dale Allison (1991, II/218) also argue that Matt

10:34 is about the "present" of Jesus' time: it is not "the messianic era of peace", since it is not fulfilling Mal 4:6 concerning Elijah's return ("And he will turn the hearts of fathers to their children and the hearts of children to their fathers"). However, they also emphasise that *1 En.* 100.1–2 and other Jewish parallels (e.g. *Jub.* 23.16,19; *4 Ezra* 5.9; 6.24; *2 Bar.* 70.3) show that: "The conviction that the great tribulation would turn those of the same household against one another was clearly widespread" (p. 220). It is possible to argue that Jesus' appearance causes the crisis (as Davies and Allison suggest), but it is also possible to see the enmity within the family as an unavoidable element of the end-time crisis. Once again, one should not interpret this passage in isolation. If we regard the larger context (including Matt 10:21–23 discussed above, and the other Matthean texts, 5:9 and 10:12–15, referred to by Davies and Allison), then it is more likely that the present passage addresses the theme of the disciples' fate: spreading the gospel of Jesus leads to divisions; this has to be suffered even if the disciples only "initiate" it in the sense that they cannot but preach the gospel of Jesus. To sum up in Donald Hagner's words (1993, A/292): "'I came to divide,' would ordinarily be taken in the sense of purpose, here it is more a way of describing the effect of the coming of Jesus and the proclamation of the kingdom. Response to the message of Jesus and his disciples will be mixed and hence cause dissension among members of the same household."

d) The urgency of discipleship

The passage immediately following upon the unit in Matthew discussed just above is arguably also a double tradition, i.e. it is witnessed to by Matthew and Luke. The content is similar but the wording is different in the two Gospels. Since the different expressions of the same content will be significant for our exposition, we quote both. Matthew 10:37–38 reads: "He who loves father or mother more than me is not worthy of me; and he who loves son or daughter more than me is not worthy of me; (38) and he who does not take up his cross and follow me is not worthy of me." The original hand of Codex Vaticanus, Codex Bezae and a few other witnesses omit the second half of v. 37, probably due to homoioteleuton, as both half-verses end with the word ἄξιος. (As v. 38 ends with the same word, the omission in P[19] until the end of v. 38 is probably due to haplography as well). Luke 14:26–27 contains one of the most striking sayings of Jesus, often understood as a witness to his radical anti-family ethos: "If any one comes to me and does not hate his own father and mother and wife and children and brothers and sisters, yes, and even his own life, he cannot be my disciple. (27) Whoever does not bear his own cross and come after me, cannot be my disciple." Verse 27 is omitted by some MSS (due to homoioteleuton, according to Howard Marshall 1979, 593); and there are minor textual variations in verse 26. The possessive pronoun, αὐτοῦ, in the expression "his father" is omitted by a few MSS; although it is supported by many MSS, NA27 prints the more emphatic ἑαυτοῦ as the main text, based on P[75], Codex Vaticanus, and a few other MSS. Variations concerning the particle τε (its omission or replacement by δε), and variations in the word order in the expressions "his own life" (ψυχὴν ἑαυτοῦ) and "be my disciple" do not challenge the view that both the Luke 14:26 and Matt 10:37 are well attested. There is no attempt to bring the wordings closer in the history of the manuscript tradition.

Luke 14:26 and Matt 10:37 are either witnesses of independent traditions or "Lukan" and "Matthean" versions of a common tradition. The latter view is held by scholars who assign the saying to Q (e.g. U. Luz 1996, II/134). There are significant differences in the structure of the verse. Craig Evans summarises them as follows (1990, 577, italics his): Luke's single sentence "may be more original in form" than Matthew's two sentences beginning with a participial construction ("he who ..."). Luke's sentence is "overloaded by having three separate pairs (Matthew, two reciprocal pairs), and by the inclusion of *wife* along with children, and of *his own life* to form a tetrad." Evans holds that the latter may be Luke's addition; it is "all-embracing rather than a fourth worldly tie" (578).

It is important to see that Luke 14:26 is not in the same context in Luke as its parallel in Matthew. The former is located after the Lukan parallel of Matt 22:1–10 and a connecting Lukan verse (14:25, "Now great multitudes accompanied him; and he turned and said to them,..."). Thus in Luke's Gospel Jesus said this saying to the multitude around him. As we have seen, the Matthean version is part of Jesus' speech at the sending out of the disciples. The saying concerning the cross (following our saying both in Matthew and Luke with some difference in wording) is a variation of a saying that is repeated by all the Synoptics after the pericope concerning Peter's confession at Caesarea Philippi (Matt 16:24; Mark 8:34; Luke 9:23). François Bovon (1996, 527) has suggested that in Luke 14:26–27 we have a parallel to Matt 10:37–38, and that two originally independent sayings were put together in the tradition prior to the time of Matthew and Luke. If this analysis is correct, then neither Matthew nor Luke can be regarded as reporting the original context of the sayings. Whatever the original context, it is a saying concerning the consequences of discipleship; thus the Matthean context on discipleship can illuminate the meaning even if it was Matthew who organised the material in this way.

I accept that Luke 14:26 and Matt 10:37 are parallels; perhaps they are editorial adaptations of a Semitic original. We can find in them the same idea expressed by different idioms: "loves more" in Matthew equals "does not hate" in Luke. The Semitic background of the term "hate" would suggest that it is about a priority and not about emotions in the modern sense. As Craig Evans has put it (1990, 577): "This may be an example of the Semitic expression of preference by means of antithesis – 'I love A and hate B' meaning 'I prefer A to B' (cf. Gen. 29:30ff; Deut. 21:15; Rom. 9:13) – which has been altered, but correctly interpreted, in the Matthaean form (Matt. 10:37)." God places second the one whom he "hates" as opposed to the one whom he elects (cf. also Mal 1:2–3), as we shall argue below. Howard Marshall (1979, 592) points to further parallels (2 Sam 19:7; Prov 13:24; Isa 60:15; 1 John 2:9) and translates the term as "to love less".[57] He adds that the Hebrew original also means "to leave aside, abandon": "The thought is, therefore, not of psychological hate, but of renunciation." If a disciple loves Jesus then he should not love his family more than he loves Jesus; he must place his family second after Jesus (in Luke's words: he must "hate" his family).

This exposition has to face some challenges. It can be argued that the term "to hate" (μισέω) in Luke refers to real enmity at other places, so this must be its meaning in 14:26 as well. Indeed, the term refers to the disciples' being hated (Luke 6:22.27; 21:17), to the people of God being hated by its enemies (1:71), and to a nobleman in a parable being hated by his citizens (19:14). Luke 16:13 is an interesting case. I would argue that although it may refer to a real emotion of "hating", it is also possible that it is about preferences, in the sense of loving one less than the preferred one (so also I. H. Marshall 1979, 592): "No servant can serve two masters; for either he will hate the one and love the other, or he will be devoted to the one and despise the other. You cannot serve God and mammon."

Even if we accept that in the majority of the seven occurrences in Luke the term refers to "hating", it can be argued that the close context is against this meaning in Luke 14:26. Here it is affirmed at the end of the list that one has to hate even one's own life. This cannot mean real hating; it must mean a willingness to sacrifice even one's own life for the sake of Jesus. As Darrell Bock argues (1998, II/1284): "The call to 'hate' is not literal but rhetorical.... Otherwise, Jesus' command to love one's neighbor as oneself as a summation of what God desires makes no sense (Luke 10:25–37)." Thus,

---

[57] For further examples in the relationship between husband and wife, with the probable meaning "to love less", see Deut 24:3 and Eph 5:29. I owe these references to Annette Merz.

the saying is about priorities: Jesus must be more important to the disciple than the disciple's own life. As Luke has many OT allusions (especially in the case of the infancy narratives; see e.g. Bock 1999, I/68), he was probably capable of seeing the meaning of "putting to the second place in preferences" also in the case of μισέω. God hated Esau, but nevertheless he made him a nation as well (though he did punish the nation when it turned against the chosen people) according to the Old Testament tradition (Mal 1:2–3). This tradition was understood as pointing to priorities in election, as it is witnessed to by Paul who cites this passage from Malachi in Rom 9:13.[58]

We have to note that the reference to the disciples' "hating" their relatives occurs only in Luke 14:26 in the canonical Gospels. This saying occurs twice in the Gospel of Thomas, no. 55 and 101. In the latter the need to love one's parents is also expressed. John 12:25 uses the term concerning the necessity of hating one's own life; this being another example of deciding upon right priorities. As we have seen, the following saying in Luke (14:27) speaks about the necessity of taking up one's cross. It is understandable if the early church applied this saying to all Christians in a spiritual sense, but this latter meaning may not have been the original sense of the saying. Rather, it refers to a readiness for concrete hardships expected by Jesus from some of his disciples. To sum up, I argue that Luke 14:26 refers to the priority of Jesus' call to one's own family ties. It does not express a general rule, but the urgency of the call to some of Jesus' disciples.

There is a further radical saying of Jesus that is witnessed to by Matthew and Luke (thus being assigned to Q by many scholars, e.g. U. Luz 1996, II/21; D. A. Hagner 1993, A/213): the saying concerning burying the dead. Matthew 8:21–22 and Luke 9:59–60 are not only close parallels in wording, but these verses appear in both Gospels as the second part of a sequel with a common theme: Jesus speaking to individuals on the cost of discipleship. As one of the most recent commentator on Luke, Darrel Bock has observed that "Luke 9:59–60 is one of the least doubted statements of Jesus" (1998, II/975). He notes that the Jesus Seminar "accepts these sayings as authentic, printing them in pink type".

In Matthew, after Jesus talked to a scribe (8:19–20), we read (vv. 21–22): "Another of the disciples said to him, 'Lord, let me first go and bury my father.' (22) But Jesus said to him, 'Follow me, and leave the dead to bury

---

[58] That μισέω is not to be taken literally in Luke 14:26 may be supported by the following verse: in Luke 14:27 the bearing of the cross is probably meant in a figurative sense, since the reader is expected to remember the qualification "daily" from Luke 9:23.

their own dead.'" There are only minor variations: some MSS (e.g. Codices Sinaiticus and Vaticanus, and minuscule 33) omit αὐτοῦ as a concrete reference to Jesus in the expression "his disciples"; some MSS (e.g. Codex Sinaiticus and minuscule 33) omit the name Jesus in v. 22. It is a general tendency to define the participant of a story with more and more precision. Even if the subject of the story was not specified in an earlier form, it is clear from the previous pericope that Jesus is the main figure of this little scene as well. Some MSS have the present form "says" (λέγει) instead of the aorist; this is the lectio difficilior, since the parallel (Luke 9:60) has the following introduction to Jesus saying: "But he said to him..." (εἶπεν δὲ αὐτῷ). Unlike Luke, Matthew does not have a third dialogue. He closes the scene with a further reference to "disciples" (8:23): "And when he got into the boat, his disciples followed him."

After Jesus' saying concerning the foxes and birds (parallel to Matthew), Luke writes (9:59–60): "To another he said, 'Follow me.' But he said, 'Lord, let me first go and bury my father.' (60) But he said to him, 'Leave the dead to bury their own dead; but as for you, go and proclaim the kingdom of God." The editors of NA27 note the omission of the address "Lord" in some of the MSS (e.g. the original hand in Codex Vaticanus), they note the variations in the expression "let me first go" (changes in the grammatical form or the place of the verb in some MSS, and omission of "first" in codex W), but they fail to note that codex 69 simply reads "leave the dead", and omits "to bury their dead". This is noted by J. C. O'Neill (1984, 86), who argues that although this might be due to *homoioteleuton*, he himself regards it as the original reading. Jesus did not speak here about the spiritually dead;[59] he used the term only in a literal sense. O'Neill holds that this hard saying of Jesus "makes the proclaimers of the Kingdom equivalent to those who have taken a Nazirite vow" (p. 87; I note that O'Neill points to further support of this shorter reading: MS 579 and the Latin Book of Mulling, p. 125, n. 12).

This suggestion solves the problem of the seemingly hard attack of Jesus on those who do not follow him, but it does leave us with the radical saying of Jesus addressed to a would-be disciple: he should leave his dead father be-

---

[59] Since it is not crucial to my project, I leave the question open as to who are the dead who should bury their dead. Ulrich Luz (1996, II/25) holds that it is not the spiritually dead. In his opinion, Jesus' sentence is an *oxymoron.*, i.e. a witty, paradoxical saying. Luz paraphrases it this way: "let the dead mutually bury one another (Laß die Toten sich untereinander selbst begraben)". The majority of commentators seem to hold the view that it is the spiritually dead who should bury the dead, i.e. those who have not responded to Jesus' call (see e.g. I. H. Marshall 1979, 411; W. D. Davies and D. C. Allison 1991, II/56). To be sure, in both cases the person is asked to leave his dead father.

hind without a burial. "All we really need is the phrase 'Leave the dead' in order to grasp the offensiveness of the saying."[60] We have seen in the environment of the New Testament that providing for a funeral was among the foremost duties of children. Did Jesus teach against this general expectation?

Most scholars emphasise the radicalism of this saying in the light of the strong expectation in Judaism that a son should provide a funeral for his father (see e.g. I. H. Marshall 1979, 411; C. F. Evans 1990, 441; D. A. Hagner 1993, A/217). We have referred to many expressions of this duty in the previous chapter. We should not try to weaken the striking character of Jesus' saying whether in the shorter or even the longer form. However, it can be argued that in spite of its radicalism, this saying is not a witness to an anti-family attitude of Jesus. The following observations point to the likelihood that this saying does not imply that Jesus failed to fulfil the duty of honouring parents at this crucial point.

First we note that the Lukan version of this text seems to be nearer to the original in an important aspect (so e.g. U. Luz 1996, II/21): Matthew says that it is a "disciple" who asks Jesus' permission first to bury his father; it is more likely that Luke is right in referring to an unspecified "other" person who has the chance to become a disciple when meeting Jesus (so also Peter Kristen 1995, 110–12). Thus the saying is part of a "call" to discipleship; not in the general sense of the word, but in the special sense of the few "itinerant" disciples we have argued for earlier in this chapter (see also J. C. O'Neill 1984, 87). Thus it can be argued that the emphasis of Jesus' radical saying lies in an urgency in time and a priority to be given to Jesus' call (so also D. A. Hagner 1993, A/218; D. L. Bock 1998, II/981).

Both Matthew and Luke express this priority in some way. In Matthew, it is the would-be disciple who addresses Jesus and offers to follow him. As an answer Jesus first says, "Follow me", and then utters the radical saying immediately. In Luke, the call to follow Jesus is not uttered together with the saying concerning the dead, because it is Jesus who addressed the would-be disciple with this call at the beginning of the scene. Howard Marshall regards this as a Lukan editorial change (1979, 411). However, it may also be argued that in the original scene it was Jesus who took the initiative to address a would-be disciple. Matthew may have assimilated the form to the preceding passage: in Matthew's version Jesus is addressed first; his sayings are answers.[61] In Luke, Jesus' radical saying is followed by another

---

[60] E. P. Sanders 1985, 398, n. 36.
[61] For a different view, see M. Hengel 1968, 4–5; for the view that "the arrangement in Matthew is probably secondary", see W. D. Davies and D. C. Allison 1991, II/53.

sentence: "but as for you, go and proclaim the kingdom of God" (which may be editorial, so e.g. I. H. Marshall 1979, 412; C. F. Evans 1990, 441). However, it remains true that both evangelists clearly indicate that the discipleship of Jesus has to be given precedence even over family ties. Howard Marshall's observation concerning the whole pericope with the three little dialogues in Luke applies to this particular saying as well (1979, 408): Jesus indicates "the stringent nature of discipleship" to three would-be disciples. Darrell Bock points to the significance of the person of Jesus who utters the call (1998, II/980): "In fact, the remark may point to Jesus seeing himself as bringing in the new era. The ability to set priorities that go beyond the Ten Commandments may suggest the presence of messianic authority".

As we have seen above, J. C. O'Neill has argued that the would-be disciple is called to become the "equivalent" to those who have taken a Nazirite vow. He points to Num 6:6–8 where it is affirmed that people who have taken the Nazirite vow should not go near a dead body, even if it is their father or mother. Martin Hengel has pointed out that the passage from Numbers cannot be a direct background to Jesus' saying, as Jesus usually did not base his utterances on cultic-ritual grounds.[62] This does not prevent us from seeing the significance of the Nazirite vow as a background in another sense: people around Jesus knew of that exception to the rule of burying one's parents, so the saying in itself was not scandalous in their ears (as Markus Bockmuehl has argued on the basis of a detailed analysis of the available texts, 1998).[63]

To sum up, the call uttered by Jesus is put in a way that should not be generalised. The saying is radical, but it does not imply that Jesus taught that his disciples do not have to fulfil their duty as children to their parents. Discipleship, *Nachfolge*, has to have precedence; people who would have remembered the example of how God has precedence in the case of the Nazirites could understand a radical call to become preachers of God's Kingdom.

---

[62] M. Hengel (1968, 12) writes concerning Lev 21:11–12 (where the high priest is prohibited to make himself impure by going in to his dead father or mother) and Num 6:6: "Das den Hohenpriester und Nasiräer betreffende Gebot wird man daher kaum mit Schniewind zur Motivierung der Antwort Jesu heranziehen dürfen, da Jesus... erst recht eine kultisch-rituelle Begründung seiner Forderung fernlag".

[63] For a convenient summary of the main proposals which do not take these words of Jesus "at face value", see W. D. Davies and D. C. Allison 1991, II/56–57. While they reject any attempt to weaken the "shocking and scandalous" character of the saying, they also add that because of our lack of knowledge of the immediate circumstances of the scene "it would be unwise to base generalizations about Jesus' attitude towards burial or his respect for the dead (or lack thereof) on an interpretation of [Matt] 8.22" (*ibid.*, 57).

e) Jesus against "fathers on earth" and against "his (own) mother"?

Having discussed passages that are attested to in more than one Gospel, we turn to traditions witnessed to by only one Gospel: first we discuss special material from Matthew, then a pericope from John's Gospel.

On a first reading, Matthew 23:9 seems to affirm that Jesus did not have a high respect for fathers. In order that the context of the saying can be seen we quote vv. 8–10:[64] "But you are not to be called rabbi, for you have one teacher, and you are all brethren. (9) And call no man your father on earth, for you have one Father, who is in heaven. (10) Neither be called masters, for you have one master, the Christ." In verse 9, there are only stylistic variations: the possessive pronoun (ὑμῶν) in the term "your father" (v. 9a) is replaced by the dative (ὑμῖν) in some MSS (due to the "odd placement of the genitive", so Hagner 1995, B/657), and it is omitted by some others. In v. 9b, the Greek text says literally: "one is your father", and the expression "your father" is in a reverse order in some MSS. The English text quoted above (RSV) translates the Greek text of the "majority" Byzantine text: ὁ ἐν τοῖς οὐρανοῖς. Some MSS (e.g. Codex Bezae, W, and the minuscule family 1) do not have ἐν τοῖς; some have ὁ οὐράνιος ("heavenly"; NA27 prints this as the main text, supported, for example, by Codices Sinaiticus, Vaticanus, and the minuscule family 13). The text history can be reconstructed in two ways: ὁ οὐράνιος may be original, at some point a scribe changed the iota and omikron at the end of the word, a later scribe thought that the dative plural could not stand alone, so he inserted ἐν τοῖς; thus producing the expression familiar to the reader from the first line of the Lord's Prayer in ch. 6. However, it is possible to argue the other way round: ἐν τοῖς may have been omitted first by mistake, and someone changed the order of omikron and iota, as the adjectival expression, "heavenly" is also known from Matthew's Gospel (e.g. 5:48; 6:14.32). Since it is well-attested in the sayings of Jesus, and supported by the earlier main codices, NA27 may be right in their decision for ὁ οὐράνιος.

Matthew 23:9a can mean either "and call no one on earth your father", or "and call no one of you on earth father". William Davies and Dale Allison (1997, III/276) opt for the first meaning, whereas Ulrich Luz argues for the second possibility, taking ὑμῶν as a partitive genitive (1997, III/296, fn. 5).

---

[64] I note with U. Luz (1997, III/296) that according to the synchronic structure vv. 8–12 form the full unit; its main part being vv. 8–11, and v. 12 being a "Nachsatz", since it differs from the preceding due to its future perspective and its general tone (the second person plural is not continued).

We shall see that this is in harmony with his understanding of the verse as reflecting the situation of the early church.

Since the saying (Matt 23:9) occurs in a long collection of Jesus' sayings concerning the scribes and Pharisees, it can be argued that Matthew is responsible for its present location.[65] In this case, it may be argued further that the saying was originally independent. It differs from vv. 8 and 10 in as much as it is in the active form ("call no man ..."), whereas its neighbouring verses have the passive ("you are not to be called", though I note that in v. 8 some MSS have an active variant). If so, then it may be regarded as a radical saying of Jesus denouncing earthly fathers. For example, Gerhard Lohfink discusses Matt 23:9 (which he holds to be a saying of the historical Jesus) under the heading "Das Ende der Väter" (1982, 57–63). He argues that Jesus tells his disciples that (after they left their fathers anyway) they should not call anyone on earth "abba", any longer, since they have in the place of their earthly fathers a heavenly father (p. 61).

Ulrich Luz offers another exposition. He argues that vv. 8ab.9 are the oldest core of the unit vv. 8–10, but he holds that even these probably originated in the early church, since it is difficult to imagine that the young followers of Jesus (coming from lower and middle classes) would have been addressed as "Rabbi" (1997, III/298).

Whether or not vv. 8–9(–10) go back to Jesus, the context helps to determine the meaning of v. 9 as well. In this case it is possible to argue that the term "father on earth" does not only refer to fathers as family members, but in a figurative sense to leaders in general. According to Donald Hagner (1995, B/661), the context even decides that the otherwise grammatically ambiguous genitive ὑμῶν refers here to "your father". Verse 9 may be a parallel to the preceding and following sayings not only in a formal way, but also as regards its content: it may speak about teachers (Hagner, *ibid.*, makes the same point). It is possible to understand this as a warning against some aspects of the lives of the Pharisees (as at the beginning of ch. 23). Even if verse 9 is an authentic saying of Jesus, it can be understood in a way different from Lohfink's exposition seen above: Jesus warns his disciples not to follow everything the scribes and Pharisees (as their "fathers") say.[66]

---

[65] The structure of ch. 23 is set out clearly by U. Luz 1997, III/292–93 and 388–89. He points out that vv. 8–12 are addressed to the disciples only, whereas the preceding section is addressed to the people and the disciples. After v. 12 begin the "woe"-sayings addressed to the scribes and the Pharisees (p. 291).

[66] It is, of course, possible that the saying addressed the situation of the later church where there were also leaders tempted by "titles" (see U. Luz 1997, III/307), but this does not mean that the saying was created by the early church. The later application does not make it im-

Verse 9 does not imply that the disciples have reached the age when they could be called "fathers". The saying concerns the rabbis whom people follow as fathers.[67]

However, even if we retain the possibility that "fathers" in their role as leaders of families are in view (referring to the fathers of the disciples and not necessarily to themselves as fathers), the saying fits the overall picture we have found to obtain in the environment: God comes before parents both in the pagan and Jewish environment of the New Testament. To remind one that his or her earthly parents are not the supreme authorities, but God has to be given precedence, does not deny the validity of the expectation that honour is due to parents as well. In Matt 23:9 Jesus does not put God in the place of the earthly fathers. Donald Hagner rightly observes (1995, B/661): "Besides one's earthly father (for whom the title is not in question), only one other may be referred to as 'Father,' i.e. God himself".[68] We have seen in the environment that God who claims precedence for himself orders that parents should be honoured. Jesus did not contradict that view in this saying.

Thus we can affirm that Matt 23:9 does not have to be seen as a witness to Jesus' criticism of earthly fathers. Even if one would argue that the present context of the saying is not original, it can be rightly claimed that the saying should be seen in the light of Jesus' other sayings as well as in the light of Jesus' environment.

We conclude this section with a brief discussion of the pericope concerning the wedding at Cana (John 2:1–11). Walter Lütgehetmann has devoted a monograph to this passage (1990). He lists the numerous problems this short pericope raises; among them the following (p. 2): "Warum reagiert Jesus auf die Feststellung des Weinmangels durch seine Mutter so hart?" Indeed, Jesus seems to fail to honour his mother when he addresses her in these words (v. 4): "O woman, what have you to do with me? My hour has

---

possible that the original version applied to the scribes and the Pharisees concerning whom the disciples were warned by Jesus. W. D. Davies and D. C. Allison argue that both interpretations are possible (1997, III/276–77).

[67] Ulrich Luz marshals the evidence (from the middle of the first century A.D. on) for scribes being given the epithet "Abba" (1997, III/307, fn. 81). Cf. the usage found at Qumran (1QH\u00aa XV[VII], 20): "You have made me like a father for the sons of favour" (in F. G. Martínez 1994, 344).

[68] J. C. O'Neill's arguments concerning the three prohibitions in Matt 23:8–10 point to a similar result (1995, 150): "These are all relative negatives, in that they do not really prohibit the use of these terms – how could a teacher stamp out the use of words of respect by students. Teachers were being taught, in this triple saying, to direct their students' attention beyond themselves to the Teacher, the Father and the Guide."

not yet come." The first half of the verse is difficult to translate; RSV has a reverse order of "me" and "you" in the Greek idiom (τί ἐμοὶ καὶ σοί, γύναι;).⁶⁹

Lütgehetmann has argued on the basis of the occurrence of the idiom elsewhere that the person who uses this idiom does not want to have anything in common with the person addressed, or it can mean that the person has a different view on a certain question (1990, 169). In the latter case, only the opinion of the other person is objected to, and the idiom does not say that no contact with the person is intended in the future. On the basis of the parallels, he further affirms that since it is in the form of a question, it must be a rhetorical question. It is important that any positive meaning of the sentence can be ruled out (p. 170). If, then, it is a denial of something, this must mean that the previous sentence uttered by the mother of Jesus is not simply a statement about the lack of wine, but it implies a request; it is this request that is denied by Jesus (171).⁷⁰ Lütgehetmann affirms concerning the parallels of the idiom (e.g. 2 Sam 16:10; 19:22, p. 171): "Auch wenn die beiden Dative Personen bezeichnen, ist es möglich, daß es nur darum geht, eine Meinungsverschiedenheit in einer bestimmten Angelegenheit und d. h. eben einzig und allein in dieser Angelengenheit auszudrücken." Lütgehetmann notes that the history of the exposition of this pericope shows that many scholars understood this verse as a programmatic saying of Jesus to show his independence from family ties when he begins his public activity.⁷¹ He himself holds that the verse is redactional; it belongs to the third and final phase of the development when a redactor wanted to counter a christology based on miracles (pp. 339–41).

Arthur Maynard argues in a similar way when he affirms that by this saying an editor intended to show Jesus' "divine nature" (cf. Mark 1:24). The evangelist did not want to put this on the lips of the demons (as in Mark), but he wanted to indicate that "Jesus is no longer 'son of Mary', but that he is now moving and living on a divine level where he has no filial relationship

---

⁶⁹ We leave the question of authenticity open. It can be argued that the story is based on motifs of the Dionysos legends, see e.g. W. Lütgehetmann 1990, 261–72 and 277–78.

⁷⁰ G. Theissen and A. Merz hold that the pericope of the wedding at Cana is a "Geschenkwunder" (1997, 267). This requires that the action of the miracle-worker should be spontanous, i.e. not asked for. They affirm (*ibid.*, fn. 18): "Man könnte allerdings Joh 2,3 als Gegenbeleg anführen. Aber ist die Feststellung der Mutter Jesu 'Sie haben keinen Wein' eine Bitte? Wohl kaum!" We may add that even if v. 3 is not taken as an implied request for help, Jesus may have disagreed with his mother on the matter whether it was women's business to deal with the provisions at a wedding; see below.

⁷¹ See his reference to Schlatter, Bultmann, Barrett, Haenchen and others, p. 172, fn. 1. He even points to the radical claim of Ben-Chorin that by this saying Jesus broke the commandment to honour father and mother (W. Lütgehetmann 1990, 172).

3. Tensions within the family

to her" (1985, 584). However, this explanation contradicts the picture we met at the end of this Gospel: Jesus providing for his mother from the cross (see on John 19:25–27, earlier in this chapter, section 2.b; though it is also possible to argue that the latter is the creation of the early church to weaken the radicalism of Jesus' other sayings).

We are left with four possibilities: First, there may be a contradiction on an editorial level. In this case it must be shown why the editor first depicted an anti-family Jesus then a caring son. Second, there is no real contradiction on the editorial level; the editor did not want to show Jesus as someone failing to honour his mother. The editor wanted to correct a Christology that laid too much emphasis on miracles.[72] Third, there is a contradiction in Jesus' behaviour, if the passages in question might have a historical core (and if he affirmed the validity of the Fifth Commandment, as we have argued above). Fourth, it is possible to argue (on the basis of the analysis of the parallels by W. Lütgehetmann) that the saying concerned only one particular matter; it was a matter of a difference of opinion.

To sum up, the text can be interpreted as an example when Jesus did not honour his mother (or the early church depicted him as acting in this way). However, it is legitimate to opt for an intepretation that corresponds to the pattern we find elsewhere in the Gospel tradition. If we find that Jesus observed the Fifth Commandment, and he observed the expectation that God comes before parents (this being no denial of the honour due to parents), then we can argue for an interpretation that fits this picture in our present case as well. Thus, I would argue that either position two or position four should be adopted.

As regards the latter view, Rudolf Pesch (1981, 223) has suggested that one concrete matter on which Jesus disagreed with his mother at the wedding in Cana may have been the issue that in Jesus' opinion it was men's duty to care about wine at a wedding. Pesch's argument also offers a reason why the unusual address, "woman", is uttered by Jesus to his mother: "Mit der zitierten Formel werden Rechts- oder Zuständigkeitsbereiche abgegrenzt; für die Versorgung von Gästen mit Wein sind nicht die Frauen (deshalb die keinesfalls respektlose Anrede Jesu an seine Mutter mit 'Frau'!), sondern allein die Männer, wozu sich der (wohl schon heranwachsende) Sohn zählt, zuständig."[73] In this case, the saying does not imply an

---

[72] Udo Schnelle (1998, 59–60) affirms that the unusual address "stellt keine Herabsetzung Marias dar, zugleich signalisiert sie aber unüberhörbar eine Distanz." Schnelle argues that the Christological justification (v. 4c) of Jesus' behaviour is editorial (p. 60).

[73] This exposition of v. 4 can be accepted irrespective of the decision whether or not one follows the overall thrust of Pesch's thesis that the whole passage originates in the circle of

anti-family behaviour on Jesus' side, though it must be admitted that the idiomatic address sounds harsh in our ears.[74]

Concerning the editorial level, Walter Kirchschläger (1996, 369) has pointed to the significance of the saying that follows the idiom in verse 4: "My hour has not yet come." By referring to the "hour", Jesus (as presented by the evangelist) pointed to God whose will has to come true:

> Entscheidend ist jedoch die vorgenommene Grenzziehung: Auch die Mutter muß die Grunddimension des jesuanischen Wirkens erkennen; in johanneischer Diktion heißt dies, daß das Geschehen der "Stunde", die sich im Wirken Jesu ereignet und schließlich vollenden wird, allein von Gott, vom Willen des Vaters also abhängt.

This means that Jesus is portrayed as giving God's will the priority above all other spheres including that of the family.[75] As we have seen in the environment, this behaviour does not involve a denial of the validity of children's duty to honour their parents. In the case of a pericope that is only attested to by the Fourth Gospel it is difficult to decide whether a view goes back to the historical Jesus or to a redactor (thus to the early church). We have emphasised at the beginning of this chapter that the question of authenticity does not play a significant role in the present project. Accordingly, we have left open the question of authenticity also during the course of the exegesis of the Gospel passages. Without any claim of conclusiveness, it is suggested here that the fourth interpretation of this passage can be maintained: it fits the picture that Jesus observed the commandment to love father and mother; at the same time, he also gave priority to God over parents.[76] By this attitude

---

stories about the childhood of Jesus (indicated by Pesch also in the above quotation by the reference to the adolescent son).

[74] János Bolyki argues that this usage of the vocative, "woman", is not impolite (2001, 101). So also J. C. O'Neill (2001, 31): "There are plenty of good examples of the honorific usage by husbands to wives, and a son could hardly be charged with implying a rejection of the proper filial relationship to his mother because he used this form. Jesus, then, used this expression to accede most readily to Mary's suggestion that he should come to the aid of their host when the wine had run out."

[75] In John 19:26–27 we not only find that Jesus addressed his mother as "woman" again (see Michael Labahn 1999, 130), but there is also a reference to the "hour" (v. 27b): "And from that hour the disciple took her to his own home." On the basis of the occurrences of the "hour" in the Fourth Gospel, Labahn concludes (128): "Das Motiv von der Stunde Jesu und die Distanz zu menschlich-verwandtschaftlichen Relationen sind Teil der Sendungschristologie und damit der theologischen Darstellung des vierten Evangeliums."

[76] In his recent treatment of John 2:4, J. C. O'Neill has pointed to Gen 23:15–16 as evidence that the idiom, "What is this between me and you?", can have a positive meaning, implying agreement. He argues that the elliptical expression can be either positive or negative, but in John 2:4 it is positive (2001, 29): "'What [possible disagreement can there be] between me and you?' Mary seems to have understood it in this latter sense, for she immediately tells the servants to do whatever Jesus is to ask of them (John 2:5)."

4. Summary

he shared the expectations of his environment. The early church (meaning the evangelists and the circles around them) saw him in this way, and depicted him accordingly.

4. Summary

In conclusion, it has to be affirmed that the exegesis offered in this chapter does not claim to have found the only possible interpretation of the texts. Indeed, it is possible to argue that the tensions found in some of the Gospel texts are indicators of a general pattern: they point to Jesus' indifference to family, or even at times to an anti-family ethos. The same can be argued for his first, itinerant followers. If this view is maintained then texts affirming the validity of the commandment to honour father and mother have to be confronted with these texts. One may either argue that Jesus was inconsistent on this matter, or one may suggest that the early church is responsible for the traditions that show a Jesus who honours parents.

The present project offers a different approach. It is argued that Jesus' (and his first followers') environment affirmed the duty of children to honour their parents. However, the environment also held that God's priority does not affect the validity of this duty. If we look at the Gospel tradition from this angle, it is striking how many passages either confirm this view or suppose this view as a natural background for everyday life. We may add as a general observation that (ethical) statements in the form of sayings are usually more radical than the ethical implications of narrative material. It is not surprising that Jesus' radical sayings are in the form of *logia* whereas texts implying the duty of honouring parents appear more often in a narrative context.[77]

It remains true that there are radical sayings in the Gospels. It is argued here that these sayings (though they are radical indeed) do not force us to conclude that Jesus failed to fulfil the Fifth Commandment. We have seen that the texts that witness to tensions in the child-parent relationship can be classified in three groups. First, some of the texts indicate that Jesus' saying is an answer to a challenge, or that the separation within a family is a consequence of the disciples' commitment to Jesus; in other words: it is not Jesus and his disciples who initiate the separation; they rather suffer it as a consequence of other people's unbelief. Secondly, some texts may be regarded as referring to exceptional cases, i.e. they do not apply to all dis-

---

[77] I owe this observation to Professor Gerd Theissen (letter dated 6.1.2001).

ciples. This view supposes (and finds confirmation in these very texts) that Jesus had two kinds of disciples: some were expected to become itinerant followers of Jesus, while others did not have to renounce family life. However, even itinerant disciples could return to their families: they did not break off all contacts with them. Thirdly, (and often in connection with the previous category) some texts are to be seen in an apocalyptic setting. They either refer to the end time, or to the urgency of deciding upon priorities in the present; in neither case do they prescribe the behaviour of all the disciples of Jesus for the present age.

To sum up, the Gospel material concerning the child-parent relationship allows us to put together a picture of Jesus and his first followers that corresponds to that found in the environment of the New Testament. Jesus and the early church around the evangelists observed the commandment to love father and mother; they did not break this commandment when they gave priority to God even over parents.

In the next chapter we look at the early church's view and practice on this matter as it is witnessed to by the Pauline Corpus.

Chapter Five

Traditions in the Pauline Corpus

1. Introduction

In the previous chapter, we have dealt with early Christian traditions as they are reflected in the Gospels. In the present chapter we continue to survey the thoughts and practices of the early church; here we focus on the writings that have been transmitted under the name of Paul. Scholarship is divided on the question as to how many letters in the New Testament can be attributed to the apostle Paul. Our project does not need to decide this matter. We have discussed Gospel traditions as reflections originating in the first few decades of early Christianity (without any major interest in the question whether or not a saying goes back to the historical Jesus); similarly, here we focus upon the first two or three generations of Christians as they appear in the letters attributed to Paul, without laying any emphasis on what may be regarded as authentic Pauline tradition. Scholarship generally agrees that even those letters that are to be ascribed to disciples of Paul, for example, the Pastoral Epistles, date in the latter part of the first century. However, we shall group our material in accordance with the consensus of present day scholarship as regards Pauline and deuteropauline authorship.[1] Without further argumentation, we limit our field of research to the "canonical" writings of the New Testament, i.e. to writings adopted by the main (or orthodox) church as their authoritative Scripture, though it is admitted that for a full view of early Christianity the non-canonical writings would have to be discussed as well.[2]

When we deal with the thirteen writings transmitted in the early church under the name of Paul, we move around in the same decades as the tradi-

---

[1] The consensus view is represented, for example, by Hans Hübner (1993, 30), who regards Romans, 1–2 Corinthians, Galatians, 1 Thessalonians, Philippians, and Philemon as authentic. – The Pastorals are usually dated around A.D. 100, see e.g. Jürgen Roloff (1988, 45–46) who rejects attempts to date them even later (after the time of Marcion; a dating represented, for example, by H. v. Campenhausen and Ph. Vielhauer).

[2] For historical arguments justifying the view that the "canonical" writings can be viewed as belonging together (and thus that it is legitimate to study them together), see Peter Balla, 1997, esp. chs. 2 and 3, pp. 48–146.

tions of the Gospels, i.e. from the time of Jesus until about the end of the first century. According to the majority view, the Gospels are to be dated to the last three decades of that century; even the latest epistles of the Pauline Corpus are not regarded by the majority of scholars as later than that. It is, therefore, significant to see that we find far fewer traditions referring to tensions in the family in the Pauline letters than in the Gospels. The Pauline Epistles reflect the life of the settled congregations. Since in the Pauline Corpus there are fewer texts addressing issues of the real child-parent relationship, it seems appropriate that we do not divide our chapter after the same principle as in the previous chapter. Rather, first we discuss texts that address the real child-parent relationship (for example, reflecting norms as in the case of the Household Codes), and then we turn to texts that use family imagery in a figurative sense, thus presupposing a certain view of the child-parent relationship (for example, when Paul speaks of his disciples as his sons).

By the way of introduction, it is appropriate to point out that recent scholarship on the early church has put an increasing emphasis on the household character of the life of the congregations. Works written from a primarily social perspective have not only illuminated aspects of life in the city as the background of most of the Christian congregations in the second half of the first century, but also have focussed on the house as the main place of living, as well as the place of worship, of the early Christians. Since the living circumstances influenced also the relationship between children and parents, we mention some results of this rapidly growing field of scholarship.[3]

Architectural evidence shows that there was a great variety of types and sizes of houses (and compounds of houses), reflecting the difference in wealth between the different social classes in the ancient Roman Empire.[4] Carolyn Osiek and David Balch have suggested that it is worth studying houses in Pompeii and Herculaneum, because, due to the eruption of Vesuvius in A.D. 79 and the cover of volcanic mud, they "give us a more complete view" than cities excavated elsewhere (1997, 5).[5] They rightly add the caution that "we have no houses from the ancient Mediterranean world in the first centuries of the Christian era in which we know for sure that Chris-

---

[3] For overviews of the social aspects of the life of the early Christians (especially in the cities), see e.g. Pieter Botha 2000, Philip Esler 1994, Peter Lampe 1987, Abraham Malherbe 1977, Wayne Meeks 1983, Ekkehard Stegemann and Wolfgang Stegemann 1995, Gerd Theissen 1989a, Michael White 1997.

[4] For a summary of types of houses in Palestine, see Pieter Botha 2000, 29–46. He points out that (in the early Roman period) building a large *manor* was a wide-spread phenomenon throughout the Empire, including Palestine; thus he holds that the site at Khirbet Qumran can be seen as a "Roman-like" manor (p. 19).

[5] On houses in these two cities, see also Andrew Wallace-Hadrill 1991.

1. Introduction

tians lived"; nevertheless they also claim that we can typify living arrangements in most of the cities of the Empire (with certain local modifications). Osiek and Balch emphasise that due to the climate around the Mediterranean Sea, houses were designed in a way that most of the time could conveniently be spent outdoors (1997, 6 and 15). The basic design of the Graeco-Roman house, the *domus*, features a central court surrounded by rooms (p. 6). These rooms are often small, even in the case of otherwise large and impressive urban houses, with the exception of the dining-room. "The house is turned inward and its life happens inside the walls, yet for the most part out of doors." In spite of the similar "peristyle design" of Greek and Latin houses, there is one main difference: in the traditional Latin house there is "an atrium just inside the front door (*ostium*, mouth) reached by a short entrance hall (*fauces*, jaws)" (p. 9). This provided enough space "for public and business purposes".

Another type of housing is that of the large apartment houses (*insulae*). Some of these have three or four storeys, and their rooms are not always small. Among the many examples at Ostia, there is a special one, the House of Diana, which has a "rather pleasant central courtyard" (p. 18). One of the back rooms on the ground floor was used by Mithraists for worship. Osiek and Balch note: "This case is illustrative of the adaptation of residential or commercial space for religious activities. Some Christian groups may have gathered in very similar circumstances." During the first three Christian centuries, increasingly "the insula and other forms of multiple-unit housing replaced the domus in crowded Ostia, undoubtedly also at Rome, and probably in other cities of the empire as well" (p. 20). The difference has a social background: poor people could afford to live only in over-crowded *insulae*.

The larger central courtyard of the *insula* and the *atrium* of the *domus* are significant, since these made it possible for Christians to meet as congregations at the houses of their more wealthy members.[6] As Gerd Theissen has put it (1974, 197): "Die Gemeindeversammlungen fanden wahrscheinlich in den Privathäusern der besser gestellten Christen statt." In Paul's letters, there are also references to the household of certain people (see e.g. 1 Cor 1:16; 16:15). This implies that he met full households, and possibly even that those whom he visited acted as host not only to him but to the congregation as well. We note that the term translated as "house" often refers to a "household" which includes "material goods and slaves; immediate blood family; or family lineage" (οἶκος, οἰκία; to some extent, the same is true for the Hebrew *bayit* and Latin *domus*; Osiek and Balch 1997, 6).

---

[6] For a discussion of the term, "the congregation at the house", see Marlis Gielen 1986.

160 Chapter Five: Traditions in the Pauline Corpus

We shall see more of this background material when we discuss the texts in the Pauline Corpus.

2. Texts concerning real child-parent relationships

a) Undisputed Pauline letters

There are some texts in the undisputed Pauline Epistles that imply expected norms by pointing to failures in carrying them out. We now turn to some examples.

In Romans 1, Paul summarises the main message of the letter concerning the Gospel and God's righteousness in vv. 16–17, then he devotes a long passage (vv. 18–32) to those who "suppress the truth", against whom "the wrath of God is revealed from heaven" (v. 18). In v. 28 he refers to these people as those who "did not see fit to acknowledge God" and therefore "God gave them up to a base mind and to improper conduct." The latter term, ποιεῖν τὰ μὴ καθήκοντα, reminds us of the environment of the New Testament: moral duties expected from human beings by nature and the gods are often referred to as τὸ καθῆκον, or τὰ καθήκοντα by the Stoics.[7] Then follows a list of vices that characterise the people of improper conduct (vv. 29–31): "They were filled with all manner of wickedness, evil, covetousness, malice. Full of envy, murder, strife, deceit, malignity, they are gossips, (30) slanderers, haters of God, insolent, haughty, boastful, inventors of evil, disobedient to parents, (31) foolish, faithless, heartless, ruthless." Although there are minor variations concerning some items in the list, there is no variant indicated by NA27 at the item that is of special importance for our theme: "disobedient to parents" (γονεῦσιν ἀπειθεῖς). From the point of view of form, disobedience to parents stands out from the other components of the list because here the victims of someone's evil deed are mentioned, namely the parents. We note that a list of vices occurs in 2 Tim 3:2–5, introduced by the statement that these are the characteristics of "the last days" (2 Tim 3:1). In that list the reference to disobedience to parents appears again, in the same Greek words as in Romans 1:30. We recall that we have found in the environment texts in an apocalyptic context, describing the spread of evil in the end-times (see ch. 3, fn. 57). Although there is no ref-

---

[7] See e.g. Ulrich Wilckens 1978, I/111, esp. fn. 209, where he also refers to Diogenes Laertius VII.108; Epictetus *Diatr.* iii.22.43, and from the Hellenistic Jewish literature to 2 Macc 6:4; 3 Macc 4:16.

erence to the last days in Romans 1, Ulrich Wilckens may be right in taking the reference to the wrath of God in v. 18 as a reference to "das endzeitliche Zorngericht Gottes" (1978, I/112; he also notes that the similar list in 1QS 4,2–14 has the Hebrew equivalent of ten words of the Pauline list, the Qumran passage being also a representative of an apocalyptic setting).[8] Wilckens argues that the genre of vice list ("Lasterkatalog") was not only popular in the Hellenistic *diatribe* style, but was adopted by Jewish writers as well, since the lists had points of contact with the social concern of the second table of the Ten Commandments. He affirms that in the Jewish tradition injustice can be seen as a counterpart ("Widerspiel") to God's justice. However, it is important to emphasise with Wilckens that in early Christianity the major dividing line lies between the time before coming to faith in Christ, and the time of conversion. The deeds of injustice ("works of the flesh") characterise the Christians *ante fidem*, whereas the lists of virtues are the fruit of the Spirit who leads them in the present (see Gal 5:18–25).

As regards the expression, "disobedient to parents", we may say that "obedience" is one of the main duties of children. We have argued that "honour" is an overarching expression that is to be filled with concrete content. However, Klaus Berger (1972, 280) holds that the same can be said also of the main duty of obedience which can sum up "die Gesamtheit sittlicher Ermahnungen". He argues that the Fifth Commandment has close affinities to wisdom literature. Accordingly, as "honour" can cover the whole area of children's duties in the Fifth Commandment, the same is true about the warning to sons to obey their parents in wisdom literature. If this analysis is true, then Paul's short expression in Rom 1:30 equals the charge of not honouring one's parents, and thus serves as an overall summary of evil behaviour in the child-parent relationship.[9]

Finally, it is worth mentioning that Paul thinks the people he refers to could have known what is right; they even knew God but they did not honour him (v. 21). Paul affirms that these people could have known God's will because God has shown it to them (v. 19). The place of coming to know God is God's creation, the world (v. 20). Paul concludes the list of vices we have just referred to by saying (v. 32): "Though they know God's decree that

---

[8] Eduard Schweizer makes a similar point when he affirms concerning Romans 1 (1979, 199): "The traditional warning against the coming wrath of God is actually the heading of the whole second half of this chapter. However, this eschatological wrath of God has already come with and in the proclamation of the Gospel, because this reveals man as he is."

[9] Concerning the negative formulation ("disobedient") in the child-parent relationship, see K. Berger 1972, 283–84, where he points to examples of negative formulations of the "Elterngebotstradition". For example, 1 Tim 1:9 speaks of murderer of fathers and mothers; see below.

those who do such things deserve to die, they not only do them but approve those who practise them." Without discussing the problem of how God can be known according to Romans 1, we observe that children's duties toward their parents are based both on God's will and on "nature". It is, perhaps, significant, that in the same vice list, though in quite an isolated way (so U. Wilckens 1978, I/114), there stands a reference to "haters of God" (v. 30). Though the expression does not stand immediately before the expression "disobedient to parents", Wilckens (*ibid.*) rightly points out that in Greek as well as Jewish thinking "boastful" behaviour against fellow human beings draws God's anger upon itself. As Thomas Schreiner has put it (1998, 97): "The connection between rejecting God and human sin is forged again with the vice list appearing in verses 29–31." Thus it may be argued that Paul's list implies that there is a connection between people failing to honour God and being disobedient to their parents.[10] From this negative formulation it is clear that Paul affirmed the duty of honouring God and, in relation to it, children's duty of honouring parents.

Our next passage is, perhaps, not an obvious example for our discussion, since it addresses the theme of adultery. However, since it concerns a rare but concrete offence against one's parents, it is worth mentioning, at least briefly. In 1 Cor 5:1–2, Paul writes to the Corinthians: "It is actually reported that there is immorality among you, and of a kind that is not found even among pagans; for a man is living with his father's wife. (2) And you are arrogant! Ought you not rather to mourn? Let him who has done this be removed from among you."

We know little of the actual circumstances. It seems clear from the wording, "with his father's wife", that the woman is not the mother of the man in question, "but a subsequent wife of his father" (Richard Hays 1997, 80). She is most likely the stepmother of the offender (so e.g. Marion Soards 1999, 111). Most commentators mention the possibility that the father has either died or he has already divorced her (so e.g. Wolfgang Schrage 1991, I/369).

Paul refers to the offence as πορνεία, "a term commonly used for prostitution" (M. L. Soards 1999, 111). In the Greek text it is said that the man "has" his father's wife (ἔχειν, in an acc. cum inf. construction). Thus the verb "indicates a somewhat permanent relationship" (M. L. Soards 1999, 111). Soards points out that "both Jewish and Roman law forbade incest"

---

[10] Cf. Eduard Schweizer's point (1979, 199, italics his): "idolatry is not simply one, if the first, vice among others; for Paul, leaving God and filling his place with created things is *the* sin. All the so-called vices are not sins in the proper sense of the word. They are but consequences to which God gave up those who had already given him up."

(*ibid.*). It is significant that the Corinthians, though not of Jewish origin, are distinguished here from the "nations". They now belong to the people of God, and that is why this case is so serious, since the offence described "is not found even among pagans", i.e. the non-Jewish nations (οὐδὲ ἐν τοῖς ἔθνεσιν, so e.g. R. B. Hays 1997, 81; see also his reference to Cicero *Clu.* 5.14–6.15 where a concrete marriage between a mother-in-law and a son-in-law is labelled as "unbelievable, unheard of"). If so, then Schrage (1991, I/370) is right in arguing that Paul probably has in mind the strict rules of the OT and other Jewish literature that condemn marriage between a son and a stepmother (e.g. Lev 18:8; 20:11; Deut 27:20; *Jub.* 33.10; Josephus *Ant.* 3.274; Philo *Spec.* 3.21; Aristeas 152; *Sib. Or.* 5.390; Ps.-Phoc. 179; see also Ezek 22:7.10). However, it remains also significant that "Roman law forbade marriage both between adoptive parents and children and between steprelatives" (M. L. Soards 1999, 111; see also references in W. Schrage 1991, I/370, fn. 16, e.g. to Gaius, *Institutiones* I.63).

As we have seen, we do not know anything about the father. The stepmother is most likely not a member of the congregation, "otherwise, she would have been subject to the disciplinary action that Paul orders in verses 2–5 and 11–13" (R. B. Hays 1997, 81). It is against the institution of marriage that the sin had been committed; in this case it is also implied that the sin had been committed against the parents (even though none of them may be alive or may be present). The strong condemnation contained in verses 3–5 (regarded as a *crux interpretum* by many commentators) implies the high value attributed to the marriage between one's father and mother by Paul. Sexual relations (probably concubinage rather than marriage, so W. Schrage 1991, I/369–70), even if only with one's stepmother, equal dishonouring one's parents.

This interpretation is strengthened by a passage in which Paul affirms the significance of marriage. In 1 Cor 7:10–16 Paul argues against divorce. First he refers to the Lord's demand, probably when addressing Christian couples (vv. 10–11; see M. L. Soards 1999, 149). Then he gives his own advice concerning mixed marriages, i.e. in which either the husband or the wife is an unbeliever (vv. 12–16; see R. B. Hays 1997, 120). This example is the more important, since from the larger context it is clear that Paul advised single people to remain single (1 Cor 7:8.24–27). Schrage points out that the term μένειν forms an inclusion in vv. 8 and 24 (1995, II/103). He sums up the main thrust of the passage as follows: "Der Christ soll solange wie möglich in der Gemeinschaft der Ehe und Familie bleiben". Schrage rightly argues that although there is a clear differentiation in Paul's arguments between what the Lord, i.e. Jesus, commands (e.g. v. 10) and his own advice (e.g. v. 12), the latter is not meant as a private opinion without binding force. Paul's apostleship implied a high claim of authority (see e.g. vv. 17, 25, and 40). Though these rulings do not address the child-parent relationship directly, they do affirm in a normative way the importance of already existing marriages (among the reasons why single people should remain alone, v. 29 is a significant one: "the appointed time has grown very short").

It is notoriously difficult to ascertain the exact meaning of v. 14, in which it is stated that the unbelieving partner is sanctified by the Christian partner in the marriage, and even their common child is sanctified. RSV reads as follows: "For the unbelieving husband is consecrated through his wife, and the unbelieving wife is consecrated through her husband. Otherwise, your children would be unclean, but as it is they are holy." The verse has been transmitted with some variations: at the end of the verse P[46], the Codices Sinaiticus (first hand) and Vaticanus, and many other MSS have ἐν τῷ ἀδελφῷ ("through the brother"); the variant translated by the RSV is probably a scribal alteration to make explicit that the "brother" is a believing husband in this case (so e.g. M. L. Soards 1999, 152).

Larry Yarbrough affirms that in the undisputed Pauline letters 1 Cor 5:1–5 and 7:12–16 are the only passages "in which Paul addresses a specific issue regarding familial relationships" (1995, 129). He interprets Paul's view in 1 Cor 7:14b in the following way: children "are 'holy' (ἅγια) so long as the couple remains together, but 'unclean' (ἀκάθαρτα) if the marriage is dissolved". Yarbrough observes that although we do not know the exact meaning of this statement, "it is clear Paul is of the opinion that 'Christian' parents are obligated to consider the effect divorce will have on their children. In essence, he argues that the marriage should be preserved 'for the sake of the children.'" Schrage (1995, II/106–107) rightly directs our attention to the Christian part in the marriage: perhaps the main emphasis of the Pauline teaching here does not lie in the status of the non-believing partner, but in the comfort the Christian partner should hold on to. The non-Christian partner will not threaten the sanctity of the Christian one, nor does it threaten the sanctity of their children.[11] On the contrary: God's sanctifying power can reach out to unbelievers; their Christian partners should preserve hope for their salvation as well (see v. 16).

Thus we can see in these two passages examples of a high view of marriage on Paul's side (emphasised by the contrasting view according to which Paul can praise non-married life as well). Though children's duties are not mentioned here in an affirmative way, we can interpret 1 Cor 5:1–5 as

---

[11] For a discussion of "children" in 1 Cor 7:14, see Gerhard Delling 1970.

an expectation that parents have to be honoured by the acknowledgment of the untouchable character of their marriage (a son should not have sexual relations with his father's wife, even if she is only his stepmother). 1 Corinthians 7:12–16 shows concern on Paul's side for children in the household. His advice in favour of the preservation of marriages supposes a view concerning order in a household that is similar to the view we meet in the Household Codes. We observe, however, that in the undisputed Pauline letters there are very few passages that address the issue of the real child-parent relationship. Paul's main interest lies in the life of the congregation and not so much in the life of individual families.

b) The Household Codes in Colossians and Ephesians

The Household Codes, with their well-defined theme of ethical conduct in relationships within a household, and their special structure, have attracted wide and ever-growing interest in the scholarly world, as reflected in numerous articles, special sections in commentaries, and even monographs.[12] Ulrike Wagener has devoted a chapter in her dissertation to the history of research on this topic (1994, 15–65). She points out the influence of Dibelius and Weidinger upon earlier research (15–16). In his commentary on Colossians (1912), Martin Dibelius argued for a Stoic background of the Household Codes. His thesis was corroborated and worked out in detail by his pupil, Karl Weidinger (1928), who argued that the early church took over and "Christianised" the scheme of Stoic ethics on duties ("offices"), mediated to them by Hellenistic Judaism. Wagener (1994, 16–18) summarises briefly the challenges and modifications to the thesis concerning the Stoic background. Some scholars argued for a Jewish background (e.g. earlier E. Lohmeyer, later also J. E. Crouch), while others held the Household Codes to be of Christian origin (e.g. K. H. Rengstorf; L. Goppelt even ar-

---

[12] To name but a few: a) articles: David Balch 1988, 1992a, 1992b (*ANRW* II.26.1), Peter Fiedler 1986, John Fitzgerald 1992, Leonhard Goppelt 1973, L. Hartman 1988, Ehrhard Kamlah 1976, Franz Laub 1986, Hermann von Lips 1994, Dieter Lührmann 1981, Winsome Munro 1972, Wolfgang Schrage 1975, Eduard Schweizer 1977, 1979; Georg Strecker 1989, Klaus Thraede 1980; b) special treatments in commentaries: Ernest Best 1998 (519–27), Peter O'Brien 1982 (214–19), James Dunn 1996 (242–46), Ulrich Luz 1998 (233–36), Michael Wolter 1993 (194–98); c) monographs: David Balch 1981, James Crouch 1972, Marlis Gielen 1990. – For a recent history of research on the Household Codes, see Johannes Woyke 2000. Woyke discusses in chronological order research on the following themes (p. 11): "1. Begriff und Texte der neutestamentlichen 'Haustafeln'; 2. Gattungsgeschichtliche Hintergründe; 3. 'Sitz im Leben' und Funktion; 4. Das spezifisch Christliche; 5. Kirchen- und theologiegeschichtliche Einordnung; 6. Theologisch-hermeneutischer Ertrag".

guing for an origin in Jesus' teaching; D. Schroeder, too, belongs to the latter group, though he also holds that the structure, address-instruction-motivation, has its origin in the apodictic laws of the OT).

Wagener then discusses a new thesis at more length, since it has convinced the majority of scholars of our time (1994, 19–54). This thesis was first put forward by David Balch, who argued that Plato and Aristotle set out the theme of *economics*, tasks related to the management of a household and its properties, as an integrated part of their discussion of the state (Wagener, p. 18, fn. 22, notes that Balch's original thesis from 1974 was published in a modified form in 1981). Plato emphasised the significance of the relationship between rulers and ruled ones, with a reference to pairs like parents and children, masters and slaves, men and women, old and young etc. He dealt with the relationships belonging to a household (marriage, slaves, children) in his *Laws* VI.771E–VII.824C. Aristotle criticised Plato's view on the direct analogy between the state and the household (*Pol.* I.1253b.1–14). In Aristotle's view, the household (οἶκος) is the most important kernel of the state. Balch has succeeded in showing a continuation of Aristotle's influence in the realm of economics right up to the NT times (the 1974 microfilm edition of the thesis was not available to me, but the texts are set out convincingly in the 1981 edition as well).

Though Wagener points to a number of works that have developed and modified the thesis concerning the background of the Household Codes in the genre of economics (e.g. K. Thraede, F. Laub, D. C. Verner), it suffices here to point to one more contribution to the field, since, in our opinion, it has proved most influential to the present day. Dieter Lührmann has rightly emphasised that the main significance of the Aristotelian discussion of the household lies in the fact that it provides us with a tradition that incorporates the two key characteristics of the Household Codes in Ephesians and Colossians, i.e. the three-part structure and the reciprocal relationship in which both partners in the pairs are mentioned (1981, 86).[13] Although Xenophon's *Oeconomicus* and the work of Pseudo-Aristotle (the name given to the otherwise unknown author indicates that the work is falsely attributed

---

[13] The date of D. Lührmann's article is given in later works as 1981, as a convenient shorthand reference to the 1980–81 volume of *NTS*; in actual fact the article appeared in the Autumn edition in 1980. I note that his earlier article on "slaves" in the Christian congregation (1975) discusses the relationship of the Household Codes to works on economics (see esp. pp. 71–83). Though Gal 3:28 does not address the child-parent relationship, Lührmann's observation is worth noting: Paul probably did not formulate the sentence ad hoc when writing the letter, since it has a well-defined structure and it is used as a proof of a thought. Thus we can suppose it was already known to the Galatians (p. 57).

2. Texts concerning real child-parent relationships

to Aristotle) unfortunately do not address the relationship between parents and children; nevertheless they belong to the same genre. We have seen in the first chapter that Xenophon's *Oeconomicus* is the first representative of this genre. Pseudo-Aristotle depends on Xenophon's and Aristotle's works (see also D. Lührmann, 1981, 85).[14] Aristotle's *Politics* is worth quoting so that the similarity to the Household Codes (as well as the differences) can be seen more easily.

In Book One of his *Politics*, Aristotle first establishes that the "household" (οἶκος) is the smallest unit from which (through the formation of a village from several households and then through the association of villages) the state is formed (*Pol.* I.2. 1252b);[15] "the association formed according to nature for the satisfaction of the purposes of every day is a household". Then he describes the relationships in this most significant kernel of the society in these words (*Pol.* I.3. 1253b):

> Now that it is clear from what parts the state is composed, it is essential to speak of household-management first [ἀναγκαῖον πρῶτον περὶ οἰκονομίας εἰπεῖν]; ... we have first to investigate each thing in terms of its smallest elements, and the first and smallest parts of a household are: master and slave, husband and wife, father and children [πρῶτα δὲ καὶ ἐλάχιστα μέρη οἰκίας δεσπότης καὶ δοῦλος, καὶ πόσις καὶ ἄλοχος, καὶ πατὴρ καὶ τέκνα]. So we should have to examine what each one of these three is, and what sort of thing it ought to be. They are: the skill 'of a master' [δεσποτική], 'marital' skill [γαμική] (there is no term for the union of man and woman), and thirdly 'procreative' skill [τεκνοποιητική] (this has not been given a name peculiar to itself).

This quotation clearly names the same three relationships found in the Household Codes in Ephesians and Colossians, though with some difference in the Greek wording (we note he himself adds that some of the terms had not been established before him). It is not as concise as the Codes in the Pauline Epistles, since Aristotle goes on to speak of these relations at great length. It is also significant that the pairs are named consistently from the point of view of the male head of the household, in his roles as master, husband, and father, whereas the "weaker" parts are addressed first in the Household Codes (see also Georg Strecker 1989, 349).[16]

---

[14] It is worth noting that Michel Foucault has devoted a chapter to the economics literature in his discussion of the theme of sexuality (1997, II/183–233). He discusses in detail the work of Xenophon, but from the point of view of the sexual relationship between husband and wife, and not our main interest, the child-parent relationship (pp. 194–210).

[15] I quote the translation made by T.J. Saunders (1995, pp. 2, 4, 18 in turn). The Greek text in square brackets is quoted from the edition published by W. D. Ross (1992, originally 1957, 2, 5, 22).

[16] Seneca's *Epistle* 94.1 mentions "one department of philosophy" (to use James Dunn's

Aristotle distinguishes among the various kinds of authority of the one and the same head of the house in his different roles. Here he uses the term πατρική as the skill in the relationship to children. (I note that this variant exists also at the above quotation, rejected by W. D. Ross probably as an assimilation to our present passage, τεκνοποιητική being the more difficult reading.) Aristotle writes concerning the head of the house (*Pol.* I.12. 1259a–b):

> For he rules over wife and children, over both as free persons, but not with the same style of rule [καὶ γὰρ γυναικὸς ἄρχει καὶ τέκνων, ὡς ἐλευθέρων μὲν ἀμφοῖν, οὐ τὸν αὐτὸν δὲ τρόπον τῆς ἀρχῆς]: over a wife he rules in the manner of a statesman [πολιτικῶς], over children in that of a king [βασιλικῶς]; for by nature the male is more fitted to be in command than the female [τό τε γὰρ ἄρρεν φύσει τοῦ θήλεος ἡγεμονικώτερον], unless conditions in some respect contravene nature; and the elder and fully grown is more fitted than the younger and underdeveloped.... Rule over children is royal, for the begetter is ruler by virtue both of affection and of seniority, and this is a species of royal rule.

We note here the view that wife and children are both "free". The Greek terminology of the "male and female" differs from the previous passage (and is nearer to Gal 3:28).

There is a major difficulty in determining the origin of the Household Codes: although there are major similarities in the constituent parts to the literature on economics (especially to the passages in Aristotle), there is no parallel to the Codes in their present form, as we have them in Colossians and Ephesians. Ulrich Luz (1998, 234) rightly affirms that only Col 3:18–4:1 and Eph 5:21–6:9 should be called a Household Code (1 Pet 2:18–3:7 takes over elements of a household code in a developed form; texts concerning warnings to office-bearers, e.g. 1 Tim 2:8–15; 6:1–2; Titus 2:1–10, should not be seen as examples of this genre).[17] He concludes that the economics literature can be seen as the background to the Household

---

term, 1996, 243) which is concerned to "advise how a husband should conduct himself toward his wife, or how a father should bring up his children, or how a master should rule his slaves", but only in Dionysius of Halicarnassus (*Roman Antiquities* 2.25.4–26.4) do we have an example of the duties of wives mentioned before those of husbands and duties of children before those of fathers. (Dunn points out that the same three pairs appear in the same order as in Colossians.)

[17] For a similar delimitation of the texts to be called a Household Code (in German scholarship referred to by the term coined by Martin Luther, *Haustafel*), see also Georg Strecker 1989, 349. For a different view, see Ernest Best (1998, 521) who holds that texts with a reference outside the household should be covered as well, and that the name of the genre should be wider. He suggests e.g. the term "social code" (but adopts the generally accepted term, *Haustafel*). – For a discussion of the Household Codes in Hungarian, see Sándor Cserháti 1978, 148–64.

2. Texts concerning real child-parent relationships 169

Codes, but the Codes are a new genre because they are shorter and all the members are addressed in them (p. 235). Luz argues that the Household Code as a literary form may be a Christian creation, originating in the Pauline congregations. In this he follows Marlis Gielen's thesis (1990).

Scholars differ in their views on the authorship of and the relationship between the letters to the Ephesians and to the Colossians. For our theme, it is not significant whether they are to be ascribed to Paul, as more traditional scholarship affirmed, or whether they are to be regarded as Deuteropauline Epistles, i.e. as written by a disciple of the apostle Paul.[18] This distinction would make a difference only if we found that Paul's views on the child-parent relationship could be shown to be modified when compared to those generally regarded as authentic today. We shall meet some difference in detail, but we shall see that both Paul and the Household Codes in Ephesians and Colossians affirm a child-parent relationship in which children are expected to honour their parents. James Dunn's view on the authorship of Colossians can be applied to the theme of the child-parent relationship as well (1996, 39):

> At all events, whatever the precise circumstances of its composition, Colossians strongly suggests that the distinctions between a Paul who himself changed in style and developed in theology, a Paul who allowed someone else to interpret his thought and concerns, and a Pauline disciple writing shortly after Paul's death but seeking to be faithful to what he perceived would be the master's thought and concerns in the situation envisaged in the letter become of uncertain and diminishing significance.[19]

Even if either or both of the two epistles are to be ascribed to disciples of Paul, their date remains within the first two or three Christian generations, i.e. within the first century A.D. Thus the letters witness to the view of the early church in the same period as the Gospels.[20]

---

[18] I note two interesting cases where a scholar changed his mind with regard to the authorship of Ephesians: Heinrich Schlier first held it was not by Paul, then wrote a commentary on the assumption of Pauline authorship (1965); Andrew Lincoln first held it was Pauline then wrote a commentary on the assumption that the letter was written by a disciple of Paul (1990, see his "autobiographical note" on p. lx). The majority of scholars regard both Colossians and Ephesians as deuteropauline (see, for example, Hans Hübner 1993, 30).

[19] For a similar view, see Dale Allison 1998, 60, fn. 212 (who also refers to John Barclay 1997, 35).

[20] As regards Colossians, it is worth noting that there are arguments for a dating in the time of Paul even if it is ascribed to a disciple of his; this view of Eduard Schweizer has recently been reaffirmed by James Dunn who inclines to the view that this is "the last Pauline letter to be written with the great apostle's explicit approval" (1996, 41; see also his reference to Schweizer at p. 38, fn. 47). Ulrich Luz favours the hypothesis that Colossians was written by a co-worker of Paul, although he emphasises that it is impossible to come to a conclusive decision on the matter (1998, 190).

Turning to the discussion of the Household Codes in Colossians and Ephesians, we note the great similarity in wording. It is possible to argue that there is a literary dependence between the two epistles; the majority of scholars argue for the thesis that the author of Ephesians used Colossians (see e.g. H. Hübner 1997, 253; A. T. Lincoln 1990, 354; U. Luz 1998, 174; M. Wolter 1993, 195). If so, then they are not independent witnesses to the genre; however, the structure of the Code is so clearly defined that it has to be regarded as a separate genre even if we have only one example of it and another one depending on the original.

Since our primary aim is not that of determining the history of dependency, we focus on the traditions (similarities as well as differences) in the two sources. With that aim in view, it is appropriate that both texts should be quoted first, and then our observations and notes to them can follow.

Adopting the working hypothesis that Colossians is presupposed by Ephesians (so also G. Strecker 1989, 350), we quote them in this sequence.[21] We quote all three pairs (without the long extension on the theme of husbands and wives in Ephesians and the details of slaves' duties in both letters), but then we focus our discussion on the one pair relating to our main project. In Colossians 3:18–4:1 we read (omitting vv. 23–25):

Wives, be subject to your husbands, as is fitting in the Lord. (19) Husbands, love your wives, and do not be harsh with them. (20) Children, obey your parents in everything, for this pleases the Lord. (21) Fathers, do not provoke your children, lest they become discouraged. (22) Slaves, obey in everything those who are your earthly masters, not with eyeservice, as men-pleasers, but in singleness of heart, fearing the Lord.... (4:1) Masters, treat your slaves justly and fairly, knowing that you also have a Master in heaven.

There are only a few variant readings in the Greek text of this passage. In vv. 18–19, NA27 has as main text "be subject to husbands" (which, in the Greek, could be taken in a wider sense "be subject to men") and "love wives [or: women]", whereas some MSS make it explicit that the passage is about "*your* men [i.e. husbands]" and "*your* women [i.e. wives]". This explanatory addition of the genitive is naturally followed in the above translation in the RSV though the very genre of the Household Code probably signalled to the first addresses that the original shorter text was unambiguous: they must have known that we are in the realm of a household, and that the men and women addressed here are addressed in their roles as husbands and

---

[21] I note that Ernest Best argues in his recent commentary on Ephesians that the Household Code cannot be proven to be taken over from Colossians. He holds that the author of Ephesians "is as likely to have drawn it directly from the tradition as from Colossians" (1998, 523).

2. Texts concerning real child-parent relationships

wives (cf. Murray Harris's reference to the "present context" as decisive in this case, 1991, 178).

There is one significant variant in the verse that is most relevant to our discussion: some MSS have a definite article in the dative before "Lord" ("this is pleasing *to* the Lord", cf. the RSV translation above), whereas NA27 print as the main text "this is pleasing *in* the Lord" (τοῦτο γὰρ εὐάρεστόν ἐστιν ἐν κυρίῳ). The former is nearer to what one would expect in general ethical advice in the environment of the New Testament, whereas the latter is a phrase repeatedly used in Pauline texts.[22] Murray Harris (1991, 180) argues that εὐάρεστον implies a dative ("to God", or more likely, "to the Lord") which is left out elliptically before the verb "is". He accepts ἐν κυρίῳ at the end of the verse, and offers the following paraphrase: "for ... such behavior pleases the Lord ... and befits those who belong to him (ἐν κυρίῳ)."

The Household Code in Ephesians reads as follows (5:21–6:9, omitting 5:23–24; 26–33; 6:6–8):

Be subject to one another out of reverence for Christ. (22) Wives, be subject to your husbands, as to the Lord.... (25) Husbands, love your wives, as Christ loved the church and gave himself up for her, ... (6:1) Children, obey your parents in the Lord, for this is right. (2) "Honor your father and mother" (this is the first commandment with a promise), (3) "that it may be well with you and that you may live long on the earth." (4) Fathers, do not provoke your children to anger, but bring them up in the discipline and instruction of the Lord. (5) Slaves, be obedient to those who are your earthly masters, with fear and trembling, in singleness of heart, as to Christ; ... (9) Masters, do the same to them, and forbear threatening, knowing that he who is both their Master and yours is in heaven, and that there is no partiality with him.

Verse 21 introduces the whole Household Code as a "title" (U. Luz 1998, 170).[23] In the verse most relevant to our theme (6:1), there is one significant

---

[22] G. Strecker (1989, 352) notes that the expression "fearing the Lord" in Col 3:22 seems to be "a genuinely Jewish" phrase, and adds that Lohmeyer argues for a Jewish background for all the references to the "Lord" in the passage. Even if it might be true as a "background", the addressees of Colossians must have seen in the repeated references to the "Lord" a "Christological" motivation (so e.g. Murray Harris 1991, 177).

[23] Ernest Best (1998, 523) argues that v. 21 differs from the Code in form and content and thus is not part of it (*pace* Marlis Gielen 1990, 204–206). – There are textual variants at the end of the verse, giving different reasons for the duty: "in fear of *Christ*", or of "Jesus Christ", "Christ Jesus", the "Lord", or "God". Verse 21 begins with a participle which here carries the meaning of the imperative, "be subject" (as is possible in Greek). This is proved by an addition in v. 22: some MSS (including the Codex Sinaiticus), add "should be subject", the same verb in the imperative: ὑποτασσέσθωσαν, and the Byzantine "majority" in the second person plural, ὑποτάσσεσθε (NA27 prints the elliptical variant: "wives to their own husbands in the Lord", supported by P⁴⁶ and the Codex Vaticanus). – In v. 25, as in the parallel in Colossians, some MSS add "your" or "your own" to "wives [women]".

variation in the textual tradition: "in the Lord" (printed in the RSV translation above) is put in square brackets by the editors of NA27, since it is not present in the Codex Vaticanus, the first hand text of Codex Bezae and some more codices (and in some quotations in the Fathers). The bracketed main text in NA27, ἐν κυρίῳ, is supported by P[46], Codices Sinaiticus and Alexandrinus, the first corrector of the Codex Bezae and many other MSS including the Byzantine "majority" text. Andrew Lincoln argues that since the text is not identical with the form of the reason (*as* to the Lord; *as* to Christ) given in Eph 5:22 and 6:5, it is not likely that it was inserted in order to conform to these verses (1990, 395; he concludes his detailed discussion of the evidence by favouring the inclusion of ἐν κυρίῳ). We shall see below that this Christological motivation distinguishes the early Christians from their environment only in that the motivation is bound to the person of Jesus; nevertheless, inasmuch as Christ was a divine being in the eye of the writer and addressees, there is a similarity with the "environment": God serves as a ground for the duty.

We can observe the following similarities and differences in the wording of the pair that concerns the child-parent relationship (Col 3:20–21; Eph 6:1–4). Both versions address children first: they begin with the phrase "children"; in the Greek the nominative case with the definite article is used for the vocative (see e.g. Peter O'Brien 1982, 224). The duty of obedience is expressed by the same verb in the second person plural, ὑπακούετε. Both have "parents" as the collective object of obedience, whereas in the reciprocal part of the pair only the "fathers" are addressed. Colossians has "to parents in everything", while Ephesians does not have κατὰ πάντα, but it adds the genitive: "to *your* parents" (Hans Hübner calls this a "stylistic improvement", 1997, 253). We shall return to this difference later.

Only Colossians has the above mentioned textual variant in the phrase giving the motivation ("for this is pleasing *in* the Lord", or, "... *to* the Lord"). Since Ephesians does not have the phrase "for this is pleasing" (τοῦτο γὰρ εὐάρεστόν ἐστιν), it is understandable that a second dative ("to the Lord") cannot follow after "to your parents"; accordingly, one stream of the textual tradition of Ephesians adds "in the Lord" as a motivation. The reason why this motivation is not an essential part of the structure is the presence of another motivation given in all the texts of Ephesians: "for this is right" (τοῦτο γάρ ἐστιν δίκαιον).

Only Ephesians quotes the Fifth Commandment as a reaffirmation of the duty of children. Ephesians has the additional remark that "this is the first commandment with a promise", as a motivation (6:2–3). Hübner observes that the text is almost identical with the Septuagint text, though the end of

Exod 20:12 (and Deut 5:16 which is slightly different) is missing after ἐπὶ τῆς γῆς (1997, 253).

Also the reciprocal part, in which "fathers" are addressed, is shorter in Colossians. It begins with the nominative together with the definite article standing for the vocative, "Fathers!" In Ephesians, this phrase is preceded by the connecting "And ...". Both Colossians and Ephesians say what fathers should *not* do. In Colossians, the imperative, ἐρεθίζετε ("do not *provoke* your children") has a textual variant that parallels the verb in Ephesians (with a very similar meaning): παροργίζετε ("do not provoke your children to anger"). Colossians and Ephesians differ in the closing phrase of the pair: Colossians gives a reason from the perspective of the children ("lest they become discouraged", ἵνα μὴ ἀθυμῶσιν), while Ephesians names a further duty of the father: "but bring them up in the discipline and instruction of the Lord" (ἀλλὰ ἐκτρέφετε αὐτὰ ἐν παιδείᾳ καὶ νουθεσίᾳ κυρίου).

Georg Strecker (1989, 356) has collected in groups the sources of parallels to the key characteristics of the Household Codes in Colossians and Ephesians.
1. The threefold structure is paralleled in: Aristotle *Pol.* I.3 (1253b, 4–14); Seneca *Ep.* 94.1; Pseudo-Phocylides 175–227.
2. There appear pairs in: Xenophon *Oec.* 1.7; Aristotle *Pol.* I.2 (1252a, 25–31); I.3 (1253b, 15); I.5 (1254b, 13–14); Philo *Hypoth.* 7.14; *Spec.* 2.226–227; Seneca *Ep.* 94.1; *Ben.* 2.18 (father – son, husband – wife); Stobaeus *Flor.* (Anthol.) 4.27.20. There are only a few examples in which the "weaker part", i.e. the representative of lower social status precedes in sequence the "stronger part": slaves are mentioned before their masters in Seneca *Ben.* 3.18; Philo *Decal.* 165 (in *Decal.* 167 the young are mentioned before the old); Epictetus *Diatr.* II.x.7 (son – father); Josephus *C. Ap.* 2.201 (wife – husband).
3. A reciprocal relationship can be found in: Aristotle *Pol.* I.4 (1254a, 11–13); I.6 (1255b, 9.12–14); Philo *Decal.* 165–167; Seneca *Ben.* 2.18; Stobaeus *Flor.* (Anthol.) 4.27.20.
4. The apodictic form is paralleled in: Xenophon *Oec.* 1.7; Pseudo-Phocylides 175–227.
5. The context of the "house" appears in: Xenophon *Oec.* 1.7; Aristotle *Pol.* I.3 (1253b, 15); and also the role of a husband, father, and master of a slave (in the first category, mentioned above) presupposes this context because these are the roles of the head of a household.

On the basis of these parallels, Strecker rightly concludes that only the concise form of the Household Codes in Colossians and Ephesians is not paralleled in this literature (1989, 357). Thus the actual Codes as they appear in the NT must be Christian creations (so also U. Luz 1998, 235), though almost all elements of them have a pre-history. On the basis of what we have seen in the chapters on the environment, it can be argued that the Household Codes fit well into the pagan and Jewish context of early Christianity. Apart from the formal parallels seen above we can observe similarities in terms of content as well. We shall refer to them when we now add some exegetical notes in relation to our main theme.

The very fact that all the members of a household are addressed in the Codes implies that the early Christian congregations gathered in houses.[24] The richer members of the congregations received the congregations into their homes for services of worship.[25] This is supported by archeological evidence which shows that until the third century there were probably no separate buildings built as "temples" by Christians.[26] The host as well as other members of the congregation may have had families and so the gathering comprised adults and children. Ernest Best argues that the Codes in Ephesians and Colossians imply "wholly Christian households", since the problems arising from a difference in faith between wife and husband, child and parent, slave and master are not addressed (1998, 524).

The Greek text does not sspecify the age of the children addressed. The word τέχνον (in the Codes in the plural) refers to the relationship. Indeed, on the basis of evidence from the environment, it is likely that not only little children are being addressed here, because the quotation of the Fifth Commandment suggests the duty of providing for older parents. Best (1998, 563) rightly observes that the children addressed "must have been old enough to understand what is said, but they could have been small, sub-

---

[24] See U. Luz 1998, 235. He even points to the likelihood that it must have happened frequently that full "families" turned to the Christian faith, as it is witnessed in 1 Cor 1:16; 16:15; Acts 16:15.31–34; 18:8. On the latter theme, see also Gerhard Delling 1964–65; Joachim Jeremias 1958; David Matson, 1996; Craig de Vos 1995.

[25] Recently, there has appeared a rapidly growing body of literature on the theme of household congregations (churches). See e.g. the following monographs: Vincent Branick 1989, Hans-Josef Klauck 1981, 1992c, Carolyn Osiek and David Balch 1997, David Verner 1983; and articles (or chapters in books): Pieter Craffert 1992 (pp. 176–216), 1998, Marlis Gielen 1986, Joachim Gnilka 1983, Hans-Josef Klauck 1989, Thorwald Lorenzen 1987; John Reumann 1998.

[26] For a monograph summarising the archeological evidence, see Michael White 1990. See esp. his ch. 5 entitled "From House Church to Church Building", pp. 102–139, in which he argues that in the second and third centuries Christians adapted (renovated) former private houses into places of worship, which he calls "domus ecclesiae" (117–23). White concludes that (p. 147): "Throughout the first three centuries the changing status and composition of Christian groups necessitated ongoing adaptation seen architecturally in the process of development from house church to domus ecclesiae and to aula ecclesiae."

teenagers, or older teenagers and young adults." He also notes that "in later rabbinic Judaism sermons were delivered to adult children on the theme of obedience to parents."[27]

The fact that children are addressed first does not mean that the patriarchal structure of the society is challenged. We have seen parallels to this phenomenon also in the environment. The Household Code shows that the role of the father remains dominant when only "fathers" are mentioned in the reciprocal part as responsible for the children, though mothers played a more important role in children's upbringing, at least in the first seven years of their children's life (as we have seen in the environment, see e.g. Pseudo-Phocylides 208; see also James Dunn 1996, 250).

Obedience to parents is given in the Code as a summary of children's duty. Both Colossians and Ephesians refer to this duty by the term ὑπακούετε, the same verb being used also in the third pair concerning slaves, while the duty of wives in the first pair is expressed by the term "be subject", or, "be submissive" (ὑποτάσσεσθε). Ephesians refers to the Fifth Commandment as to the duty of children, and so it seems that the call to "honour" father and mother is another way of saying "be obedient to your parents". This duty is the main duty of a child, and at the same time it can be seen as a general duty that is to be acted out by fulfilling a number of other duties, as we have seen in the environment.

Only Colossians adds "in everything" (κατὰ πάντα, though missing in P[46] and some other MSS). This seems to imply that there is no limit to be recognized in carrying out the duty. However, we recall that texts in the environment also affirmed this duty as an overall expectation, yet they could name exceptions when the behaviour of the father was unworthy. It is worth noting that Epictetus (*Diatr.* II.x.7) uses this expression ("be obedient in everything"), though we have seen that he also affirms that a philosopher's commitment to the "good" has to be given priority. As the Household Code names only the main duty in each case, it should not surprise us that it does not deal with the question of limits. Dunn rightly says (1996, 250):

---

[27] E. Best (p. 563, fn. 1) points to S. Safrai's chapter entitled "House and Family" in the major work edited by Safrai and others on "The Jewish People in the First Century". Safrai writes concerning "tannaitic and other Jewish literature" (1976, II/771): "this preaching was usually directed not towards young children, but rather towards adult men and women, including those who were married, who were obliged to care for and honour their aging parents." However, the Household codes in Colossians and Ephesians probably refer to children "who are growing up" (P.T. O'Brien 1982, 224), since the warning to the fathers mentioned in the Codes corresponds best to this age: "bring them up" (Eph 6:4), "lest they [the children] become discouraged" (Col 3:21; see U. Luz's term, "heranwachsende Kinder", 1998, 236).

The assumption is that parents, acting as parents, will deal wisely and kindly with their children (cf. Matt. 7:9–11/Luke 11:11–13).... The counsel here, of course, does not envisage situations where the norm is breached by the parents or where a higher loyalty might need to be invoked (as in Luke 14:26).

If Colossians was used by Ephesians, it is difficult to find a reason why the reference to "everything" is omitted in the latter. It is not likely to be a sign that the author wanted to make the duty "milder" (so also E. Best, 1998, 565, who finds here another indication that Ephesians used the tradition of the Code independently of Colossians). It is probable that the author of Ephesians used the Code as implying general validity, thus the addition "in everything" was not necessary to be made explicit. Ephesians also refers to a commandment, by that implying an overall validity of the duty. We can argue that the Codes were written with the purpose of stating the duty, and the question of limits was not addressed in them.

On the surface it seems that the motivation (or reason) given for the duty is the only "Christian" characteristic of the Code (apart from the actual final form of the whole Code, mentioned earlier). I suggest that the reference to the "Lord" in the Codes implies the following meaning: "Christians (people and congregations in the Lord) adhere to this overall rule observed by pagans and Jews alike". The following observations point to this interpretation.

Recently, a growing number of scholars have come to the conclusion that one of the main aims of the Household Codes was the attempt to show to the environment that Christians did not want to present a threat to the "state", or in other words, to the wider society around them. This reason may be more emphatic in the case of 1 Peter (as David Balch has argued in his monograph of 1981, esp. pp. 81–116), but it can be argued that this was also a reason for the inclusion of the Household Code in Colossians and Ephesians (see e.g. A. T. Lincoln 1990, 357, who accepts this proposal as convincing, in spite of the different hypothesis put forward by Klaus Berger).[28] Even if it is acknowledged that the Codes regulate the life of the congregations (an aspect rightly emphasised by Michael Wolter 1993, 201), this does not exclude the possibility of a wider apologetic purpose. Andrew Lincoln has argued that, in the environment of early Christianity, "religious groups that attracted women and slaves were seen as particularly likely to be subversive of social stability" (1999, 101). Thus Christians may have used the Household Codes in order to respond to such suspicion and accusations. James

---

[28] For a critical presentation of the different nuances in K. Berger's two major contributions in which he attempts to locate the background to the Household Codes in Hellenistic gnomic literature, put forward in an *ANRW* article and in his *Formgeschichte* (both published in 1984), see Ulrike Wagener 1994, 54–61.

2. Texts concerning real child-parent relationships

Dunn (1996, 250) adds that Colossians 3:20b ("for this is pleasing in the Lord") uses the term εὐάρεστον, which refers to "pleasing to God" in the only two LXX uses of the word: Wis 4:10, 9:10. He also points to a passage in Philo which makes a similar point (p. 251; Philo *Mut.* 40): "If you honor parents ... you will be pleasing (εὐαρεστήσεις) before God." Thus Dunn on the aim of the Code in Colossians concludes (1996, 251):

> Here, in other words, we can recognize a double apologetic slant in the parenesis: assurance to influential outsiders that the Christian message was not subversive and to Colossian Jews that the new movement was still faithful to Jewish praxis and ideals.

The same conclusion can be reached regarding the longer parallel version in Ephesians. Ernest Best has argued that the expression "in the Lord" (ἐν κυρίῳ, both its presence and omission is well supported by MSS) is more likely a later addition, since, "if originally present it is difficult to see why it should have been omitted" (1998, 564). He draws the conclusion: "If the phrase is not read, then the text says nothing more than any Greco-Roman or Jewish moralist would have said." This point is supported by the two other reasons given in the Code in Ephesians: "for this is just" (δίκαιον, with a "general moral connotation", Best 564; he also points to Epictetus I.xxii.1 and II.xvii.6, p. 565), and the Fifth Commandment (as referring to the Jewish Law). Concerning the latter, Best argues that since it is not the "first" commandment with a promise in sequence (for example, the Second Commandment has a promise, too), Ephesians' expression, πρώτη, might be taken in a figurative sense "as indicating a pre-eminent commandment, one of great importance because it is included in the Decalogue and has a promise" (1998, 567). Ulrich Luz argues that even if the author used "first" in the sense of first in a sequence (because he had not taken Exod 20:6 as a promise or simply had not thought of it), the Fifth Commandment was regarded in Judaism as a "besonders wichtiges und schweres Gebot" (1998, 174). Whatever the meaning of "first", the very presence of the quotation of the commandment shows that, according to the author of Ephesians, Christians were expected to obey their parents because they were expected to observe the Fifth Commandment as well.

Finally, we note that the promise quoted from the Fifth Commandment, "that it may be well with you and that you may live long (ἔσῃ) on the earth" (Exod 20:12 and Deut 5:16 have ἵνα ... γένῃ), is a motivation (reason for the duty) from God's law, implying a reward from God. At the same time, it might point to the view we have met in the environment (see especially Philo's exposition of the Fifth Commandment as discussed in our third chapter) that children honouring their parents could expect that their children will honour them. In practical terms: they can expect a long life because their own children will care for them just as they honour their parents by caring for them in their old age. Though not explicit in the Decalogue, on the basis of the parallels in the environment, we can assume that the readers of the Household Code would have sensed this implication.

To sum up, the reference to the "Lord" in the Codes can be best explained in this way: Christians in Colossae and Ephesus should honour their parents because this behaviour is expected from the followers of Jesus. If this exposition is true, then we have found implicit evidence outside the Gospels that the early Christians did not think Jesus broke the Fifth Commandment, in spite of the tensions his itinerant life-style (and the unbelief of his family during his earthly life) had brought about. They held that Jesus shared the expectation of his environment that children should honour and obey their parents; that is why they expected the same from his followers.

c) The Pastoral Epistles

Our following examples are taken from the Pastoral Epistles (1–2 Timothy and Titus) which are regarded as pseudonymous, i.e. not written by Paul, by the majority of present day scholars.[29] We shall see that the household imagery presented in them is similar to the circumstances envisaged in the Household Codes in Colossians and Ephesians, although there are differences in some aspects as well.[30] If the Pastoral Epistles are not by Paul, they represent Pauline tradition. (For convenience sake, I adopt the usage found in the letters and refer to Paul as the writer.) We observe the normative tone of these letters, presented as Paul's instructions to congregations led by his converts (whom he calls his "children").

We begin by briefly mentioning two texts that condemn behaviour that turns against parents in a violent way or by disobedience. In 1 Tim 1:9–10,

---

[29] See e.g. Lewis Donelson 1986, Udo Schnelle 1996; for a recent commentary based on the hypothesis of Pauline authorship, see George Knight III 1992. James Miller (1997) argues that some parts of the Pastoral Epistles were written by Paul.

[30] William Strange (1996, 75) argues that the Pastoral Epistles "appear to take a rather different approach to the place of children in the Christian community" than the Household Codes in Colossians and Ephesians. He holds that children's discipleship is absent from the Pastorals, where children "have become part of their parents' discipleship" (p. 76). To this we may reply that the comparison is not entirely adequate, because the Pastoral letters do not have Household Codes (for example, Titus 2:1–10 is not of the same genre as the Codes in Colossians and Ephesians). On the other hand, we shall see that there are passages in the Pastoral Epistles where children's discipleship is implied; and conversely, the fact that children are explicitly addressed in Colossians and Ephesians does not mean that they were given a different (or more prominent) role in these congregations than was assumed in the Pastoral letters.

2. Texts concerning real child-parent relationships 179

there is a list of those against whom the law is applied. In verse 10, among the items of the vice list we find "murderers of fathers and murderers of mothers" (πατρολῴαις καὶ μητρολῴαις). It is worth noting, that these terms are preceded by offences against God ("unholy and profane", ἀνοσίοις καὶ βεβήλοις) and followed by offences against human beings, the next term being rather general: "manslayers" (ἀνδροφόνοις). Thus, the sequence presupposes the view that among human beings parents rank first; but they come after God. This is also in agreement with the order of the Ten Commandments. George Knight III (1992, 83) has argued that the elements of the list from the offence against parents onward form a "deliberate echo of the order of the second part of the Decalogue (Ex. 20:12–16)." He cautiously raises the possibility that the terms preceding the reference to father and mother may refer to the first part of the Decalogue; thus "unholy and profane" may correspond to offences against God's name and the Sabbath (p. 84).[31]

The terms πατρολῴας and μητρολῴας appear only here in the NT, and they are absent from the Septuagint. Knight (p. 85) argues that in their background may lie Exodus 21; accordingly, they speak probably of "striking" or "smiting" one's parents rather than of "slaying" (murdering) them. It is, however, clear that they are meant as a negative counterpart to honouring father and mother. These offences invoke punishment by the law. (We recall that we have already in the environment met this reason why this offence against parents should be avoided.)

The other expression that condemns children who fail to honour their parents appears in 2 Tim 3:2, again in a vice list (see Larry Yarbrough 1995, 130). Among the evil characteristics of people in the "last days" we read that they will be "disobedient to their parents" (γονεῦσιν ἀπειθεῖς, the same phrase as in Rom 1:30). Knight (1992, 431) observes that the reference to "disobedience" opens a sequence of eight terms beginning with an *alpha privativum* (negating some good quality), surrounding the only exception: διάβολοι. He argues: "It may well be placed first in this group as the first step, or the most basic violation, in these violations of natural order." The next phrase, "ungrateful" (ἀχάριστοι, replaced by a few MSS by the similarly sounding ἄχρηστοι), may be in connection with disobe-

---

[31] Jürgen Roloff (1988, 75–76) argues against this view: "gegen diese Annahme spricht neben dem Umstand, daß weder jüdisch-hellenistische noch ntl. Kataloge die erste Dekalogtafel aufnehmen, die Beobachtung, daß sich im NT nirgends ein Ansatz für eine einführung des Dekalogs als normative Größe in die Paränese findet." However, he observes also that: "Für den antiken Menschen stand Frevel gegen die Eltern dem Frevel gegen den Bereich des Göttlichen besonders nahe" (p. 76; in fn. 115 he points to Plato, *Phaed.* 113e, 114a, and *Pol.* 615c).

dience to parents as well: it may refer to failing to repay the debt children owe their parents.[32] 1 Timothy 5:4 is a further support for this interpretation, where the change to the plural in the subject of the verbs ("if a widow *has*"; "let *them* learn", though the latter is in the singular in some MSS) may indicate that it is probably the children who owe a return to their widowed parents:[33] "If a widow has children or grandchildren, let them first learn their religious duty (εὐσεβεῖν) to their own family and make some return to their parents; for this is acceptable in the sight of God."[34] The explicit religious motivation in this verse is implied also in the vice lists, since the vices listed are offences not only against nature and law, but (often inseparably from these two, as we have seen in the environment) also against God (see e.g. Eduard Schweizer 1979, esp. 196, 199).

The Pastoral Epistles lay an emphasis on the good order of the household in general and that office bearers in particular. According to the context, 1 Timothy 5:8 stresses the need that if widows have family members, these relatives should provide for them, but the verse formulates a general principle that may apply to every reader: "If any one does not provide for his relatives, and especially for his own family, he has disowned the faith and is worse than an unbeliever" (cf. also Titus 2:3–5).

As regards office bearers, one of the characteristics expected from them is that they look after their children well. This requirement may imply the expectation that their children should be obedient to them, because if a father is known to be able to raise obedient children, it can be anticipated that he would be a good "leader" in the congregation as well. The following verses support this interpretation: 1 Tim 3:4–5, a bishop "must manage his own household (τοῦ ἰδίου οἴκου) well, keeping his children submissive and respectful in every way (τέκνα ἔχοντα ἐν ὑποταγῇ, μετὰ πάσης σεμνότητος); (5) for if a man does not know how to manage his own household (εἰ δέ τις τοῦ ἰδίου οἴκου προστῆναι οὐκ οἶδεν), how can he care for God's

---

[32] Jerome Quinn and William Wacker (2000, 719–720) agree with this interpretation. They add that the next three vices may also be offences against parents: ἀνόσιοι, "'devoid of piety' (towards parents)"; ἄστοργοι "loveless"; ἄσπονδοι "without formal treaty", or "without a drink-offering" (their translations, p. 719).

[33] Jürgen Roloff (1988, 288) regards this as a possible interpretation, but he argues that "a widow" remains the subject of the verb in the plural as well: "der Übergang vom generischen Singular zum Plural ist als *constructio ad sensum* zu erklären".

[34] James Miller (1997, 84) argues that the abrupt change from the singular to plural subject points to a "lack of linguistic precision" which "suggests that materials have been removed from their original context." – For a discussion of the significance attributed by the author of the Pastoral Epistles to the raising up of children ("Kinderaufzucht" as opposed to "Kindesaussetzung"), see Ulrike Wagener 1994, esp. 178–86.

2. Texts concerning real child-parent relationships 181

church?" (cf. also 1 Tim 3:15 where "God's church" is also called "God's household"); 1 Tim 3:12, "Let deacons be the husband of one wife, and let them manage their children and their households well" (τέκνων καλῶς προϊστάμενοι καὶ τῶν ἰδίων οἴκων); Titus 1:6, elders (πρεσβύτεροι), and probably also a bishop (ἐπίσκοπος, see v. 7), can only be elected if they fulfil the following requirements: "if any man is blameless, the husband of one wife, and his children are believers and not open to the charge of being profligate or insubordinate" (τέκνα ἔχων πιστά, μὴ ἐν κατηγορίᾳ ἀσωτίας ἢ ἀνυπότακτα). Although "believer" is a possible translation, since the term πιστός occurs in the Pastoral Epistles with this meaning too (e.g. in 1 Tim 6:2), nevertheless, the expression can mean "faithful" (so e.g. in 2 Tim 2:2), and this is more probable here, since the following expressions in Titus 1:6b imply obedient, non-rebellious children (so also George Knight 1992, 289–90, who argues that the meaning of the phrase here is similar to that of τέκνα ἔχοντα ἐν ὑποταγῇ in 1 Tim 3:4).

We observe the "patriarchal structure" of the households and congregations implied by the emphasis on children's obedience in the Pastoral Epistles. William Strange (1996, 75) may be right in finding that: "Here the emphasis seems to fall, more emphatically than in Colossians or Ephesians, on a family which is governed by the father, and on children as objects of paternal control." Dieter Lührmann (1981, esp. 91–97) differentiates between the views in the Household Codes and the Pastoral Epistles when he argues concerning the later "phase" represented by the Pastorals (95): "Offenbar sind nun die Gemeinden größer und sozial ausdifferenzierter und damit die Probleme komplexer geworden. Aus den Haustafeln werden Gemeindeordnungen, die nun noch deutlicher die Gemeinde in Analogie zum οἶκος begreifen, z. B. mit der Aufforderung an einen Bischof, die οἰκονομία zu beherrschen (1 Tim. 3.4 f.)." For our main theme it is significant that the child-parent relationship is portrayed in the Pastoral Epistles as involving children's duties similar to those expected in the environment of the early Christians.

Like the Household Codes in Colossians and Ephesians, the set of admonitions and duties in the Pastoral Epistles serves two purposes: they regulate life in the Christian households (and in the house churches), and by doing so they also show to the environment that Christians share their basic expectations concerning the ethical conduct in the household, the kernel of the wider society.[35] Included in these shared expectations is children's duty to honour and obey their parents.

---

[35] For the latter point, see Lewis Donelson 1986, 177–83. He also argues that the Pastoral

3. Family imagery in a figurative sense

In this section we discuss texts in which family imagery appears in a figurative sense; these texts presuppose a certain view of the child-parent relationship both on the side of the writer and of the readers. Accordingly, our focus of interest lies in the question: What kind of a child-parent relationship was envisaged as normative by the authors (and first addressees) of these texts?

a) Undisputed Pauline letters

In Romans 16:13, in a long list of persons to be greeted, Paul mentions a certain Rufus, whose mother he also calls his own mother: "Greet Rufus, eminent in the Lord, also his mother and mine."[36] At the end of the verse there is a compressed expression in the Greek: an emphatic ἐμοῦ together with another genitive, added to the term "mother" (τὴν μητέρα αὐτοῦ καὶ ἐμοῦ). Peter Lampe (1987, 133) points out that such a structure appears only at Rom 1:12 again, thus putting it among the grammatical phenomena known from Romans 1–15 as genuinely Pauline. The verse can be translated like this: "Greet Rufus, the chosen (one) in the Lord, and greet his mother (who is) also mine."

Ulrich Wilckens (1982, III/133) notes that the long list of greetings in chapter 16 is not only unique to the Pauline Corpus, but also to the rest of the letters in the New Testament. He presents other scholars' arguments for the view that this chapter was originally a separate letter, given to Phoebe as a letter of support to be taken to Ephesus (1978, I/24–27), but he does not find the arguments convincing. Wilckens regards the chapter as an integral part of the original letter of Paul (p. 27; see also 1982, III/132). Whatever the origin of the chapter, there are many persons whom Paul personally knows, among them a mother and his son, Rufus.[37]

Epistles not only want to display the good order of their own communities, but also "use this standard of good order polemically" when the author says of his opponents "that they produce disorder and disharmony in the church" (178–79).

[36] For references pro and contra the possibility that this Rufus is the same as the one mentioned in Mark 15:21, see Thomas Schreiner 1998, 791. Schreiner remarks that: "If Mark's Gospel was written in Rome, the naming of the sons of Simon (Alexander and Rufus) by Mark would indicate that they were known in the Roman community."

[37] For a detailed discussion of the arguments (including the textual evidence) with the conclusion that Rom 16 was originally addressed to Rome as part of the letter, see Peter Lampe 1987, 124–35. He argues that the holder of the Latin name, Rufus, may have come from a free family in the East (pp. 152–53).

3. Family imagery in a figurative sense

Paul never refers to his earthly parents in a concrete way (see the autobiographical sections at Phil 3:3–6; Acts 21:3); he uses family imagery in a figurative sense here as well. Perhaps Paul was grateful for the loving care experienced from Rufus's mother. Thomas Schreiner suggests (1998, 793): "presumably Rufus's mother either helped Paul in a specific situation or ministered to him regularly at some point in his labors." Peter Lampe has a more concrete suggestion (1987, 153): "diese Charakterisierung lässt am ehesten an eine einem Haus vorstehende Matrone denken, die in dieser Funktion in der Lage war, den Apostel zu bewirten – zu 'bemuttern'." Although we do not know the reason why he calls her his mother, it is clear that Paul wants to describe a close relationship by alluding to the strong bond between a mother and her child. This supposes a high view of the role of a mother, and also the natural expectation that a son would love his mother and remain grateful for her care.

We do not know the reason why Paul is silent on the matter of his relationship to his parents, but it is worth recalling that we have argued even concerning the first itinerant followers of Jesus that their going away from home did not mean that they ceased to honour their parents (though it is possible that they had to suffer enmity from the side of their relatives who did not believe in Jesus). Thus this passage can be seen as a witness to Paul's high respect for mothers; he used this term to describe his own relationship to Rufus's mother, because he wanted to refer to an intimate relationship. His readers must have understood it in positive terms; perhaps even in the light of the Gospel tradition that the followers of Jesus will receive mothers and brethren a hundredfold. Whatever the reason why Paul cannot be near his real parents, he can call a senior lady, to whom he owes gratitude for provision, his "mother".

When referring to his relationship to those Christians whom he had served with the Gospel, Paul can apply the imagery of parenthood to himself. On occasion, he applies the picture of fatherhood (1 Thess 2:11), and even of the childbearing role of a mother (Gal 4:19; we shall return to both texts). There are also references that lead us to the realm of the household, though it is not certain whether parenting or nursing roles are in view (see e.g. 1 Thess 2:7 below). In 1 Corinthians 3:1–2 Paul refers to the addressees as "babes in Christ". Although the term νήπιος can stand as a counterpart to τέλειος (unexpressed here, but expressed in 14:20; see Wolfgang Schrage 1991, I/280), the reference to the Corinthians being fed with milk by Paul points here to the realm of the household where little children are nourished. Schrage observes that the reference to "milk" is purely positive as regards new-born Christians in 1 Pet 2:2, but it implies the need of growing up in Heb 5:12 and in our passage (pp. 279–80; he also gives references in Epictetus and Philo for the latter implication).[38]

We know that nurses were given the task of feeding little children in antiquity, but it is just as possible that the mother is in view as feeding her little infant with milk.[39] One can argue for a parental picture on the basis of the Corinthians' claim that they belong to Paul (v. 4); this may imply a child-parent relationship in a figurative sense between the congregation founded by Paul's preaching and between the apostle himself (see v. 6 where he says he had "planted" the congregation). Though 1 Cor 3:2 is in itself ambiguous, the context seems to favour interpreting this text as a reference to parents bringing up their children. I follow Wolfgang Schrage (1991, I/354, fn. 233), who understands this verse as using the metaphor of "mother". (I note that he holds the same for 1 Thess 2:7.)

This interpretation may be strengthened by 1 Cor 4:14–16, a passage that belongs to the same main unit (chs. 1–4). Here we read: "I do not write this to make you ashamed, but to admonish you as my beloved children. (15) For though you have countless guides in Christ, you do not have many fathers. For I became your father (ἐγὼ ὑμᾶς ἐγέννησα) in Christ Jesus through the gospel. (16) I urge you, then, be imitators of me." In other words, Paul expects the Corinthians to learn from him as from their father (note especially v. 16). Schrage rightly points out that the child-parent imagery implies an unchangeable relationship (1991, I/354): "Dieses Verhältnis ist unauswechselbar und behaftet beide ein für allemal. Keiner von beiden kann sich davon emanzipieren." The term "beloved children" is applied in the singular to Timothy in the same context, in v. 17 (otherwise it does not appear in the Pauline Corpus). Larry Yarbrough (1995, 132) says concerning 1 Corinthians 4: "The paternal imagery, ... bespeaks the intimate feelings Paul has for the Corinthians." These two texts, then, can be seen as further indirect evidence for Paul's positive view on the role of parents; and, accordingly, for his expectation that "children" should follow their parents' instructions.

---

[38] I note that Marion Soards (1999, 76) argues that νήπιος points to "immaturity that is incapable of spiritual understanding", i.e. to a "lack of understanding, not lack of growth". In this he follows the argument of J. Francis (*JSNT* 7 [1980], 41–60). – Contrast Richard Hays's affirmation (1997, 48): "The metaphors used here (adults vs. infants and solid food vs. milk) are stock language in relation to philosophical and religious instruction throughout the ancient world. The assumption is that spiritual progress can be graded and that a different sort of curriculum is appropriate to each level of maturity."

[39] Walter Grundmann (1958, 200) opts for the picture of a nurse ("Amme") as a background to 1 Cor 3:2, but he also points to 1QH VII.20ff where the Teacher of Righteousness, the likely author of the hymn, refers to himself as a father, mother, and nurse of his congregation. Grundmann interprets 1 Pet 2:2 and Heb 5:12 in the same way as W. Schrage, seen above.

3. Family imagery in a figurative sense

There are several further texts in which Paul uses family imagery to describe his relationship to the congregations he addresses. In 2 Corinthians 6 Paul urges the congregation to lead a life in accordance with the grace of God which had been extended to them (v. 1). Part of his argument is to point out the consequences of the apostolic ministry, with both its joys and its sorrows (vv. 3–10). Then he wants to influence the congregation by an appeal to his own feelings of love towards them, asking a similar return of feelings from them. In vv. 11–13 he writes: "Our mouth is open to you, Corinthians; our heart is wide. (12) You are not restricted by us, but you are restricted in your own affections. (13) In return – I speak as to children – widen your hearts also." In v. 13 Paul uses the same term, "children" (ὡς τέκνοις λέγω), as we have already seen in 1 Cor 4:14. Since the Greek term refers to a relationship, we can translate it as "my children" even thought there is no possessive pronoun in the Greek text. In this passage, Paul makes it clear that he uses a metaphor when he says "*as* to children". Yet it is at the same time significant that he addresses them as his own children. The immediate context refers to the "heart" (καρδία) and to "affections" (σπλάγχνα), both of them places of emotion. Perhaps it is not accidental that the following admonitions address the themes of relationship and fellowship: just as Paul regards the Corinthians as members of his household, they should be careful whom else they receive into that household circle.

Verses 11–13 can only be used as an argument by Paul, if Paul and his addressees share the view that children should honour their father, and this honour includes obedience to his advice. The idea of "return" (ἀντιμισθία) probably refers to the widespread expectation that children owe a debt to their parents: just as the parents provided for them when young, so they should repay that debt later on (so also O. L. Yarbrough 1995, 133). To adopt Paul's language here: as he widened his heart toward them, they, too, should widen their hearts to Paul, i.e. treat him as a person whose advice they regard as authoritative, i.e. worthy to be followed.

2 Corinthians 10–13 is recognised by most scholars as forming a unit within the letter (due to its change in both tone and content when compared with ch. 9 and the preceding chapters). Whether or not one adopts the view that chs. 10–13 comprised the "letter written in tears", thus to be placed before chs. 1–9 in time, or the view that they were written some time later than chs. 1–9 (Paul having received further news in the meantime), it is significant for our purposes that chs. 10–13 form a self-contained unit.[40] In chap-

---

[40] For a summary of the main views as regards the integrity of chs. 10–13 within 2 Corinthians, see Udo Schnelle 1996, 101–5 and 108–11. Schnelle (pp. 110–11) argues

ters 10–13, there is one passage that uses the child-parent imagery, and this opens up the possibility that this imagery might be understood as a background to other parts of the unit as well.

In 2 Corinthians 12:14–15 we read: "Here for the third time I am ready to come to you. And I will not be a burden, for I seek not what is yours but you; for children ought not to lay up for their parents, but parents for their children. (15) I will most gladly spend and be spent for your souls. If I love you the more, am I to be loved the less?" In verse 14b Paul uses the picture of parents laying up for their children, meaning "setting apart a fortune as a later inheritance" (οὐ γὰρ ὀφείλει τὰ τέκνα τοῖς γονεῦσιν θησαυρίζειν ἀλλὰ οἱ γονεῖς τοῖς τέκνοις, with a change in the order of some words in some MSS). This half-verse is an argument: from verse 14a (and from the connecting "for", γάρ) it is clear that Paul regards himself as a parent to the Corinthians who does not want to be a burden; rather, it is he who provides for his "children", i.e. the congregation. In this context the Greek term θησαυρίζειν points to the realm of inheritance (though Paul can use it in other ways, see Rom 2:5; 1 Cor 16:2).[41] Thus it is understandable that Paul speaks of the duty of parents only, though in other contexts he implies children's duty of "repaying the debt" (as in 2 Cor 6:13). Larry Yarbrough paraphrases Paul's thought in this way (1995, 137): "I am responsible for you, you are not responsible for me." If, perhaps, the Corinthians attacked Paul for not accepting their financial support (see 2 Cor 11:7–10), here "Paul uses the maxim to defend himself by reminding the Corinthians of his duties as their father." This reminds us of one of the reasons why children owe obedience to their parents: because they are going to inherit from them (see e.g. ch. 2, fn. 90).

We note that the following verse uses the language of mutual love (ἀγαπάω, 2 Cor 12:15b). This reminds us of the previous passage discussed above concerning the mutual widening of feelings of love (2 Cor 6:11–13). Paul's willingness to bear a sacrifice for the Corinthians may be an expression of paternal love as well (12:15a). Yarbrough paraphrases Paul's argument in this way (1995, 137): "If he became their father by bringing the gospel to the Corinthians, he fulfilled the duties of a father by supporting himself and, more importantly, by enduring deprivation and

---

for the second view above, accepting the possibility of a change of tone within the same letter.

[41] Larry Yarbrough (1995, 134) emphasises that the same usage can be found in Plutarch's *On the Love of Wealth* 526a. As further examples of "parents' obligation to provide an inheritance for their children", he mentions Philo *Moses* 2.245 and Musonius Rufus, *Should Every Child That Is Born Be Raised?* 100.15.

3. Family imagery in a figurative sense

hardship for their sakes. Their response, he states pleadingly, is to love him in return."

In the light of these verses, we may suggest that the same father-children relationship is implied in other parts of chs. 10–13 as well. For example, in 2 Cor 11:2 Paul writes: "I feel a divine jealousy for you, for I betrothed you to Christ to present you as a pure bride to her one husband." We have seen that in the environment of the NT it was a father's duty to decide whom his daughter should marry, and obedience was expected as a duty of the daughter. If we allow for the possibility that the Corinthian "correspondence" was so lively between Paul and the congregation that they could remember what the apostle wrote in an earlier letter, then we might suppose that from the beginning of their relationship they knew that Paul regarded himself as a father to them (see 1 Cor 4:15, or even 3:1–6 as we argued above). Against this background, we can suppose that, when reading (or hearing) 2 Cor 11:2, the Corinthians understood that Paul spoke with a father's concern and in a father's role. As Yarbrough has put it (1995, 133): Paul presents himself here as a "solicitous father". The Corinthians owed obedience to him rather than to the "false apostles" (cf. 2 Cor 11:13). Perhaps 2 Corinthians 10 is to be read against this background as well: Paul's repeated reference to the authority he can claim among the Corinthians may be seen as grounded in his relationship to them, i.e. in the relationship of a father to his children (cf. 2 Cor 10:1–2.8; also 2 Cor 13:10).[42]

Paul not only uses paternal images, but he can refer to himself also as the "mother" of his converts. In Gal 4:19–20 he writes: "My little children, with whom I am again in travail (οὓς πάλιν ὠδίνω) until Christ be formed in you! (20) I could wish to be present with you now and to change my tone, for I am perplexed about you."[43] These verses conclude a passage in which Paul refers to the intimate relationship between himself and the Galatians. He reminds them of the emotional reception the Galatians extended to him when he preached the gospel among them (Gal 4:12–16). After Paul had left, some people came who wanted to "shut the Galatians out" (v. 17), and turn their "zeal" away from Paul to themselves. In this central part of

---

[42] For the view that Paul acted out the role of the *paterfamilias* in relation to "the household of believers in Corinth", see Stephan Joubert 1995 (quotation at p. 217). Joubert argues a twofold thesis. On the hand, he holds that Paul played different roles that "served to symbolize and institutionalize his subordinate position as official emissary of the heavenly *paterfamilias*." On the other hand, Paul "also presented himself as earthly *paterfamilias* of the new community of believers."

[43] We note a variant reading that has the diminutive, τεκνία μου; NA27 prints τέκνα μου ("my children") as the main text (supported, for example, by the first hand of Codex Sinaiticus and by Codex Vaticanus).

the letter, Paul addresses the main problem of the Galatians, i.e. how they turned away from the gospel he had preached to them. Now he has to give them birth a second time, i.e. he brings them to a Christian life again. The reference to "birth-pains" is a most emotional reminder that the Galatians owe their Christian life to the apostle.[44] We note the personal argument using the imagery of a mother giving birth to her child, since it is even more significant in the light of the other occurrences of family images, where the role of the father appears more often in Paul's letters.[45] This usage should warn us against portraying Paul (only) in the role of the *paterfamilias*. The fact that he uses the image of the mother (and arguably that of a nurse) may suggest that he did not want to use parental images in a patronizing way; rather, his role as a "parent" of his converts puts his role of caring and providing for them in the foreground. It remains true, however, that he expects his "children" should return his loving feelings and obey his advice.

In the same chapter, in Gal 4:1–7, Paul uses the imagery of the process of inheriting as an argumentative analogy to the Christians' relationship to God. Paul refers to a minor being under guardians and stewards, probably until the time of his coming of age (v. 2); and he uses adoption terminology when referring to "sonship" (υἱοθεσία, v. 5).

It is significant that in the preceding passage Paul refers to people who are also known to us as members of a household relationship (3:28): slaves, and "male and female", probably implying also the most common sphere where these two become partners, the sphere of marriage. In Gal 3:29 the term "heirs" not only provides a connection to the next passage, but it implies the other members of a typical household: children. Galatians 3:28–29 reads: "There is neither Jew nor Greek, there is neither slave nor free, there is neither male nor female; for you are all one in Christ Jesus. (29) And if you are Christ's, then you are Abraham's offspring, heirs (κληρονόμοι) according to promise." Thus, though not in the form of a Code, these two verses speak of the people of God with expressions used also in the realm of the household. The passage that follows them continues the imagery.

In Gal 4:1–7 we read:

---

[44] James Dunn (1993, 239) points out that the imagery of "spiritual generation" was used in Hellenistic religion; and it was used "for the relationship between teacher and pupil" e.g. in Philo *Legat.* 58.

[45] James Dunn (1993, 240) observes that "talk of someone as 'born/begotten' from a male as from a woman was not uncommon" in antiquity (he points to 1QHª III, 7ff as an example), "so there is no need to postulate Paul's dependence here on hellenistic mysticism or Gnosticism."

3. Family imagery in a figurative sense 189

I mean that the heir, as long as he is a child (ἐφ' ὅσον χρόνον ὁ κληρονόμος νήπιός ἐστιν), is no better than a slave, though he is the owner of all the estate; (2) but he is under guardians and trustees until the date set by the father (ἀλλὰ ὑπὸ ἐπιτρόπους ἐστὶν καὶ οἰκονόμους ἄχρι τῆς προθεσμίας τοῦ πατρός). (3) So with us; when we were children (οὕτως καὶ ἡμεῖς, ὅτε ἦμεν νήπιοι), we were slaves to the elemental spirits of the universe. (4) But when the time had fully come, God sent forth his Son, born of woman, born under the law, (5) to redeem those who were under the law, so that we might receive adoption as sons. (6) And because you are sons, God has sent the Spirit of his Son into our hearts, crying, "Abba! Father!" (7) So through God you are no longer a slave but a son, and if a son then an heir.[46]

This passage addresses one of the key issues of the whole letter: the role played by the law in the relationship between Christians and God. However, this is achieved in an indirect way, through an analogy. James Dunn sums up the main thrust of the imagery of minors (νήπιοι) and slaves in Gal 4:1–11 as follows (1993, 209): "to submit now to the rule of the law was to turn the clock back to a previous stage of God's purpose, and so to return to a more limited and unnecessarily restricted status before God". Without giving a full exegesis of all the details of the passage, we note some characteristics that are relevant to our project.

Paul uses a language related to the image of the *paterfamilias*, and applies it to God. The father of the household appointed a guardian "to see to the child's support and education, and to administer the inheritance in his interest" (J. D. G. Dunn 1993, 211). This father has such power (cf. *patria potestas* in Roman law) that he even determines when his son should come of age (v. 2). Paul goes on to explain what he wants to argue by means of this analogy: God arranged that Christians are his children come of age (v. 5), by believing in his Son and by receiving his Spirit (the first person plural, "we", probably includes Jewish and non-Jewish Christians). Earlier Paul's addressees had similar rights to those of slaves, i.e. they were not entitled to inherit (v. 1; cf. 4:30). Now they are heirs (v. 7; cf. 3:29; cf. also Col 1:12–14).

James Dunn observes that in the NT "the metaphor of 'adoption' is distinctive to the Pauline corpus" (he points to Rom 8:15.23; 9:4; Eph 1:5; see

---

[46] Among the variants we mention that in v. 6 "of his son" is omitted by P[46], and that some MSS have the second person plural: "into *your* hearts" (both of them regarded as scribal changes by Dunn 1993, 209). There are many variants at the end of v. 7 (our RSV text above moved the translation to the beginning of the sentence): some MSS have "through God" (διὰ θεοῦ, printed as the main text by NA27), and some have "through Christ", or "of God through Christ" (and some have even the name "Jesus" added), all these taken to be "improvements" by Dunn 1993, 209. With P[46], the first hand of Codex Sinaiticus, Codex Vaticanus and some other MSS we adopt the main text of NA27: "... and if a son then an heir through God."

1993, 217). "Almost certainly Paul had in mind the legal act of *adoptio*, by which a Roman citizen entered another family and came under the *patria potestas* of its head". Dunn argues that in the background of Paul's language may lie the legal procedure according to which a father could sell his son (*emancipatio*) and yet later "the son could be manumitted (like a slave) back to his father, who would receive him back by a fresh act of *adoptio*". The adopted person had the same legal rights as a natural son, including the rights of inheritance, "so that 'adoption' is fully equivalent to 'sonship'". Dunn explains the significance of the Greek term for "receiving" in Gal 4:5 (ἀπολάβωμεν, the compound form rather than the simple form as in Rom 8:15; p. 218) in this way: "The son 'emancipated' and then manumitted back, literally 'receives back'... by 'adoption' the status of a son." All this implies that the relationship between the Christians and God is explained by Paul using a language belonging to the realm of the household.

Once again, as in 2 Cor 6:11–13, we note the presence of the expression "heart" (καρδία) in a context where the child-parent relationship is addressed. This time it is God's children who cry out "Father!" by the help of God's Spirit in their hearts (Gal 4:6). The fact that Paul uses the Aramaic form "Abba", when writing to the predominantly Gentile Christians in Galatia, implies that it is an expression used probably in worship. It may be part of the regular prayers of early Christians, possibly going back to a usage on Jesus' lips (so J. D. G. Dunn 1993, 221). As we have seen, early Christians worshipped in houses where full "households" would be present. They did not only have a relationship to the owner of the house (and, in a figurative sense, to Paul) as to a household leader, but they understood themselves as members of God's family. The imagery of God as "father" supposes a view that "children" are expected to honour and obey their parents.

There are many passages in the NT where God is described as "father". These texts would corroborate our thesis, but due to their large number, they would need special treatment in a monograph. Here we only refer to some of them. We discuss those in which not only the term "father" appears, but the family imagery is used in a more extended way, for example, by giving some detail about the "children", as in the passage above. We shall unavoidably mention also those in which the addressees of a letter are referred to as the children of the sender as well as the children of God.[47]

---

[47] May it suffice to point out here that this usage is also significant in the Gospels, where God is the "father" of Jesus (see e.g. Matt 11:25–27 par. Luke 10:21–22; Matt 3:17 par. Mark 1:11, Luke 3:22, John 1:34; see further Walter Grundmann 1965–66, Joachim Jeremias 1966, Robert Hamerton-Kelly 1979, 1981, Dieter Zeller 1981), but also of the followers of Jesus

3. Family imagery in a figurative sense

There is a passage in Paul where he applies to himself more than one metaphor from family imagery when describing his relationship to his addressees. In 1 Thessalonians, in the immediate context he uses both the picture of a father warning his children and the picture of nursing. The latter belongs to the household imagery as well, though it is open to interpretation whether the nursing is carried out by a mother or by a nurse. In 1 Thess 2:7–12 we read:

But we were gentle among you, like a nurse taking care of her children. (8) So, being affectionately desirous of you, we were ready to share with you not only the gospel of God but also our own selves, because you had become very dear to us. (9) For you remember our labor and toil, brethren; we worked night and day, that we might not burden any of you, while we preached to you the gospel of God. (10) You are witnesses, and God also, how holy and righteous and blameless was our behavior to you believers; (11) for you know how, like a father with his children, (12) we exhorted each one of you and encouraged you and charged you to lead a life worthy of God, who calls you into his own kingdom and glory.[48]

Whether or not the term "gentle" should be adopted in v. 7 (so e.g. F. F. Bruce 1982, 29 and 31; Eckart Reinmuth 1998, 126), it is significant that Paul uses the imagery of a nursing mother.[49] I have already argued that the

---

(see e.g. Matt 6:9 par. Luke 11:2; John 1:12; see further Fred Burnett 1992, Mary D'Angelo 1992, H.W. Montefiore 1956, Taeseong Roh 2001, Gerhard Schneider 1992, H. F. D. Sparks 1955). God as "father" appears elsewhere in different writings of the NT, see e.g. Rom 8:15; Eph 5:1; Phil 2:15; 1 John 3:10. We shall discuss Heb 12:7 and 1 Pet 1:17 in the following chapter, since their context makes use of family imagery in more detail than in other texts. See further Daniel von Allmen 1981, Günther Bornkamm 1976, Judith Lieu 1981, Abraham Malherbe 1995, W. Marchel 1971, Dietrich Rusam 1993. Among these, we note especially the treatment in monographs of the theme "Christians as the family of God": Roh (2001) has studied the Synoptic Gospels, von Allmen (1981) the Pauline letters, and Rusam (1993) the Johannine letters under this aspect. – Harry Jungbauer argues that natural parents are replaced by the "familia dei" in the Synoptic tradition (2002, 290–307), but he also points to a "congruence" between these two kinds of family references in the Synoptics (pp. 308–12). Jungbauer describes the Johannine congregation as a *familia dei* (pp. 313–23).

[48] There are a few minor textual variants in this passage. We mention only that in v. 7 some MSS have ἤπιοι ("gentle", adopted by the RSV quoted above, and by NA until the 25th edn), and some have νήπιοι ("infants", adopted by NA27 as the main text). It is clear that it is either dittography or haplography on the side of a scribe, since the preceding word ends with a "ν". "Gentle" is the easier reading, since if adopted, there is no change in the metaphor: gentle nursing is in view. The more difficult reading is "infants", since Paul applies it in other letters to minors who need to grow up to maturity (see e.g. Rom 2:20; 1 Cor 3:1; 13:11; Gal 4:1.3). If we adopt it, then we can say that Paul applied to himself all the metaphors offered by the imagery of the household (father, mother, infant child, nurse, brother, and we might add that he also calls himself a slave of Christ, see e.g. Rom 1:1). Recently, Jeffrey Weima has argued this case in a convincing way (2000).

[49] For arguments in favour of the view that "gentleness" here stands in deliberate contrast

imagery in 1 Cor 3:2 refers to a mother feeding her child with milk (rather than to a nurse), and I suggest that 1 Thess 2:7 refers to a mother, too. In the latter case, although a "nurse" is mentioned, nevertheless it is stressed that she "cherishes her own children" (ὡς ἐὰν τροφὸς θάλπῃ τὰ ἑαυτῆς τέκνα), so she is probably a "nursing mother" (so F. F. Bruce 1982, 31), i.e. "a wet nurse who nurses her own children" (A. J. Malherbe 1995, 121). It is worth noting that the picture of a nursing mother is chosen by Paul to replace apostolic authority (to which he would be entitled, too, see v. 7).[50] Verse 8 probably carries on the imagery when it is said that Paul is "affectionately desirous" of the Thessalonians,[51] and that he puts his life ("his own existence", E. Reinmuth 1998, 126) at their disposal, because they are "dear" to him (καὶ τὰς ἑαυτῶν ψυχάς, διότι ἀγαπητοὶ ἡμῖν ἐγενήθητε. Throughout the passage he uses the plural, probably including the people who were with him when they first preached the gospel in Thessalonica).[52]

In v. 9 Paul addresses the Thessalonians as "brethren", which he does on twelve more occasions in the letter, this being "the highest incidence of the term in all of Paul's letters" (so A. J. Malherbe 1995, 122). Since this is the most common way Christians addressed each other (having adopted this custom from Judaism), its use here may be idiomatic. Perhaps even in this verse the paternal image may be in the background, since Paul emphasises how hard he and his co-workers worked in order not to burden the Thessalonians.

At the end of this passage, in v. 11, Paul changes the metaphor again: he refers to himself and his co-workers as "father".[53] Three participles describe what they did in the role of the father (v. 12, with little difference in meaning, see F. F. Bruce 1982, 36): "we exhorted each one of you and encouraged you and charged you" (παρακαλοῦντες ὑμᾶς καὶ παραμυθούμενοι καὶ

---

to a type of itinerant Cynic who used reproach rather than admonition, see Abraham Malherbe 1970, esp. 211.

[50] F. F. Bruce (1982, 32) points to Num 11:12 as a passage in which a similar picture is applied by Moses to himself: "Did I conceive all this people? Did I bring them forth, that thou shouldst say to me, Carry them in your bosom, as a nurse carries the sucking child, to the land which thou didst swear to give their fathers?"

[51] The majority of MSS have the Hellenistic term, ὁμειρόμενοι, while some MSS have the classical equivalent, ἱμειρόμενοι.

[52] Eckart Reinmuth argues (1998, 126): "Wir gehen davon aus, daß das 'wir' des Briefes regelmäßig dem Autor Paulus gilt und zugleich die beiden Mitabsender in die Botschaft des Schreibens einbezieht".

[53] F. F. Bruce points out that (1982, 36): "Both the maternal and paternal figures are used of the God of Israel in the OT; cf. Isa 66:13 ('as one whom his mother comforts, so I will comfort you') and Ps. 103:13 ('as a father pities his children, so the Lord pities those who fear him')."

3. Family imagery in a figurative sense 193

μαρτυρόμενοι εἰς τὸ περιπατεῖν ὑμᾶς ἀξίως τοῦ θεοῦ).[54] We note that the comparative particle, "as", clearly signals that Paul makes use of a metaphor (v. 11, the same is true for the metaphor of the nurse in v. 7). However, the metaphor in v. 11 is taken so seriously that it is emphatically stated that they did exhort their "children" "one by one" (ἕνα ἕκαστον ὑμῶν ὡς πατὴρ τέκνα ἑαυτοῦ παρακαλοῦντες). Thus the whole passage implies that the Thessalonians share the image that they and Paul form a well-ordered household, where parental care is returned by the "children" through obedience to the father's admonitions. The exhortation to receive the gospel and to lead a life accordingly, i.e. "worthy of God" (v. 12), was obediently accepted by the Thessalonians who recognised in it God's call into his "kingdom and glory".

It is worth noting that the verse immediately following on this passage may be understood against the background just depicted. In 2:13 we read: "And we also thank God constantly for this, that when you received the word of God which you heard from us, you accepted it not as the word of men but as what it really is, the word of God, which is at work in you believers." Perhaps 1 Thess 2:13 implies that the Thessalonians received Paul as their "father and mother" in the faith; consequently they accepted their preaching as the words spoken by God. We might find a parallel to this phenomenon in Philo's exposition of the Fifth Commandment where parents are to be honoured because they participate in God's creative activity when giving life to their children.[55] In the Thessalonian context, it is not physical existence, but spiritual new life that they received from Paul as their parent. This may be a factor in their accepting Paul's gospel as the word of God.

Apart from whole congregations (as seen above in the case of the Corinthians, the Galatians, and Thessalonians), Paul can refer to individuals as his "children" (using the term τέκνον in each case), since he has led them to faith in Jesus. We meet this phenomenon in the undisputed letters of Paul, and we find more examples in the Pastoral Epistles.

We have already seen that in the very context where Paul refers to the Corinthians as his children, he also applies the imagery to an individual (1 Cor 4:17): "I sent to you Timothy, my beloved and faithful child in the Lord" (ὅς

---

[54] E. Reinmuth (1998, 127) points out the difference of the social role of the father and that of the mother reflected also in Paul's metaphors in vv. 7–8 and 11–12: "Offenbar ist die unterschiedliche Gestalt der Zuwendung in beiden Bildern durch die sozialen Rollen veranlaßt, in denen Paulus Väter und Mütter unterschieden weiß."

[55] Abraham Malherbe (1995, 118–19) has pointed to the phenomenon that in antiquity, "since a father was viewed as progenitor, God as creator would be referred to as father." He mentions e.g. Plato *Timaeus* 28C, 37C; Philo *Cher.* 44; *Migr.* 28.193, 194; *Opif.* 45, 46; *Spec.* 1.41; 2.225 (p. 119, fn. 8).

ἐστίν μου τέκνον ἀγαπητὸν καὶ πιστὸν ἐν κυρίῳ). 1 Corinthians 4:17 perhaps even implies that first Paul teaches his "child", then he sends him to participate in the teaching of the congregations: "I sent to you Timothy, ... to remind you of my ways in Christ, as I teach them everywhere in every church." This verse summarises the situation envisaged in the Pastoral Epistles as well: through the leaders of congregations, Paul teaches in many house churches.

In Phlm 10 we read Paul's words to Philemon: "I appeal to you for my child, Onesimus, whose father I have become in my imprisonment" (παρακαλῶ σε περὶ τοῦ ἐμοῦ τέκνου, ὃν ἐγέννησα ἐν τοῖς δεσμοῖς, Ὀνήσιμον).[56] Since in the Greek the name of Onesimus stands at the end of the sentence, it is only at this point that it becomes clear for the first readers that Paul uses a metaphor (Peter Lampe 1998, 217; Michael Wolter 1993, 262). Until the congregation heard the name, they could have thought that Paul had really begotten a child. What is even more surprising news (to be learnt at the end of the sentence only): the very "child" is Onesimus, the slave who had fled from Philemon, and who has just returned with this letter of recommendation from Paul (cf. v. 12, see also Michael Wolter 1993, 261–62).[57] Lampe points out that although there is a house church meeting at Philemon's house, Onesimus had not been a Christian beforehand, which shows that it was not self-evident that full households were accepting the Christian faith (as it was the case on some other occasions, cf. e.g. 1 Cor 1:16; 16:15; Acts 16:15.31–34; 18:8; cf. also Acts 11:14; John 4:53).

We recall that Paul uses the same Greek expression for "becoming a father to someone" as in 1 Cor 4:15, "I have begotten" (ἐγέννησα). The term, γεννάω, means "begetting" if the subject is a man, and "giving birth to" if the subject is a woman (Murray Harris 1991, 261). The former meaning is adopted here by Lampe (1998, 217).

However, it is possible to argue that Paul uses the maternal imagery here, since he wants to emphasise that Onesimus is a new being, he is born as a

---

[56] There are a few MSS which emphasise the subject of the verb by inserting "I" before it. The RSV quoted above translates a variant which has the possessive pronoun after "bonds" (by metonymy, "imprisonment", see Murray Harris 1991, 261), whereas NA27 prints as the main text the shorter variant (which the readers must have understood as referring to Paul's imprisonment even without the term "my").

[57] Recent interpreters (beginning with Peter Lampe ZNW 76 [1985], 135–37) argue that Onesimus was probably not a *fugitivus* in the Roman legal sense, but fled to a friend of his master in order to gain support from this *amicus domini* and with the plan of returning to his master. For a survey of the history of this interpretation, that can be regarded now as a consensus, see Hans Hübner 1997, 33–35.

3. Family imagery in a figurative sense

Christian.[58] Michael Wolter argues that since Philemon, too, became a Christian through Paul (cf. v. 19b), the apostle now presents to Philemon his "brother", Onesimus (1993, 262). If this latter view is adopted then we have a further example of the emotional richness of Paul's use of the family imagery. However, even if one adopts the paternal imagery here, one should recognise that Paul does not play the role of an all-powerful *paterfamilias*, but that of a loving father, since in v. 12 he refers to Onesimus as his own "heart" (σπλάγχνα being an expression for the centre of emotions, cf. also v. 7; M. J. Harris 1991, 254, 263).

Whatever meaning of γεννάω one adopts here, it remains significant that Onesimus has to be received as a "brother" into the house church of Philemon. Thus there are three overlapping usages of household imagery in this letter: one applying to the relationship between Paul and Onesimus, another applying to the relationship between Paul and Philemon, and a third applying to the congregation at the house of Philemon. As Peter Lampe has put it (1998, 213): "die von Paulus vorgelebten brüderlichen Verhältnisse *Paulus : Philemon* und *Paulus : Onesimus*, die beide auf Gleichstellung basieren, sollen zum motivierenden Vorbild für das Verhältnis *Philemon : Onesimus* werden." Lampe rightly refers here to "brotherly" relationship, since Paul addresses Philemon as "brother" (v. 7), and he also refers to Onesimus as his own "brother" and Philemon's brother (v. 16). Thus the parental imagery does not overrule the usual Christian imagery according to which all Christians are brethren. Paul regards as his brothers even those to whom he had given "birth" (or whom he had begotten) for a new life in Christ.

To sum up, the Epistle to Philemon supposes a setting in which the house church of Philemon functions as an extended family. Onesimus, a slave, should be received as a brother in Christ. Furthermore, Paul uses affectionate language taken from family imagery to describe his relationship to Onesimus. Though not explicitly stated, it is implied that Philemon is also a child of Paul in the faith. Thus he is expected to obey the wish of his "father": he is to receive into the family a new brother.[59] Throughout the letter it is supposed that the addressees agree that children should honour and obey their parents; that is why family language is used so extensively by Paul.

---

[58] As Michael Wolter has put it (1993, 262): "Es geht nicht allein darum, die enge Bindung zwischen Paulus und Onesimus hervorzuheben; denn wenn der Letztgenannte als neugeborenes Kind dargestellt wird, so wird damit vor allem eine biographische Diskontinuität gekennzeichnet."

[59] Chris Frilingos (2000, 93) has argued recently that the household imagery in the relationship between Paul and Philemon involves "not only intimacy and affection but also economics and paternal authority." He has put forward the thesis that "the epistle's family language constructs a rhetorical household that rivals Philemon's actual household."

When we turn to the Deuteropauline Epistles, it is conspicuous that Colossians and Ephesians do not use paternal imagery to express the relationship between the author and the addressees. The term "father" is used about God (e.g. Col 1:2.3.12; 3,17; Eph 1:2.3.17; 2:18; 3:14; 4:6; 5:20; note also that according to Eph 3:15, "every family [πᾶσα πατριά] in heaven and on earth is named" from the "Father", i.e. God); and "father" also occurs in the Household Codes concerning real child-parent relationships. Ephesians 5:31 quotes Gen 2:24, but this verse does not refer to enmity in the family: "For this reason a man shall leave his father and mother and be joined to his wife, and the two shall become one." 2 Thessalonians uses the term "father" only about God (1:1.2; 2:16). So we move on to a discussion of the Pastoral Epistles.

b) The Pastoral Epistles

If the Pastoral Epistles are not by Paul, then we have a further example of the consistency in the usage of famtitily imagery in the Pastorals and in the undisputed Pauline letters. We can refer to the following examples in which paternal imagery is applied to individuals: Timothy (1 Tim 1:2.18; 2 Tim 1:2; 2:1),[60] and Titus (Titus 1:4). In some of these cases we find an adjectival expression: "to Timothy, my *true* child in the faith" (γνησίῳ τέκνῳ ἐν πίστει, 1 Tim 1:2); "to Timothy, my *beloved* child" (ἀγαπητῷ τέκνῳ, 2 Tim 1:2); "to Titus, my *true* child in a common faith" (γνησίῳ τέκνῳ κατὰ κοινὴν πίστιν, Titus 1:4). We note that at the beginning of the Pastoral Epistles these expressions are immediately followed by the Pauline apostolic greeting in which grace "from God the father" is conveyed. This fits the picture seen in the previous passages: Paul can refer to himself as "father" and at the same time he can see the Christians as belonging to God's household.

The family imagery expressed by the reference to Timothy and Titus as Paul's children has clear implications: Paul teaches them as a father to become good leaders of their congregations. Paul teaches whole congregations as the head of their households, as a "father" to them, as well. He can expect that his "children" will follow his advice.

The same imagery appears in 2 Timothy concerning the relationship between Timothy and his earthly mother and grandmother. Paul praises Tim-

---

[60] Cf. also Phil 2:22, "how as a son with a father he has served with me in the gospel", which reminds us of the phenomenon met in the environment that sons often worked together with their father in the same "trade".

3. Family imagery in a figurative sense 197

othy for the faith he has learnt from his ancestors. (I refer to Paul as the implied author of the letter, leaving open the question of authorship.) In 2 Tim 1:5 we read (as a conclusion of a long sentence in vv. 3–5): "I am reminded of your sincere faith, a faith that dwelt first in your grandmother Lois and your mother Eunice and now, I am sure, dwells in you." Timothy's real father was probably a pagan (cf. Acts 16:1–3), so Timothy had learnt faith in God from his Jewish mother.[61] Acts 16:1 says about Timothy's mother that she was a Jewess and a "believer" (πιστῆς). It would have been superfluous to mention the latter if it simply meant she believed in the God of Israel; the reference to being a "believer" probably implies she believed in Jesus (so George Knight 1992, 369), but we have to emphasise that we do not know when and how she became a Christian. The more concrete content of what that faith included is told in 2 Tim 3:15. The full context, vv. 14–17, is worth quoting:

But as for you, continue in what you have learned and have firmly believed, knowing from whom you learned it (15) and how from childhood you have been acquainted with the sacred writings which are able to instruct you for salvation through faith in Christ Jesus. (16) All scripture is inspired by God and profitable for teaching, for reproof, for correction, and for training in righteousness, (17) that the man of God may be complete, equipped for every good work.

Verse 14 is ambiguous: it is an introduction to the following verses, and at the same time it rounds off the previous section. On the one hand, Timothy is reminded of the fact that he has learnt things from his mother and grandmother ("from whom" is in the plural form in one part of the Greek manuscript tradition, including the Codices Sinaiticus and Vaticanus, and is adopted as the main text in NA27), and v. 15 spells out what he has learnt. On the other hand, the preceding passage began by a reminder that Timothy followed Paul's teaching (2 Tim 3:10). Thus we may say that Paul as well as Timothy's mother and grandmother are included in those from whom he has learnt (so George Knight 1992, 443). In the light of Paul's references to Timothy as his own child, we may suggest that Paul taught Timothy as his spiritual "father" since he met him as a young man.

The text implies that Timothy's mother taught him "from childhood on" (ἀπὸ βρέφους). She taught him "sacred writings".[62] These must include

---

[61] James Miller (1997, 120) calls for caution as regards Eunice's "allegiance to Judaism", since she married a non-Jew and had not had her son circumcised (cf. Acts 16:1–3). In the following, we discuss the relevant passages in 2 Timothy from the point of view of the kind of family life they portray (whether this picture is historical or "ideal").

[62] ἱερὰ γράμματα, the definite article being omitted by some MSS and bracketed by

the Scriptures of Israel, though it has to be affirmed that it is not specified what exactly is included, neither is it spelled out what the expression "all Scripture" (πᾶσα γραφή) in v. 16 refers to (for a summary of the possibilities in interpreting v. 16, see George Knight 1992, 444–50).[63] May it suffice to say that, in accordance with what we have seen concerning the Jewish environment, the passage envisages a child who is taught the Scriptures by his Jewish mother (and grandmother). When the child became a young man, he met Paul who led him to faith in Jesus (cf. 1 Tim 1:2); perhaps it was Paul who added the Christological interpretation to the Scriptures (cf. 2 Tim 3:15b), and showed all the benefits of Scripture in equipping Timothy for his ministry (vv. 16–17). These verses address a concrete family situation in which a child is praised for learning from his mother, and they also imply the same praise for Timothy's obedient relationship to his spiritual father, the apostle Paul.

4. Summary

We have seen in the *Corpus Paulinum* that views and practices in the realm of the child-parent relationship correspond to a large extent to those met in the environment. With some differences in detail, this applies to the undisputed Pauline letters, to the Household Codes in Colossians and Ephesians, as well as to the Pastoral Epistles.

We have discussed texts which refer to norms and passages that imply a certain view on the child-parent relationship shared by the writer and the addressees. The differences in detail may be summarised in the following way. In the undisputed Pauline Epistles priority is given to the congregation as a "family"; Paul is interested in congregational ethics rather than family ethics. Family images are used in order to speak about the *familia dei*. However, even this usage confirms in an indirect way that Paul must have shared the views of his Jewish and pagan environment concerning the honour due to parents. The Household Codes in Colossians and Ephesians (regarded as Deuteropauline Epistles by the majority of scholars) show that children in

---

NA27. The phrase appears only here in the NT, but is frequent in Philo and Josephus (see James Miller 1997, 120).

[63] James Miller's thesis, published after Knight's commentary, understands the Pastoral letters as "composite documents", i.e. not written by one author, but containing a "collection" of texts. In this particular case, he argues that vv. 14–15 and vv. 16–17 represent "previously independent sayings on loyalty to the traditions that were gathered at some point by an editor" (1997, 121). His key argument is the change in the phrase applied to "scripture" in vv. 15 and 16.

the congregations were taught to honour their parents. Real family relations are addressed here. However, the term "father" is used also in a figurative sense: with reference to God. In the Pastoral Epistles God as "father" is mentioned only in the letter-opening sections. However, the emphasis on the order in the "house" is a point of contact between the Christian congregation and their "environment".

For the sake of an easy comparison, we summarise the views and practices met in the Pauline Corpus in the order we followed in the chapters on the environment: first we collect children's duties, then motivations or "reasons" for those duties, and finally we address the theme of limits of the duties.

We have encountered the following duties, all of which appeared in the environment as well. The duty of "honouring" parents is mentioned explicitly only in the Household Code in Ephesians, when the Fifth Commandment is quoted, but it is implied in texts which sum up children's duties in the duty of obedience. On occasion, giving due honour to parents and being obedient to them can be regarded as equivalents, e.g. in the Codes in Colossians and Ephesians, and in vice list like Rom 1:30 and 2 Tim 3:2. Honour as an expectation is implied also in the emphasis on the good order in the households in the Pastoral Epistles. However, we observe that in the sources found in the environment the term "honour" is *used* more frequently, whereas in the Pastorals it is more often *implied*.

Obedience does not only serve as an overarching duty; it can also include following the advice of one's parents. That is why Paul uses parental imagery when he wants his addressees to follow his teaching and conduct, e.g. in Corinthians, Galatians, Thessalonians, and Philemon. Obedience entails children's willingness to learn from their parents (2 Tim 1:5; 3:15; cf. also Timothy's learning from Paul as his "father"). Another concrete sphere of obedience is marriage: the father determines whom the daughter should marry (2 Cor 11:2).

We have met the view that children owe a debt to their parents in return for their care and provision (1 Tim 5:4, implied also by Rom 16:13; 2 Cor 6:13). They are grateful to their parents for their lives (implied by their gratitude for their Christian life, e.g. Gal 4:19, and the congregations and individuals whom Paul helped to faith in Jesus).

We have found in the environment that (apart from honour and obedience) the two most important duties of children were provision and care for the parents while they live, and burial and veneration when they die. Thus we have to note the lack of references to deceased persons in Paul's letters. This silence cannot mean that they did not care for the deceased; early Christians must have buried their dead relatives. We do not know the reason for this silence, but we may cautiously suggest that it may be due to Christians' reluctance to venerate dead ancestors as divine beings. If so, then this is a significant difference when compared with the environment. Early Christians held that Jesus died and rose again; they did not elevate any other human being to the same level of divinity.

We also note that the duties of children are not spelled out in so many concrete ways in the Pauline letters as in the sources in the environment. It seems that the main emphasis in the "Pauline" congregations lay on good order in the household. We have seen (and adopted in this project) the view that early Christians wanted to show to their environment that they did not present a threat to the wider society; in the case of the child-parent relationship this can be achieved by emphasising Christian children's obedient character.

We have met numerous reasons for duties that are similar to those found in the environment. In some cases these reasons were only implied, but this does not make them less important.

By adopting many formal characteristics of the economics literature for the Household Codes, Christians probably wanted to show that they shared the reasons for duties with their environment: these reasons include the seeking of what is pleasing to God (implied by Colossians, cf. also 1 Tim 5:4) and what is "right" (Ephesians). Both Codes refer to the "Lord" Jesus as a Christological motivation; the term is used to show that Christians wanted to follow Jesus also in this respect. Thus they must have thought that Jesus shared the view with his environment that parents should be honoured and obeyed.

The Household Code in Ephesians quotes the Fifth Commandment: this implies that the law of God is seen as a motive for the duty. In the same context a reward from God (in the form of a promise as the second part of the commandment) is a further reason for the duty.

The order of vice lists (especially in Rom 1:29–31 and 1 Tim 1:9–10) implies that an offence against parents is an offence against God as well. The order of the vice lists also implies that parents rank first among human beings.

1 Timothy 1:9–10 further implies that punishment by the law should serve as a reason for avoiding offences against parents. Punishment by the congregation (an exclusion decided by this human court) appears in 1 Cor 5:1–5. The reference to the "nations" in 1 Cor 5:1 may also imply that Christians did not want to have an ethical conduct inferior to that of their environment.

We have also seen that the reason for "returning" love and care to parents is the provision already experienced by the children from the parents (e.g.

2 Cor 6:11–13; 1 Tim 5:4). Children also owe gratitude and obedience to parents for the provision of an inheritance (implied by 2 Cor 12:14; and implied by the view that Christians are "heirs" adopted by their heavenly father, see e.g. Gal 3:29–4:7).

Thus reasons from both the divine and the human spheres are widely shared by the early Christians and their environment.

It is most conspicuous that the matter of "limits" in carrying out duties is not addressed in the Pauline Epistles. We have met the view that one of the characteristics of the "last days" is that children will be disobedient to their parents (2 Tim 3:1–2). We recall that in the discussion of some of the Gospel passages we emphasised the apocalyptic context of sayings concerning tensions and enmity within the family. The context implies that the tension is "necessary", but it is not intended by Jesus and his followers. However, apart from this similarity, we do not have parallels to the "environment" and to the Jesus tradition concerning a "limit" set by the higher "good" or by the preference that is to be given to God.

This silence may be significant. It confirms our view argued in the previous chapter that the early Christians did not think Jesus broke with God's commandment to honour father and mother. Even tensions in the family that arose from Jesus' (and some of his disciples') itinerant lifestyle did not mean that he (and his disciples) ceased to give due honour to parents. If Paul, who is well aware of the problems in marriage, caused by difference in faith (cf. 1 Cor 7), remains silent on the theme of tensions within the child-relationship, this must have had some reason.

On the one hand, he probably wanted to make sure his congregations live in good order, so that they may be on good terms with their environment. One might argue that avoiding any mention of limits in children's duties may be a conscious move on Paul's side to please the environment.

On the other hand, it is not likely that Paul and his disciples would have avoided this theme if they thought Jesus approved of tensions within the family. Thus, in an indirect way, the Pauline Corpus confirms the view we have argued concerning the Jesus traditions: early Christianity as reflected in the Pauline letters probably did not understand the radical sayings of Jesus as implying a necessary breach with the Fifth Commandment. Rather, they must have thought that priority to be given to Jesus (whom they believed to be God), and the urgency of his call to discipleship did not challenge the view that the majority of Christians have to live in well-ordered households, where the expectation is shared with the environment that children should honour and obey their parents.

Chapter Six

The Rest of the New Testament

1. Introduction

In this chapter we survey the thoughts and practices of the early church as reflected in the New Testament, apart from the two great parts studied already. Once again, it is significant that the writings to be discussed originate probably in the last quarter of the first century, which means that they are contemporaneous with the Gospels and the later writings of the Pauline Corpus. Second Peter may be an exception (if it is to be dated later), but it does not make wide use of family imagery, so we shall refer to it only briefly. We do not engage in the debates as to whether Acts was written in the eighties or possibly in the sixties (when it ends its story, Paul still being alive), whether the Epistles of John precede or follow the Fourth Gospel, and whether Revelation is an early document or was written in the nineties. Even if we adopt the later dates in each case, these sources reflect "early Christianity" within two or three generations from Jesus' time. We do not attempt to date the views on the child-parent relationship with a greater precision than this.

In this chapter we follow the same pattern in ordering our material as in the previous chapter. We collect the texts in the two main groups established in our chapter on the Pauline Corpus: first, we discuss texts addressing a real child-parent relationship; then we turn to texts which use the picture of children and parents in a figurative way. If a text has both usages, we discuss it under one heading only, noting the different applications of the family imagery. We shall see that in the writings of the NT outside the Gospels and the Pauline Corpus the theme of the "real" child-parent relationship is not addressed frequently. Since the figurative sense of the term "children" is often applied to the recipients in two ways, as the children of the writer and at the same time as God's children, we shall unavoidably include in our discussion the latter usage (which we excluded from our discussion of the Gospels and mentioned only occasionally in relation to the Pauline Corpus).

2. Texts concerning real child-parent relationships

Acts has several passages where children are together with their parents. Although these passages do not mention children's duties in a direct way, they are told in such a natural manner that they imply children's obedience to their parents.

In Acts 1:14 only the Codex Bezae mentions that, as well as women, there were also children in the gathering of Jesus' followers in Jerusalem before Pentecost (cf. Rudolf Pesch 1986, I/81). In this verse we are told after being given the names of Jesus' apostles (eleven names, since Judas Iscariot is already dead): "All these with one accord devoted themselves to prayer, together with the women and Mary the mother of Jesus, and with his brothers." Codex Bezae adds after women: "and children" (καὶ τεκνοῖς). This may reflect the situation of the church when the textual tradition of the Codex Bezae was fixed, but it also corresponds to other parts of Acts where whole households are mentioned as accepting faith in Jesus, and, on occasion, as being baptised (cf. e.g. 16:15, the Codex Bezae and a few other MSS add "whole" (πᾶς) before "household" (ὁ οἶκος); 16:34, the composite phrase, πανοικεί, is replaced by "with his household" in the Codex Bezae).[1] William Strange (1996, 71) notes that it is "unlikely that the words 'and children' come from Luke". Strange argues that the addition by "an early scribe" shows "that Christians in the early church, like that scribe, expected children to be present at worship."[2]

Concerning Jesus' family, it is worth pointing out that "Mary the mother of Jesus is referred to here only in Acts" (C. K. Barrett 1994, I/89). Jesus' "brothers" are not mentioned later in Acts either; even James (12:17; 15:13; 21:28) "is not described as the Lord's brother, though he is so described in Galatians" (Barrett, p. 90). They are mentioned in Acts 1:14 in order to show to the reader that now they belong to Jesus' "new family" (so e.g. R. Pesch 1986, I/81; Barrett refers to Jesus' "spiritual family", 1994, I/89–90).[3]

---

[1] For discussions of household conversion narratives and of texts concerning the baptizing of households in Acts, see e.g. Craig de Vos 1995, Gerhard Delling 1964–65, Joachim Jeremias 1958, David Matson 1996.

[2] W. A. Strange (*ibid.*) also notes that the younger "Pliny said of the people of Bithynia during his governorship (c.112 AD) that 'many of all ages' were in danger of contagion from the Christian menace (Pliny, 96.9: *NE* 19). He had evidently noticed that children were involved in the Christian worship which he was trying to stamp out in his province." – We may note the presence of children in the Gospel tradition, for example, on the occasion of the feeding of the five thousand, see e.g. Matt 14:21 (from the Synoptic parallels of this passage, only Matthew mentions children explicitly; cf. John 6:9).

[3] Gerhard Schneider notes concerning v. 14 (1980, I/207): "Der die Erzähleinheit ab-

Though the passage does not address the former tension in Jesus' family, it is possible to see in it a conscious addition to the Gospel narrative in which Jesus' earthly family did not belong to those "who hear the word of God and do it" (see Luke 8:19–21 par. Mark 3:31–35, discussed in our fourth chapter).[4]

It is significant that other passages, too, show the presence of children in the community of faith. In Acts 2:17–18, Peter applies the prophecy of Joel to their own situation at Pentecost (cf. Joel 3:1–5): "And in the last days it shall be, God declares, that I will pour out my Spirit upon all flesh, and your sons and your daughters shall prophesy, and your young men shall see visions, and your old men shall dream dreams; (18) yea, and on my menservants and my maidservants in those days I will pour out my Spirit; and they shall prophesy." We note that the reference to the "last days" in v. 17, and the final verb affirming that also the servants "shall prophesy", are changes and additions to the passage in Joel, that has simply "after these things", μετὰ ταῦτα (Joel 3:1). Some MSS have changed the text of Acts back to Joel's μετὰ ταῦτα. Barrett rightly notes that these MSS miss the point of Peter's speech which claims that the early Christians "are part of God's final act of redemption" (1994, I/136).

Although this is a quotation from the OT, its application implies that there may have been also young people at Pentecost together with the apostles. Whether or not this quotation describes "reality" in the circle of the first followers of Jesus, it does show that (according to Luke) Peter envisaged a community where full households turn to faith in Jesus, including "sons and daughters", and also servants. We note that both sexes are mentioned not only in v. 17 ("your sons and your daughters"), but also in v. 18 ("on my menservants and my maidservants" [ἐπὶ τοὺς δούλους μου καὶ ἐπὶ τὰς δούλας μου]; cf. C. K. Barrett 1994, I/137). In v. 18, the possessive pronoun, "my", is Luke's addition to the text of the Septuagint; by this addition Luke applies Joel's text on servants to men and women in the Christian congregation (so R. Pesch 1986, I/120).

Children appear also towards the end of the Book of Acts. Shortly before

---

schließende Vers hat den Charakter eines Summariums, das eine ideale Zustandsbeschreibung bietet".

[4] We recall from the previous chapter that Luke's version of the passage is "milder" than that of Mark inasmuch as Luke does not say that Jesus' relatives said he was mad. Alfons Weiser notes concerning the mention of Jesus' brothers in Acts 1:14 (1981, I/58–59): "Die Erwähnung wird auch zusammenhängen mit der luk Tendenz, das Verhältnis der Angehörigen zu Jesus im ganzen günstiger darzustellen, als es in manchen anderen urchristlichen Überlieferungskreisen geschah (vgl. Mk 3,20 diff Lk; Joh 7,3–10)".

2. Texts concerning real child-parent relationships 205

Paul is arrested, the congregation at Tyre warned Paul not to go up to Jerusalem. When Paul nevertheless decided to continue his ship journey, they all followed him to the beach. In Acts 21:5 we read: "And when our days there were ended, we departed and went on our journey; and they all, with wives and children, brought us on our way till we were outside the city; and kneeling down on the beach we prayed and bade one another farewell." We note that whereas v. 4 only mentions "disciples", verse 5 includes their wives and children in a natural way. This probably means that they were part of the congregation; they followed their parents to worship as well as to special meetings when wandering apostles visited the congregation. As Rudolf Pesch puts it (1986, II/210): "Die ganze Gemeinde samt Frauen und Kindern geleitet Paulus und seine Begleiter zum Hafen".[5] Ben Witherington remarks that this little scene "shows Paul had won the affections of whole families, and so shows the extent of his impact" (1998, 631, fn. 292). It may be added that the presence of whole families is also implied in the next verse from which we learn that the congregation members returned "to their own [things]" (21:6b, εἰς τὰ ἴδια), where the plural must imply their "homes" (C. K. Barrett 1998, II/991).

Two further texts in Acts are worth mentioning where the child-parent relationship appears as having special significance. In Acts 7:21, in the speech of Stephen, it is narrated about Moses that "when he was exposed, Pharaoh's daughter adopted him and brought him up as her own son" (ἀνείλατο αὐτὸν ἡ θυγάτηρ Φαραὼ καὶ ἀνεθρέψατο αὐτὸν ἑαυτῇ εἰς υἱόν). Moses' significance for the author can be seen from the fact that he is referred to fourteen times in speeches in Acts, and some more times outside the speeches (see Marion Soards 1994, 64). The reference to the adoption originates in the story narrated in Exodus 2, but Acts 7:22 adds that "Moses was instructed (ἐπαιδεύθη) in all the wisdom of the Egyptians" before God called him to lead his people out of Egypt. It may be significant that the tradition about Moses' education mentioned in Acts 7:22 is not paralleled in Exodus, but Philo, too, has details about Moses' education that go beyond the text of Exodus (*Vita* 1.21–24; see also R. Pesch 1986, I/252; C. K. Barrett 1994, I/355).

Inasmuch as this passage in Acts refers to Moses' time, it may be a witness to the fact that the same family setting was supposed to be valid also by the early Christians. Acts 7:21–22 refers to the situation of the Pharaoh's

---

[5] Cf. also A. Weiser's discussion of F. Bovon's thesis that Luke follows here the pattern of Greek stories about the departure of heroes who leave their family and friends. Weiser (1985, II/590) adds to this view Luke's emphasis on Paul's willingness to accept the journey leading to suffering, which stands in parallel to Jesus' journey to Jerusalem.

daughter's son. Moses' training was in connection with the adoptive act on the side of the Pharaoh's daughter. This little scene points to the parents' house as the place where children are supposed to learn; we have seen this phenomenon also in the sources from the environment. In the speech of Stephen, it is in contrast to this family scene that Moses remembers his real "brethren": the sons of Israel (v. 23).

The son of Paul's sister is mentioned in Acts 23:16; he warns Paul that a plot is planned against him. This is the only information we have about members of Paul's family (C. K. Barrett 1998, II/1075). Acts 22:3 may imply that not only Paul but also some of his relatives lived for some period of time in Jerusalem, though this cannot be proved conclusively. Ben Witherington cautiously remarks (1998, 695): "The presence of this relative of Paul's in Jerusalem supports the suggestion that not just Paul, but his family, had moved to Jerusalem some time ago." It seems that the wider family, apparently at the time resident in Jerusalem, kept in touch with Paul when he was in the city. Though the text does not tell us any detail about Paul's sister, the very fact that she is mentioned may imply that she and her son lived in the same household.

These examples in Acts corroborate the view that children were present in the congregations in the early Christian church. They also point to a "household" setting which we have found in the previous chapters. This setting implies that children grew up "obediently" in their parents' home.

Our next example, Hebrews 12:4–11 includes references to real child-parent relationships, but they are woven into an argument concerning God in the role of the father exercising discipline. To avoid repetition, in discussing the passage in this section we also mention the figurative usage to be found in it. In verses 5–6 the author quotes Prov 3:11–12 (LXX[A] with a slight modification) in order to introduce an admonition to his addressees: they have to accept the discipline of God their father (Heb 12:7). In vv. 4–7 we read:

In your struggle against sin you have not yet resisted to the point of shedding your blood. (5) And have you forgotten the exhortation (τῆς παρακλήσεως) which addresses you as sons? – "My son, do not regard lightly the discipline of the Lord (παιδείας κυρίου), nor lose courage when you are punished by him. (6) For the Lord disciplines him whom he loves (ὃν γὰρ ἀγαπᾷ κύριος παιδεύει), and chastises every son whom he receives." (7) It is for discipline that you have to endure. God is treating you as sons; for what son is there whom his father does not discipline?

Then the author reminds them of two rules in the earthly sphere: 1) discipline from one's father is a sign of sonship, because the father of the house

2. Texts concerning real child-parent relationships

cares less about an illegitimate child; 2) children honour their fathers even if they discipline them (v. 9). Although generally in the Greek παιδεία and παιδεύω refer to "education", from the parallelism in v. 5 (5b: ἐλεγχόμενος) we can see that here they refer to "discipline" ("Züchtigung", so Erich Gräßer 1997, III/258–59) or, more precisely, to "instructive discipline, correction" (so William Lane 1991, B/419).

The relationship to one's real father is referred to as an argumentative analogy with the relationship to God. The argument only works if the addressees are expected to share these rules with the author. Verses 8–10 read as follows:

If you are left without discipline, in which all have participated, then you are illegitimate children and not sons. (9) Besides this, we have had earthly fathers to discipline us and we respected them. Shall we not much more be subject to the Father of spirits and live? (10) For they disciplined us for a short time at their pleasure, but he disciplines us for our good, that we may share his holiness.[6]

The passage in question is part of a longer exhortative section classified by William Lane as "parenetic midrash" (1991, B/406) and as "eine längere Glaubensparänese" by Erich Gräßer (1997, III/250). The exhortation is one of the key reasons why the letter was written: it summons the addressees to hold on to their faith, probably amidst persecution and temptations to give up their faith in Jesus (see e.g. Gräßer 1997, III/259, speaking "von der allein den Glauben bedrohenden Kardinalsünde des Abfalls"). Just as Jesus gave an example in enduring suffering (Heb 12:1–3), the recipients of the letter should be strengthened and should hold on to God's grace (vv. 12–15). Gräßer (1997, III/251) points also to chs. 2–5 as a parallel: "Wie Jesus, der durch Erniedrigung zur Erhöhung gelangte (2,9) und der – *obwohl* Sohn – in der Anfechtung den Gehorsam lernte und dadurch zum τελειωθείς wurde (5,8 f), so wird es auch mit einer geringfügigen sachlichen Abweichung bei den Glaubenden sein: *Weil* sie Söhne sind, erleiden sie die Zucht Gottes."[7] The author of the letter asks his readers to accept their situation from God's hand. God has received them as his sons (ὡς in v. 5 is to be translated as

---

[6] There are only minor variants in the longer passage; NA27 can be adopted in each case. To mention but a few: In verse 4 some MSS have the less emphatic ἀγωνιζόμενοι, while NA27 adopt the compound version, which not only means "suffer hardship", but includes the idea of "resisting" (ἀνταγωνιζόμενοι). In verse 7, some MSS have εἰ ("if"), but NA27 suggest that we should adopt the prepositional phrase, "*for* (εἰς) discipline". The latter is adopted by W. L. Lane who argues that the variant is due to an "assimilation to the conditional construction found in v 8" (1991, B/401). In verse 9, NA27 brackets δέ; the particle is not really needed, because the antithesis is already expressed by the interrogative comparison, "shall we not much more..." (οὐ πολὺ μᾶλλον).

[7] Italics his; we return later to the passages mentioned.

"als" and not "wie", so Gräßer 1997, III/256; see also v. 6: πάντα υἱὸν ὃν παραδέχεται); consequently they would find strength if they looked upon their suffering as a discipline from their heavenly father. Discipline from the side of God as father is not a sign of anger, but of love (v. 6a), as it is written in Proverbs. As Gräßer puts it (1997, III/261): "Die wichtigste aus dem Zitat gewonnene Erkenntnis lautet: Das Leiden ist Erweis der Vaterliebe Gottes (V 7 f)."

Children's duty is expressed by the verb "to endure" (v. 7: ὑπομένετε, here probably as an imperative, so W. L. Lane 1991, B/401; for the verb, cf. also 10:32 concerning the addressees and 12:2 concerning Jesus). The author of the letter turns to the example of earthly fathers from verse 7b onward. This half-verse sums up an axiom in the form of a question which is answered in v. 8b: "for what son is there whom his father does not discipline?", – it is an illegitimate son (νόθοι, only here in the NT).[8] The very fact that God disciplines them shows that the addressees of the letter are not regarded by God as illegitimate sons. Erich Gräßer (1997, III/258) calls this argument a "'pädagogische Analogieschluß' a minori ad maius".[9]

Another duty of children appears in the analogy of earthly ("bodily", τῆς σαρκός) fathers in v. 9a, when the author simply affirms as a general truth: we "respect" (ἐνετρεπόμεθα) them (even when they discipline us). In v. 9b, the author returns from the analogy to the relationship to God, the "father of spirits" (with a little textual variation: "father of the spirituals", minuscule 440; "father of the fathers" in a few MSS). This expression (τῷ πατρὶ τῶν πνευμάτων) appears only here in the NT. It is probably used in order to emphasise the contrast between earthly fathers and God, by applying the terminology of a dualistic anthropology: σάρξ (v. 9a) and πνεῦμα (so E. Gräßer 1997, III/268–69). "'The Father of spirits' is the transcendent God to whom the heavenly world is also subject."[10] The third duty appears in v. 9b in the form of a rhetorical question: "Shall we not much more be subject (ὑποταγησόμεθα) to the Father of spirits and live?"

Thus it is expected from children that they obey their fathers; this obedi-

---

[8] We note that the idea of illegitimacy may be in the background of the infancy narratives in the Gospels: Jesus may have been regarded as an "illegitimate" son in Joseph's neighbourhood, since Jesus was conceived before Joseph married Mary. (Cf. also J. Schaberg 1990.)

[9] E. Gräßer (*ibid.*, 257–58) paraphrases the argument of the author in this way: "Wenn schon zwischen Vater und Sohn Erziehung geübt wird, die letzterem nützlich und Bestätigung der Sohnschaft ist, um wieviel mehr ... muß sie dann auch zwischen Gottvater und Gottessöhnen stattfinden 'zum (wahren) Nutzen (συμφέρον), damit sie Anteil erhalten an seiner Heiligkeit' (V 10)."

[10] W. L. Lane 1991, B/424; he points to the following parallel passages: Num 16:22; 27:16 LXX.

ence includes accepting discipline. All this is put in the form of rhetorical questions and axiomatic affirmations; they are expected to be shared by the addressees. We note that v. 10 implies that there may be no limit to be recognised in carrying out this duty, since it is supposed that children respect their fathers who discipline them "at their pleasure", i.e. as they like (κατὰ τὸ δοκοῦν αὐτοῖς; cf. August Strobel's reference to "Dafürhalten und Willkür", 1991, 161).

We discuss 1 Pet 2:18 in the next section, since it is concerns a short reference to earthly fathers in a passage where the figurative sense of "children" and "father" dominates.

3. Family imagery in a figurative sense

In the NT writings discussed in this chapter there are some texts that address the child-parent relationship only in an indirect way. When discussing them we continue to focus on the question: What kind of views on the child-parent relationship do they suppose?

The Letter to the Hebrews draws on family imagery when speaking about Jesus' sonship and also when referring to the Christians as Jesus' brethren or God's "sons". As an example of the latter, we have already mentioned Heb 12:4–11 in the previous section.

Hebrews 2:5–18 comforts the addressees by pointing to Jesus' suffering and to the addressees' relationship to Jesus and to his father who is also their father. Hebrews 2:10 first refers to God, "for whom and by whom all things exist" (a circumlocution for God, "not found elsewhere in the Greek Bible", W. L. Lane 1991, A/55),[11] and then to Jesus who "brought many sons to glory". In the Greek text it is not specified whose sons are meant, but the next verse makes explicit that they are God's sons, and the brethren of Jesus (v. 11): "For he who sanctifies and those who are sanctified have all one origin. That is why he is not ashamed to call them brethren". In verse 10, "many" is inclusive: "The writer envisions the great host of those for whom Jesus secured the fulfillment of the divine intention and whose 'sonship' is established by virtue of his relationship to them" (W. L. Lane 1991, A/55). We note that according to v. 11 the children of God are "sanctified" just as the children of the believing partner in a marriage are holy in 1 Cor 7:14 (the cognate ἅγια being used there).

---

[11] E. Gräßer holds that the expression originates in Stoic pantheism, whence it came to the early Christians via Hellenistic Judaism (1990, I/127).

We note that in the OT it is God who sanctifies (see e.g. Exod 31:13; Lev 20:8); yet it is rightly emphasised by Erich Gräßer (1990, I/134) that in Hebrews this predicate of God is transferred to Jesus (so also W.L. Lane 1991, A/58; cf. Heb 10:29; 13:12). However, the idea of God as the sanctifier is also present in Hebrews (see e.g. 12:10), so Gräßer is right in his conclusion concerning 2:11 (*ibid.*, 135; italics his): "ἁγιαζόμενοι umschreibt also den Stand der *Söhne*". This confirms our interpretation that Heb 2:11 refers to God's "sons" being holy.

The statement in verse 11 is supported by two quotations from Scripture: Ps 22:12 is quoted in v. 12 because it includes a reference to the "brethren" of the speaker, perhaps alluding to the early Christian tradition that Jesus prayed this Psalm when hanging on the cross (cf. Mark 15:34; Harald Hegermann [1988, 7] refers to Ps 22 as "das älteste uns greifbare Schriftzeugnis zur Passionstradition").[12] Then Isa 8:17–18 is quoted (in two parts, in v. 13a and 13b), where Isaiah speaks about his own children (παιδία).[13] This latter citation seems to change the imagery, since the "children" of the speaker are mentioned, but v. 17 turns back to the original picture when it refers to the Christians as to Jesus' "brethren". As William Lane has put it (1991, A/60): "Although the concept of the people of God as τὰ παιδία, 'the children,' of the exalted Son is not found elsewhere in the NT, the image of the family suggests an intimacy of relationship and a tenderness that broadens the concept of solidarity."

In this passage family imagery is used with the purpose of comfort, as the goal of the section affirms (v. 18): "For because he [i.e. Jesus] himself has suffered and been tempted, he is able to help those who are tempted." The "brethren" of Jesus, God's "sons" can find strength in this "family": "Sohn und Söhne bilden eine himmlische Bruderschaft" (E. Gräßer 1990, I/113).

Although the key notion of Hebrews is Jesus' priesthood, the notion of sonship is significant as well. This can be seen in 3:1–6 where after Jesus is called a high priest (v. 1), the imagery of the household is introduced. Verse 2 speaks about the faithfulness of Moses "in his house", and then Jesus' glory is compared to that of Moses (v. 3a: Jesus "has been counted worthy of as much more glory than Moses"). The comparison is continued in vv. 5–6 (with a quotation about Moses, from Num 12:7 LXX, in v. 5a) where we read: "Now Moses was faithful in all God's house as a servant (ὡς

---

[12] Cf. E. Gräßer's question (1990, I/139): "ist der Kontext von Ps 22 typologisch mitbedacht: Wie der ursprüngliche Psalmbeter aus äußerster Bedrängnis zur Rettung und zum Gotteslob geführt wird, so Jesus aus dem Tod zum Leben?"

[13] W.L. Lane (1991, A/59) mentions that the citation in v. 13a is so brief that we cannot be certain that it comes from Isa 8:17; it may come from 2 Sam 22:3.

3. Family imagery in a figurative sense 211

θεράπων), to testify to the things that were to be spoken later, (6) but Christ was faithful over God's house as a son (Χριστὸς δὲ ὡς υἱὸς ἐπὶ τὸν οἶκον αὐτοῦ). And we are his house (οὗ οἶκός ἐσμεν ἡμεῖς) if we hold fast our confidence and pride in our hope."

There are two significant variants in this passage. In verse 6, some MSS have "*which* house we are" (ὅς e.g. in P[46]), instead of "*whose* house we are" (NA27 adopts the latter, attested e.g. by P[13], the Codices Sinaiticus and Vaticanus, and followed by the RSV quoted above). Even if we adopt the latter reading, it is clear from the context that God's house and Christ's house is the same: one house is referred to throughout the passage. Erich Gräßer rightly argues (1990, I/168): there is only one people of God envisaged in the Epistle to the Hebrews.[14] In the same verse NA27 puts in the apparatus two expressions which were in the main text until the 25th edition: "until the end", and "strong" as an adjective belonging to "confidence" (in the Greek three consecutive words).

The argument in vv. 5–6 is somewhat difficult. Gräßer paraphrases it in this way (1990, I/167; italics his): "Mose ist nicht Erbauer des Hauses Gottes, sondern Diener *in* ihm. Wenn aber schon Mose *als Diener* im Hause Gottes gehorsamerheischende Autorität war, wieviel mehr Jesus, der als Sohn *Herr* über das Haus Gottes ist (vgl. 10:21)." Scott Layton (1991, 477) contrasts the role of the servant (Moses) to that of the "steward" (Jesus). He argues that the Hebrew expression, על־הבית (אשר), is a title which "denotes a royal administrative official" in 1–2 Kings (p. 475). The same expression is used in the Joseph story when Joseph is appointed over Potiphar's house (Gen 39:4), and when he is appointed by the Pharaoh (Gen 41:40; p. 474). On the basis of this usage, Layton writes (p. 474): "I propose that the phrase 'over his house' is the NT reflex of Hebrew על־הבית (אשר) '(the one) over the house', and that by this phrase Christ is portrayed as the steward over the household of God."

Gräßer calls the reference to Christians as "the house of God" an allegory (1990, I/168). He also points to the significance of the household imagery for the author of the letter (p. 169): "In seiner Doppelbedeutung – räumlich-sachlich meint οἶκος das Haus, die kultische Wohnung; personal-sozial die Familie, die kultische Gemeinde – scheint der οἶκος-Begriff dem Hebr bestens geeignet zu sein, das Verhältnis Christus/Gemeinde zu bestimmen."

Although the author of the letter goes beyond the passage he quotes from Num 12:7 inasmuch as he adds the reference to the builder (v. 4), the key

---

[14] E. Gräßer further argues (*ibid.*): "Denn 'Haus Christi' ist nur Spezifikation des einen Hauses Gottes, sofern wir Christus angehören, der der Herr über den οἶκος θεοῦ ist."

picture of Heb 3:1–6 is that of the "house". We may add that v. 1a fits the household imagery, when the recipients are addressed as "holy brethren" (ἀδελφοὶ ἅγιοι). The section refers to the addressees as God's household in order to exhort them to steadfast hope in the footsteps of Jesus (vv. 1b and 6b): "consider Jesus, the apostle and high priest of our confession.... And we are his house if we hold fast our confidence and pride in our hope."

Hebrews 5:8 is a difficult passage from the point of view of systematic theology, since it raises the question as to what Jesus, the son of God, had to learn. However, it fits the family imagery we have met so far. In Hebrews 5, the context makes it clear that Jesus is referred to as the son of God, since v. 5 applies to him Ps 2:7: "Thou art my Son, today I have begotten thee". We note that the same verb, γεννάω, is used here as in 1 Cor 4:15 and Phlm 10 (discussed in the previous chapter). Erich Gräßer (1990, I/289) points to the inthronisation of the OT kings as the background to Ps 2:7: "Durch dieses schöpferische, eine neue Existenz setzende Wort wird der erwählte König auf die Seite Gottes gezogen, als sein 'Allernächster', als Erbe und Repräsentant der göttlichen Macht und Herrschaft." Hebrews 5:5 belongs to the NT passages in which the "today" of Ps 2:7 is understood as the time of elevating the king into the sphere of the divine presence (Gräßer, *ibid.*).

Hebrews 5:8 reads: "Although he was a Son, he learned obedience through what he suffered" (καίπερ ὢν υἱός, ἔμαθεν ἀφ' ὧν ἔπαθεν τὴν ὑπακοήν). The beginning of the sentence is concessive: καίπερ, "although", shows that Jesus in his status as God's son would not be expected to have to learn through suffering (so Gräßer 1990, I/295).[15] However, what follows is a general truth: what does "being a son" involve? – it involves learning obedience. Thus the sentence serves as an argument in the longer passage beginning from 5:1 in which the emphasis lies on Jesus' nearness to other human beings. Even though he is God's son, he fulfils the customs applying to earthly "sons": he learns obedience. "Das war die Einübung in die Solidarität mit den Brüdern" (Gräßer (1990, I/295).

The first finite verb in the whole long sentence in vv. 7–10 is ἔμαθεν, "he learned" (*ibid.*, 294); this puts an emphasis on it. Jesus being "obedient" is known in the early Christian tradition elsewhere (see Phil 2:8), but only Hebrews emphasises that he had to *learn* obedience. The expression "learning from suffering" is an axiom of popular wisdom ("Allerweltsweisheit"), well attested in Greek and Jewish sources (Gräßer 1990, I/306). However, both

---

[15] For a discussion of Harnack's proposal that the clause "although he was the Son" should belong to v. 7, see W. L. Lane 1991, A/110. Lane argues that though it is true that καίπερ usually qualifies what precedes, and not what follows, there are also examples for "the introduction of a protasis with καίπερ".

3. Family imagery in a figurative sense 213

terms belong to the sphere of the son-father relationship as well: the reference to suffering may imply the discipline carried out by the father. More concretely, here it may be a reference to Jesus' "passion" (as πάσχειν always is in Hebrews; W. L. Lane 1991, A/121); thus this suffering can be seen as being included in the "teaching" work of God as the "father" of Jesus. Lane suggests that the term "he learned" should be understood against a development in "biblical Greek, where learning takes place in the reception of Scripture as the word of God" (*ibid.*). We have seen in the chapters on the Jewish sources and on the Pauline Corpus that learning from Scripture belongs to the household setting of Jewish families. The very occurrence of the term "obedience" points in this direction as well.

To sum up, whatever dogmatic difficulties this verse may present, it seems to use family imagery in such a way as to suppose that the duty of children to learn obedience must have been acknowledged by both the writer and the addressees.[16]

The Epistle of James does not address the child-parent relationship directly. In as much as the letter refers to two commandments from the second table of the Ten Commandments (2:11), and in 2:8 the author quotes from Lev 19:18 the commandment to love one's neighbour, it may be surprising that the commandment to honour father and mother does not surface in the letter. However, we can argue the other way round as well: the social interest of the letter, and its appeal to the Ten Commandments may raise the possibility that the honour due to parents may be supposed to be in the background of some passages in the letter.

Abraham appears together with his son in Jas 2:21; here he is not only the father of Isaac, but the author calls him "our father" (ὁ πατὴρ ἡμῶν). Franz Mussner (1987, 141) argues that this expression was originally a claim made by Jewish people (cf. e.g. Isa 51:2; 4 Macc 16:20; Matt 3:9; John 8:39), but in early Christianity it included Gentile Christians as well (cf. Rom 4:12; so also Sophie Laws 1980, 133). Thus Mussner argues that James's reference to Abraham as "our father" does not imply that only Jewish Christians are addressed by the letter (*ibid.*).

Abraham is called "our father" in James, but this must be understood in the sense of a "forefather" (cf. Rom 4:1, where in many MSS he is referred to as "father", but there is also a textual tradition, adopted also by NA27 as the main text, that has τὸν προπάτορα ἡμῶν). Honour toward the fore-

---

[16] We note that the sonship of Jesus involves a high authority in the eye of the writer even in the present passage, since the following verse speaks about others being obedient to him. – For a discussion of the Melchizedek references (starting in Hebrews in this passage, cf. 5:6.10), see e.g. Peter Balla 1995.

fathers implies honour to one's parents as well. This is paralleled in honour toward older people. In Jas 5:14 the readers are told that ill people should "call for the elders of the church" (προσκαλεσάσθω τοὺς πρεσβυτέρους τῆς ἐκκλησίας). It is probable that the term "elders" refers to "officials" here (so e.g. Peter Davids 1982, 193; Franz Mussner 1987, 219). However, the model of the Jewish leadership of villages and of synagogues probably influenced the author of the letter just as it influenced the early Christian church in Jerusalem (so Hubert Frankemölle 1994, II/710). If so, then it is likely that some of the elders were also "old" in age. The "office" of eldership, at least in its origins, is probably in connection with the view that old people should be honoured. This duty is related to the duty of honouring parents, as we have seen in the environment of the NT.

The author repeatedly addresses his readers as "brethren" (most often "my brethren" or "my beloved brethren" (see e.g. 1:2.19; 2:1.5.14; 3:1; 4:11; 5:7.19). We have seen in the Pauline Corpus that this usage can imply that Christians belong to the family of God; they are brothers and sisters because they are children of God. Perhaps this idea is reflected in Jas 1:17–18. Here God is referred to as the "father of lights" (ἀπὸ τοῦ πατρὸς τῶν φώτων). Wolfgang Schrage points to Gen 1:14 and Ps 135:7 (LXX) as examples where "lights" mean "stars" (1993, 20). This must be its meaning in Jas 1:17 as well (see e.g. H. Frankemölle 1994, I/291, 295; F. Mussner 1987, 91). Concerning the use of the expression in James, Schrage argues (*ibid*.): "damit wird der Vaterbegriff in sonst im Neuen Testament unüblicher Weise kosmologisch verstanden und mit den Gestirnen verbunden."

However, we may add that the expression also fits family imagery, since v. 17 speaks about "gifts" coming from this father "from above": "Every good endowment and every perfect gift is from above, coming down from the Father of lights with whom there is no variation or shadow due to change." The gift is not specified; it may be "wisdom" (so P. H. Davids 1982, 88; cf. Jas 3:15.17). Whatever it include, it implies the father's care in providing for his children. The "slightly imperfectly quantified hexameter" in v. 17 contains a wordplay (so S. Laws 1980, 72); thus πᾶσα δόσις and πᾶν δώρημα are either synonymous, or δόσις may be translated as a verbal noun, "so that it is 'all good giving and every perfect gift' (NEB) that may be attributed to God" (Laws, *ibid*.).

Verse 18 continues the parental imagery, since the expression "bringing forth" is used: "Of his own will he brought us forth by the word of truth that we should be a kind of first fruits of his creatures." The expression "brought us forth" (ἀπεκύησεν) "denotes the female's part in giving birth" (S. Laws 1980, 75), but it is probably used here as a continuation of the picture in

3. Family imagery in a figurative sense 215

v. 15, where the same verb occurs: "Then desire when it has conceived gives birth to sin; and sin when it is full-grown brings forth death." As Peter Davids has put it (1982, 89): "Sin produces death, but God produces life".

In Jas 1:18 we further observe the presence of the idea of creation, which is expressed in the term "his creatures" (and in the variant reading in some MSS which have ἐποίησεν instead of ἀπεκύησεν). We have seen in the environment (e.g. in Philo) that the creative activity of God and the procreative activity of parents are regarded as being closely related. The idea of "God as the creator" and "God as father" belong together. Sophie Laws argues that v. 18 continues describing "God as Father", in spite of the use of ἀποκυέω (1980, 75). The verse refers to one particular gift of God, "that of birth" (*ibid.*). God's gift of new life has an ethical implication: the addressees are expected to lead a way of life that is in accordance with the word of God (cf. also the next verse, 1:19, which begins a paraenetic section: "Know this, my beloved brethren. Let every man be quick to hear, slow to speak, slow to anger").

We may put it in this way: Christians are the "children" of God. Just as we have seen in the Pauline Corpus that one implication of the parental imagery is the expectation that Christians will obey him, this imagery may be in the background in the Epistle of James as well, since this letter is full of ethical advice.

Although 1 Peter has a long passage dealing with duties in the realm of family relationships and in wider circles of the society, we have argued in the previous chapter that this text is not a Household Code. For one thing, its concern includes also the leaders of the "state"; for another, it omits the child-parent relationship (see 1 Pet 2:13–3:7). However, there is a passage stressing the duty of children to honour their parents. In 1 Pet 1:14 we read: "As obedient children (ὡς τέκνα ὑπακοῆς), do not be conformed to the passions of your former ignorance" ("of your ignorance" is partly or wholly missing in some MSS; in the Greek it is parenthetical, interrupting the expression "to former passions").

The expression "obedient children" has a similar genitival structure in the Greek to the phrase "the sons of disobedience" (υἱοὶ τῆς ἀπειθείας) in Eph 2:2. Thus it may be that it is idiomatic, describing the readers as an "obedient people" (see Ramsey Michaels 1988, 56).[17] However, the term τέκνα in

---

[17] Although the idiomatic use of "son(s) of ..." is not discussed in this monograph, we note that since the idiom points to a strong, inseparable relationship, it is based on a family imagery in which sons imitate their fathers to such an extent that they become one with them. The idiomatic use in Eph 2:2 can be paralleled by the following expressions (using υἱός / υἱοί): "son of peace" (Luke 10:6); "sons of the resurrection" (Luke 20:36); "sons of light"

1 Pet 1:14 may be a conscious choice of the author in order to anticipate the reference to "father" in v. 17. The only other occurrence of τέκνα in 1 Peter is in 3:6, where the idea of obedience plays a role as well; though here Christian wives are addressed as the "children of Sarah", and Sarah's obedience to her husband is emphasised. The choice of the word τέκνα may be due to its association with "obedience" (Michaels 1988, 57). Although 1 Pet 1:14 does not say explicitly whose children are addressed, the following verses probably imply that the readers of the letter are referred to as God's children.

The author goes on to exhort the addressees to be holy, since he who has called them is holy, too (v. 15). Although in the NT 1 John 2:20 may be the only other reference to God the father as "the Holy One", ὁ ἅγιος (though even this occurrence is open to discussion, see J. R. Michaels 1988, 58), the expression is widely attested in the Septuagint in the form of "the Holy One of Israel" (e.g. Ps 70:22 LXX; Isa 1:4). In verse 16, the author makes clear that he refers to God's call when he quotes from Lev 19:2 (LXX): "You shall be holy, for I am holy" (cf. also Lev 11:44, with minor differences). We have already seen that the reference to being "holy" (ἅγιοι) can stand in a context where a believing parent's child shares the parent's holiness (1 Cor 7:14; cf. also Heb 2:11, discussed above). Apart from the "priestly" connotations of the quotation from Leviticus (so J. R. Michaels 1988, 60, pointing also to 1 Pet 2:9), this further aspect may lie behind the use of ἅγιοι in this context.

The reference to holiness in 1 Pet 1:15–16 is immediately followed by a reference to God as "father" in v. 17, where we read: "And if you invoke as Father him who judges each one impartially" (καὶ εἰ πατέρα ἐπικαλεῖσθε; with minor variants regarding the verb). We note the natural way in which the reference to "father" occurs: it is not a point to be proved, but something already supposed. The paternal imagery applied to God is significant for the author of the letter, since God as father appeared already at the beginning, in vv. 2–3. The reappearance of the motif in v. 17 (after it was already implied in v. 14) must have a purpose. The metaphor is used in order to motivate the addressees (so also Norbert Brox 1979, 79), as v. 17b clearly says: "conduct yourselves with fear throughout the time of your exile." Thus I suggest that we have here an argument similar to that in 1 Corinthians: a parent's holiness is passed on to the children; this time God himself is the "holy parent".

(Luke 16:8; John 12:36; 1 Thess 5:5); "the son of perdition" (John 17:12); "sons of the day" (1 Thess 5:5). We note that the idiomatic usage appears with τέκνα in Eph 2:3 ("children of wrath"), Eph 5:8 ("children of light"), and in 2 Pet 2:14 (though here in reversed order, κατάρας τέκνα, "accursed children" [RSV]).

3. Family imagery in a figurative sense

The imagery of the child-parent relationship between the addressees and God is continued in v. 23, where a verb related to γεννάω is used: "You have been born anew (ἀναγεγεννημένοι), not of perishable seed but of imperishable, through the living and abiding word of God". As the same verb is used in v. 3, the two occurrences form an *inclusio*. The picture is carried over to chapter two, where in verse two the addressees are called to long for "milk" (γάλα; cf. 1 Cor 3:2), "like newborn babes" (ὡς ἀρτιγέννητα βρέφη). The metaphor has its limits, since real infants do not need to be told "to long for" milk. The author uses the picture to imply that the recipients should acknowledge their need for growth (Eduard Schweizer 1998, 42). This does not mean that they have only recently become Christians. Rather, it emphasises that they cannot make themselves perfect; they receive salvation from God through the "spiritual" milk (λογικόν here may refer back to διὰ λόγου in 1:23; so Schweizer, *ibid.*). The picture of being nourished serves to show the addressees how much they have to rely on God.

First Peter 1:22 employs family imagery, too: "Having purified your souls by your obedience to the truth (ἡγνικότες ἐν τῇ ὑπακοῇ τῆς ἀληθείας) for a sincere love of the brethren, love one another earnestly from the heart". We observe that "love of the brethren" (φιλαδελφία) is mentioned here together with another Greek expression for the idea of "loving" (ἀγαπήσατε), and together with "heart" (ἐκ καρδίας). "Heart" has an adjective in some MSS, "clean" (καθαρᾶς), which is put in brackets in the main text of NA27. If we adopt the shorter reading, then the text is a confirmation of the family imagery. Ramsey Michaels rightly notes (1988, 72): "The latter picks up the emphasis on 'genuine brotherly love' in the preceding clause, while the longer reading accents the reference to purification with which the verse begins." We may add that the reference to "obedience" in the same verse may confirm our exposition that the verse uses family imagery.

We observe that the whole passage, 1:14–2:2, has a paraenetic character: the author calls the readers to a life-style worthy of those who have been "ransomed" (v. 18) "with the precious blood of Christ" (v. 19).[18] The call to obedience to God is expressed by words belonging to the imagery of the child-parent relationship.

It is against this background that a reference to earthly fathers appears in this longer passage. In verse 18 we read: "You know that you were ran-

---

[18] Eduard Schweizer points out concerning 1 Pet 1:13–21 (1998, 31): "In dem langen Abschnitt finden sich nur drei Tätigkeitswörter in der direkten Aussageform: 'hofft! – werdet! – wandert!' Es sind alles Aufforderungen, im Griechischen in der Zeitform, die den Neueinsatz betont."

somed from the futile ways inherited from your fathers" (ἐλυτρώθητε ἐκ τῆς ματαίας ὑμῶν ἀναστροφῆς πατροπαραδότου, the order of the last two words is reversed in some MSS). The adjective πατροπαράδοτος ("transmitted by the fathers") is found neither in the LXX, nor elsewhere in the NT. In non-Christian sources it is a positive term praising the old traditions (see examples in J. R. Michaels 1988, 64; e.g. a letter of King Attalus III to the people of Pergamum in 135 B.C.). The author of 1 Peter seems to be the first Christian to apply it to the old, pagan way of life from which the Christians are freed (so N. Brox 1979, 81).

Thus it is striking that earthly fathers are mentioned in a negative context: they pass on a "futile" lifestyle to their children. There are two possible lines of interpretation. On the one hand, it may be argued that the negative picture about earthly fathers serves as a contrast to highlight the greatness of the gifts of God the father. In this case there is a tension between real earthly fathers and God the heavenly Father (the term being used in a figurative sense): our heavenly Father has to save us from the futile lifestyle inherited from our earthly fathers. On the other hand, it is also possible to argue that the reference to earthly fathers is introduced in order to point to human fallenness; forefathers throughout many generations are included (so e.g. N. Brox 1979, 80).

If we adopt the latter argument, then the context may shed a new light on v. 18. It becomes significant that the reference to earthly fathers appears in a context which is characterised by family imagery calling for obedience to God as father. Earthly fathers are assumed to be honoured, in spite of the fact that they participate in the process by which human fallenness is passed on to ever new generations. Thus it is possible to interpret this passage in such a way that it is not taken to imply dishonouring one's parents. Rather, since God is to be obeyed as "father", earthly fathers are supposed to receive due honour, in spite of their fallen nature.[19]

We briefly note that at the end of the letter the author refers to Mark as to his "son" (5:13–14a): "She who is at Babylon, who is likewise chosen, sends you greetings; and so does my son Mark. (14) Greet one another with the kiss of love." The structure of the letter-ending is similar to those of the Pauline letters (see E. Schweizer 1998, 97). The use of family imagery in

---

[19] Eduard Schweizer can point also to some good deeds of the forefathers (1998, 34–35): "Dabei haben diese [i.e. die 'Väter'] gewiss nicht nur Verbrechen und Perversitäten ausgeübt, sondern auch Kinder grossgezogen, Felder bestellt und für ihr Vaterland gekämpft, schöne Gottesdienste gefeiert und Opfer gebracht. 'Nichtig' war ihr Leben nicht, weil es im Vergleich zu anderen Völkern inhaltlos oder besonders böse gewesen wäre, sondern weil Gott anderes mit ihnen wollte."

3. Family imagery in a figurative sense 219

this verse is similar to the reference to Timothy and Titus as Paul's children. Though 1 Pet 5:13 uses the expression "son" (Μᾶρκος ὁ υἱός μου) instead of "child" which is used in the Pauline Corpus, it points to a spiritual relationship, too. Because of the word "son", Wolfgang Schrage rightly uses the term "spiritual fatherhood" ("geistliche Vaterschaft"; 1993, 121); however, there may be a difference when compared with the Pauline Corpus: in the case of Peter and Mark this may not imply that Mark has become a Christian through Peter (so E. Schweizer 1998, 98, with a reference to Acts 12:12). There is a tradition attributed to a certain "elder" by Papias that Mark was the "interpreter" of Peter (recorded in Eusebius, *Hist. eccl.* 3.39.15), and another tradition referring to Mark as a "follower" of Peter (*Hist. eccl.* 2.15.1). Ramsey Michaels (1988, 312) argues that the term "son" here "should be understood as 'convert' or 'disciple' (BGD, 833.1c) in the same way that Timothy is referred to as Paul's 'child'". Whether or not the latter interpretation is right, Michaels (*ibid.*) may be right at least in his other suggestion that "Peter seems to have adopted it here to give to his concluding words the ring of a family greeting (cf. his emphasis on the Christian community as a 'brotherhood' in 2:17; 5:9)."

The reference to a "kiss" in verse 14 fits the family imagery. We note that a few MSS add "holy" (ἁγίῳ) to the expression "kiss", instead of the reference to "love" (ἀγαπῆς; the latter being adopted as the main text of NA27). "With the holy kiss" may be an assimilation to Pauline letter-endings (cf. e.g. Rom 16:16; 1 Cor 16:20). "Peter's distinctive 'kiss of love' picks up the admonitions to mutual love in 1:22 and 4:8, and love for the whole Christian brotherhood in 2:17" (J. R. Michaels 1988, 313). Wolfgang Schrage suggests that this "kiss" may have been part of early Christian worship, "als Zeichen gegenseitiger Bruderliebe" (1993, 121). Thus the Christian congregation is depicted here as an extended family where "brethren" greet each other in this way.

To sum up, 1 Peter uses household imagery in the following ways: the author can refer to God as the "father" of the Christians (implying also their brotherhood to one another), and the author can refer to an individual as his own "son" (implying a close spiritual bond). In the NT only 1 Peter applies a reference to the traditions of the forefathers to the former pagan way of life of the addresses. However, this use does not imply a failure in honouring one's parents.

We do not discuss 2 Peter and Jude in detail, since they do not refer to a real child-parent relationship, and they use family imagery only in passing. The author of Jude uses family language only in v. 1: he refers to himself as the "brother of James", and he makes use of the expression "God the father". The reference to being the brother of James is probably a claim to be the brother of the Lord as well (so Udo Schnelle 1996, 475–76, who holds that this is a pseudepigraphical writing; for a monograph treating the problem, see Richard Bauckham 1990). Otherwise Jude calls his addressees "beloved" (vv. 3, 17, 20: ἀγαπητοί). The reference to "God the father" (v. 1) must imply that the author shares the view which we have met in other NT writings that Christians are the "children" of God, but he does not make any more use of this imagery in the letter.

The author of 2 Peter calls his addressees "brethren" once: in 1:10. He refers to "God the father" in 1:17; this occurrence belongs to the child-parent imagery concerning the relationship of Jesus to God. Second Peter 1:17–18 refers to the scene of the "transfiguration": "For when he received honor and glory from God the Father and the voice was borne to him by the Majestic Glory, 'This is my beloved Son, with whom I am well pleased,' (18) we heard this voice borne from heaven, for we were with him on the holy mountain."

In 2 Peter 3:4 we find a reference to the "fathers" (some MSS add ἡμῶν, thus referring to "*our* fathers") who "fell asleep" (οἱ πατέρες ἐκοιμήθησαν), meaning the forefathers (2 Pet 3:3–4): "First of all you must understand this, that scoffers will come in the last days with scoffing, following their own passions (4) and saying, 'Where is the promise of his coming? For ever since the fathers fell asleep, all things have continued as they were from the beginning of creation.'" These "fathers" are either the Jewish patriarchs (so e.g. D. A. Carson *et al.*, 1993, 436, who argue that "nowhere else in the New Testament is the expression 'the fathers' used of the early Christians"), or earlier Christian generations (see e.g. Udo Schnelle 1996, 485, who counts the historical Peter among the fathers already fallen asleep). In either case, the expression is not used here to refer to people in their role as fathers of children.

We have already mentioned that there is an idiomatic use of the term "children" in 2 Peter, in which τέκνα are mentioned. In 2 Peter 2:14, at the end of a long list of vicious actions of false teachers, we find the expression (RSV): "Accursed children!" (κατάρας τέκνα). Richard Bauckham paraphrases the idiom in this way (1983, 258): "They are under God's curse." He notes that literally the idiom means, "children of a curse", and calls it a Hebraism (p. 267; so also Anton Vögtle 1994, 204; and Wolfgang Schrage 1993, 144).

Thus the few uses of family imagery in 2 Peter and Jude are close parallels to the uses met so far, though they are not elaborated in any detail in these letters.

3. Family imagery in a figurative sense

In the Epistles of John, the recipients are addressed frequently as "children". The author calls them his own children; and he also refers to them as God's children.[20] In 1 John 2:1 the author names the purpose of his writing. It is significant that this is the first time in 1 John that the author calls his readers "children" (with a diminutive form, "my little children", τεκνία μου): "My little children, I am writing this to you so that you may not sin; but if any one does sin, we have an advocate with the Father, Jesus Christ the righteous". By this way of addressing his recipients, the author implies that he has a loving relationship to them, and also that he writes with the expectation that they will obey him.

We note that in the same verse the author refers also to God as "father" (he already did so in 1:2.3, and implied it in 1:7 by a reference to Jesus as "son"). Thus the author uses the child-father imagery in a twofold way. First, he himself is the "father" of his addressees in a spiritual sense. We observe that he does not refer to himself as "father", but refers to his addressees as his "children". Second, Christians are regarded as the children of God. This is implied in the first two chapters and is expressed explicitly in 3:1a.2: "See what love the Father has given us, that we should be called children of God; and so we are.... (2) Beloved, we are God's children now; it does not yet appear what we shall be, but we know that when he appears we shall be like him, for we shall see him as he is." Although in v. 1 some MSS have "has given *you*", it is clear that the author includes himself, because the verb stands in the first person plural form (κληθῶμεν), and because the author uses "we are" (ἐσμέν) in v. 2 (we note that καὶ ἐσμέν at the end of v. 1 is omitted in some MSS). We may add that v. 2b may belong to this family imagery as well; if so, then it echoes the similarity between children and their fathers.

We can find further examples of these two uses, i.e. that the author as well as God are seen in the role of the father. We name but a few. First John 2:12–14 is a well-structured passage: it has two triplets of addresses. The author begins the first part with the address: "little children" (v. 12). The readers may think it is the same usage as in 2:1. Minuscule 630 even adds "my", to make explicit that the author speaks about his own children.

---

[20] When referring to the "author", I leave open the question whether the three letters were written by one author or 2–3 John were written by a different person. Similarly, I do not address the question of the historical order of the letters and their relationship to the Fourth Gospel. For a discussion of the issues involved, see Hans-Josef Klauck 1995a (arguing for one author of the three letters who is not the same as the Fourth Evangelist; see esp. p. 126); and Udo Schnelle 1996 (arguing for the priority of 2–3 John; see pp. 495–533, esp. 500–504, 516–18, 522). – Dietrich Rusam holds that the Johannine Epistles follow the Gospel of John. He observes that 1 John has a larger number of examples of the terms "children of God" and "born of God" than John's Gospel has (1993, 11).

The author goes on to address "fathers" as a second group (v. 13a). A third group, "young men" (νεανίσκοι), are addressed in v. 13b; then each of the three groups is addressed a second time (v. 14). On the second occasion, "children" are referred to with another word, παιδία (some MSS wanted to have an exact parallel, so they have παιδία also in v. 12, in the place of τεκνία). The Greek word is ambiguous, it can also mean "servants", but it probably means "children" in this context, as they are praised because they "know the father".

First John 2:12–14 reads:

I am writing to you (γράφω ὑμῖν), little children, because your sins are forgiven for his sake (διὰ τὸ ὄνομα).
(13) I am writing to you, fathers, because you know him who is from the beginning.
I am writing to you, young men, because you have overcome the evil one.
I write to you (ἔγραψα ὑμῖν), children, because you know the Father.
(14) I write to you, fathers, because you know him who is from the beginning.
I write to you, young men, because you are strong, and the word of God abides in you, and you have overcome the evil one.

Hans-Josef Klauck (1991, 132) summarises the "most favoured" exposition these days in the following way. The first items of both triplets concern Christians in general, i.e. all the members of the congregation ("als Anrede an die Gesamtgemeinde"). The second and the third items of the parallel structure are addressed to two "age groups" in the sense of the length of their being Christians. Thus this section is probably addressing various groups among the recipients. Klauck (*ibid.*) himself suggests that the view is worth considering that all three addresses refer to the whole congregation, but under different aspects. An alternative view would be to understand the three addresses as referring to age groups. Klauck argues that this is unlikely because of the sequence, children – fathers – young men, and because of the content of what is said to the different groups.[21]

If we accept that τεκνία and παιδία (in this case as synonyms) refer to the whole congregation, then we have an ambiguity (perhaps intended by the author). On the one hand, they may be used to refer to the "children" of the author (see e.g. Klauck 1991, 133, who speaks of the "role of the fatherly teacher", known from Wisdom literature). On the other hand, the

---

[21] The hypothesis of J.C. O'Neill is worth mentioning (1989, 282): "1 John, with its fierce command not to love the world nor the things in the world and to flee the lust of the flesh ... (1 John 2:15f.) might well have first been written for a monastic community. Note that the community is male, and consists perhaps of three grades, children, men and fathers (2:12–14)." "Father" was the Abbot, i.e. the head of the house (see J.C. O'Neill 1998, 126–32).

3. Family imagery in a figurative sense 223

terms may refer to the "children" of God. Klauck argues that in v. 12 the expression "forgiveness of sins" and the reference to the "name" (τὸ ὄνομα) remind the recipients of their becoming Christians (*ibid.*): "Kinder sind jene, die in Taufe und Sündenvergebung das neue Leben als Geschenk aus der Hand des Vaters empfangen."

In verse 13, "father" must refer to God, because it stands in the singular, and also because children would not need to be praised for "knowing" their own earthly fathers. "Knowing" here probably refers to knowing God as someone who calls his children to love each other (cf. the immediate context: vv. 9–10).

We observe that this passage addresses children and fathers, yet it does not speak about their duties toward one another. We further note that God as father appears in a context where earthly fathers are mentioned as well. This implies that various groups, including fathers, in a Christian household (and house church) should carry out their duties as God's children.

In 1 John 3:9–10, the author uses the verb γεννάω in the perfect tense when referring to the Christians being "born of God": "No one born of God commits sin; for God's nature abides in him, and he cannot sin because he is born of God. (10) By this it may be seen who are the children of God, and who are the children of the devil: whoever does not do right is not of God, nor he who does not love his brother." Concerning the use of the expression "born of God", Dietrich Rusam points out that (1993, 111): "Die Vaterschaft Gottes erfährt im 1 Joh eine logische Begründung: Gott ist Vater der Glaubenden, weil sie aus ihm geboren sind." The imagery includes associations both to the family and to creation. Christians thank their new life to God; that is why they follow his instructions. Horst Balz also emphasises the implication that God as father enables his children to withstand evil (1993, 190). "Konkret angespielt wird damit auf die Neugeburt der Glaubenden durch den Geist Gottes (vgl. Joh. 3,6–8). Die Möglichkeit eines Lebens im Widerspruch zur Sünde geht allein von Gott aus."

The author argues that because God loves the recipients (cf. 4:7–8), they ought to love one another as "brethren" (3:10b; cf. also 4:19–21, where, though not mentioned explicitly, God can be seen as "father", and this can serve as the ground for Christians to love one another). Rusam emphasises that God's fatherhood involves caring love (1993, 111). "So wird im 1 Joh das Gebot der Gottes- und Bruderliebe weniger auf Gottes väterliche Macht zurückgeführt, durch die er die Möglichkeit hat zu gebieten, sondern auf seine väterliche Liebe".

We have already seen in the environment of the NT the duty of children to take their father's advice. We have also seen in other letters in the NT that the authors made use of paternal imagery concerning the relationship between the Christians and God in order to call them to obedience in the matters concerning their way of life. A crucial piece of ethical advice in 1 John belongs to the picture of the household: brothers and sisters should love one another.

With these examples in the background, we cautiously raise the possibility that in 4:4 and in 5:21 their may be a conscious ambiguity in the use of τεκνία. On the one hand, it is probable that in both cases the term addresses the recipients as the "children" of the author, though the possessive pronoun "my" is not added in these cases. On the other hand, it may be that the author left out "my" on purpose: the addressees should think of themselves also as the children of God. In 4:4 this second possible meaning is implied by the beginning of the verse: "you are of God" (ὑμεῖς ἐκ θεοῦ ἐστε, the Greek preposition possibly implying being "born" of God, as in 3:9). The final verse of the letter, 5:21, is preceded by a reference to Jesus, the "son" of God (5:20). Perhaps, then, the addressees are not only referred to as the author's "children", but also as the brethren of the Son, as God's children.

To sum up, the author uses the imagery of the child-father relationship because he expects obedience to his ethical advice. The recipients are called the "children" of the author and those of God, because they are expected to obey the teaching of the author, and to fulfil the will of God. This implies a child-parent relationship in which children honour and obey their parents.

Whereas 1 John does not begin like a typical letter, 2 John does contain the sender and the addressees (v. 1a): "The elder to the elect lady and her children, whom I love in the truth". "Elder" (ὁ πρεσβύτερος) can be a reference to an office in the early church, but at the same time it can retain its original meaning: it can refer to an old person (see e.g. H. Balz 1993, 213). Hans-Josef Klauck (1992a, 28) suggests that the grammatical form of the comparative, "older", does not have to be stressed in the Greek, so the term can be translated as "der Alte". As we have seen in the part on the "environment", this latter meaning, too, would imply a claim of authority. The "elect lady" (ἐκλεκτῇ κυρίᾳ) is probably a metaphor for the congregation (so e.g. H. Balz 1993, 213; see also S. S. Smalley 1984, 318–9). This view is strengthened by the last verse of the letter (v. 13), which refers to the "sister" of this lady: "The children of your elect sister greet you" (the term "elect", ἐκλεκτῆς, is replaced in a few MSS by ἐκκλησίας, making the implied meaning explicit; see also Klauck 1992a, 34 against the view that the addressee would be an individual, a real lady).

By the way of an *inclusio*, both the beginning and the end of the letter mention "children": the addressees as well as those sending greetings are called τέκνα. As Klauck has put it (1992a, 74): "Es ist ein Stück Familienkorrespondenz, Familie dabei aber verstanden als *familia Dei*." It is worth noting that in v. 1 the "children" belong to the congregation: they are the children of the "elect lady". This implies that the congregation can be thought of as a "mother" (so also H. Balz 1993, 213). Verse 4a continues this usage: "I rejoiced greatly to find some of your children (ἐκ τῶν τέκνων σου) following the truth". Here we note that an exhortation is closely connected to praise: the author probably met some members of the congregation (so H-J. Klauck 1992a, 45), and by expressing his joy over them he implies that all of them should live like those he met. In verse 5 the author turns to the whole congregation (addressed as the "lady" again) in order to exhort them to fulfil the commandment of love.

We observe, however, that in v. 4b another metaphor appears when God is referred to as "father": "just as we have been commanded by the Father" (4b). In v. 3 we find a reference to peace from "God the father" and Jesus is also mentioned together with an addition naming him as the "son of the father" (though some MSS omit this second occurrence of "father", while other MSS replace it by a reference to "God"). Thus it seems that the children of the congregation are at the same time the children of God as well.

The author of 3 John refers to himself as an elder; thus the letter begins with the same expression as 2 John: ὁ πρεσβύτερος. However, there is a difference in the usage of the term "children": whereas in 2 John 4 the children of the "lady" were mentioned, in 3 John the author speaks about his own "children". In 3 John 3–4 we read: "For I greatly rejoiced when some of the brethren arrived and testified to the truth of your life, as indeed you do follow the truth. (4) No greater joy can I have than this, to hear that my children (τὰ ἐμὰ τέκνα) follow the truth."

The plural form, "my children", implies a general truth, but the immediate context, v. 3, makes it probable that the addressee of the letter, Gaius, is also included (so also H-J. Klauck 1992a, 85). This a further example of using family imagery to express the relationship between the author and his addressees. Our interpretation, that Gaius is included in the circle of the "children" of the author, is strengthened by the frequent reference to him as "the loved one" (vv. 1, 2, 5, 11). Gaius is praised for his services to the "brethren" (v. 5).[22] The reference to the "brethren" in vv. 3 and 5 implies that they are all "children" of God the father.

---

[22] Dietrich Rusam (1993, 212) has pointed out that the situation in 3 John fits the general picture we have of early Christianity inasmuch as there are probably house churches implied

Thus this letter supposes the child-parent imagery as regards the relationship between the addressees and God. At the same time, the idea that they are the "children" of the author is more dominant in 3 John than in 2 John.

We observe that both 2 John and 3 John are concerned with a way of life in accordance with God's will (see e.g. 2 John 4; 3 John 11). The addressees are praised, but at the same time they are warned against the bad example of others (see e.g. 2 John 7–11; 3 John 9–10). Thus we see here a use of family imagery similar to that in the Pauline Corpus: congregational members are expected to follow the advice of the letter-writer and to live in accordance with the will of God; that is why they are referred to as the children of the writer and the children of God.

At the end of our inquiry, we mention briefly that Revelation makes use of the child-parent relationship in a way similar to that seen in the Johannine Epistles: the term "children" is used in a figurative sense. In the letter to the congregation in Thyatira we read (Rev 2:20–23):

But I have this against you, that you tolerate the woman Jezebel, who calls herself a prophetess and is teaching and beguiling my servants to practice immorality and to eat food sacrificed to idols. (21) I gave her time to repent, but she refuses to repent of her immorality. (22) Behold, I will throw her on a sickbed, and those who commit adultery with her I will throw into great tribulation, unless they repent of her doings; (23) and I will strike her children dead (καὶ τὰ τέκνα αὐτῆς ἀποκτενῶ ἐν θανάτῳ). And all the churches shall know that I am he who searches mind and heart, and I will give to each of you as your works deserve.

The woman mentioned in Rev 2:20 can be an "individual false teacher, who could be a woman", but it is more likely that she stands as a personification for a group of false teachers, whose members are the "children" of this "woman" (so e.g. G. K. Beale 1999, 260–61). The Greek expression, τὴν γυναῖκα, is ambiguous: it can mean "woman", but the same word is used in the nominative referring to Jezebel, the "wife" of King Ahab in 3 Kgdms 20:25 (LXX), to which Rev 2:20 alludes. The punishment of "her children", i.e. of the false teachers, involves their death (cf. Rev 6:8; Ezek 33:27), which was also the punishment of Jezebel and Ahab's sons in the OT. Thus this occurrence of the term "children" is in contrast with that in 2 John where they were praised; in Revelation the death penalty awaits the group of false teachers. This text, however, implies a similar view of the child-parent relationship to that which we have met in other writings of the NT: in

---

in this letter as well: Diotrephes probably did not receive some people into the congregation that met at his house (vv. 9–10); whereas Gaius is probably praised for his hospitality in receiving people into the congregation at his house (vv. 5–6). The letter mentioned in v. 9 must have been directed to the whole church of the place, and not just to one house church in it.

Revelation, too, it implies obedience to a "mother" (this time the "mother" is probably a personification of false teaching; but the imagery has the same implication if one particular false teacher is in view).

We note that Revelation uses the term "child" also in 12:4.5.13, in the scene concerning the woman whose child was threatened by the dragon right after its birth. This passage, however, does not address the theme of child-parent relationship from the perspective of the child, which is our main interest in this inquiry. We note, however, the protecting and nourishing role of the "mother" (Rev 12:13–14).

Finally, it is worth mentioning that Revelation uses the term "father" always in relation to Jesus: God is Jesus' father (1:6; 2:28; 3:5.21; 14:1). It is in accordance with this usage that in the passage discussed above Jesus is referred to as the "Son of God" (Rev 2:18). This expression has a special emphasis here, since otherwise the attributes of Jesus in the seven letters (chs. 2–3) usually repeat those mentioned in the first chapter. In Rev 1:13 the expression "like a son of man" is used; this may be replaced in 2:18 by the reference to the "Son of God" (see also G. K. Beale 1999, 259).

4. Summary

In the writings discussed in this chapter (Acts, Hebrew, the Catholic Epistles, and Revelation), we have found similar uses of the child-parent imagery to those in the Pauline Corpus. We have found a few references to real child-parent relationships in which it is assumed that children live at home together with their parents (Acts) and that they learn from their parents, accepting even discipline from their fathers (Hebrews).

We have seen that the figurative sense of the terms "child", "son", "father", and "mother" dominate. Christians are referred to as "children" in their relationship to the senders of letters (1 John, 3 John). "Son" can refer in a figurative sense to the spiritual bond between Christians (1 Peter). The figurative imagery may even refer to people as the "children" of the church (2 John) and of a group of false teachers, personified in the figure of a woman (Revelation).

God is referred to metaphorically as "father" extensively in these writings. God is the "father" of Jesus (Hebrews, 2 Peter, 1 John, 2 John, Revelation); and he is also the father of the Christians (Hebrews, James, 1 Peter, 1 John). The parental imagery is used in these writings in order to imply a strong bond and loving feelings in the relationships to which it is applied. The imagery conveys comfort (Hebrews). One particular consequence of the Christians being regarded as the children of God is that they are "brethren" to one another. This use is widely attested in early Christianity (cf. our examples from Hebrews, 1 Peter, 1 John, 3 John). Because Christians are loved by God, their "father", they ought to love one another as "brethren".

In general terms, in our sources it is expected from the recipients of parental care that they will return it by their obedience to their teachers and to God's will. This implies a view of the child-parent relationship in which it is assumed that children honour and obey their parents.

Finally, we note the absence of references to tensions in the family that would be similar to those envisaged by some radical sayings of Jesus in the Gospel tradition. In an indirect way, this may confirm our thesis that Jesus' radical call to some disciples was not understood by the early church as a breach of the expectation of their pagan and Jewish environment that children owe honour to their parents.

Conclusion

Each chapter has concluded with a summary. It now remains to collect in the form of theses the findings which have emerged from studying the sources. The purpose of studying the pagan and Jewish environment of the New Testament in Part I was to prepare a background for answering the question in Part II, Did the first Christians conform to the standard expectation and teach that children had a duty to honour their parents?

We have found that in the pagan environment of the early Christians there was a strong expectation that children should honour and obey their parents. "Honour" included provision made for aged parents, and veneration of the parents after their death. The duty of children to honour their parents had a long prehistory; indeed we have found the same duties clearly stated centuries before the age of the first Christian generations, as can be seen in the summarising tables at the end of the first and second chapters.

We have seen that there were reasons given for children's duties both in the divine ("religious") sphere and in the human sphere. The main religious reason was that it is the will of the gods that parents have to be respected. It is the more significant that the main limitation to the honour offered by children are the gods themselves: although parents come first among human beings, they are always ranked after the gods. In other words: gods have priority over parents. We have noted in the summary of the second chapter that honour due to parents was expected even more emphatically in the period around the turn of the era than in the centuries before. There were fewer limits to the duty; and the ground for duty in nature was strengthened by a reference to the gods, as was the limit to a father's right to obedience should he try to prevent his son from studying philosophy.

Our study of the Jewish environment (chapter three) has led us to the conclusion that in most areas of the child-parent relationship Jews shared the same duties as we have found in the pagan environment. One significant difference was that honouring parents after their death did not mean venerating them as divine beings. In this regard, early Christianity followed the Jewish example rather than that of the pagan environment. There were also grounds for duties specific to the Jewish people, namely in the Mosaic Law, specifically the Fifth Commandment. This ground for the duty of honouring parents plays a significant role also in the New Testament in the Gospel tradition and in the Household Code in Ephesians. As regards limits to children's duties, we have seen that the senility of old parents was not a "limit" in Sirach as it was in Plato (ch. 1), but a view similar to that of Sirach is to be found in Periktyone (ch. 2). The Torah, the temple, and conversion to "Judaism" served as limits only in our Jewish sources; but the loyalty to the Torah can be seen as parallel to the loyalty to the higher good in philosophy (see ch. 2). In *1 Enoch*, enmity within the family is presented as an unavoidable sign of the last days when God's judgment will be executed.

In discussing the relevant texts of the New Testament, our primary interest has been to find out whether Jesus and the early Christians shared the view of their environment on children's duty to honour parents. We have found texts in the Gospel tradition (chapter four) which show a radical view of the child-parent relationship on Jesus' side: children have to leave their parents and follow Jesus. This radicalism can be explained in two ways. One possible line of interpretation is to point out that there is an either/or decision to be made by some disciples of Jesus: their alternatives are their parents or their new master. Another possibility is to emphasise the similarity between the expectations toward children in the Gospel tradition and in the non-Christian sources. We have argued that the radical sayings of Jesus can be interpreted in a way that does not involve a breach of the expectation found in the pagan and Jewish environment. Jesus traditions concerning tensions in the child-parent relationship can be classified in the following three groups: divisions within a family can be a consequence of the disciples' commitment to Jesus; some texts may refer to exceptional cases, i.e. they do not apply to all disciples; some texts either refer to the end time, or to the urgency of deciding upon priorities in the present. We may add that if we accept the view that Jesus was regarded by the early Christians as a divine being, priority given to Jesus corresponds to the view found in the environment: God comes before parents. If we view early Christianity against the background described in Part I, we may conclude that Jesus and his first followers shared the view of their environment that there is a hierarchy by which God takes precedence over parents. The Gospel tradition confronts us not so much with an alternative as with a priority: Jesus and his Kingdom have to occupy the first place in the life of Christians. This priority does not affect the validity of the Fifth Commandment for Jesus and his first followers.

Our discussion of the Pauline Corpus (chapter five) and of the rest of the New Testament (chapter six) has led us to the conclusion that outside the

Gospels the radical consequences of the itinerant lifestyle in following Jesus were not continued in the settled congregations. When discussing the texts we did not aim at a completely detailed exegesis; rather we wanted to find out what kind of a real child-parent relationship is expected in our sources and what kind of a relationship is presupposed in texts that make use of family imagery in a figurative sense.

We have found that in the undisputed Pauline Epistles priority is given to the congregation as the people of God. Paul's usage of figurative language implies that he thought of God's people as a "family". This usage confirms in an indirect way the conclusion that Paul must have shared the views of his Jewish and pagan environment concerning the honour due to parents. Among the Deuteropauline Epistles the Household Codes in Colossians and Ephesians show that children in the congregations were present with their parents at worship; they were taught to honour their parents. The fact that children are addressed before their fathers may also witness to a high respect for children. This may be due to the early Christian picture of Jesus: they held that their teacher had a high regard for children. However, the Household Codes teach children to obey parents; good order in the household was expected. In an indirect way this may confirm the conclusion that early Christianity did not understand the radical sayings of Jesus as implying a breach of the Fifth Commandment.

In the Pauline Corpus the term "father" is used also in a figurative sense: with reference to God. In the Pastoral Epistles God as "father" is mentioned at the beginning of the letters. Honour as an expectation is implied also in the emphasis on the need for good order in the households. In the Pastorals, this seems to be the primary reason for using family imagery. The emphasis on order in the "house" is a point of contact between the Christian congregation and their "environment".

In the rest of the NT we have found similar uses of the child-parent imagery to those in the Pauline Corpus. We have found only a few references to real child-parent relationships. We have seen that the figurative sense of the family imagery dominates. God is referred to metaphorically as "father" extensively in these writings (God is the "father" of Jesus; and he is also the father of the Christians). The parental imagery is used to imply a strong bond in the relationship between author and recipients; on the basis of this relationship it is expected that the recipients will follow the advice of the author.

Finally, we have noted the absence of references to tensions in the family. Early Christians wanted to show to their environment that they did not present a threat to society: they lived in households in which children honoured their parents; and their congregations were like extended families kept in good order. We hope to have shown that Jesus' radical call to some disciples was not understood by the early church as a breach of the expectation of their pagan and Jewish environment that children owe honour to their parents.

Bibliography

1. Editions of ancient texts

Aelian: *On the Characteristics of Animals.* With an English translation by A. F. Scholfield. LCL 3 vols, vol. 2 (books VI–XI): 1959, London: William Heinemann; Cambridge, Mass.: Harvard University Press

The Speeches of Aeschines. With an English translation by Charles Darwin Adams. LCL, 1919, London: William Heinemann; New York: G. P. Putnam's Sons

Aeschylus. With an English translation by Herbert Weir Smyth. LCL 2 vols, vol. 1: 1963, London: William Heinemann; Cambridge, Mass.: Harvard University Press

Aristophanes: *Clouds.* Edited with Introduction and Commentary by K. J. Dover. 1968, Oxford: Clarendon Press

The Comedies of Aristophanes. Vol. 3: Clouds. Edited with Translation and Notes by Alan H. Sommerstein. 1991 (third, corrected impression of 1982 orig.), Warminster, England: Aris & Phillips

Aristoteles: *Politik.* Nach der Übersetzung von F. Susemihl mit Einleitung, Bibliographie und zusätzlichen Anmerkungen von W. Kullmann. 1994, Reinbek bei Hamburg: Rowohlt Taschenbuch Verlag

Aristotelis Politica. Recognovit brevique adnotatione critica instruxit W. D. Ross. 1992 (twelfth impression of 1957 orig.), Oxford: Oxford University Press

Aristotle: *Politics.* Books I and II, translated with a Commentary by T. J. Saunders. 1995, Oxford: Clarendon Press

Aristotle in Twenty-Three Volumes. XIX: The Nicomachean Ethics. With an English translation by H. Rackham. LCL, 1975, London: William Heinemann; Cambridge, Mass.: Harvard University Press

M. Tullii Ciceronis De Officiis Libri Tres. Recognovit C. F. W. Müller. 1906, Lipsiae: in Aedibus B. G. Teubneri

Cicero in Twenty-Eight Volumes. XXI: De Officiis. With an English Translation by Walter Miller. LCL, 1968, London: William Heinemann; Cambridge, Mass.: Harvard University Press

Cicero, Werke in Drei Bänden. Bd. 3: 1989, Berlin und Weimar: Aufbau-Verlag

Corpus Papyrorum Judaicarum. Edited by Victor A. Tcherikover and Alexander Fuks. Vol. 1: 1957, vol. 2: 1960, (Published for The Magnes Press, The Hebrew University) Cambridge, Mass.: Harvard University Press

The Dead Sea Scrolls Translated: The Qumran Texts in English. Edited by Florentino García Martínez; transl. by W. G. E. Watson. 1994, Leiden: E. J. Brill

Dillon, J. – Hershbell, J., 1991, see Iamblichus: *On the Pythagorean Way of Life.*

Diogenes Laertius: *Lives of Eminent Philosophers*. With an English translation by R. D. Hicks. LCL 2 vols, vol. 1: 1972, vol. 2: 1970, London: William Heinemann; Cambridge, Mass.: Harvard University Press

Epictetus: *The Discourses as Reported by Arrian, The Manual, and Fragments*. With an English translation by W. A. Oldfather. LCL 2 vols, vol. 1: 1967, vol. 2: 1978, London: William Heinemann; Cambridge, Mass.: Harvard University Press

Fideler, D. R., 1987, see *The Pythagorean Sourcebook...*

The Attic Nights of Aulus Gellius. With an English translation by John C. Rolfe. LCL 3 vols, vol. 1: 1961, London: William Heinemann; Cambridge, Mass.: Harvard University Press

Hesiod. *The Homeric Hymns and Homerica*. With an English translation by Hugh G. Evelyn-White. LCL, 1959, London: William Heinemann; Cambridge, Mass.: Harvard University Press

Homer: *The Iliad*. With an English translation by A. T. Murray. LCL 2 vols, vol. 1: 1960, vol. 2: 1963, London: William Heinemann; Cambridge, Mass.: Harvard University Press

Horbury, W., 1992, see *Jewish Inscriptions...*

Horsley, G. H. R., 1981, 1982, 1983, 1987, see *New Documents...*

Iamblichus: *On the Pythagorean Way of Life*. Text, Translation, and Notes by John Dillon and Jackson Hershbell. 1991, Atlanta, Ga.: Scholars Press

Isaeus. With an English translation by Edward Seymour Forster. LCL, 1957, London: William Heinemann; Cambridge, Mass.: Harvard University Press

Jewish Inscriptions of Graeco-Roman Egypt: With an index of the Jewish inscriptions of Egypt and Cyrenaica. Edited by William Horbury and David Noy. 1992, Cambridge: Cambridge University Press

Josephus in Nine Volumes. With an English translation by H. St. J. Thackeray. LCL Vol. 1 (*The Life; Against Apion*): 1956, London: William Heinemann; Cambridge, Mass.: Harvard University Press

Liddell, H. G. – Scott, R.: *A Greek-English Lexicon. A New Edition Revised and Augmented throughout by H. J. Jones*. 1961 (repr. of 1940 ninth edn), Oxford: Clarendon Press

Lysias. With an English translation by W. R. M. Lamb. LCL, 1960, London: William Heinemann; Cambridge, Mass.: Harvard University Press

Martínez, F. G., 1994, see *The Dead Sea Scrolls Translated*.

Menander. Edited with an English translation by W. G. Arnott. LCL Vol. 1 (*Aspis to Epitrepontes*): 1977; London: William Heinemann; Cambridge, Mass.: Harvard University Press

Musonius (in: *Epiktet, Teles, Musonius*): *Ausgewählte Schriften, Griechisch-Deutsch*. Edited and translated by Rainer Nickel. 1994, Zürich: Artemis & Winkler

New Documents Illustrating Early Christianity. Edited by G. H. R. Horsley. Vol. 1: 1981; vol. 2: 1982; vol. 3: 1983; vol. 4: 1987, North Ryde, Australia: Macquarie University

Philo in Ten Volumes (and Two Supplementary Volumes). With an English translation by F. H. Colson. LCL Vol. 7 (*De Decalogo; De Specialibus Legibus* I–III): 1950, vol. 9: 1954, London: William Heinemann; Cambridge, Mass.: Harvard University Press

Philo von Alexandria, Die Werke in Deutscher Übersetzung. Herausgegeben von L. Cohn, I. Heinemann, M. Adler und W. Theiler. 7 vols, vols 1–6: 1962², vol. 7: 1964, Berlin: Walter de Gruyter

Philonis Alexandrini Opera Quae Supersunt. Ediderunt L. Cohn et P. Wendland. 7 vols, 1962 (unveränderter Nachdruck von 1896–1930 Orig.), Berolini: Typis et Impensis Georgii Reimeri (vol. 7: Walter de Gruyter)

Plato: *Laws*. With an English translation by R. G. Bury. LCL 2 vols (vol. 1: books I–VI; vol. 2: books VII–XII), 1961, London: William Heinemann; Cambridge, Mass.: Harvard University Press

Plato, Werke in acht Bänden. Bd. VIII/2: Gesetze. Bearb. und übers. von Klaus Schöpsdau. Nachdruck, 2001, Darmstadt: Wissenschaftliche Buchgesellschaft

Plutarch's Lives in Eleven Volumes. With an English translation by Bernadotte Perrin. LCL Vol. 1 (Solon and others): 1959, London: William Heinemann; Cambridge, Mass.: Harvard University Press

Plutarch's Moralia in Sixteen Volumes. Vol. 1: 1A–86A. With an English translation by F. C. Babbitt. LCL, 1969, London: William Heinemann; Cambridge, Mass.: Harvard University Press

Pliny. Natural History in Ten Volumes. With an English translation by H. Rackham. LCL Vol. 2: 1989, London, England and Cambridge, Mass.: Harvard University Press

Pomeroy, S. B., 1994, see Xenophon: *Oeconomicus*.

The Pythagorean Texts of the Hellenistic Period. Collected and edited by Holger Thesleff. 1965, Åbo: Åbo Akademi

The Pythagorean Sourcebook and Library: An Anthology of Ancient Writings Which Relate to Pythagoras and Pythagorean Philosophy. Compiled and translated by Kenneth S. Guthrie. Introduced and edited by David R. Fideler. 1987, Grand Rapids, Mich.: Phanes Press

The Institutio Oratoria of Quintilian in Four Volumes. Translated by H. E. Butler. 1921, London: William Heinemann; New York: G. P. Putnam's Sons

Qumran Cave 4, XXIV: Sapiential Texts, Part 2. (Discoveries in the Judaean Desert XXXIV.) Ed.-in-chief: Emanuel Tov, 1999, Oxford: Clarendon Press

Saunders, T. J., 1995, see Aristotle: *Politics*.

Select Papyri. Transl. by A. S. Hunt and C. C. Edgar. LCL 3 vols, vol. 1: *Non-literary Papyri: Private Affairs*. 1970, London: William Heinemann; Cambridge, Mass.: Harvard University Press

L. Annaei Senecae Ad Lucilium Epistulae Morales. Recognovit et adnotatione critica instruxit L. D. Reynolds. 2 vols, vol. 2: 1965, Oxford: Oxford University Press

Seneca in Ten Volumes. Moral Essays. With an English translation by John W. Basore in Three Volumes. LCL Vol. 1: *De Clementia (et al.)*. 1970; vol. 3: *De Beneficiis*. 1975, London: William Heinemann; Cambridge, Mass.: Harvard University Press

Lucius Annaeus Seneca: *Philosophische Schriften. Bd. 4: Briefe an Lucilius.* Zweiter Teil: Brief 82–124 (übersetzt von O. Appelt). 1993 (Repr. von 1924 Orig.), Hamburg: Felix Meiner Verlag

Seneca: *Moral and Political Essays.* Edited and translated by J. M. Cooper and J. F. Procopé. 1995, Cambridge: Cambridge University Press

Solon. Testimonia veterum collegit Antonius Martina. 1968, Roma: Edizioni dell'Ateneo

Sommerstein, A. H., 1982, see *The Comedies of Aristophanes.*

Sophocles. Edited and translated by Hugh Lloyd-Jones. LCL 3 vols, vol. 1: *Ajax, Electra, Oedipus Tyrannus.* vol. 2: *Antigone, The Women of Trachis, Philoctetes, Oedipus at Colonus.* 1994, London, England and Cambridge, Mass.: Harvard University Press

Sophokles: *Antigone.* Für den Schulgebrauch erklärt von Gustav Wolff, siebente Auflage bearbeitet von Ludwig Bellermann. 1913, Leipzig, Berlin: Verlag von B. G. Teubner

Ioannis Stobaei Anthologium. Recensuerunt C. Wachsmuth et O. Hense. 4 vols, vol. 4, part. 1: 1909, Berolini: Apud Weidmannos

Taylor, Thomas (transl.): *Political Fragments of Archytas, Charondas, Zaleucus, and Other Ancient Pythagoreans, Preserved by Stobaeus; and also, Ethical Fragments of Hierocles, Preserved by the Same Author.* 1822, Manor Place, Walworth: C. Whittingham

Tcherikover, V. A. and Fuks, A., 1957, 1960, see *Corpus Papyrorum Judaicarum.*

Terence in Two Volumes. With an English translation by John Sargeaunt. Vol. 2: 1920, London: William Heinemann; New York: G. P. Putnam's Sons

P. Terentius Afer: *Adelphoe. Die Brüder.* Lateinisch-Deutsch, übersetzt, erläutert und mit einem Nachwort herausgegeben von Herbert Rädle. 1977, Stuttgart: Philipp Reclam jun.

The Comedies of Terence. Edited with Introduction and Notes by Sidney G. Ashmore. 1962 (sixth printing of 1908 second edn) New York: Oxford University Press

Terence: *The Mother-in-Law.* Edited with translation, introduction and commentary by S. Ireland. 1990, Warminster, Wiltshire: Aris & Phillips

Thesleff, H., 1965, see *The Pythagorean Texts...*

Tov, E., 1999, see *Qumran Cave 4.*

Valeri Maximi facta et dicta memorabilia. Edited by John Briscoe. 2 vols, 1998, Stuttgart and Leipzig: B. G. Teubner

Virgil in Two Volumes. With an English translation by H. Rushton Fairclough. LCL Vol. 1: 1956, London: William Heinemann; Cambridge, Mass.: Harvard University Press

Wachsmuth, C. – Hense, O., 1909, see *Ioannis Stobaei Anthologium.*

Xenophon: *Ökonomische Schriften.* Griechisch und Deutsch von G. Audring. 1992, Berlin: Akademie Verlag

Xenophon: *Oeconomicus. (A Social and Historical Commentary.)* With a new English translation by Sarah B. Pomeroy. 1994, Oxford: Clarendon Press

2. Literature on the environment of the New Testament

a) Graeco-Roman environment

Almquist, Helge: *Plutarch und das Neue Testament: Ein Beitrag zum Corpus Hellenisticum Novi Testamenti.* 1946, Uppsala: Appelbergs Boktryckeri A.-B.; Kopenhagen: Einar Munksgaard

Aune, David E. (ed.): *Greco-Roman Literature and the New Testament: Selected Forms and Genres.* 1988, Atlanta, Ga.: Scholars Press

Balch, David L.: "1 Cor 7:32–35 and Stoic Debates about Marriage, Anxiety, and Distraction", *Journal of Biblical Literature* 102 (1983), 429–39

Blomenkamp, P.: "Erziehung", in: Th. Klauser (ed.): *Reallexikon für Antike und Christentum.* Bd. 6: 1966, Stuttgart: Anton Hiersemann, cols. 502–59

Bonhöffer, Adolf: *Epiktet und das Neue Testament.* 1911, Gießen: Verlag von Alfred Töpelmann (vormals J. Ricker)

Bradley, Keith R.: *Discovering the Roman Family: Studies in Roman Social History.* 1991 a, Oxford, New York: Oxford University Press

Bradley, Keith R.: "Remarriage and the Structure of the Upper-Class Roman Family", in: B. Rawson (ed.): *Marriage, Divorce, and Children in Ancient Rome.* 1991 b, Canberra: Humanities Research Centre; Oxford: Clarendon Press, 79–98

Buckley, Jorunn Jacobsen: "An Interpretation of Logion 114 in *The Gospel of Thomas*", *Novum Testamentum* 27 (1985), 245–72

Buckley, Jorunn Jacobsen: "The Mandaean Appropriation of Jesus' Mother, Miriai", *Novum Testamentum* 35 (1993), 181–96

Burguière, André, *et al.* (eds.): *Geschichte der Familie. Band I: Altertum.* (transl. by G. Seib vom 1994 second French edn, orig. 1986) 1996, Frankfurt/Main, New York: Campus Verlag; Paris: Editions de la Fondation Maison des Sciences de l'Homme

Carcopino, J.: *Rom: Leben und Kultur in der Kaiserzeit.* 1977^2, Stuttgart: Philipp Reclam jun.

Colish, Marcia L.: "Stoicism and the New Testament: An Essay in Historiography", in: W. Haase (ed.): *Aufstieg und Niedergang der römischen Welt. II.26.1.* 1992, Berlin, New York: Walter de Gruyter, 334–79

Conte, Gian Biagio: "Die Literatur der Kaiserzeit", in: F. Graf (ed.): *Einleitung in die lateinische Philologie.* 1997, Stuttgart, Leipzig: B. G. Teubner, 192–227

Corbier, Mireille: "Divorce and Adoption as Roman Familial Strategies (*Le Divorce et l'adoption 'en plus'*)", in: B. Rawson (ed.): *Marriage, Divorce, and Children in Ancient Rome.* 1991, Canberra: Humanities Research Centre; Oxford: Clarendon Press, 47–78

Crossan, John Dominic: "Kingdom and Children: A Study in the Aphoristic Tradition", *Semeia* 29 (1983), 75–95

Crossan, John Dominic: *The Historical Jesus: The Life of a Mediterranean Jewish Peasant.* 1992, New York: HarperCollins

Dassmann, Ernst – Schöllgen, Georg: "Haus II (Hausgemeinschaft)", in: Th. Klauser, E. Dassmann, *et al.* (eds.): *Reallexikon für Antike und Christentum.* Bd. 13: 1986, Stuttgart: Anton Hiersemann, cols. 801–905

Degani, Enzo: "Griechische Literatur bis 300 v. Chr.", in: H-G. Nesselrath (ed.): *Einleitung in die griechische Philologie.* 1997, Stuttgart, Leipzig: B. G. Teubner, 171–245

Dorandi, Tiziano: "Tradierung der Texte im Altertum; Buchwesen", in: H-G. Nesselrath (ed.): *Einleitung in die griechische Philologie.* 1997, Stuttgart, Leipzig: B. G. Teubner, 3–16

Downing, F. Gerald: *Cynics and Christian Origins.* 1992, Edinburgh: T&T Clark

Downing, F. Gerald: "A Cynic Preparation for Paul's Gospel for Jew and Greek, Slave and Free, Male and Female", *New Testament Studies* 42 (1996), 454–62

Dixon, Suzanne: *The Roman Mother.* 1988, London and Sydney: Croom Helm

Dixon, Suzanne: "The Sentimental Ideal of the Roman Family", in: B. Rawson (ed.): *Marriage, Divorce, and Children in Ancient Rome.* 1991, Canberra: Humanities Research Centre; Oxford: Clarendon Press, 99–113

Dixon, Suzanne: *The Roman Family.* 1992, Baltimore and London: The John Hopkins University Press

Eddy, Paul Rhodes: "Jesus as Diogenes? Reflections on the Cynic Jesus Thesis", *Journal of Biblical Literature* 115 (1996), 449–69

Eyben, Emiel: "Fathers and Sons", in: B. Rawson (ed.): *Marriage, Divorce, and Children in Ancient Rome.* 1991, Canberra: Humanities Research Centre; Oxford: Clarendon Press, 114–43

Eyben, Emiel: *Restless Youth in Ancient Rome.* 1993, London and New York: Routledge

Eyben, Emiel: "Jugend", in: E. Dassmann (ed.): *Reallexikon für Antike und Christentum.* Bd. 19: 1999, Stuttgart: Anton Hiersemann, cols. 388–442

Fideler, D. R., 1987, see section 1

Foucault, Michel: *Sexualität und Wahrheit.* 3 vols, vol. 2: *Der Gebrauch der Lüste*, vol. 3: *Die Sorge um sich.* Übersetzt von Ulrich Raulff und Walter Seitter. 1997[5] (first edn: 1989, translated from 1984 French orig.), Frankfurt am Main: Suhrkamp

Frank, K. S.: "Gehorsam", in: Th. Klauser (ed.): *Reallexikon für Antike und Christentum.* Bd. 9: 1976, Stuttgart: Anton Hiersemann, cols. 390–430

Gardner, Jane F. and Wiedemann, Thomas: *The Roman Household: A Sourcebook.* 1991, London and New York: Routledge

Gardner, Jane F.: *Family and Familia in Roman Law and Life.* 1998, Oxford: Clarendon Press

Gaudemet, J.: "Familie I (Familienrecht)", in: Th. Klauser (ed.): *Reallexikon für Antike und Christentum.* Bd. 7: 1969, Stuttgart: Anton Hiersemann, cols. 286–358

Graf, Fritz (ed.): *Einleitung in die lateinische Philologie.* 1997, Stuttgart, Leipzig: B. G. Teubner

Greeven, Heinrich: *Das Hauptproblem der Sozialethik in der neueren Stoa und im Urchristentum.* 1935, Gütersloh: Verlag C. Bertelsmann

2. Literature on the environment of the New Testament 239

Hallett, Judith P.: *Fathers and Daughters in Roman Society: Women and the Elite Family.* 1984, Princeton, N.J.: Princeton University Press

Horsley, G. H. R., 1981, 1982, 1983, 1987, see section 1

Horst, P.W. van der: "Musonius Rufus and the New Testament: A Contribution to the Corpus Hellenisticum", *Novum Testamentum* 16 (1974), 306–15

Horst, P.W. van der: "Hierocles the Stoic and the New Testament: A Contribution to the Corpus Hellenisticum", *Novum Testamentum* 17 (1975), 156–60

Hunter, Richard: "Hellenismus", in: H-G. Nesselrath (ed.): *Einleitung in die griechische Philologie.* 1997, Stuttgart, Leipzig: B. G. Teubner, 246–68

Kaser, Max: *Das Römische Privatrecht. Erster Abschnitt: Das altrömische, das vorklassische und klassische Recht.* 1971^2; *Zweiter Abschnitt: Die nachklassischen Entwicklungen.* 1975^2, München: C. H. Beck'sche Verlagsbuchhandlung

Kreissig, Heinz: "Das 'Haus' (oikos) des Hesiod", *Jahrbuch für Wissenschaftsgeschichte* (1981/IV), 91–95

Kunkel, W.: "Mater familias", in: W. Kroll (ed.): *Paulys Real-Encyclopädie der Classischen Altertumswissenschaft.* XIV/2, 1930, Stuttgart: J. B. Metzlersche Verlagsbuchhandlung, cols. 2183–4

Lacey, W. K.: *Die Familie im Antiken Griechenland.* (Transl. by Ute Winter from the 1968 English orig.) 1983, Mainz am Rhein: Verlag Philipp von Zabern

Lacey, W. K.: "*Patria Potestas*", in: B. Rawson (ed.): *The Family in Ancient Rome: New Perspectives.* 1986, Ithaka, New York: Cornell University Press, 121–44

Lerat, L.: "Une loi de Delphes sur les devoirs des enfants envers leurs parents", *Revue de Philologie de Littérature et d'Histoire Anciennes* 17 (1943), 62–86

Lumpe, A. – Karpp, H.: "Eltern", in: Th. Klauser (ed.): *Reallexikon für Antike und Christentum.* Bd. 4: 1957, Stuttgart: Anton Hiersemann, cols. 1190–219

Malherbe, Abraham J.: "'Gentle as a Nurse': The Cynic Background to I Thess ii", *Novum Testamentum* 12 (1970), 203–17

Malherbe, Abraham J.: *Moral Exhortation, A Greco-Roman Sourcebook.* 1986, Philadelphia, Pa.: The Westminster Press

Malherbe, Abraham J.: "Hellenistic Moralists and the New Testament", in W. Haase (ed.): *Aufstieg und Niedergang der römischen Welt. II.26.1.* 1992, Berlin, New York: Walter de Gruyter, 267–333

Marrou, H. I.: *A History of Education in Antiquity.* Transl. by George Lamb. 1977 (second impression of 1956 orig.), London: Sheed and Ward

Nesselrath, Heinz-Günther (ed.): *Einleitung in die griechische Philologie.* 1997, Stuttgart, Leipzig: B. G. Teubner

Nilsson, Martin Persson: *Opuscula selecta linguis Anglica, Francogallica, Germanica conscripta.* 1951, Lund: Gleerup

Pircher, Joseph: *Das Lob der Frau im vorchristlichen Grabepigramm der Griechen.* 1979, Innsbruck: Universitätsverlag Wagner

Pomeroy, Sarah B.: *Xenophon: Oeconomicus. A Social and Historical Commentary.* With a new English translation by S. B. Pomeroy. 1994, Oxford: Clarendon Press

Pomeroy, Sarah B.: *Families in Classical and Hellenistic Greece: Representations and Realities.* 1997, Oxford: Clarendon Press

Praechter, Karl: *Hierokles der Stoiker.* 1901, Leipzig: Dieterich'sche Verlags-Buchhandlung, Theodor Weicher
Rawson, Beryl (ed.): *The Family in Ancient Rome: New Perspectives.* 1986a, Ithaka, New York: Cornell University Press
Rawson, Beryl: "The Roman Family", in: B. Rawson (ed.): *The Family in Ancient Rome: New Perspectives.* 1986b, Ithaka, New York: Cornell University Press, 1–57
Rawson, Beryl: "Children in the Roman *Familia*", in: B. Rawson (ed.): *The Family in Ancient Rome: New Perspectives.* 1986c, Ithaka, New York: Cornell University Press, 170–200
Rawson, Beryl (ed.): *Marriage, Divorce, and Children in Ancient Rome.* 1991a, Canberra: Humanities Research Centre; Oxford: Clarendon Press
Rawson, Beryl: "Adult–Child Relationships in Roman Society", in: B. Rawson (ed.): *Marriage, Divorce, and Children in Ancient Rome.* 1991b, Canberra: Humanities Research Centre; Oxford: Clarendon Press, 7–30
Robbins, Vernon K.: "Pronouncement Stories and Jesus' Blessing of the Children: A Rhetorical Approach", *Semeia* 29 (1983), 43–74
Rühfel, Hilde: *Das Kind in der griechischen Kunst: Von der minoisch-mykenischen Zeit bis zum Hellenismus.* KAW 18, 1984a, Mainz am Rhein: Philipp von Zabern
Rühfel, Hilde: *Kinderleben im klassischen Athen: Bilder auf klassischen Vasen.* KAW 19, 1984b, Mainz am Rhein: Philipp von Zabern
Sachers, E.: "Pater familias", in: Ziegler, K.: *Paulys Real-Encyclopädie der Classischen Altertumswissenschaft.* XVIII/4, 1949, Waldsee (Württ.): Alfred Druckenmüller Verlag, cols. 2121–57
Sachers, E.: "Potestas patria", in: K. Ziegler (ed.): *Paulys Realencyclopädie der Classischen Altertumswissenschaft.* XXII/1, 1953, Stuttgart: J. B. Metzlersche Verlagsbuchhandlung, cols. 1046–1175
Saller, Richard P.: "Corporal Punishment, Authority, and Obedience in the Roman Household", in: B. Rawson (ed.): *Marriage, Divorce, and Children in Ancient Rome.* 1991, Canberra: Humanities Research Centre; Oxford: Clarendon Press, 144–65
Saller, Richard P.: *Patriarchy, property and death in the Roman family.* 1994, Cambridge: Cambridge University Press
Saunders, T. J., 1995, see section 1
Sevenster, J. N.: "Education or conversion: Epictetus and the Gospels", *Novum Testamentum* 8 (1966), 247–62
Sissa, Giulia: "Die Familie im griechischen Stadtstaat", in: A. Burguière, *et al.* (eds.): *Geschichte der Familie. Band I: Altertum.* (transl. by G. Seib vom 1994 second French edn, orig. 1986) 1996, Frankfurt/Main, New York: Campus Verlag; Paris: Editions de la Fondation Maison des Sciences de l'Homme, 237–76
Stowers, Stanley K.: "A Cult from Philadelphia: Oikos Religion or Cultic Association?", in: A. J. Malherbe, F. W. Norris, J. W. Thompson (eds.): *The Early Church in Its Context: Essays in Honor of Everett Ferguson.* 1998, Leiden: E. J. Brill, 287–301

Strobel, August, "Der Begriff des Hauses im griechischen und römischen Privatrecht", *Zeitschrift für die neutestamentliche Wissenschaft* 56 (1965), 91–100
Taylor, T., 1822, see section 1
Thesleff, Holger: *An Introduction to the Pythagorean Writings of the Hellenistic Period.* 1961, Åbo: Åbo Akademi
Thesleff, H., 1965, see section 1
Thom, Johan C.: *The Pythagorean Golden Verses: With Introduction and Commentary.* 1995, Leiden, New York, Köln: E. J. Brill
Treggiari, Susan: *Roman Marriage: Iusti Coniuges From the Time of Cicero to the Time of Ulpian.* 1991 a, Oxford: Clarendon Press
Treggiari, Susan: "Divorce Roman Style: How Easy and how Frequent was it?", in: B. Rawson (ed.): *Marriage, Divorce, and Children in Ancient Rome.* 1991 b, Canberra: Humanities Research Centre; Oxford: Clarendon Press, 31–46
Wallace-Hadrill, Andrew: "Houses and Households: Sampling Pompeii and Herculaneum", in: B. Rawson (ed.): *Marriage, Divorce, and Children in Ancient Rome.* 1991, Canberra: Humanities Research Centre; Oxford: Clarendon Press, 191–227
Ward, Roy Bowen: "Musonius and Paul on Marriage", *New Testament Studies* 36 (1990), 281–9
Weaver, Paul R. C.: "The Status of Children in Mixed Marriages", in: B. Rawson (ed.): *The Family in Ancient Rome: New Perspectives.* 1986, Ithaka, New York: Cornell University Press, 145–69
Weaver, Paul R. C.: "Children of Freedmen (and Freedwomen)", in: B. Rawson (ed.): *Marriage, Divorce, and Children in Ancient Rome.* 1991, Canberra: Humanities Research Centre; Oxford: Clarendon Press, 166–90
Wiedemann, Thomas: *Adults and Children in the Roman Empire.* 1989, New Haven and London: Yale University Press
Wilson, Nigel: "Griechische Philologie im Altertum", in: H-G. Nesselrath (ed.): *Einleitung in die griechische Philologie.* 1997, Stuttgart, Leipzig: B. G. Teubner, 87–103

b) Jewish environment

Alvarez-Péreyre, Franck and Heymann, Florence: "Ein Streben nach Transzendenz: Das hebräische Muster der Familie und die jüdische Praxis", in: A. Burguière, *et al.* (eds.): *Geschichte der Familie. Band I: Altertum.* (transl. by G. Seib vom 1994 second French edn, orig. 1986) 1996, Frankfurt/Main, New York: Campus Verlag; Paris: Editions de la Fondation Maison des Sciences de l'Homme, 196–235
Charlesworth, James H. (ed.): *The Old Testament Pseudepigrapha.* 2 vols, vol. 1: 1983, vol. 2: 1985, Garden City, N.Y.: Doubleday
Cohen, Shaye J. D. (ed.): *The Jewish Family in Antiquity.* 1993 a, Atlanta, Ga.: Scholars Press
Cohen, Shaye J. D.: "Introduction", in: S. J. D. Cohen (ed.): *The Jewish Family in Antiquity.* 1993 b, Atlanta, Ga.: Scholars Press, 1–5

Collins, John J.: "Marriage, Divorce, and Family in Second Temple Judaism", in: L.G. Perdue, et al.: *Families in Ancient Israel*. 1997, Louisville, Ky.: Westminster John Knox Press, 104–62

Dschulnigg, Peter: "Gleichnis vom Kind, das zum Vater flieht (JosAs 12,8)", *Zeitschrift für die neutestamentliche Wissenschaft* 80 (1989), 269–71

Dearman, J. Andrew: "The Family in the Old Testament", *Interpretation* 52 (1998), 117–29

Fechter, Friedrich: *Die Familie in der Nachexilszeit: Untersuchungen zur Bedeutung der Verwandtschaft in ausgewählten Texten des Alten Testaments.* BZAW 264, 1998, Berlin, New York: Walter de Gruyter

Fiensy, David A.: *The Social History of Palestine in the Herodian Period: The Land Is Mine.* Studies in the Bible and Early Christianity 20, 1991, Lewiston/Queenston/Lampeter: The Edwin Mellen Press

Fox, Michael V.: "The Pedagogy of Proverbs 2", *Journal of Biblical Literature* 113 (1994), 233–43

Habicht, Christian: *2. Makkabäerbuch. JSHRZ Band I: Historische und legendarische Erzählungen.* Lieferung 3, 1976, Gütersloh: Gütersloher Verlagshaus Gerd Mohn

Halpern-Amaru, Betsy: "The First Woman, Wives, and Mothers in *Jubilees*", *Journal of Biblical Literature* 113 (1994), 609–26

Holladay, John S. Jr.: "House, Israelite", in D.N. Freedman (ed.): *The Anchor Bible Dictionary.* Vol. 3 (H–J): 1992, New York: Doubleday, 308–18

Hollander, H.W. – de Jonge, M.: *The Testaments of the Twelve Patriarchs: A Commentary.* 1985, Leiden: E.J. Brill

Horbury, W., 1992, see section 1

Horst, Pieter W. van der: *Ancient Jewish Epitaphs: An introductory survey of a millennium of Jewish funerary epigraphy (300 BCE – 700 CE).* 1991, Kampen: Kok Pharos

Hossfeld, Frank-Lothar: "Die alttestamentliche Familie vor Gott", in: J. Schreiner (ed.): *Freude am Gottesdienst: Aspekte ursprünglicher Liturgie.* 1983, Stuttgart: Verlag Katholisches Bibelwerk, 217–28

Joubert, Stephan and van Henten, Jan Willem: "Two a-typical Jewish families in the Greco-Roman period", *Neotestamentica* 30 (1996), 121–40

Kippenberg, Hans Gerhard: *Garizim und Synagoge: Traditionsgeschichtliche Untersuchungen zur samaritanischen Religion der aramäischen Periode.* 1971, Berlin, New York: Walter de Gruyter

Kraemer, Ross S.: "Jewish Mothers and Daughters in the Greco-Roman World", in: S.J.D. Cohen (ed.): *The Jewish Family in Antiquity.* 1993, Atlanta, Ga.: Scholars Press, 89–112

Martin, Dale B.: "Slavery and the Ancient Jewish Family", in: S.J.D. Cohen (ed.): *The Jewish Family in Antiquity.* 1993, Atlanta, Ga.: Scholars Press, 113–29

Martínez, F.G., 1994, see section 1

Metzger, B.M. (ed.): *The Apocrypha of the Old Testament: Revised Standard Version.* (The Oxford Annotated Apocrypha. Expanded edition.) 1977, New York: Oxford University Press

Meyer, R.: "Tobitbuch", in: K. Galling (ed.): *Die Religion in Geschichte und Gegenwart*. Dritte Auflage. Vol. 6: 1962, Tübingen: J. C. B. Mohr (Paul Siebeck), col. 907

Perdue, Leo G. – Blenkinsopp, Joseph – Collins, John J. – Meyers, Carol: *Families in Ancient Israel*. 1997, Louisville, Ky.: Westminster John Knox Press

Peskowitz, Miriam: "'Family/ies' in Antiquity: Evidence from Tannaitic Literature and Roman Galilean Architecture", in: S. J. D. Cohen (ed.): *The Jewish Family in Antiquity*. 1993, Atlanta, Ga.: Scholars Press, 9–36

Pilhofer, Peter: *Presbyteron kreitton: Der Altersbeweis der jüdischen und christlichen Apologeten und seine Vorgeschichte*. WUNT 2/39, 1990, Tübingen: J. C. B. Mohr (Paul Siebeck)

Reinhartz, Adele: "Parents and Children: A Philonic Perspective", in: S. J. D. Cohen (ed.): *The Jewish Family in Antiquity*. 1993, Atlanta, Ga.: Scholars Press, 61–88

Safrai, S. and Stern, M. (eds.): *The Jewish People in the First Century: Historical Geography, Political History, Social, Cultural and Religious Life and Institutions*. 2 vols, vol. 1: 1974, vol. 2: 1976, Assen/Amsterdam: Van Gorcum

Sanders, James A.: "Canon: Hebrew Bible", in: D. N. Freedman (ed.): *The Anchor Bible Dictionary*. 6 vols, vol. 1: 1992, New York: Doubleday, 837–52

Sauer, Georg: *Jesus Sirach (Ben Sira). JSHRZ Band III: Unterweisung in lehrhafter Form*. Lieferung 5, 1981, Gütersloh: Gütersloher Verlagshaus Gerd Mohn

Skehan, Patrick W. – Di Lella, Alexander A.: *The Wisdom of Ben Sira: A New Translation with Notes*. AB 39, 1987, New York: Doubleday

Smith, Morton: *Tannaitic Parallels to the Gospels*. JBLMS 6, 1951, Philadelphia, Pa.: SBL

Strotmann, Angelika: *Mein Vater bist Du! (Sir 51,10): Zur Bedeutung der Vaterschaft Gottes in kanonischen und nichtkanonischen frühjüdischen Schriften*. FTS 39, 1991, Frankfurt am Main: Verlag Josef Knecht

Taylor, Nicholas H.: "The Social Nature of Conversion in the Early Christian World", in: Ph. F. Esler (ed.): *Modelling Early Christianity: Social-scientific studies of the New Testament in its context*. 1995: London and New York: Routledge, 128–36

Tcherikover, V. A. and Fuks, A., 1957, 1960, see section 1

Yarbrough, O. Larry: "Parents and Children in the Jewish Family of Antiquity", in: S. J. D. Cohen (ed.): *The Jewish Family in Antiquity*. 1993, Atlanta, Ga.: Scholars Press, 39–59

Zakowitch, Yair: "Rahab als Mutter des Boas in der Jesus-Genealogie (Matth. I.5)", *Novum Testamentum* 17 (1975), 1–5

3. Literature related to the New Testament

a) Commentaries

Balz, Horst – Schrage, Wolfgang: *Die "Katholischen Briefe"*. NTD 10, 1993[14] (James, 1–2 Peter, Jude: Schrage; 1–3 John: Balz), Göttingen und Zürich: Vandenhoeck & Ruprecht

Barclay, John: *Colossians and Philemon*. NTG, 1997, Sheffield: Sheffield Academic Press

Barrett, C. K.: *The Gospel According to St John: An Introduction with Commentary and Notes on the Greek Text*. 1978[2], London: SPCK

Barrett, C. K.: *A Critical and Exegetical Commentary on the Acts of the Apostles*. ICC, 2 vols, vol. 1: 1994, vol. 2: 1998, Edinburgh: T&T Clark

Bauckham, Richard J.: *Jude, 2 Peter*. WBC 50, 1983, Waco, Tex.: Word Books

Beale, G. K.: *The Book of Revelation: A Commentary on the Greek Text*. NIGTC, 1999, Grand Rapids, Mich.: Eerdmans; Carlisle: The Paternoster Press

Becker, Jürgen – Luz, Ulrich: *Die Briefe an die Galater, Epheser und Kolosser*. NTD 8/1 (Galatians: Becker; Ephesians and Colossians: Luz), 1998, Göttingen: Vandenhoeck & Ruprecht

Best, Ernest: *A Critical and Exegetical Commentary on Ephesians*. ICC, 1998, Edinburgh: T&T Clark

Bock, Darrell L.: *Luke*. BECNT 2 vols, vol. 1: 1999 (second printing of 1994 orig.), vol. 2: 1998 (second printing of 1996 orig.) Grand Rapids, Mich.: Baker Books

Bolyki, János: *"Igaz tanúvallomás" : Kommentár János evangéliumához*. 2001, Budapest: Osiris Kiadó

Bovon, François: *Das Evangelium nach Lukas*. EKKNT III/1: 1989, III/2: 1996, Zürich: Benziger Verlag, Neukirchen-Vluyn: Neukirchener Verlag

Brown, Raymond E.: *The Gospel According to John. XIII–XXI*. AB 29A, 1970, London: Geoffrey Chapman

Brox, Norbert: *Der erste Petrusbrief*. EKKNT XXI, 1979, Zürich: Benziger Verlag, Neukirchen-Vluyn: Neukirchener Verlag

Bruce, F. F.: *1 and 2 Thessalonians*. WBC 45, 1982, Waco, Tex.: Word Books

Cserháti, Sándor: *Pál apostolnak a kolossébeliekhez írt levele és Filemonhoz írt levele*. 1978, Budapest: Evangélikus Sajtóosztály

Cserháti, Sándor: *Pál apostolnak a galáciabeliekhez írt levele*. 1982, Budapest: Evangélikus Sajtóosztály

Davids, Peter H.: *The Epistle of James: A Commentary on the Greek Text*. NIGTC, 1982, Grand Rapids, Mich.: Eerdmans; Exeter: The Paternoster Press

Davies, William David, and Allison, Dale C.: *A Critical and Exegetical Commentary on the Gospel According to Saint Matthew*. ICC, 3 vols, vol. 1: 1988, vol. 2: 1991, vol. 3: 1997, Edinburgh: T&T Clark

Dibelius, Martin: *Die Briefe des Apostels Paulus, II: An die Kolosser, Epheser, an Philemon*. 1912, Tübingen: J. C. B. Mohr (Paul Siebeck)

Dóka, Zoltán: *Márk evangéliuma*. 1996, Budapest: Ordass Lajos Baráti Kör

3. Literature related to the New Testament 245

Dunn, James D. G.: *The Epistle to the Galatians.* BNTC, 1993, Peabody, Mass.: Hendrickson

Dunn, James D. G.: *The Epistles to the Colossians and to Philemon: A Commentary on the Greek Text.* NIGTC, 1996, Grand Rapids, Mich.: Eerdmans; Carlisle: The Paternoster Press

Evans, C. F.: *Saint Luke.* TPINTC, 1990, London: SCM Press, Philadelphia: Trinity Press International

Frankemölle, Hubert: *Der Brief des Jakobus.* ÖTK 17/1–2, 2 vols, 1994, Götersloh: Gütersloher Verlagshaus; Würzburg: Echter Verlag

Gnilka, Joachim: *Das Evangelium nach Markus.* EKKNT II/2, 1979, Zürich: Benziger Verlag; Neukirchen-Vluyn: Neukirchener Verlag

Gnilka, Joachim: *Der Kolosserbrief.* HTKNT X/1, 1980, Freiburg, Basel, Wien: Herder

Goppelt, Leonhard: *A Commentary on I Peter.* Translated and augmented by John E. Alsup. 1993, Grand Rapids, Mich.: Eerdmans

Gräßer, Erich: *An die Hebräer.* EKKNT XVII/1: 1990, XVII/2: 1993, XVII/3: 1997, Zürich: Benziger Verlag; Neukirchen-Vluyn: Neukirchener Verlag

Guelich, Robert A.: *Mark 1–8:26.* WBC 34A, 1989, Dallas, Tex.: Word Books

Gundry, Robert H.: *Mark: A Commentary on His Apology for the Cross.* 1993, Grand Rapids, Mich.: Eerdmans

Hagner, Donald A.: *Matthew.* WBC 33A–B, 2 vols, vol. 1: 1993, vol. 2: 1995, Dallas, Tex.: Word Books

Harris, Murray J.: *Colossians and Philemon.* EGGNT, 1991, Grand Rapids, Mich.: Eerdmans

Hays, Richard B.: *First Corinthians.* IBC, 1997, Louisville, Ky.: John Knox Press

Hegermann, Harald: *Der Brief an die Hebräer.* THKNT 16, 1988, Berlin: Evangelische Verlagsanstalt

Klauck, Hans-Josef: *Der erste Johannesbrief.* EKKNT XXIII/1, 1991, Zürich und Braunschweig: Benziger Verlag; Neukirchen-Vluyn: Neukirchener Verlag

Klauck, Hans-Josef: *Der zweite und dritte Johannesbrief.* EKKNT XXIII/2, 1992a, Zürich: Benziger Verlag; Neukirchen-Vluyn: Neukirchener Verlag

Knight III, George W.: *The Pastoral Epistles: A Commentary on the Greek Text.* NIGTC, 1992, Grand Rapids, Mich.: Eerdmans; Carlisle: The Paternoster Press

Lampe, P., 1998, see under Walter, Nikolaus

Lane, William L.: *Hebrews.* WBC 47A–B, 2 vols, 1991, Dallas, Tex.: Word Books

Laws, Sophie: *A Commentary on the Epistle of James.* BNTC, 1980, London: Adam & Charles Black

Lenkeyné Semsey, Klára: *Péter első levele.* 1998[3], Debrecen: Debreceni Református Hittudományi Egyetem

Lincoln, Andrew T.: *Ephesians.* WBC 42, 1990, Dallas, Tex.: Word Books

Luz, Ulrich: *Das Evangelium nach Matthäus.* EKKNT I/1: 1985 (1989[2]a, 2002: 5., völlig neubearbeitete Auflage), I/2: 1990 (1996[2]), I/3: 1997, Zürich: Benziger Verlag; Neukirchen-Vluyn: Neukirchener Verlag

Luz, U., 1998, see under Becker, Jürgen

Marshall, I. Howard: *The Gospel of Luke: A Commentary on the Greek Text*. NIGTC, 1979 (second impression of 1978 orig.), Exeter: Paternoster Press

Martin, Ralph P.: *Colossians and Philemon*. NCB, 1973, London: Marshall, Morgan & Scott

Michaels, J. Ramsey: *1 Peter*. WBC 49, 1988, Waco, Tex.: Word Books

Mussner, Franz: *Der Jakobusbrief*. HTKNT XIII, 1987[5], Freiburg, Basel, Wien: Herder

Nolland, John: *Luke 9:21–18:34*. WBC 35B, 1993, Dallas, Tex.: Word Books

O'Brien, Peter T.: *Colossians, Philemon*. WBC 44, 1982, Waco, Tex.: Word Books

Pesch, Rudolf: *Die Apostelgeschichte*. EKKNT V, 2 vols, 1986, Zürich: Benziger Verlag; Neukirchen-Vluyn: Neukirchener Verlag

Quinn, Jerome D. and Wacker, William C.: *The First and Second Letters to Timothy*. ECC, 2000, Grand Rapids, Mich., Cambridge, U.K.: Eerdmans

Reinmuth, E., (1998), see under Walter, Nikolaus

Roloff, Jürgen: *Der erste Brief an Timotheus*. EKKNT XV, 1988, Zürich: Benziger Verlag; Neukirchen-Vluyn: Neukirchener Verlag

Schlier, Heinrich: *Der Brief an die Epheser: Ein Kommentar*. 1965 (fifth edn of 1957 orig.), Düsseldorf: Patmos-Verlag

Schmithals, Walter: *Das Evangelium nach Markus* ÖTK 2/1: 1979, 2/2: 1986[2] (revised edn, orig. 1979) Gütersloh: Gütersloher Verlagshaus Gerd Mohn; Würzburg: Echter Verlag

Schneider, Gerhard: *Die Apostelgeschichte*. HTKNT V/1: 1980, V/2: 1982, Freiburg, Basel, Wien: Herder

Schnelle, Udo: *Das Evangelium nach Johannes*. THKNT 4, 1998, Leipzig: Evangelische Verlagsanstalt

Schrage, W., 1993, see under Balz, Horst

Schrage, Wolfgang: *Der erste Brief an die Korinther*. EKKNT VII/1: 1991, VII/2: 1995, VII/3: 1999, Zürich: Benziger Verlag; Neukirchen-Vluyn: Neukirchener Verlag

Schreiner, Thomas R.: *Romans*. BECNT, 1998, Grand Rapids, Mich.: Baker Books

Schweizer, Eduard: *Der Brief an die Kolosser*. EKKNT XII, 1980[2], Zürich: Benziger Verlag; Neukirchen-Vluyn: Neukirchener Verlag

Schweizer, Eduard: *Der erste Petrusbrief*. ZBK 15, 1998[4], Zürich: Theologischer Verlag Zürich

Smalley, S. S.: *1, 2, 3 John*. WBC 51, 1984, Dallas, Tex.: Word Books

Soards, Marion L.: *1 Corinthians*. NIBCNT 7, 1999, Peabody, Mass.: Hendrickson

Strobel, August: *Der Brief an die Hebräer*. NTD 9/2, 1991[13], Göttingen und Zürich: Vandenhoeck & Ruprecht

Vögtle, Anton: *Der Judasbrief, Der 2. Petrusbrief*. EKKNT XXII, 1994, Zürich: Benziger Verlag; Neukirchen-Vluyn: Neukirchener Verlag

Wacker, W. C. (2000), see under Quinn, Jerome D.

Walter, Nikolaus – Reinmuth, Eckart – Lampe, Peter: *Die Briefe an die Philipper, Thessalonicher und an Philemon*. NTD 8/2 (Philippians: Walter; Thessalonians: Reinmuth; Philemon: Lampe), 1998, Göttingen: Vandenhoeck & Ruprecht

Weiser, Alfons: *Die Apostelgeschichte.* ÖTK 5/1: 1981, 5/2: 1985, Gütersloh: Gütersloher Verlagshaus Gerd Mohn; Würzburg: Echter Verlag
Wilckens, Ulrich: *Der Brief an die Römer.* 3 vols, EKKNT VI/1: 1978, VI/2: 1980, VI/3: 1982, Zürich: Benziger Verlag; Neukirchen-Vluyn: Neukirchener Verlag
Witherington III, Ben: *The Acts of the Apostles: A Socio-Rhetorical Commentary.* 1998, Grand Rapids, Mich.: Eerdmans; Carlisle, Cumbria: The Paternoster Press
Wolter, Michael: *Der Brief an die Kolosser. Der Brief an Philemon.* ÖTK 12, 1993, Gütersloh: Gütersloher Verlagshaus Gerd Mohn; Würzburg: Echter Verlag
Wright, N. T.: *The Epistles of Paul to the Colossians and to Philemon: An Introduction and Commentary.* TNTC, 1986, Leicester, England: Inter-Varsity Press; Grand Rapids, Mich.: Eerdmans

b) *Other works related to the New Testament*

Abel, E. L.: "The Genealogies of Jesus Ο ΧΡΙΣΤΟΣ", *New Testament Studies* 20 (1974), 203–10
Aichele, George: "Jesus' Uncanny 'Family Scene'", *Journal for the Study of the New Testament* 74 (1999), 29–49
Allison, Dale C.: *Jesus of Nazareth: Millenarian Prophet.* 1998, Minneapolis: Fortress Press
Allmen, Daniel von: *La famille de Dieu: la symbolique familiale dans le paulinisme.* OBO 41, 1981, Fribourg: Éditions Universitaires; Göttingen: Vandenhoeck & Ruprecht
Balch, David, L.: *Let Wives be Submissive: The Domestic Code in I Peter.* SBLMS 26, 1981, Atlanta, Ga.: Scholars Press
Balch, David L.: "Household Codes", in: D. E. Aune (ed.): *Greco-Roman Literature and the New Testament: Selected Forms and Genres.* 1988, Atlanta, Ga.: Scholars Press, 25–50
Balch, David L.: "Household Codes", in: D. N. Freedman (ed.): *The Anchor Bible Dictionary.* Vol. 3 (H–J): 1992 a, New York: Doubleday, 318–20
Balch, David L.: "Neopythagorean Moralists and the New Testament Household Codes", in: W. Haase (ed.): *Aufstieg und Niedergang der römischen Welt. II.26.1.* 1992 b, Berlin, New York: Walter de Gruyter, 380–411
Balla, Peter: *The Melchizedekian Priesthood.* 1995, Budapest: Károli Gáspár Reformed University, Faculty of Theology
Balla, Peter: *Challenges to New Testament Theology: An Attempt to Justify the Enterprise.* WUNT 2/95, 1997, Tübingen: Mohr Siebeck (repr. Peabody, Mass.: Hendrickson, 1998)
Barton, Stephen C.: "The Communal Dimension of Earliest Christianity", *The Journal of Theological Studies* 43 (1992), 399–427
Barton, Stephen C.: *Discipleship and Family Ties in Mark and Matthew.* 1994, Cambridge: Cambridge University Press
Barton, Stephen C. (ed.): *The Family in Theological Perspective.* 1996, Edinburgh: T&T Clark

Barton, Stephen C.: "Living as Families in the Light of the New Testament", *Interpretation* 52 (1998), 130–44
Batey, Richard A.: "Is not this the Carpenter?", *New Testament Studies* 30 (1984), 249–58
Bauckham, Richard: *Jude and the Relatives of Jesus in the Early Church*. 1990, Edinburgh: T&T Clark
Bauckham, Richard: "Salome the Sister of Jesus, Salome the Disciple of Jesus, and the Secret Gospel of Mark", *Novum Testamentum* 33 (1991), 245–75
Bauckham, Richard: "Tamar's Ancestry and Rahab's Marriage: Two Problems in the Matthean Genealogy", *Novum Testamentum* 37 (1995), 313–29
Benoit, Pierre: "L'Enfance de Jean-Baptiste selon Luc I", *New Testament Studies* 3 (1956), 169–94
Berger, Klaus: *Die Gesetzesauslegung Jesu: Ihr historischer Hintergrund im Judentum und im Alten Testament. Teil I: Markus und Parallelen*. WMANT 40, 1972, Neukirchen-Vluyn: Neukirchener Verlag
Best, Ernest: "Mark iii.20,21,31–35", *New Testament Studies* 22 (1976), 309–19
Bockmuehl, Markus: "'Let the Dead Bury their Dead' (Matt. 8:22/Luke 9:60): Jesus and the Halakhah", *The Journal of Theological Studies* 49 (1998), 553–81
Bornkamm, Günther: "Das Vaterbild im Neuen Testament", in: H. Tellenbach (ed.): *Das Vaterbild in Mythos und Geschichte: Ägypten, Griechenland, Altes Testament, Neues Testament*. 1976, Stuttgart, Berlin, Köln, Mainz: W. Kohlhammer
Botha, Pieter J. J.: *Everyday life in the world of Jesus*. 2000, Pretoria: Biblia Publishers
Brandt, Pierre-Yves and Lukinovich, Alessandra: "Οἶκος et οἰκία chez Marc comparé à Matthieu et Luc", *Biblica* 78 (1997), 525–33
Branick, Vincent P.: *The House Church In the Writings of Paul*. 1989, Wilmington, Del.: Michael Glazier, Inc.
Breytenbach, Cilliers: *Nachfolge und Zukunftserwartung nach Markus: Eine methodenkritische Studie*. AThANT 71, 1984, Zürich: Theologischer Verlag Zürich
Broadhead, Edwin K.: "Jesus the Nazarene: Narrative Strategy and Christological Imagery in the Gospel of Mark", *Journal for the Study of the New Testament* 52 (1993), 3–18
Broadhead, Edwin K.: *Naming Jesus: Titular Christology in the Gospel of Mark*. JSNTSup 175, 1999, Sheffield: Sheffield Academic Press
Brown, R. E.: *The Death of the Messiah: From Gethsemane to the Grave. A Commentary on the Passion Narratives in the Four Gospels*. 2 vols, 1994, New York: Doubleday
Buchanan, George Wesley: "Jesus and the Upper Class", *Novum Testamentum* 7 (1964–65), 195–209
Burnett, Fred W.: "Exposing the Anti-Jewish Ideology of Matthew's Implied Author: The Characterization of God As Father", *Semeia* 59 (1992), 155–91
Busse, Ulrich: "Nachfolge auf dem Weg Jesu: Ursprung und Verhältnis von Nachfolge und Berufung im Neuen Testament", in: H. Frankemölle, K. Kertelge (eds.): *Vom Urchristentum zu Jesus: Für Joachim Gnilka*. 1989, Freiburg im Breisgau: Herder, 68–81

Campbell, R. A.: "Καὶ μάλιστα οἰκείων – A New Look at 1 Timothy 5.8", *New Testament Studies* 41 (1995), 157–60

Cantwell, L.: "The Parentage of Jesus: Mt. 1:18–21", *Novum Testamentum* 24 (1982), 304–15

Carroll, John T.: "Children in the Bible", *Interpretation* 55 (2001), 121–34

Carson, D. A. – Moo, Douglas J. – Morris, Leon: *An Introduction to the New Testament*. 1993 (reprint of 1992 first British edn), Leicester: Apollos

Cave, C. H.: "St Matthew's Infancy Narrative", *New Testament Studies* 9 (1962), 382–90

Cheney, Emily: "The Mother of the Sons of Zebedee (Matthew 27.56)", *Journal for the Study of the New Testament* 68 (1997), 13–21

Coulot, C.: *Jésus et le disciple: Étude sur l'autorité messianique de Jésus*. 1987, Paris: Librairie Lecoffre, J. Gabalda et Cie. Éditeurs

Craffert, Pieter F.: "A Social-Scientific Key to Paul's Letter to the Galatians: An Alternative to Opponent Hypotheses as a Cypher Key." Ph.D. diss., University of South Africa, 1992

Craffert, Pieter F.: "The Pauline household communities: Their nature as social entities", *Neotestamentica* 32 (1998), 309–41

Craffert, Pieter F.: *Illness and Healing in the Biblical World: Perspectives on health care*. 1999a, Pretoria: Biblia Publishers

Craffert, Pieter F.: *Mediating Divine Power: Perspectives on religion in the biblical world*. 1999b, Pretoria: Biblia Publishers

Craffert, Pieter F.: *Meeting the Living among the Dead: Perspectives on burials, tombs and the afterlife*. 1999c, Pretoria: Biblia Publishers

Crosby, Michael H.: *House of Disciples: Church, Economics, and Justice in Matthew*. 1988, Maryknoll, N.Y.: Orbis Books

Crossan, John Dominic: "Mark and the Relatives of Jesus", *Novum Testamentum* 15 (1973), 81–113

Crouch, James E.: *The Origin and Intention of the Colossian Haustafel*. 1972, Göttingen: Vandenhoeck & Ruprecht

Cuvillier, Elian: "Tradition et rédaction en Marc 7:1–23", *Novum Testamentum* 34 (1992), 169–92

D'Angelo, Mary Rose: "Women in Luke-Acts: A Redactional View", *Journal of Biblical Literature* 109 (1990), 441–61

D'Angelo, Mary Rose: "*Abba* and 'Father': Imperial Theology and the Jesus Traditions", *Journal of Biblical Literature* 111 (1992), 611–30

Danker, Frederick W.: "The υἱός Phrases in the New Testament", *New Testament Studies* 7 (1960), 94

Delling, Gerhard: "Zur Taufe von 'Häusern' im Urchristentum", *Novum Testamentum* 7 (1964–65), 285–311

Delling, Gerhard: "Lexikalisches zu τέκνον: Ein Nachtrag zur Exegese von I. Kor. 7,14", in: G. Delling: *Studien zum Neuen Testament und zum Judentum: Gesammelte Aufsätze 1950–1968. (Herausgegeben von F. Hahn, T. Holtz, N. Walter.)* 1970, Göttingen: Vandenhoeck & Ruprecht, 270–80

Derrett, J. Duncan M.: "KOPBAN, O ΕΣΤΙΝ ΔΩΡΟΝ", *New Testament Studies* 16 (1970), 364–8

Derrett, J. Duncan M.: "'Eating up the Houses of Widows': Jesus's Comment on Lawyers?", *Novum Testamentum* 14 (1972), 1–9

Derrett, J. Duncan M.: "ἦσαν γὰρ ἁλιεῖς (Mk i 16): Jesus's Fishermen and the Parable of the Net", *Novum Testamentum* 22 (1980), 108–37

Donelson, Lewis R.: *Pseudepigraphy and Ethical Argument in the Pastoral Epistles.* HUTh 22, 1986, Tübingen: J. C. B. Mohr (Paul Siebeck)

Dormeyer, Detlev: "Die Familie Jesu und der Sohn der Maria im Markusevangelium (3,20f.31–35; 6,3)", in: H. Frankemölle, K. Kertelge (eds.): *Vom Urchristentum zu Jesus: Für Joachim Gnilka.* 1989, Freiburg im Breisgau: Herder, 109–35

Dwyer, Timothy: *The Motif of Wonder in the Gospel of Mark.* JSNTSup 128, 1996, Sheffield: Sheffield Academic Press

Ebertz, Michael N.: *Das Charisma des Gekreuzigten: Zur Soziologie der Jesusbewegung.* WUNT 45, 1987, Tübingen: J. C. B. Mohr (Paul Siebeck)

Eltrop, Bettina: *Denn solchen gehört das Himmelreich: Kinder im Matthäusevangelium. Eine feministisch-sozialgeschichtliche Untersuchung.* 1996, Stuttgart: Verlag Ulrich E. Grauer

Esler, Philip F.: *The First Christians in their Social Worlds: Social-scientific approaches to New Testament interpretation.* 1994, London and New York: Routledge

Esler, Philip F. (ed.): *Modelling Early Christianity: Social-scientific studies of the New Testament in its context.* 1995: London and New York: Routledge

Fander, Monika: *Die Stellung der Frau im Markusevangelium: Unter besonderer Berücksichtigung kultur- und religionsgeschichtlicher Hintergründe.* Münsteraner Theol. Abh. 8, 1990², Altenberge: Telos-Verlag

Fiedler, Peter: "Haustafel", in: Th. Klauser, E. Dassmann, *et al.* (eds.): *Reallexikon für Antike und Christentum.* Bd. 13: 1986, Stuttgart: Anton Hiersemann, cols. 1063–73

Fischer, Karl Martin: *Tendenz und Absicht des Epheserbriefes.* FRLANT 111, 1973, Göttingen: Vandenhoeck & Ruprecht

Fitzgerald, John T.: "Haustafeln", in: D. N. Freedman (ed.): *The Anchor Bible Dictionary.* Vol. 3 (H–J): 1992, New York: Doubleday, 80–81

Frankemölle, Hubert: *Jahwebund und Kirche Christi: Studien zur Form- und Traditionsgeschichte des "Evangeliums" nach Matthäus.* NTAbh NF 10, 1974, Münster: Aschendorff

Frilingos, Chris: "'For My Child, Onesimus': Paul and Domestic Power in Philemon", *Journal of Biblical Literature* 119 (2000), 91–104

Gielen, Marlis: "Zur Interpretation der paulinischen Formel ἡ κατ' οἶκον ἐκκλησία", *Zeitschrift für die neutestamentliche Wissenschaft* 77 (1986), 109–25

Gielen, Marlis: *Tradition und Theologie neutestamentlicher Haustafelethik: Ein Beitrag zur Frage einer christlichen Auseinandersetzung mit gesellschaftlichen Normen.* 1990, Frankfurt am Main: Verlag Anton Hain

Glombitza, Otto: "Der zwölfjährige Jesus. Luk. ii 40–52: Ein Beitrag zur Exegese der lukanischen Vorgeschichte", *Novum Testamentum* 5 (1962), 1–4

Gnilka, Joachim: "Martyriumsparänese und Sühnetod in synoptischen und jüdischen Traditionen", in: R. Schnackenburg, J. Ernst, J. Wanke (eds.): *Die Kirche des Anfangs: Für Heinz Schürmann*. 1978, Freiburg, Basel, Wien: Herder, 223–46

Gnilka, Joachim: "Die neutestamentliche Hausgemeinde", in: J. Schreiner (ed.): *Freude am Gottesdienst: Aspekte ursprünglicher Liturgie*. 1983, Stuttgart: Verlag Katholisches Bibelwerk, 229–42

Goppelt, Leonhard: "Jesus und die 'Haustafel'-Tradition", in: P. Hoffmann (ed.): *Orientierung an Jesus: Zur Theologie der Synoptiker. Für Josef Schmid*. 1973, Freiburg im Breisgau: Herder, 93–106

Grassi, Joseph A.: "The Wedding at Cana (John II 1–11): A Pentecostal Meditation?", *Novum Testamentum* 14 (1972), 131–6

Grundmann, Walter: "Die νήπιοι in der urchristlichen Paränese", *New Testament Studies* 5 (1958), 188–205

Grundmann, Walter: "Matth. xi.27 und die johanneischen 'der Vater – der Sohn'-Stellen", *New Testament Studies* 12 (1965–66), 42–49

Gundry, Robert H.: "On True and False Disciples in Matthew 8.18–22", *New Testament Studies* 40 (1994), 433–41

Hamerton-Kelly, Robert: *God the Father: Theology and Patriarchy in the Teaching of Jesus*. 1979, Philadelphia: Fortress Press

Hamerton-Kelly, Robert: "Gott als Vater in der Bibel und in der Erfahrung Jesu: Eine Bestandaufnahme", *Concilium* 17 (1981), 247–56

Hartman, L.: "Some Unorthodox Thoughts on the 'Household-Code Form'", in J. Neusner, et al. (eds.): *The Social World of Formative Christianity and Judaism*. 1988, Philadelphia: Fortress Press, 219–32

Haufe, Günter: "Das Kind im Neuen Testament", *Theologische Literaturzeitung* 104 (1979), cols. 625–38

Heil, Christoph: "Die Rezeption von Micha 7,6 LXX in Q und Lukas", *Zeitschrift für die neutestamentliche Wissenschaft* 88 (1997), 211–22

Hengel, Martin: *Nachfolge und Charisma*. BZNW 34, 1968, Berlin: Verlag Alfred Töpelmann

Hengel, Martin: *The Charismatic Leader and his Followers*. 1981, Edinburgh: T&T Clark (English transl. of 1968 German orig.: *Nachfolge und Charisma*.)

Hengel, Martin: "Entstehungszeit und Situation des Markusevangeliums", in: H. Cancik (ed.): *Markus-Philologie*. WUNT 33, 1984, Tübingen: J. C. B. Mohr (Paul Siebeck), 1–45

Hill, David: "The Request of Zebedee's Sons and the Johannine δόξα-theme", *New Testament Studies* 13 (1966), 281–5

Hübner, Hans: "Mark vii.1–23 und das 'jüdisch-hellenistische' Gesetzes-Vertständnis", *New Testament Studies* 22 (1976), 319–45

Hübner, Hans: *Biblische Theologie des Neuen Testaments*. 3 vols, vol. 1: *Prolegomena*. 1990, vol. 2: *Die Theologie des Paulus und ihre neutestamentliche Wirkungsgeschichte*. 1993, vol. 3: *Hebräerbrief, Evangelien und Offenbarung, Epilegomena*. 1995, Göttingen: Vandenhoeck & Ruprecht

Iersel, B. M. F. van: "The Finding of Jesus in the temple: Some observations on the original form of Luke ii:41–51 a", *Novum Testamentum* 4 (1960–61), 161–73

Jeremias, Joachim: *Die Kindertaufe in den ersten vier Jahrhunderten.* 1958, Göttingen: Vandenhoeck & Ruprecht

Jeremias, Joachim: *Abba: Studien zur neutestamentlichen Theologie und Zeitgeschichte.* 1966, Göttingen: Vandenhoeck & Ruprecht

Jeremias, Joachim: *Neutestamentliche Theologie I.: Die Verkündigung Jesu.* 1979³, Gütersloh: Gütersloher Verlagshaus Gerd Mohn

Jonge, Henk J. de: "Sonship, Wisdom, Infancy: Luke ii.41–51 a", *New Testament Studies* 24 (1978), 317–54

Joubert, Stephan J.: "Managing the Household: Paul as *paterfamilias* of the Christian household group in Corinth", in: Ph. F. Esler (ed.): *Modelling Early Christianity: Social-scientific studies of the New Testament in its context.* 1995: London and New York: Routledge, 213–23

Jungbauer, Harry: *"Ehre Vater und Mutter": Der Weg des Elterngebots in der biblischen Tradition.* WUNT 2/146, 2002, Tübingen: Mohr Siebeck

Kamlah, Ehrhard: "Philos Beitrag zur Aufhellung der Geschichte der Haustafeln", in: B. Benzing, O. Böcher, G. Mayer (eds.): *Wort und Wirklichkeit: Studien zur Afrikanistik und Orientalistik. Eugen Ludwig Rapp zum 70. Geburtstag.* 1976, Meisenheim am Glan: Verlag Anton Hain, 90–95

Kiilunen, Jarmo: "Der nachfolgewillige Schriftgelehrte. Matthäus 8.19–20 im Verständnis des Evangelisten", *New Testament Studies* 37 (1991), 268–79

Kingsbury, Jack Dean: "On Following Jesus: the 'Eager' Scribe and the 'Reluctant' Disciple (Matthew 8.18–22)", *New Testament Studies* 34 (1988), 45–49

Kirchschläger, Walter: "Was ist zwischen dir und mir, Frau", *Diakonia* 27 (1996), 366–72

Kitzberger, Ingrid: *Bau der Gemeinde: Das paulinische Wortfeld* οἰκοδομή/(ἐπ)οικοδομεῖν. 1986, Würzburg: Echter Verlag Klauck, Hans-Josef: *Hausgemeinde und Hauskirche im frühen Christentum.* 1981, Stuttgart: Verlag Katholisches Bibelwerk

Klauck, Hans-Josef: "Die Hausgemeinde als Lebensform im Urchristentum", in: H-J. Klauck: *Gemeinde, Amt, Sakrament: Neutestamentliche Perspektiven.* 1989, Würzburg: Echter Verlag, 11–28

Klauck, Hans-Josef: "Die dreifache Maria: Zur Rezeption von Joh 19,25 in EvPhil 32", in: F. Van Segbroeck, *et al.* (eds.): *The Four Gospels, 1992: Festschrift Frans Neirynck.* 3 vols, vol. 3: 1992 b, Leuven: University Press, 2343–58

Klauck, Hans-Josef: *Gemeinde zwischen Haus und Stadt: Kirche bei Paulus.* 1992 c, Freiburg im Breisgau: Herder

Klauck, Hans-Josef: *Die Johannesbriefe.* EdF 276, 1995 a (second edn of 1991 orig.), Darmstadt: Wissenschaftliche Buchgesellschaft

Klauck, Hans-Josef: *Die religiöse Umwelt des Urchristentums.* 2 vols, vol. 1: *Stadt- und Hausreligion, Mysterienkulte, Volksglaube.* 1995 b, vol. 2: *Herrscher- und Kaiserkult, Philosophie, Gnosis.* 1996, Stuttgart, Berlin, Köln: W. Kohlhammer

Klemm, Hans G.: "Das Wort von der Selbstbestattung der Toten: Beobachtungen zur Auslegungsgeschichte von Mt. viii.22 Par.", *New Testament Studies* 16 (1970), 60–75

Kloppenborg, John S.: *The Formation of Q: Trajectories in Ancient Wisdom Collections*. 1987, Philadelphia: Fortress Press

Knight, George W. III: "ΑΥΘΕΝΤΕΩ in Reference to Women in 1 Timothy 2.12", *New Testament Studies* 30 (1984), 143–57

Kristen, Peter: *Familie, Kreuz und Leben: Nachfolge Jesu nach Q und dem Markusevangelium*. 1995, Marburg: N. G. Elwert Verlag

Labahn, Michael: *Jesus als Lebensspender: Untersuchungen zu einer Geschichte der johanneischen Tradition anhand ihrer Wundergeschichten*. BZNW 98, 1999, Berlin, New York: Walter de Gruyter

Lambrecht, J.: "The relatives of Jesus in Mark", *Novum Testamentum* 16 (1974), 241–58

Lampe, Peter: *Die stadtrömischen Christen in den ersten beiden Jahrhunderten: Untersuchungen zur Sozialgeschichte*. WUNT 2/18, 1987, Tübingen: J. C. B. Mohr (Paul Siebeck)

Lategan, Bernard: "Intertextuality and Social Transformation: Some Implications of the Family Concept in New Testament Texts", in: S. Draisma (ed.): *Intertextuality in Biblical Writings: Essays in honor of Bas van Iersel*. 1989, Kampen: Uitgeversmaatschappij J. H. Kok, 105–16

Laub, Franz: "Sozialgeschichtlicher Hintergrund und ekklesiologische Relevanz der neutestamentlich-frühchristlichen Haus- und Gemeinde-Tafelparänese – ein Beitrag zur Soziologie des Frühchristentums", *Münchener Theologische Zeitschrift* 37 (1986), 249–71

Laufen, Rudolf: *Die Doppelüberlieferungen der Logienquelle und des Markusevangeliums*. BBB 54, 1980, Königstein/Ts. – Bonn: Peter Hanstein Verlag

Layton, Scott C.: "Christ over His House (Hebrews 3.6) and Hebrew אשר על־הבית", *New Testament Studies* 37 (1991), 473–7

Leaney, A. R. C.: "The Birth Narratives in St Luke and St Matthew", *New Testament Studies* 8 (1961), 158–66

Lee, G. M.: "Mark xv 21, 'The Father of Alexander and Rufus'", *Novum Testamentum* 17 (1975), 303

Légasse, S.: *Jésus et L'Enfant: "enfants", "petits" et "simples" dans la tradition synoptique*. 1969, Paris: Librairie Lecoffre, J. Gabalda et Cie. Éditeurs

Légasse, S.: "Approche de l'Épisode préévangélique des Fils de Zébédée (Marc x.35–40 par.)", *New Testament Studies* 20 (1974), 161–77

Lieu, Judith M.: "'Authority to become children of God': A Study of I John", *Novum Testamentum* 23 (1981), 210–28

Lincoln, Andrew T.: "The Household Code and Wisdom Mode of Colossians", *Journal for the Study of the New Testament* 74 (1999), 93–112

Lindboe, Inger Marie: *Women in the New Testament: A Select Bibliography*. 1990, Oslo: University of Oslo, Faculty of Theology

Linnemann, Eta: "Die Hochzeit zu Kana und Dionysos", *New Testament Studies* 20 (1974), 408–18

Lips, Hermann von: "Die Haustafel als 'Topos' im Rahmen der urchristlichen Paränese: Beobachtungen anhand des 1. Petrusbriefes und des Titusbriefes", *New Testament Studies* 40 (1994), 261–80

Lohfink, Gerhard: *Wie hat Jesus Gemeinde gewollt?: Zur gesellschaftlichen Dimension des christlichen Glaubens*. 1982, Freiburg im Breisgau, Basel, Wien: Herder

Lohse, Eduard: *Theologische Ethik des Neuen Testaments*. 1988, Stuttgart, Berlin, Köln: W. Kohlhammer

Lorenzen, Thorwald: "Die christliche Hauskirche", *Theologische Zeitschrift* 43 (1987), 333–52

Lührmann, Dieter: "Wo man nicht mehr Sklave oder Freier ist: Überlegungen zur Struktur frühchristlicher Gemeinden", *Wort und Dienst* 13 (1975), 53–83

Lührmann, Dieter: "Neutestamentliche Haustafeln und antike Ökonomie", *New Testament Studies* 27 (1981), 83–97

Lütgehetmann, Walter: *Die Hochzeit von Kana (Joh 2,1–11): Zu Ursprung und Deutung einer Wundererzählung im Rahmen johanneischer Redaktionsgeschichte*. Bibl. Unters. 20, 1990, Regensburg: Verlag Friedrich Pustet

Luz, Ulrich: "Überlegungen zum Epheserbrief und seiner Paränese", in: Merklein, H. (ed.): *Neues Testament und Ethik: Für Rudolf Schnackenburg*. 1989b, Freiburg im Breisgau, Basel, Wien: Herder, 376–96

MacDonald, Margaret Y.: "The Ideal of the Christian Couple: Ign. *Pol.* 5.1–2 Looking Back to Paul", *New Testament Studies* 40 (1994), 105–25

Malbon, Elizabeth Struthers: "τῇ οἰκίᾳ αὐτοῦ: Mark 2.15 in Context", *New Testament Studies* 31 (1985), 282–92

Malherbe, Abraham J.: "'Gentle as a Nurse': The Stoic Background to 1 Thess. II.", *Novum Testamentum* 12 (1970), 203–17

Malherbe, Abraham J.: *Social Aspects of Early Christianity*. 1977, Baton Rouge and London: Louisiana State University Press

Malherbe, Abraham J.: "God's New Family in Thessalonica", in: L. M. White and O. L. Yarbrough (eds.): *The Social World of the First Christians: Essays in Honor of Wayne A. Meeks*. 1995, Augsburg, Minn.: Fortress Press, 116–25

Marchel, W.: *Abba, Père! La prière du Christ et des chrétiens: Étude exégétique sur les origines et la signification de l'invocation à la divinité comme père, avant et dans le Nouveau Testament*. 1971, Rome: Biblical Institute Press

Matera, F. J.: *New Testament Ethics: The Legacies of Jesus and Paul*. 1996, Louisville, Ky.: Westminster John Knox Press

Matson, David Lertis: *Household Conversion Narratives in Acts: Pattern and Interpretation*. JSNTSup 123, 1996, Sheffield: Sheffield Academic Press

May, David M.: "Mark 2.15: The Home of Jesus or Levi?" *New Testament Studies* 39 (1993), 147–9

Maynard, Arthur H.: "TI EMOI KAI ΣOI (John 2.4)", *New Testament Studies* 31 (1985), 582–6

McArthur, Harvey K.: "'Son of Mary'", *Novum Testamentum* 15 (1973), 38–58

McCane, Byron R.: "'Let the Dead Bury Their Own Dead': Secondary Burial and Matt 8:21–22", *Harvard Theological Review* 83 (1990), 31–43

Mealand, David L.: *Poverty and Expectation in the Gospels*. 1981 (second impression of 1980 orig.), London: SPCK

Meeks, Wayne A. (ed.): *Zur Soziologie des Urchristentums: Ausgewählte Beiträge zum frühchristlichen Gemeinschaftsleben in seiner gesellschaftlichen Umwelt.* Transl. from English by G. Memmert. 1979, München: Chr. Kaiser Verlag

Meeks, Wayne A.: *The First Urban Christians: The Social World of the Apostle Paul.* 1983, New Haven and London: Yale University Press

Meeks, Wayne A.: *The Moral World of the First Christians.* 1987, London: SPCK

Meeks, Wayne A.: *The Origins of Christian Morality: The First Two Centuries.* 1993, New Haven, Conn.: Yale University Press

Meisinger, Hubert: *Liebesgebot und Altruismusforschung: Ein exegetischer Beitrag zum Dialog zwischen Theologie und Naturwissenschaft.* NTOA 33, 1996, Freiburg (Schweiz): Universitätsverlag; Göttingen: Vandenhoeck & Ruprecht

Melzer-Keller, Helga: *Jesus und die Frauen: Eine Verhältnisbestimmung nach den synoptischen Überlieferungen.* Herders Bibl. Stud. 14, 1997, Freiburg im Breisgau: Herder

Merkel, Helmut: "Das Gleichnis von den 'ungleichen Söhnen' (Matth. xxi.28–32)", *New Testament Studies* 20 (1974), 254–61

Merklein, Helmut (ed.): *Neues Testament und Ethik: Für Rudolf Schnackenburg.* 1989, Freiburg im Breisgau, Basel, Wien: Herder

Miller, James D.: *The Pastoral Letters as Composite Documents.* 1997, Cambridge: Cambridge University Press

Montefiore, H.W.: "God as Father in the Synoptic Gospels", *New Testament Studies* 3 (1956), 31–46

Moxnes, Halvor (ed.): *Constructing Early Christian Families: Family as social reality and metaphor.* 1997, London and New York: Routledge

Mödritzer, Helmut: *Stigma und Charisma im Neuen Testament und seiner Umwelt: Zur Soziologie des Urchristentums.* NTOA 28, 1994, Freiburg (Schweiz): Universitätsverlag; Göttingen: Vandenhoeck & Ruprecht

Müller, Peter: *In der Mitte der Gemeinde: Kinder im Neuen Testament.* 1992, Neukirchen-Vluyn: Neukirchener Verlag

Munro, Winsome: "Col. iii.18–iv.1 and Eph. v.21–vi.9: Evidences of a Late Literary Stratum?", *New Testament Studies* 18 (1972), 434–47

Mussner, Franz: "Jesus und 'das Haus des Vaters' – Jesus als 'Tempel'", in: J. Schreiner (ed.): *Freude am Gottesdienst: Aspekte ursprünglicher Liturgie.* 1983, Stuttgart: Verlag Katholisches Bibelwerk, 267–75

Neyrey, Jerome H.: "Loss of Wealth, Loss of Family and Loss of Honor: The cultural context of the original makarisms in Q", in: Ph. F. Esler (ed.): *Modelling Early Christianity: Social-scientific studies of the New Testament in its context.* 1995, London and New York: Routledge, 139–58

Noack, B: "On I John ii.12–14", *New Testament Studies* 6 (1959), 236–41

Nock, Arthur Darby: *Conversion: The Old and the New in Religion from Alexander the Great to Augustine of Hippo.* 1952 (repr. of 1933 first edn), Oxford: Clarendon Press

Nolland, John: "The Four (Five) Women and Other Annotations in Matthew's Genealogy", *New Testament Studies* 43 (1997), 527–39

O'Neill, John C.: *Messiah: Six lectures on the ministry of Jesus*. 1984 (repr. of 1980 original edn), Cambridge: Cochrane Press

O'Neill, John C.: "The origins of monasticism", in: R. Williams (ed.): *The Making of Orthodoxy: Essays in honour of Henry Chadwick*. 1989, Cambridge, Cambridge University Press, 270–87

O'Neill, John C.: *Who Did Jesus Think He Was?* BIS 11, 1995, Leiden, New York, Köln: E.J. Brill

O'Neill, John C.: "New Testament Monasteries", in: J.V. Hills, *et al.* (eds.): *Common Life in the Early Church: Essays honoring Graydon F. Snyder*. 1998, Harrisburg, Pa.: Trinity Press International, 118–32

O'Neill, John C.: "Jesus' Reply to his Mother at Cana of Galilee (John 2:4)", *Irish Biblical Studies* 23 (2001), 28–35

Osiek, Carolyn: "The Family in Early Christianity: 'Family Values' Revisited", *The Catholic Biblical Quarterly* 58 (1996), 1–24

Osiek, Carolyn and Balch, David L.: *Families in the New Testament World: Households and House Churches*. 1997, Louisville, Ky.: Westminster John Knox Press

Perdue, L.G., 1997, see section 2b

Pesch, Rudolf: "Das Weinwunder bei der Hochzeit zu Kana (Joh 2,1–12): Zur Herkunft der Wundererzählung", *Theologie der Gegenwart* 24 (1981), 219–25

Pöhlmann, Wolfgang: *Der Verlorene Sohn und das Haus: Studien zu Lukas 15,11–32 im Horizont der antiken Lehre von Haus, Erziehung und Ackerbau*. WUNT 68, 1993, Tübingen: J.C.B. Mohr (Paul Siebeck)

Ravens, D.A.S.: "Luke 9.7–62 and the Prophetic Role of Jesus", *New Testament Studies* 36 (1990), 119–29

Reumann, John: "One Lord, One Faith, One God, but Many House Churches", in: J.V. Hills, *et al.* (eds.): *Common Life in the Early Church: Essays Honoring Graydon F. Snyder*. 1998, Harrisburg, Pa.: Trinity Press International, 106–17

Richter Reimer, Ivoni: *Frauen in der Apostelgeschichte des Lukas: Eine feministisch-theologische Exegese*. 1992, Gütersloh: Gütersloher Verlagshaus Gerd Mohn

Rieplhuber, Rita: *Die Stellung der Frau in den neutestamentlichen Schriften und im Koran*. 1986, Altenberge: Christlich-Islamisches Schrifttum

Roh, Taeseong: *Die familia dei in den synoptischen Evangelien: Eine redaktions- und sozialgeschichtliche Untersuchung zu einem urchristlichen Bildfeld*. NTOA 37, 2001, Freiburg (Schweiz): Universitätsverlag; Göttingen: Vandenhoeck & Ruprecht

Rusam, Dietrich: *Die Gemeinschaft der Kinder Gottes: Das Motiv der Gotteskindschaft und die Gemeinden der johanneischen Briefe*. BWANT 133, 1993, Stuttgart, Berlin, Köln: W. Kohlhammer

Sanders, E.P.: *Jesus and Judaism*. 1985, London: SCM Press

Sariola, Heikki: *Markus und das Gesetz: Eine redaktionskritische Untersuchung*. 1990, Helsinki: Suomalainen Tiedeakatemia

Sauer, Jürgen: *Rückkehr und Vollendung des Heils: Eine Untersuchung zu den ethischen Radikalismen Jesu*. 1991, Regensburg: S. Roderer Verlag

Schaberg, J.: *The illegitimacy of Jesus: a feminist theological interpretation of the infancy narratives.* 1990, New York: Crossroads

Schmeller, Thomas: *Brechungen: Urchristliche Wandercharismatiker im Prisma soziologisch orientierter Exegese.* SBS 136, 1989, Stuttgart: Verlag Katholisches Bibelwerk

Schmidt, Thomas E.: "Mark 10.29–30; Matthew 19.29: 'Leave Houses ... and Region'?", *New Testament Studies* 38 (1992), 617–20

Schneider, Gerhard: "Jesu überraschende Antworten. Beobachtungen zu den Apophthegmen des dritten Evangeliums", *New Testament Studies* 29 (1983), 321–36

Schneider, Gerhard: "Auf Gott bezogenes 'mein Vater' und 'euer Vater' in den Jesus-Worten der Evangelien", in: F. Van Segbroeck, *et al.* (eds.): *The Four Gospels, 1992: Festschrift Frans Neirynck.* 3 vols, vol. 3: 1992, Leuven: University Press, 1751–81

Schnelle, Udo: *Einleitung in das Neue Testament.* UTB 1830, 1996², Göttingen: Vandenhoeck & Ruprecht

Schottroff, Luise: "Wanderprophetinnen: Eine feministische Analyse der Logienquelle", *Evangelische Theologie* 51 (1991), 332–44

Schrage, Wolfgang: "Zur Ethik der neutestamentlichen Haustafeln", *New Testament Studies* 21 (1975), 1–22

Schrage, Wolfgang: *Ethik des Neuen Testaments.* 1989⁵, Göttingen: Vandenhoeck & Ruprecht

Schroeder, Hans-Hartmut: *Eltern und Kinder in der Verkündigung Jesu: Eine hermeneutische und exegetische Untersuchung.* 1972, Hamburg-Bergstedt: Herbert Reich, Evangelischer Verlag

Schulz, Siegfried: *Neutestamentliche Ethik.* 1987, Zürich: Theologischer Verlag Zürich

Schüssler Fiorenza, Elisabeth: *In Memory of Her: A Feminist Theological Reconstruction of Christian Origins.* 1983, New York: Crossroad

Schweizer, Eduard: "Die Weltlichkeit des Neuen Testamentes: die Haustafeln", in: H. Donner, R. Hanhart, R. Smend (eds.): *Beiträge zur Alttestamentlichen Theologie: Festschrift für Walther Zimmerli zum 70. Geburtstag.* 1977, Göttingen: Vandenhoeck & Ruprecht, 397–413

Schweizer, Eduard: "Traditional ethical patterns in the Pauline and post-Pauline letters and their development (lists of vices and house-tables)", in: E. Best, R. McL. Wilson (eds.): *Text and Interpretation: Studies in the New Testament presented to Matthew Black.* 1979, Cambridge: Cambridge University Press, 195–209

Soards, Marion L.: *The Speeches in Acts: Their Content, Context, and Concerns.* 1994, Louisville, Ky.: Westminster/John Knox Press

Söding, Thomas: *Glaube bei Markus: Glaube an das Evangelium, Gebetsglaube und Wunderglaube im Kontext der markinischen Basileiatheologie und Christologie.* SBB 12, 1985, Stuttgart: Verlag Katholisches Bibelwerk

Sparks, H. F. D.: "The Doctrine of the Divine Fatherhood in the Gospels", in: D. E. Nineham (ed.): *Studies in the Gospels: Essays in Memory of R.H. Lightfoot.* 1955, Oxford: Basil Blackwell, 241–62

Stambaugh, John E. and Balch, David L.: *The New Testament in Its Social Environment*. 1986, Philadelphia, Pa.: The Westminster Press

Stegemann, Ekkehard W. and Stegemann, Wolfgang: *Urchristliche Sozialgeschichte: Die Anfänge im Judentum und die Christusgemeinden in der mediterranen Welt*. 1995, Stuttgart, Berlin, Köln: W. Kohlhammer

Strange, William A.: *Children in the Early Church: Children in the Ancient World, the New Testament and the Early Church*. 1996, Carlisle: Paternoster Press

Strecker, Georg: *Der Weg der Gerechtigkeit: Untersuchung zur Theologie des Matthäus*. 1971³, Göttingen: Vandenhoeck & Ruprecht

Strecker, Georg: "Die neutestamentlichen Haustafeln (Kol 3,18–4,1 und Eph 5,22–6,9)", in: H. Merklein (ed.): *Neues Testament und Ethik: Für Rudolf Schnackenburg*. 1989, Freiburg im Breisgau, Basel, Wien: Herder, 349–75

Telford, W. R.: *The Theology of the Gospel of Mark*. 1999, Cambridge: Cambridge University Press

Theissen, Gerd, "Soziale Integration und sakramentales Handeln: Eine Analyse von I Cor. XI 17–34", *Novum Testamentum* 16 (1974), 179–206

Theissen, Gerd: "'Wir haben alles verlassen' (Mc. X 28): Nachfolge und soziale Entwurzelung in der jüdisch-palästinischen Gesellschaft des I. Jahrhunderts n. Ch.", *Novum Testamentum* 19 (1977), 161–96

Theissen, Gerd: *Biblischer Glaube in evolutionärer Sicht*. 1984, München: Chr. Kaiser

Theissen, Gerd: "Tradition und Entscheidung: Der Beitrag des biblischen Glaubens zum kulturellen Gedächtnis", in: Jan Assmann and Tonio Hölscher (eds.): *Kultur und Gedächtnis*. 1988, Frankfurt am Main: Suhrkamp, 170–96

Theissen, Gerd: *Studien zur Soziologie des Urchristentums*. WUNT 19, 1989a (third edn of 1979 orig.) Tübingen: J. C. B. Mohr (Paul Siebeck)

Theissen, Gerd: "Legitimation und Lebensunterhalt. Ein Beitrag zur Soziologie urchristlicher Missionare", in: G. Theissen: *Studien zur Soziologie des Urchristentums*. 1989³b, Tübingen: J. C. B. Mohr (Paul Siebeck), 201–30

Theissen, Gerd: "Soziale Schichtung in der korinthischen Gemeinde. Ein Beitrag zur Soziologie des hellenistischen Urchristentums", in: G. Theissen: *Studien zur Soziologie des Urchristentums*. 1989³c, Tübingen: J. C. B. Mohr (Paul Siebeck), 231–71

Theissen, Gerd: "Wanderradikalismus. Literatursoziologische Aspekte der Überlieferung von Worten Jesu im Urchristentum", in: G. Theissen: *Studien zur Soziologie des Urchristentums*. 1989³d, Tübingen: J. C. B. Mohr (Paul Siebeck), 79–105

Theissen, Gerd: "Die soziologische Auswertung religiöser Überlieferungen: Ihre methodologischen Probleme am Beispiel des Urchristentums", in: G. Theissen: *Studien zur Soziologie des Urchristentums*. 1989³e, Tübingen: J. C. B. Mohr (Paul Siebeck), 35–54

Theissen, Gerd: *Soziologie der Jesusbewegung: Ein Beitrag zur Entstehungsgeschichte des Urchristentums*. 1997 (seventh edn of 1977 orig.), Gütersloh: Chr. Kaiser/Gütersloher Verlagshaus

3. Literature related to the New Testament

Theissen, Gerd: *A Theory of Primitive Christian Religion*. Transl. by John Bowden. (The German orig. appeared in 2000, in a revised form.) 1999, London: SCM Press

Theissen, Gerd, and Merz, Annette: *Der historische Jesus: Ein Lehrbuch*. 1997 (second edn of 1996 orig.), Göttingen: Vandenhoeck & Ruprecht

Thraede, Klaus: "Zum historischen Hintergrund der 'Haustafeln' des NT", in: E. Dassmann, K. S. Frank (eds.): *Pietas: Festschrift für Bernhard Kötting*. 1980, Münster Westfalen: Aschendorffsche Verlagsbuchhandlung, 359–68

Torjesen, Karen Jo: *When Women Were Priests: Women's Leadership in the Early Church and the Scandal of Their Subordination in the Rise of Christianity*. 1993, San Francisco: Harper

Verner, David C.: *The Household of God: The Social World of the Pastoral Epistles*. SBLDS 71, 1983, Chico, Calif.: Scholars Press

Vogt, Thea: *Angst und Identität im Markusevangelium: Ein textpsychologischer und sozialgeschichtlicher Beitrag*. NTOA 26, 1993, Freiburg (Schweiz): Universitätsverlag; Göttingen: Vandenhoeck & Ruprecht

Vos, Craig Steven de: "The Significance of the Change from οἶκος to οἰκία in Luke's Account of the Philippian Gaoler (Acts 16.30–4)", *New Testament Studies* 41 (1995), 292–6

Vos, Craig Steven de: "Stepmothers, Concubines and the Case of Πορνεία in 1 Corinthians 5", *New Testament Studies* 44 (1998), 104–14

Wagener, Ulrike: *Die Ordnung des 'Hauses Gottes': Der Ort von Frauen in der Ekklesiologie und Ethik der Pastoralbriefe*. WUNT 2/65, 1994, Tübingen: J.C.B. Mohr (Paul Siebeck)

Walter, Nikolaus: "Zur Analyse von Mc 10,17–31", *Zeitschrift für die neutestamentliche Wissenschaft* 53 (1962), 206–18

Wansbrough, Henry: "Mark iii.21 – Was Jesus out of his mind?", *New Testament Studies* 18 (1972), 233–5

Weber, Hans-Ruedi: *Jesus and the Children: Biblical Resources for Study and Preaching*. 1979, Geneva: World Council of Churches

Weigandt, Peter: "Zur sogenannten 'Oikosformel'", *Novum Testamentum* 6 (1963), 49–74

Weima, Jeffrey A. D.: "'But We Became Infants Among You': The Case for NEPIOI in 1 Thess 2.7", *New Testament Studies* 46 (2000), 547–64

Weiser, Alfons: "Evangelisierung im 'Haus'", *Biblische Zeitschrift* 34 (1990), 63–86

Wenham, David: "The Meaning of Mark iii.21", *New Testament Studies* 21 (1975), 295–300

Weren, Wim J. C.: "Kinder bei Matthäus: Eine semantische Untersuchung", *Concilium* 32 (1996), 147–54

Whitaker, G. H.: "Of the Household: Is the Rendering Correct?", *Expositor* 8/23 (1922), 76–79

White, L. Michael: *Building God's House in the Roman World: Architectural Adaptation among Pagans, Jews, and Christians*. 1990, Baltimore and London: The John Hopkins University Press

White, L. Michael: *The Social Origins of Christian Architecture. Vol.II: Texts and Monuments for the Christian Domus Ecclesiae in Its Environment*. 1997, Valley Forge, Pa.: Trinity Press International
White, L. M. and Yarbrough, O. L. (eds.): *The Social World of the First Christians: Essays in Honor of Wayne A. Meeks*. 1995, Augsburg, Minn.: Fortress Press
Willemse, J.: "La Patrie de Jésus selon Saint Jean iv.44", *New Testament Studies* 11 (1964), 349–64
Williams, Joel F.: *Other Followers of Jesus: Minor Characters as Major Figures in Mark's Gospel*. JSNTSup 102, 1994, Sheffield: Sheffield Academic Press
Witherington III, Ben: *Women in the Earliest Churches*. SNTSMS 59, 1988, Cambridge: Cambridge University Press
Witherington III, Ben: *Women and the Genesis of Christianity*. 1990, Cambridge: Cambridge University Press
Woyke, Johannes: *Die neutestamentlichen Haustafeln: Ein kritischer und konstruktiver Forschungsüberblick*. SBS 184, 2000, Stuttgart: Verlag Katholisches Bibelwerk
Yarbrough, O. Larry, 1993, see section 2b
Yarbrough, O. Larry: "Parents and Children in the Letters of Paul", in: L. M. White and O. L. Yarbrough (eds.): *The Social World of the First Christians: Essays in Honor of Wayne A. Meeks*. 1995, Augsburg, Minn.: Fortress Press, 126–41
Zeller, Dieter: "God as Father in the Proclamation and in the Prayer of Jesus", in: A. Finkel and L. Frizzell (eds.): *Standing Before God: Studies on Prayer in Scriptures and in Tradition with Essays. In Honour of John M. Oesterreicher*. 1981, New York: Ktav Publishing House, Inc., 117–29
Zumstein, Jean: "Johannes 19,25–27", *Zeitschrift für Theologie und Kirche* 94 (1997), 131–54

Index of References

1. Old Testament

Genesis

1,14	214
2,24	135, 196
23,15–16	154
25,9	96
28,1–7	85
29,30ff	144
35,29	96
41,40	211
49,29	96

Exodus

13,14	83
20,6	177
20,12	87, 90, 103, 117, 130, 173, 177
20,12–16	179
20,12a	117
21,15	87, 92, 102, 118
21,17	87, 102
31,13	210

Leviticus

11,44	216
18,8	163
19,2	216
19,3	87, 92
19,18	28, 119, 121, 213
19,32	92
20,8	210
20,9	102, 117
20,11	163
21,11–12	148

Numbers

6,6	148
6,6–8	148
11,12	192
16,22	208

Deuteronomy

5,16	87
5,16a	117, 118
6,5	90, 119
6,6–9	83
21,15	144
21,18–21	102
24,3	144
27,16	102
27,20	163

Joshua

4,6.21	83

1 Samuel

28,13	96

2 Samuel

14,16	96
16,10	152
19,7	144
19,22	152
22,3	210

3 Kingdoms

20,25	226

Esther

2,7	11

Psalms

2,7	212
22,12	210
70,22	216
103,13	192
135,7	214

Proverbs

1,8–9	84
3,11–12	84, 206
4,1–4	83
13,24	144
17,25	84
24,23	8

Isaiah

1,4	216
3,5	92
5,1–5	125
8,17	210
8,17–18	210
8,19–20	96
51,2	213
60,15	144
66,13	192

Ezekiel

22,7	163
22,10	163
33,27	226

Daniel

7,9	92

Joel

3,1–5	204

Micah

7,6	139, 140, 141
7,7	141
7,12	141

Zechariah

13,3	109

Malachi

1,2–3	144, 145
3,24	12
4,6	142

2. Old Testament Apocrypha and Pseudepigrapha

Judith

8,2	85

1 Maccabees

18,10	83

2 Maccabees

6,4	160
15,18	106

3 Maccabees

4,16	160

4 Maccabees

2,9b–13	106
5,7	8
16,20	213

Sirach

3,1–18	92
3,3–4	99
3,5	99
3,6	104
3,6–7	92
3,7	94
3,8	92, 99
3,11	90
3,12	94
3,12–13	91
3,13	104
3,14–15	99
3,16	98
7,23	83
7,24–25	84
7,27–28	100
7,27–29	119

7,27a	90, 119	23,7	96
7,27b	90	23,16	109, 142
7,29a	90, 119	23,19	142
7,33	97	33,10	163
22,3–5	84	36,1–2	96
30,1–6	84	36,18	96
30,12	84	39,6	83
42,9–11	85		
48,10	12		

Letter of Aristeas

132	119
152	163
187–294	88
228	88, 119

Tobit

1,9	85
3,15–17	85
4,3	95
4,12	85
4,17	97

Wisdom of Solomon

4,10	177
9,10	177

Pseudo-Phocylides

lines 175–227	89, 173
line 179	163
line 208	175
lines 220–222	91

Apocalypse of Abraham

8,1–6	107

Sibylline Oracles

II.273–275	94, 101
II.275–276	92
III.573–574	88
III.593	119
III.593–594	88
V.390	163

2 Baruch

70,3	142
70,6	109

1 Enoch

100,1–2	59, 142

Testament of Gad

8,3	96

4 Ezra

5,9	142
6,24	142
6,25	139

Testament of Joseph

20,3	96

Joseph and Aseneth

11,4	108

Testament of Judah

1,4	93
13,1	93, 94
17,3–4	94

Jubilees

4,15–33	85
7,20	89
8,6	85
11,7.14	85
11,16	83, 107

Testament of Reuben

3,8	93
7,1–2	96

Testament of Zebulun

10,2	93

3. New Testament

Matthew

3,9	213
3,17	190
4,18–22	131
4,21–22	131
5,9	141, 142
5,21ff	92
5,31–32	135
5,48	149
6,9	191
6,14	149
6,32	149
7,9–11	176
8,14–15	123
8,19–20	145
8,20	60
8,21–22	145
8,22	148
8,23	146
9,18–26	121
9,22	122
10,12–15	141, 142
10,17–22	139
10,21	138, 140, 141, 142
10,21–23	141, 142
10,22	140
10,22b	139
10,23	140
10,34	108, 142
10,34ff	108
10,34–36	140
10,35	139
10,35–36	141
10,37	143, 144
10,37–38	142, 143
11,25–27	190
12,46–50	133
13,53–58	134
13,57	135
14,21	203
15,1–9	117
15,4	118
15,5	118
15,21–28	122
15,26	122
16,24	143
17,14–21	122
18,1–5	121
18,4	121
19,1–9	135
19,13–15	121
19,16–26	120
19,27–30	136
19,29	138
19,30	136
20,16	136
20,20	123
21,28–32	126
21,33–46	124
21,39	125
22,1–10	143
23,8–10	149, 151
23,9	149, 150, 151
23,9a	149
23,29	96
26,37	123
27,32	123
27,56	123

Mark

1,11	59, 125, 190
1,16–20	131
1,18	131
1,19	55
1,20b	131
1,24	152
1,29–31	123
2,15	124
3,7	132
3,20	133, 204
3,20–21	133, 134
3,21	134
3,31–35	133, 140, 204
3,35	134, 137
5,21–43	121
5,24	132
5,34	122
5,40	122
5,43	122
6,1–6a	134
6,3	55
6,4	135
6,6	135
7,8	119
7,9–13	1
7,10	117, 118
7,11–13	118
7,13	119

Index of References

7,24–30	122	9,37–43a	122
7,28	122	9,46–48	121
8,34	143	9,58	60
9,7	125	9,59–60	145, 146
9,14–29	122	9,60	146
9,17	122	10,6	215
9,33–37	121	10,21–22	190
10,1–12	135	10,25–37	144
10,7	135	11,2	191
10,13–16	121	11,11–13	176
10,17–27	1, 120	12,51–53	140
10,19	120, 121	13,30	136
10,20–21	121	14,25	143
10,28	136, 138	14,26	1, 115, 120, 142, 143, 144, 145, 176
10,28–31	136		
10,29	1, 137, 138		
10,29–30	137, 138	14,26–27	142, 143
10,30	137	14,27	145
10,31	136	15,11–32	128
10,35	123	15,12	128
10,46	123	15,19	129
12,1–12	124	15,29a	129
12,8	126	15,31	129
13,9–13	138	15,32	129
13,12	59, 138, 139	16,8	216
14,61–62	125	16,13	144
15,21	123, 182	16,18	135
15,34	210	18,15–17	121
15,40	123	18,18–27	120
		18,28–30	136
Luke		18,29	138
		19,14	144
1,17	12	20,9–19	124
1,71	144	20,15	125
2,41–52	127	20,36	215
2,48	127	21,10–19	139
2,49	127	21,16	139
2,51	127	21,17	144
3,22	190	23,26	123
4,16–30	134		
4,38–39	123	*John*	
5,1–11	131		
5,10	123	1,12	191
5,28	135	1,34	190
6,22	144	1,35–51	131
6,27	144	2,1–11	151
8,19–21	133, 204	2,3	152
8,40–56	121	2,4	61, 154
8,48	122	2,5	154
8,51	122	3,6–8	223
8,55	122	4,44	134
9,23	143, 145	4,53	194

6,9	203	4,1	213
6,42	134	4,12	213
7,3–10	204	8,15	189, 191
7,5	134	8,23	189
8,39	213	9,4	189
12,25	145	9,13	144
12,36	216	11,32	131
17,12	216	16,13	182
19,17	123	16,16	219
19,25–27	129, 153		
19,26–27	154	*1 Corinthians*	
21,1–11	131		
21,2	123	1,16	159, 174, 194
21,3	131	3,1	191
		3,1–2	183
Acts		3,2	184, 192, 217
		4,14	184, 185
1,14	203, 204	4,14–16	184
2,17–18	204	4,15	187, 194, 212
7,21	205	4,17	193
7,22	205	5,1–2	162
11,14	194	5,1–5	164, 200
12,12	219	5,3–5	163
12,17	203	7,8	163
15,13	203	7,10–16	163
16,1	84, 174, 194, 197	7,12–16	164, 165
		7,14	164, 209, 216
16,1–3	197	7,14b	164
16,15	174, 203	7,21–22	44
16,31–34	174	7,24–27	163
16,34	203	9,4–5	115
18,2–3	55	9,5	124
18,8	174	13,11	191
21,3	183	14,20	183
21,5	205	16,2	186, 219
21,6b	205	16,15	159, 174, 194
21,28	203	16,20	219
22,3	206		
23,16	206	*2 Corinthians*	
		6,11–13	185, 186, 190, 201
Romans			
		6,13	186, 199
1,1	182, 191	10,1–2	187
1,12	182	10,8	187
1,16–17	160, 198	11,2	187, 199
1,21	161	11,7–10	186
1,29–31	160, 162, 200	11,13	187
1,30	160, 161, 179, 199	12,14	201
		12,14–15	186
1,32	161	12,15b	186
2,5	186	13,10	187
2,20	191		

Galatians

3,28	166, 168, 188
3,28–29	188
3,29	188, 201
3,29–4,7	201
4,1	191
4,1–7	188
4,1–11	189
4,3	191
4,4–6	52
4,5	190
4,6	190
4,12–16	187
4,19	183, 187, 199
4,19–20	187
4,30	189
5,18–25	161

Ephesians

1,2–3	196
1,5	189
1,17	196
2,2	215
2,3	216
3,15	196
5,1	191
5,8	216
5,21–6,4	171
5,21–6,9	168
5,22	172
5,29	144
5,31	196
6,1–4	172
6,2–3	90, 103, 172
6,4	98, 175
6,5	172

Philippians

2,15	191
2,22	196
3,3–6	183

Colossians

1,2–3	196
1,12–14	189
3,18–4,1	168, 170
3,20–21	172
3,20b	177
3,21	98, 175
3,22	171

1 Thessalonians

2,7	183, 184, 191, 192
2,7–12	191
2,11	183
2,13	193, 215
5,5	216

2 Thessalonians

1,1–2	196
2,16	196

1 Timothy

1,2	196, 198
1,9	161, 178, 200
1,9–10	178, 200
1,18	196
2,8–15	168
2,9	50
3,4	180
3,4–5	180
3,12	181
3,15	181
5,4	180, 199, 200, 201
5,8	180
6,1–2	168
6,2	181

2 Timothy

1,2	196
1,5	84, 197, 199
2,1	196
2,2	181
3,1	160, 197, 198, 201
3,1–2	201
3,2	160, 179, 199
3,2–5	160
3,10	197
3,14–17	197
3,15	84, 197, 198, 199
3,15b	198

Titus

1,4	196
1,6	181
1,6b	181
2,1–10	168, 178
2,3–5	180
2,4–5	50

Philemon

10	212
12	195

Hebrews

2,5–18	209
2,8	213
2,11	210, 216
3,1–6	187, 210, 212
3,3	102
5,5	212
5,6	213
5,8	212
5,12	184
10,29	210
10,32	208
12,1–3	207
12,2	208
12,4–7	206
12,4–11	206
12,6–7	84
12,7	191, 206
13,12	210

James

1,2	214
1,17	214
1,17–18	214
1,19	215
2,21	213
3,15	214
3,17	214
5,14	214

1 Peter

1,13–21	217
1,14	215, 216
1,14–2,2	217
1,15–16	216
1,17	184, 191, 204, 214, 216
1,18	218
1,22	219
1,23	217
2,2	183, 184, 217
2,9	216
2,13–3,7	215
2,17	219
2,18	168, 209
2,18–3,7	168
4,8	219
4,14	140
5,9	219
5,13–14a	218

2 Peter

1,10	220
2,14	216
3,3–4	220

1 John

2,1	221, 222
2,9	144
2,20	216
3,1–2	221
3,9–10	223
3,10	191
4,4	224
4,7–8	223
4,19–21	223
5,21	224

2 John

1a	212, 224
4	225, 226
4a	225
7–11	226
13	224

3 John

3–4	225
5	225
9–10	226
11	226

Jude

1	204, 219

Index of References

Revelation

1,6	227
1,13	227
2,18	227
2,20–23	226
2,28	227
3,5	227
3,21	227
6,8	226
12,4–5	227
12,13–14	227
14,1	227

4. Philo

Hypothetica

8.7.14	82, 173

On the Change of Names

40	177

On the Cherubim

44	193
114	43

On the Creation of the World

45, 46	193

On the Decalogue

50–51	97
106	87
106–120	81, 87
107	87, 97
108	81
110–112	82
111	99
113–117	100
116	95, 100
118	101
119	101
120	98
121	98
165–167	81, 93, 173

On the Embassy to Gaius

	188

On the Life of Moses

1.21–24	205
2.245	186

On the Migration of Abraham

28, 193, 194	193

On the Special Laws

1.41	193
1.200–201	101
2.224–241	81
2.225	98, 193
2.226	101, 173
2.226–227	173
2.228	102
2.229	102
2.231	102
2.235	86, 119
2.236	105
2.237	92
2.248	92, 102
2.261	103
2.262	103
3.21	163

5. Josephus

Against Apion

2.190	119
2.200	85
2.201	173
2.204	84
2.205	96
2.206	91, 96, 101, 103, 105, 119
2.210	107

Jewish Antiquities

3.274	163

Jewish War

2.197	106
5.545	96

6. Qumran

1QH³ 3,7 ff	188
1QH 7,20 ff	184
1QS 4,2–14	161
4Q416	89, 94, 104
4Q418	89

7. Rabbinic Writings

Babylonian Talmud

b. Qiddushin

31b	95

b. Shabbat

12a	85
150a	85

Mishnah

Shabbat

16,22	85

Sotah

9,15	140

8. New Testament Apocrypha, Classical and Patristic Texts

Aelian

On the Characteristics of Animals

IX,1	12

Aeschines

I,13	13, 33
I,14	13

Aeschylus

The Suppliant Maidens

lines 707–709	24

Aristophanes

Clouds

lines 991–995	19
lines 1380–1390	18
lines 1404–1405	18
lines 1409–1410	18
lines 1421–1424	18
lines 1427–1429	12

Aristotle

Nicomachean Ethics

1161a	9
1165a	17, 28, 35

Politics

I.2. 1252a	173
I.2. 1252b	167
I.3. 1253b	166, 167, 173
I.4. 1254a	173
I.5. 1254b	173
I.6. 1255b	173
I.12. 1259a–b	168

Aulus Gellius

Attic Nights

2.7.1–10	75

Callicratidas

On the Felicity of Families

	48, 62

Cicero

Epistulae ad familiares

14.11	68

De legibus

2.22 and 55	68

Index of References

De officiis

1.17.58	64, 75
1.45.160	64, 75

Epistulae ad Atticum

11.17	68

Partitiones oratoriae

25.88	69

Pro Cluentio

5.14–6.15	163

Diogenes Laertius

VII.108	160
VII.120	63

Life of Pythagoras

VIII.22	22

Dionysius of Halicarnassus

Antiquitates romanae

2.25.4–26.4	168

Epictetus

Diatribai

I.xxii.1	177
II.x.7	74, 173, 175
II.x.10–12	73
II.xvii.6	177
III.iii.5–6	61
III.iii.6	135
III.vii.25–28	61
III.xxii.43	160
III.xxii.45–47,50	60

Eusebius

Ecclesiastical History

2.15.1	219
3.39.15	219

Gaius

Institutiones

I.63	163

Golden Verses of Pythagoras

lines 1–4	15

The Gospel of Thomas

55	145
65	125
101	145

Hesiod

Works and Days

lines 174–176	11
line 180	22
lines 182–189	11
line 201	11
lines 331–332	21
lines 331–334	11

Homer

Iliad

4,477–478	11
17,301–302	11

Iamblichus

On the Pythagorean Way of Life

ch. 8, section 37	22
ch. 8, section 38	15
ch. 8, sections 38–39	22
ch. 8, section 40	15, 23
ch. 33, section 229	23
ch. 33, section 230	23

Isaeus

Speech XIII	29

Justin Martyr

Apology

I,4	140

Livy		XI.926D	34
		XI.928D	34
1.50.9	59	XI.928D–E	34
		XI.928E	34
Lysias		XI.929D–E	34
		XI.929E	34
XIX.55	17	XI.931A	26
		XI.931A–D	26
Musonius Rufus		XI.931B–C	27
		XI.931D	27
Must One Obey One's Parents Under All Circumstances?	73, 74	XI.931E–932A	27
		XI.932A	8, 9, 16, 27
		XI.932A–B	27
		XI.932A–C	16
		XI.932B–C	7, 25
Should Every Child That Is Born Be Raised?		*Phaedo*	
100.15	186	113E	179
		114A	179
Ocellus Lucanus			
		Statesman	
On the Nature of the Universe	48	615C	179
Pempelus		*Timaeus*	
On Parents	70	28C	193
		37C	193
Perictyone			
		Pliny the Elder	
On the Harmony of a Woman	49, 71, 74	*Natural History*	
Phintys		5.17.4	132
		7.121	66
On Woman's Temperance	50	Pliny the Younger	
Plato		*Epistulae*	
Laws		6.33	75
I.627A	10, 25		
IV.717B–718A	16, 25	Plutarch	
IV.717C–D	16, 25		
IV.718A	16, 25	*Cato the Elder*	
VI.771E–VII.824C	166	20,4–7	43
VII.821B	26		
X.909D	26	*Lives*	
X.910B–C	26		
XI.917A	8	Solon XXII.1	31
XI.926B–C	34	Solon XXII.4	32

Index of References

On the Love of Wealth

526a	186

Polycarp

To the Philippians

8,2	140

Quintilian

Institutio oratoria

6.2.14	69

Seneca

De beneficiis

2.18	173
3.1.5	66
3.18	173
3.18.1	69
6.23.5	66

Epistulae morales

94.1	167, 173

On Mercy

1.16.3	59

Sophocles

Antigone

lines 897–904	14

Electra

lines 32–37	33

Oedipus tyrannus

lines 867–868	13
lines 1329–1330	24
lines 1345–1346	24
lines 1371–1374	24

Tacitus

Annales

XV,44	139

Terence

The Brothers

lines 40–79	69

Valerius Maximus

5.4.7	66
5.8.4	59
7.7.4	75
7.8.2	68

Xenophon

Oeconomicus

I.7	173
VII.5–6	19
VII.11–12	20
VII.14–15	20
VII.42	20

Index of Authors

Aichele, G. 134
Allison, D.C. 141–142, 146–149, 151, 169
Allmen, D. von 191
Alvarez-Péreyre, F. 103–104
Anderson, H. 106
Ariès, P. 42
Ashmore, S.G. 69

Balch, D.L. 158–159, 165–166, 174, 176
Balla, P. 157, 213
Balz, H. 223–225
Barclay, J. 169
Barrett, C.K. 152, 203–206
Barton, S.C. 60–62, 107
Bauckham, R. 220
Beale, G.K. 226–227
Berger, K. 161, 176
Best, E. 165, 168, 170–171, 174–177
Blenkinsopp, J. 96
Blomenkamp, P. 43, 51
Bock, D.L. 141, 144–145, 147–148
Bockmuehl, M. 148
Bolyki, J. 129, 154
Bonhöffer, A. 60
Botha, P.J.J. 158
Bovon, F. 127, 143, 205
Bradley, K.R. 55, 75
Branick, V.P. 174
Broadhead, E.K. 125
Brown, R.E. 125, 129
Brox, N. 216, 218
Bruce, F.F. 191–192
Burchard, C. 101, 108
Burguière, A. 29–30, 104

Carroll, J.T. 121
Carson, D.A. 220
Charlesworth, J.H. 83, 88, 92–94, 106–108

Cohen, S.J.D. 80, 109
Collins, J.J. 83, 85, 88, 92, 94, 98–99
Colson, F.H. 81, 102
Conte, G.B. 66
Corbier, M. 53
Craffert, P.F. 96, 174
Crossan, J.D. 60
Crouch, J.E. 165
Cserháti, S. 168

Dassmann, E. 19, 49
Davids, P.H. 214–215
Davies, W.D. 140–142, 146–149, 151
Degani, E. 11, 13, 33
Delling, G. 164, 174, 203
Dibelius, M. 134, 165
Dixon, S. 42, 51–52, 54–55, 67–68, 72, 75
Dóka, Z. 123
Donelson, L.R. 178, 181
Dorandi, T. 6
Dover, K.J. 18
Downing, F.G. 60
Dunn, J.D.G. 165, 167–169, 175, 177, 188–190
Dwyer, T. 133–134

Eltrop, B. 121
Esler, P.F. 158
Evans, C.F. 143–144, 147–148
Eyben, E. 42–43, 45–46, 51, 59, 64, 68

Fideler, D.R. 14–17, 26, 34, 48–50, 63, 69–74
Fiedler, P. 165
Fitzgerald, J.T. 165
Foucault, M. 167
Francis, J. 184
Frankemölle, H. 214
Frilingos, C. 195

Index of Authors

Gardner, J. F. 43, 46, 52
Gaudemet, J. 46–47, 53
Gielen, M. 159, 165, 169, 171, 174
Gnilka, J. 120, 125, 135, 139, 174
Goppelt, L. 165
Graf, F. 66, 198
Gräßer, E. 207–212
Grundmann, W. 184, 190
Guelich, R. A. 133

Habicht, C. 106
Hagner, D. A. 142, 145, 147, 149–151
Hallett, J. 46–47, 51
Harris, M. J. 171, 194–195
Haufe, G. 52, 121
Hays, R. B. 162–163, 184
Hegermann, H. 210
Hengel, M. 132, 139, 147–148
Henten, J.W. van 80, 85
Heymann, F. 104
Hollander, H.W. 93
Horsley, G. H. R. 54, 58, 67, 72
Horst, P.W. van der 88
Hübner, H. 157, 169–170, 172, 194

Ireland, S. 69
Isaac, E. 108

Jeremias, J. 174, 190, 203
Jonge, M. de 93
Joubert, S. 80, 85, 187

Kee, H. C. 93
Kirchschläger, W. 127, 154
Klauck, H-J. 130, 174, 221–225
Knight III, G.W. 178–179, 181, 197–198
Kraemer, R. S. 83
Kristen, P. 147
Kunkel, W. 47

Labahn, M. 154
Lacey, W. K. 45
Lampe, P. 158, 182–183, 194–195
Lane, W. L. 207–210, 212–213
Laub, F. 165–166
Laws, S. 213–215
Layton, S. C. 211
Lerat, L. 28
Liddell, H. G. 11, 22
Lieu, J. M. 191
Lincoln, A. T. 169–170, 172, 176

Lips, H. von 118–119, 152, 165, 190
Lohfink, G. 150
Lohmeyer, E. 165, 171
Lorenzen, T. 174
Lührmann, D. 165–167, 181
Lumpe, A. 10, 58, 65–66, 68, 71
Lütgehetmann, W. 151–153
Luz, U. 43, 118–119, 132, 134, 139–141, 143, 145–147, 149–151, 165, 168–171, 174–175, 177

Malbon, E. S. 124
Malherbe, A. J. 158, 191–193
Marrou, H. I. 41, 43
Marshall, I. H. 129, 143–144, 146–148
Martina, A. 12
Martínez, F. G. 89–90, 151
Matson, D. L. 174, 203
May, D. M. 124
Maynard, A. H. 152
Mealand, D. L. 120, 131–132
Meeks, W. A. 158
Merz, A. 125–126, 133, 144, 152
Metzger, B. M. 83
Meyer, R. 95
Michaels, J. R. 215–219
Miller, J. D. 178, 180, 197–198
Müller, P. 42, 52–53, 64, 121
Mussner, F. 213–214

Nesselrath, H-G. 6–7, 11, 13, 30, 33
Nickel, R. 73–75
Nock, A. D. 60

O'Brien, P. T. 165, 172, 175
O'Neill, J. C. 132, 146–148, 151, 154, 222
Osiek, C. 158–159, 174

Perdue, L. G. 80, 82–83, 85, 95–96, 98–99
Pesch, R. 153–154, 203–205
Pilhofer, P. 22, 92
Pöhlmann, W. 128
Pomeroy, S. B. 19–20
Praechter, K. 63

Quinn, J. D. 180

Rädle, H. 69
Rawson, B. 42–43, 51, 54, 56

Reinhartz, A. 98, 100–102, 105–106
Reinmuth, E. 191–193
Rengstorf, K.H. 165
Roh, T. 134, 137, 191
Roloff, J. 157, 179–180
Ross, W.D. 83, 167–168
Rubinkievicz, R. 107
Rühfel, H. 6
Rusam, D. 191, 221, 223, 225

Sachers, E. 46, 50
Safrai, S. 80, 85, 175
Saller, R. 46, 66
Sanders, E.P. 147
Sanders, J.A. 81, 147
Sauer, G. 83
Saunders, T.J. 26, 167
Schaberg, J. 208
Schlier, H. 169
Schmithals, W. 126, 131, 133
Schneider, G. 191, 203
Schnelle, U. 129–130, 153, 178, 185, 220–221
Schöllgen, G. 19
Schöpsdau, K. 26
Schrage, W. 162–165, 183–184, 214, 219–220
Schreiner, T.R. 162, 182–183
Schroeder, H-H. 121, 166
Schweizer, E. 87, 161–162, 165, 169, 180, 217–219
Sevenster, J.N. 60
Shutt, R.J.H. 88
Smalley, S.S. 224
Soards, M.L. 162–164, 184, 205
Sommerstein, A.H. 12, 18–19, 35
Stegemann, E.W. and Stegemann, W. 158
Strange, W.A. 121, 178, 181, 203

Strecker, G. 165, 167–168, 170–171, 173
Strobel, A. 209

Taylor, T. 17, 26, 74
Tcherikover, V.A. 41
Theissen, G. 37, 44, 86, 90, 115–116, 119–120, 125–126, 130, 133, 137–138, 152, 155, 158–159
Thesleff, H. 48–50, 70–71
Thom, J.C. 15
Thraede, K. 165–166
Tov, E. 89–90, 94
Treggiari, S. 42, 67

Verner, D.C. 166, 174
Vögtle, A. 220
Vos, C.S. de 174, 203

Wacker, W.C. 180
Wagener, U. 165–166, 176, 180
Wallace-Hadrill, A. 56, 158
Weaver, P.R.C. 54
Weidinger, K. 165
Weiser, A. 204–205
White, L.M. 158, 174
Wiedemann, T. 43, 46, 52
Wilckens, U. 160–162, 182
Williams, J.F. 120, 122–123
Wintermute, O.S. 83
Witherington III, B. 205–206
Wolter, M. 165, 170, 176, 194–195
Woyke, J. 165

Yarbrough, O.L. 10, 59, 75, 164, 179, 184–187

Zeller, D. 127, 190
Zumstein, J. 129–130

Index of Subjects

adoption 51–52, 188–190, 205
Aelian 12
Aeschines 13, 33, 37
Aeschylus 24, 36, 38
Alexandria 6, 59, 65, 81, 88–89, 106
Antigone 13–14, 24
Apollodorus 69
Aristophanes 12, 17–18, 25, 35–39
Aristotle 6, 9, 17, 23, 28, 30, 35–38, 166–168, 173
Aristoxenus 17, 33, 36–38
attendant 57
Aulus Gellius 75, 78

brothers and sisters 137, 142, 214, 224

Callicratidas 48, 62
Cato 43
Chaeremon 69, 76
Charondas 71, 78
children of God 190, 209, 214–215, 220–221, 223–226, 228
Cicero 19, 47, 54, 64, 68, 70, 75–78, 163
Corban 1, 117–118
Creon 13–14
Cynic philosophers 60–61, 70, 74, 121, 116

debt 11, 16–17, 21, 25, 28–29, 32, 36, 38–40, 65, 76, 78, 90, 100–101, 110–111, 122, 180, 185–186, 199
Decalogue 81, 86–87, 177–179
Delphi 21, 28, 36, 38
Dike (Justice) 24–25, 30, 71–72, 77, 89, 161
Diogenes Laertius 22, 63, 75–76, 160
Dionysius of Halicarnassus 45, 168
discipline 35, 83, 85, 90, 171, 173, 206–209, 213, 227
do ut des 38–39, 71, 78, 111
domus 64, 159, 174

Egypt 44, 81, 83, 88, 90, 96, 108, 205
emancipatio 53, 190
Epictetus 60–62, 73–74, 76–78, 134, 160, 173, 175, 177, 184
Euripides 6, 24–25, 30, 36–38

familia Dei 191, 198, 225
family
– imagery 116, 158, 182–183, 185, 187, 189–191, 193, 195–197, 202, 209–215, 217–221, 223, 225–226, 231
– of Jesus 133, 190, 203–204
– relationships 2, 23, 48, 107, 215
Fifth (Fourth) Commandment 81, 87, 89–91, 93, 95, 97, 99, 103–104, 109–111, 117–121, 153, 155, 161, 172, 174–175, 177–178, 193, 200–201, 230–231
friendship 9, 23, 88
funeral 14, 16–17, 37, 64, 67–68, 77, 95–96, 109–110, 147

genres 9–10, 17–19, 21, 24, 29, 31, 33, 90, 94, 128, 161, 166–170, 178
Golden Verses 15, 23, 33, 36–38

Hellenistic period 6–7, 9, 11, 21, 33, 39, 41–42, 44, 46, 48, 50, 52, 54, 56, 58, 60, 62, 64, 66, 68, 70, 72, 74, 76, 78
Hesiod 11, 21, 36–38
Hierocles 63, 69–70, 72, 76–77
Homer 6, 8–12, 14, 16, 18, 20, 22, 24, 26, 28, 30, 32, 34, 36, 38, 40
house(hold) churches 1, 174, 181, 194–195, 223, 225–226
Household Codes 1, 4, 19, 30, 46, 48, 52, 56, 59, 83, 89, 128, 158, 165–171, 173–176, 178, 181, 196, 198–200, 230–231

Iamblichus 14–15, 22–23, 34
illegitimate children 32, 40, 52, 207–208
inclusio 129, 217, 224
insula 159
Isaeus 17, 29, 36, 38
Ischomachus 19–20
Isis 72, 76–78
itinerant charismatics 115

Jesus, alleged teaching against the family,
 See radical sayings, radicalism
Jewish families 1, 213
Josephus 80, 84–85, 91–92, 96, 101, 103, 106–107, 109–111, 119, 132, 163, 173, 198
Judaism 10, 51, 83–86, 88, 91, 96–97, 99, 106, 108, 111, 119, 140, 147, 165, 175, 177, 192, 197, 209

Kingdom of God 49, 105, 107, 116, 121, 127, 133, 136, 138, 142, 146, 148 191, 193, 230

Livy 59
Lysias 17, 37

marriage
 – aim of 101
materfamilias 51
Menander 18, 30–31, 36, 38, 69
mother
 – and children 8, 203
 – Jewish 84, 197–198
mothers
 – and daughters 3
 – and sons 51
 – Roman 51
Museion 6
Musonius Rufus 61–62, 73–74, 78, 186

Nachfolge 115, 121, 132, 148
nature 9, 12, 27, 30, 38–39, 48–49, 61, 63, 66, 70, 72, 77–79, 86, 95, 97, 100–101, 110–111, 116, 133, 148, 152, 160, 162, 167–168, 180, 218, 223, 229
Nemesis 25
Neopythagorean philosophy 48–49
New Comedy 30–31, 69

Ocellus Lucanus 48
Oedipus 13, 24, 26
Old Comedy 18
older people 22, 24–25, 32, 91, 109, 123, 214

Palestine 83, 89–90, 106–107, 126, 158
papyri 1, 44–45, 56
parents
 – aged 7–8, 11–12, 20, 26–27, 72, 95, 119, 130, 229
 – insane 34, 39–40, 74, 78–79, 91
 – prayers of 9, 26–27, 38, 71
paterfamilias 46, 50, 53, 62, 76, 187–189, 195
patria potestas 45–46, 102, 190
patriarchal society 8–9, 45, 49, 181
Pempelus 26, 70, 77–78
Perictyone 42, 48–49, 62, 71–73, 76–78, 110
Pheidippides 12, 18, 35, 39
Philemon 30, 37–38
Philo 12, 43, 65, 80–82, 86–87, 92–95, 97–103, 105–106, 109–111, 117, 119–120, 163, 173, 177, 184, 186, 188, 193, 198, 205, 215
Phintys 42, 48–50, 62, 76
pietas, piety 23, 46–47, 64–66, 68–70, 72, 76–77, 100, 180
Plato 6–10, 16–17, 25–27, 30, 34, 36–39, 70, 73, 91, 104, 107, 110, 166, 179, 193, 230
Plautus 30, 69
Pliny 66, 75, 78, 132, 203
Plutarch 31–32, 42–43, 51, 186
priority 33, 35, 39–40, 78–79, 88, 92, 110, 116, 132, 134, 144–145, 147, 154–156, 175, 198, 201, 221, 229–231
prudence 49, 62
Pseudo–Phocylides 88–89, 91, 97, 105, 109–111, 173
punishment 7–8, 14, 21, 25, 27–29, 37–39, 72, 78–79, 84, 92, 102–103, 111, 179, 200, 226
Pythagoras 6, 14–16, 22–23, 33–34, 36–38, 48
Pythagorean school 14–16, 22–23, 33–39, 48–49, 76

Qumran 80, 89, 93, 97, 104, 108–110, 151, 158

radical sayings 1, 35, 92, 114, 116,
    145–147, 150, 155, 201, 228, 230–231
radicalism 115, 130, 132, 138, 147, 153,
    230
respectful speech 37, 59, 77, 92
reward 14, 25, 32, 39, 77–78, 103, 136,
    138, 177, 200

Seneca 54, 59, 66, 69–70, 76, 78, 167,
    173
settled congregations 1, 115, 158, 231
Simoeisius 10
slaves 11, 20, 43–44, 46, 48, 52–54, 82,
    93, 159, 166–168, 170–171,
    173–175–176, 188–191, 194–195
social life 8, 44, 126
Socrates 18–20, 35
Solon's laws 12–13, 31–33, 36–39
Sophocles 13–14, 24, 33, 37–38
Stobaeus 24, 26, 29–30, 48, 63, 69–70
Stoic philosophers 60–61, 63–64,
    69–70, 74–76, 78, 132, 160, 165, 209

Ten Commandments 81, 86–87, 97,
    117–118, 120, 148, 161, 213
tensions in the familiy 58, 121,
    130–131, 133, 135, 137, 139, 141,
    143, 145, 147, 149, 151, 153, 155,
    158, 178, 201, 228, 230–231
Terence 30, 69, 78, 128
Timocles 29–30, 36, 38

upper classes 19, 20, 44, 47, 51, 54–55

Valerius Maximus 66, 68, 70, 75–76, 78
veneration 37, 64, 77, 97, 110, 199, 229

Wanderradikalismus 115, 130
will (Testament) unjust 39–40, 68, 79

Xenophon 19–20, 36–38, 166–167, 173

Zaleucus 16, 23, 33, 36–38
Zeus 20–21, 23, 35, 75, 78–79

www.ingramcontent.com/pod-product-compliance
Lightning Source LLC
Chambersburg PA
CBHW070236230426
43664CB00014B/2324